utsa
memorial
fund
in memory
of

J. Arthur York

from a gift
to utsa
By

the members
of the
UTSA Memorial Fund

Paleoanthropology

World Anthropology

General Editor

SOL TAX

Patrons

CLAUDE LÉVI-STRAUSS
MARGARET MEAD
LAILA SHUKRY EL HAMAMSY
M. N. SRINIVAS

MOUTON PUBLISHERS · THE HAGUE · PARIS
DISTRIBUTED IN THE USA AND CANADA BY ALDINE, CHICAGO

Paleoanthropology

Morphology and Paleoecology

Editor

RUSSELL H. TUTTLE

MOUTON PUBLISHERS · THE HAGUE · PARIS

DISTRIBUTED IN THE USA AND CANADA BY ALDINE, CHICAGO

Distributed in the United States of America and Canada
by Aldine Publishing Company, Chicago, Illinois
ISBN 90-279-7699-6 (Mouton)
0-202-02017-7 (Aldine)
Jacket photo by Marie-Antoinette de Lumley
Cover and jacket design by Jurriaan Schrofer
Indexes by John Jennings
Printed in the Netherlands

to

Dr. L. S. B. Leakey

General Editor's Preface

This volume provides a wealth of new information — and lively discussion — on the evolution of the ancestors of our own and of collateral hominoid species from Miocene, Pliocene, and Pleistocene times in Africa, Asia, and Europe. It brings together work of physical anthropologists and evolutionary biologists, geologists and prehistorians, and comparative morphologists and anatomists. Perhaps most significantly, here are papers by indigenous authors discussing fossils uncovered in their own countries. Studies of early hominids have developed so rapidly in this generation that only specialized journals can keep up with them. Each journal necessarily confines itself to a particular subject matter and sets limits to what it can publish. The present book and its two companion volumes therefore offer a unique variety of new information and ideas, often from younger people of different continents writing articles for discussion with a greater latitude that gives the published results vigor. This book required the creative energy of the brilliant young paleoanthropologist who organized the meetings and edited the results, as much as it did the inspiration of an unusual international Congress.

Like most contemporary sciences, anthropology is a product of the European tradition. Some argue that it is a product of colonialism, with one small and self-interested part of the species dominating the study of the whole. If we are to understand the species, our science needs substantial input from scholars who represent a variety of the world's cultures. It was a deliberate purpose of the IXth International Congress of Anthropological and Ethnological Sciences to provide impetus in this direction. The *World Anthropology* volumes, therefore, offer a first glimpse of a human science in which members from all societies have played an active role. Each of the books is designed to be self-contained; each is an attempt to update its particular sector of scientific knowledge and is written by specialists from all parts of the world. Each volume should be read and reviewed individually as a separate volume on its own given subject. The set as a whole will indicate what changes are in store for anthropology as scholars from the developing countries join in studying the species of which we are all a part.

The IXth Congress was planned from the beginning not only to include as many of the scholars from every part of the world as possible, but also with a view toward the eventual publication of the papers in high-quality volumes. At previous Congresses scholars were invited to bring papers which were then read out loud. They were necessarily limited in length; many were only summarized; there was little time for discussion; and the sparse discussion could only be in one language. The IXth Congress was an experiment aimed at changing this. Papers were written with the intention of exchanging them before the Congress, particularly in extensive pre-Congress sessions; they were not intended to be read at the Congress, that time being devoted to discussions — discussions which were simultaneously and professionally translated into five languages. The method for eliciting the papers was structured to make as representative a sample as was allowable when scholarly creativity — hence self-selection — was critically important. Scholars were asked both to propose papers of their own and to suggest topics for sessions of the Congress which they might edit into volumes. All were then informed of the suggestions and encouraged to re-think their own papers and the topics. The process, therefore, was a continuous one of feedback and exchange and it has continued to be so even after the Congress. The some two thousand papers comprising *World Anthropology* certainly then offer a substantial sample of world anthropology. It has been said that anthropology is at a turning point; if this is so, these volumes will be the historical direction-markers.

As might have been foreseen in the first post-colonial generation, the large majority of the Congress papers (82 percent) are the work of scholars identified with the industrialized world which fathered our traditional discipline and the institution of the Congress itself: Eastern Europe (15 percent); Western Europe (16 percent); North America (47 percent); Japan, South Africa, Australia, and New Zealand (4 percent). Only 18 percent of the papers are from developing areas: Africa (4 percent); Asia-Oceania (9 percent); Latin America (5 percent). Aside from the substantial representation from the U.S.S.R. and the nations of Eastern Europe, a significant difference between this corpus of written material and that of other Congresses is the addition of the large proportion of contributions from Africa, Asia, and Latin America. "Only 18 percent" is two to four times as great a proportion as that of other Congresses; moreover, 18 percent of 2,000 papers is 360 papers, 10 times the number of "Third World" papers presented at previous Congresses. In fact, these 360 papers are more than the total of ALL papers published after the last International Congress of Anthropological and Ethnological Sciences which was held in the United States (Philadelphia, 1956).

The significance of the increase is not simply quantitative. The input of scholars from areas which have until recently been no more than subject matter for anthropology represents both feedback and also long-awaited theoretical contributions from the perspectives of very different cultural, social, and historical traditions. Many who attended the IXth Congress were convinced that anthropology would not be the same in the future. The fact that the next Congress (India, 1978) will be our first in the "Third World" may be symbolic of the change. Meanwhile, sober consideration of the present set of books will show how much, and just where and how, our discipline is being revolutionized.

In addition to the two companion volumes of this book, *Socio-ecology and psychology of primates* and *Primate functional morphology and evolution*, readers will be particularly interested in other volumes of the *World Anthropology* series which deal with archeology, with biological, psychological, and linguistic anthropology, and with particular geographic areas of the Old World.

Chicago, Illinois   SOL TAX
August 25, 1975

Preface

This volume contains articles that were prepared for discussion in Session 311 at the IXth International Congress of Anthropological and Ethnological Sciences. The session was convened on September 3, 1973, at the Conrad Hilton Hotel in Chicago, Illinois.

Although some papers were volunteered in response to the initial call for papers from the conference office, I solicited many of them with the intention of focusing discussion on a limited number of problem areas in paleoanthropology. Small subsets of papers and two or four topics were discussed by two successive panels which included authors of papers in the session, other experts on one or more subjects treated in the papers, and reputable raconteurs.

Teuku Jacob and Marie-Antoinette de Lumley served with me as co-chairpersons and discussants during the entire session.

The first panel included Susan Cachel, Robert Eckhardt, William W. Howells, K. Prasad, George Sacher, Frederick Szalay, Phillip Tobias, Christian Vogel, John Wallace, and Milford Wolpoff. They were principal discussants of papers in Sections I, II, and III of this volume.

The second panel included William W. Howells, Christopher Janus, Philip Lieberman, G. H. R. von Koenigswald, Phillip Tobias, Milford Wolpoff, and V. P. Yakimov. They were principal discussants of papers in Sections IV, V, and VI herein.

The format of discussion varied considerably during the session. But generally panelists were asked to summarize their own papers and to comment on related papers of other symposiasts. The topics and papers were then opened for discussion by the panel and the audience. In many instances the briefs were illustrated with slides or casts or both.

The arrangement of this volume does not faithfully reflect the chronology of events in Session 311. I regret that we did not have time to discuss more fully "revised concepts of early man in Java" and "the Neanderthal problem."

I prepared and edited typescripts of all discussions in the session and mailed them to the commentators for further editing, brief augmentation, and permission to publish. Summaries of papers were deleted from the typescript. So we have here a greatly condensed (but I hope no less mentally nutritious) rendering of the conference discussions.

Many persons contributed to the success of this adventure. Pre-eminent among them is Sol Tax, who was encouraging, challenging, and insightful about every aspect of the session and volume. His staff, especially Roberta MacGowan and Gay Neuberger, and my secretaries, June Ford and Susan Kurth, greatly expedited the preparation of manuscripts and correspondence with the contributors. It was also delightful to work with Jean Block and other staff members of the Midway Editorial Service and Karen Tkach and Peter Zoutendijk of Mouton Publishers.

Marlene Tuttle contributed in many ways to the development and completion of the project, especially assisting with typescripts of the discussions and the index. We are grateful to Nicole and Matthew Tuttle for their cooperation which permitted us to work together on the project.

The good cheer, cooperation, and communicativeness of the participants were overwhelming. We are very grateful for their colleague-ship.

University of Chicago RUSSELL H. TUTTLE
Chicago, Illinois
May 25, 1974

Table of Contents

Modeling and Hypothesis Testing in Paleoanthropology

Hypothesis Testing in Paleoanthropology

DAVID PILBEAM and J. RIMAS VAIŠNYS

INTRODUCTION

It is our aim here to analyze systematically a specific paleoanthropological problem, namely, the classification of certain Plio-Pleistocene hominid species; however, the procedures we adopt can, we believe, be generally applied to many other problems in paleontology. Our first step is to express verbally the alternative hypotheses that might plausibly explain the relevant fossil hominid data. An important step in the evaluative process, and one that is unfortunately rarely taken, is to find a correspondence between anthropological hypotheses and quantitative, and therefore testable, mathematical hypotheses. The mathematical hypotheses can then be evaluated in probabilistic terms. With such data in hand, a choice among anthropological hypotheses is rendered somewhat easier.

Clearly, probability calculations cannot give certainty where certainty does not exist for physical reasons, but such calculations can provide a reasonable measure of the uncertainty associated with the possible answers and can clarify the arguments by eliminating unnecessary ambiguities. In some cases, an examination of the calculations can also suggest worthwhile extensions of the arguments.

STATEMENT OF HYPOTHESES

Our attempt to formulate anthropological hypotheses and to relate

Our thanks go to Carol Coke Pilbeam. The order of authors is alphabetical.

these to a variety of mathematical hypotheses is illustrated by a problem familiar to paleoanthropologists — the classification of late Pliocene and early Pleistocene hominid species. In particular, we are concerned with relationships between specimens generally assigned to two species, *Austrolopithecus africanus* and *Australopithecus* (or *Homo*) *habilis* (Pilbeam 1972).

Australopithecus africanus includes fossils from Taung, Sterkfontein, and Makapansgat in South Africa (although the latter two sites probably do not yield only *A. africanus)* and may well also be represented at certain East African localities (i.e. older sediments of the Shungura Formation from the Omo Basin of Ethiopia). *A. habilis* is best known at Olduvai Gorge, Tanzania, but is also probably sampled in younger Shungura Formation deposits at the Omo, and in sites on the eastern shores of Lake Rudolf in Kenya. However, the best described material of these two species comes from South Africa and from Olduvai Gorge. A number of workers have argued that South African *A. africanus* and East African *A. habilis* are insufficiently distinct to be separated at the species level; however, a majority feel that differences between the two samples justify specific separation.

As yet there is no agreement on the relative dating of the two geographic samples. Estimates range from the assumption that fossils from South and East Africa are approximately penecontemporaneous to the view that the South African specimens are significantly older than those from Olduvai. Arguments will therefore center around somewhat different hypotheses depending on which relative geological ages are used. If the samples are coeval, then we need to decide whether they are drawn from one or more lineages; if they differ in age, the samples might be drawn from only a single lineage. In that case, the samples could be assigned to one or more time-successive species.

Thus, we can propose a wide variety of anthropological hypotheses to account for the data. A still broader range of classificatory schemes is then available for labeling the data once it is ordered. The anthropological hypotheses will be affected by assumptions that we make about the relative dating of samples and by the several explanations that can be proposed to account for the observed variability within, and differences between, the two samples.

A. africanus and *A. habilis* have been discriminated from each other principally on the basis of jaw size, tooth size, tooth proportions (especially differences in breadth/length indices of the lower premolars, *A. africanus* having relatively somewhat broader teeth than *A. habi-*

lis), and endocranial volume (measurable specimens assigned to *A. africanus* yield a mean endocranial volume markedly lower than that for the *A. habilis* sample). Debates concerning endocranial volumes have centered on six estimates of South African *A. africanus* and four of East African *A. habilis;* the most reliable volumes are given in Table 1. Earlier literature quoted only one *A. habilis* volume, that for Olduvai hominid 7, but other values have since become available (Holloway 1970; Tobias 1971).

Holloway (1970) and Pilbeam (1969) pointed out that the endocranial volume of one *A. habilis* (Olduvai hominid 7) differs significantly from the *A. africanus* sample when compared by Student's t test. This suggested to them that the two samples (of six specimens and one specimen respectively) were drawn from populations differing very considerably in this parameter, and that they should therefore be classified in different species. This correspends to the mathematical hypothesis that the collected data are drawn from two probability distributions.

Table 1.   Cranial capacities of early Hominidae (Holloway 1970; Tobias 1971)

Locality	Specimen	Volume (cubic centimeters)
1. Taung	Taung 1	440 (estimated)
2. Sterkfontein	Sts 60	428
3. Sterkfontein	Sts 5	485
4. Sterkfontein	Sts 19	436
5. Sterkfontein	Sts 71	428
6. Makapans	MLD 37/38	435
7. Olduvai	Hominid 7	> 657
8. Olduvai	Hominid 13	> 640
9. Olduvai	Hominid 16	> 620

However, Wolpoff (1969) argued that all seven specimens, six from South Africa and Hominid 7 from Olduvai, should be treated as a single sample, thus ignoring geographical, possible temporal, and morphological differences. Wolpoff stated that the pooled sample coefficient of variation, V ($s/\bar{x}$, × 100), is low enough to suggest strongly that the pooled sample is homogeneous; he therefore concluded that for this reason, and others, these hominids should be classified together in one species (which he called *Homo africanus)*. This argument corresponds to the mathematical hypothesis that the collected data are drawn from a single probability distribution.

However, Pilbeam (1970) suggested that factors other than just the coefficient of variation ought to be considered in problems of this kind. The six South African hominid endocranial volumes are clustered closely together and set far apart from the single *A. habilis* value. Such a distribution seems unlikely to be the result of sampling from a single probability distribution. In an attempt to simulate the paleontological situation, samples of seven individuals were drawn at random by Pilbeam (1970) from a group of twenty extant chimpanzee endocranial volumes; none of these samples resembled the fossil hominid distribution. Nor did random samples of six chimpanzees and one gorilla, drawn from twenty known chimpanzee and twenty gorilla volumes, resemble the fossil distribution. It was concluded that this (admittedly empirical) method indicated that the seven hominids around which the debate first centered were very unlikely to have been sampled from one distribution. It was further concluded that the fossil hominids were in fact sampled from two distributions so different that they could not represent a single species. (The addition of more *A. habilis* estimates — for hominids 13, 16, and 24 from Olduvai — renders it even less likely that one normal distribution is involved [Tobias 1971].)

It will be observed that the above discussion of cranial capacities in early hominids by Wolpoff and Pilbeam basically corresponds to a comparison of two mathematical hypotheses about the populations giving rise to the data, Wolpoff favoring the mathematical hypothesis that the collected data represent a single distribution, whereas Pilbeam and Holloway favor the hypothesis that the collected data represent two distributions. This type of question not only lends itself to analysis by probability methods but also to extension of the arguments in the direction of a quantitative description of the populations.

EVALUATION OF HYPOTHESES

The paleoanthropological problem can be abstracted as follows: given (a) a small number of carefully scrutinized and selected data, and (b) a number of possible statistical hypotheses, all accounting for these data, how should these hypotheses be chosen for further consideration? Because the data set is usually small and the number of possible hypotheses is indefinitely large, no certain answer can be expected. In such cases probability arguments are useful in comparing and selecting mathematical hypotheses.

The evaluation of such hypotheses can be approached as follows. Let D_s represent the proposition "the observed cranial data are as represented in Table 1"; H_i the proposition "cranial capacity observations are drawn from a distribution or distributions specified in Table 4"; and X the proposition "certain other data and propositions relevant to the problem which have been accepted by the participants." A direct and reasonable ranking of possible hypotheses and a measure of their credibility is provided by the probabilities associated with the hypotheses. A more probable hypothesis, other things being equal, is preferable, or more defensible, than a less probable one. The conditional probability associated with the i–th hypothesis, given the data and other pertinent information, is denoted by $p(H_i/D_sX)$ (i.e. the probability of H_i given D_s and X). Any propositions appearing after the solidus are accepted as being true. In terms of these concepts, the discussion between Pilbeam and Wolpoff, being essentially an attempt to choose between the two hypotheses mentioned earlier (denoted by H_A and H_B, respectively) can be reduced to the evaluation of $p(H_A/D_sX)$ and $p(H_B/D_sX)$.

The calculation of the conditional probability $p(H_i/D_sX)$ is carried out by means of the relation:

$$p(H_i/D_sX) = p(H_i/X)\frac{p(D_s/H_iX)}{p(D_s/X)} \ .$$

This relation is a form of the well-known Bayes' rule (Tribus 1969). In fact, we do not wish to preassign the number of hypotheses that may be considered, and therefore only the relative credibility of two hypotheses need be assessed: in other words, it makes sense, for two hypotheses H_i and H_j, to calculate the relative conditional probability $r_c(i, j) = p(H_i/D_sX)/p(H_j/D_sX)$, that is, the ratio of probabilities of the two hypotheses given the same data set in each case. This conditional probability then may be expressed as:

$$r_c(i, j) = \frac{p(H_i/D_sX)}{p(H_j/D_sX)} = \frac{p(H_i/X)\,p(D_s/H_iX)}{p(H_j/X)\,p(D_s/H_jX)} = r_u(i, j)\frac{p(D_s/H_iX)}{p(D_s/H_jX)}$$

In this final term, $r_u(i, j)$ stands for the relative probability for the hypotheses i and j in the absence of the observational data on the cranial capacities collected in Table 1, i.e. the relative *a priori* probability. In most calculations, the competing hypotheses will be of comparable *a priori* probability, in which case $r_u(i, j)$ will be close to unity. In other cases, qualitative considerations will often suggest the value of this probability ratio to an order of magnitude, i.e. a factor of ten. The second half of this final term, $\dfrac{p(D_s/H_iX)}{p(D_s/H_jX)}$, evaluates the relative probability of the given data set being sampled from two different distributions, as specified by hypotheses H_i and H_j. The preceding formulation thus enables us to assess the likelihoods of various pairs of hypotheses, given a common set of data. We are also enabled to feed in our *a priori* ideas about the probabilities of the hypotheses being examined. For example, some hypotheses might be *a priori* less acceptable to us than others because they made less biological "sense," for example, in terms of what we know of variation in living primates.

In the calculations that follow it will be convenient to choose two hypotheses as reference hypotheses and to evaluate others relative to them. To illustrate the above approach, we perform the probability calculations for a number of hypotheses about the populations from which the fossil hominid skulls are obtained.

We have made our initial calculations utilizing statistical assumptions about distributions in fossil hominids derived from endocranial

Table 2.   Cranial capacities (cubic centimeters) of living Hominoidea (Ashton and Spence 1958; Martin and Saller 1959)

	sample size (n)	mean ($\bar{x}$)	standard deviation (s)	coefficient of variation (V)
Pan troglodytes				
male	33	410	47.7	11.6
female	78	380	35.1	9.2
pooled	111	390	41.1	10.5
female mean/male mean				93 percent
Pongo pygmaeus				
male	30	415	37.6	9.1
female	18	370	34.9	9.4
pooled	48	400	43.3	10.8
female mean/male mean				89 percent
Gorilla gorilla				
male	63	550	61.9	11.3
female	50	460	35.2	7.7
pooled	113	510	69.1	13.5
female mean/male mean				84 percent
Homo sapiens: range of means for 37 populations				
male	1317–1609			
female	1181–1445			
female mean/male mean				83–99 percent

volume measurements of living hominoids. Cranial capacity data for living hominoids are given by Ashton and Spence (1958), and these are listed in Table 2. Intraspecies variability in apes cannot be assessed, although there is some sexual dimorphism in brain volume. Unfortunately, the extent of sexual dimorphism in *Homo sapiens* cannot be calculated from Ashton and Spence's data; however, Martin and Saller (1959) give data on thirty-seven *Homo sapiens* populations. Female/male cranial capacity ratios vary from 83 to 99 percent, with a mean of about 90 percent, whereas the ratio of smallest to largest of the thirty-seven population means is 82 percent. Coefficients of variation for sexed pongid samples range from 7.7 (female gorillas) to 11.6 (male chimpanzees). For convenience of initial calculation we have assumed a value $V = 10$ for the early hominids, with ratios of female to male mean volumes ranging from 80 to 100 percent (the lowest mean ratio among extant hominoids is that for gorillas, 84 percent, reflecting the largest amount of sexual dimorphism).

To simplify the calculations we assume that in all cases the populations can be described by either one or two Gaussian distributions, having standard deviations corresponding to 10 percent of the means. This assumption greatly simplifies the numerical work, but is not inherent in the method of calculation. It is justified because contemporary hominoid populations are quite well approximated by such distributions and also because the main point of the result is not very sensitive to this assumption.

Table 3. Partial hypotheses

Partial hypothesis	Parameters defining h_i: mean (standard deviation 10 percent of mean)	Observation subset from Table 1 (appropriate data set to which particular hypothesis refers)
h_1	420	1–6
h_2	440	1–6
h_3	450	1–6
h_4	470	1–6
h_5	510	1–6
h_6	470	7
h_7	510	7
h_8	520	7
h_9	550	7
h_{10}	660	7
h_{11}	510	7–9
h_{12}	550	7–9
h_{13}	570	7–9
h_{14}	640	7–9

The calculations are first done with the seven observations referred to in Wolpoff (1969) and Pilbeam (1969, 1970) (see Table 1); later, data for hominids 13 and 16 are included (Tobias 1971). The hypotheses can be defined with the help of Tables 3 and 4.

A concise and convenient specification of an hypothesis H_i is in terms of the conjunction of two subhypotheses, h_f and h_k. The subhypotheses are listed in Table 3. Under the heading "Observation subset" are

Table 4.   Hypothesis table

	h_1 (420)	h_2 (440)	h_3 (450)	h_4 (470)	h_5 (510)
h_6 (470)				H_1	
h_7 (510)					H_2
h_8 (520)	H_3				
h_9 (550)		H_4			
h_{10} (660)		H_5			
h_{11} (510)					H_6
h_{12} (550)		H_7			
h_{13} (570)			H_8		
h_{14} (640)		H_9			

listed the observations that are considered to be derived from a Gaussian distribution with stated mean and standard deviation. In order to keep the number of hypotheses manageable for hand calculation, the data were partitioned among subhypotheses so that only the more probable hypotheses, H_i, are generated, as we are interested only in such hypotheses for any further consideration. The main hypotheses H_i, which can be generated from subhypotheses are indicated in Table 4. Table 5 includes brief notes explaining our choice of hypotheses and subhypotheses.

Table 5.   Notes on choice of hypotheses (all distributions assumed normal, with $V = 10$)

H_1 Assumes that values 1–7 are sampled from a population in which male and female means are equal. The mean is the arithmetic mean of all seven measurements.

H_2 Similar to H_6.

H_3 Assumes fossils are sampled from population with an overall mean volume of 470 cubic centimeters, but in which mean values for samples differ by an amount close to the maximum for living hominoids (smaller value is 81 percent of larger value).

H_4 Similar to H_3; yields a ratio between populations of 80 percent. This would be essentially a "single-species hypothesis" if early hominids were no more polytypic or dimorphic than the most variable extant hominoids. (Thus a mathematical hypothesis [H_4] can be easily modified into an anthropological one.)

H_5 Similar to H_4, assuming data 1–6 are drawn from a population with a mean of 440 cubic centimeters, datum 7 from a population with a mean of 660 cubic centimeters (about 657 cubic centimeters). This gives a ratio of means of 67 percent and would be, essentially, a "two-species hypothesis" in anthropological terms.

H_6 Assumes that values 1–9 are sampled from a single population in which subpopulation means are equal. The mean is the (approximate) arithmetic mean of all nine measurements. (Similar to H_1.)

H_7 Similar to H_4.

H_8 Similar to H_4, but using data 1–9. Ratio of means is 78 percent.

H_9 Similar to H_5, but calculating the second population mean (640 cubic centimeters) using data 7–9. Ratio of means is 69 percent.

Hypotheses H_1 and H_6 are essentially those proposed by Wolpoff (1969); that is, they are single distribution hypotheses.

Noting that the observations can be considered as independent, the necessary probabilities may be factored as a product of probabilities assigned to individual observations D_j:

$$p(D_s/H_iX) = \Pi_j p(D_j/H_iX),$$

where Π_j indicates a product over the set of individual observations. The individual probabilities, $p(D_j/H_iX)$, are simply and directly calculable from the appropriate Gaussian distribution functions defining the hypothesis H_i. Choosing hypothesis H_1 as a reference hypothesis (i.e. considering the data set discussed by Wolpoff [1969], Pilbeam [1969, 1970], and Holloway [1970]) and taking the initial *a priori* probability of the hypotheses, $r_u(i, 1)$, as 1, using the above equations we obtain the relative conditional probabilities shown in Table 6. It is clear that the observations greatly favor two-distribution hypotheses. The evidence

Table 6. Probability of hypothesis i compared with the probability of hypothesis 1, given seven observations and assuming equal *a priori* probabilities for all hypotheses

H_i	Ratio of probability of hypothesis i to probability of hypothesis 1
H_1	1.0
H_2	0.4 (.4)
H_3	1.7×10^2 ($\sim$200)
H_4	1.4×10^3 ($\sim$1000)
H_5	7.8×10^3 ($\sim$8000)

for two-distribution hypotheses becomes even more striking when recent observations are taken into account and a total of nine observations are used. The appropriate results are summarized in Table 7.

It should be noted that we can include the effect of unequal *a priori* weighting of any two hypotheses simply by multiplying the entries of

Table 7. Probability of hypothesis i compared with the probability of hypothesis 6, given nine cranial capacity observations and assuming equal *a priori* probabilities for all hypotheses

H_i	Ratio of probability of hypothesis i to probability of hypothesis 6
H_6	1.0
H_7	9.9×10^4 (~100,000)
H_8	4.2×10^5 (~400,000)
H_9	3.3×10^6 (~3,000,000)

Tables 6 and 7 by the ratio of these *a priori* probabilities, r_u (i, j), for the two hypotheses.

ANTHROPOLOGICAL IMPLICATIONS

These calculations show that, with regard to the interpretation of the data on the cranial capacity of the hominids, hypotheses that two distributions are involved are substantially more probable than the hypothesis that there is a single distribution. The rejection of the two-distribution hypothesis in favor of the one-distribution hypothesis can be justified only if one is prepared to accept *a priori* (i.e. before considering the observations) that the one-distribution hypothesis is many thousand times more likely than the two-distribution hypothesis.

The procedure also shows that, in light of the current available data and subject to the assumption of equal *a priori* probabilities, the most probable hypothesis is H_9, that there are two distributions with means of about 440 cubic centimeters and 640 cubic centimeters, corresponding to subhypotheses h_2 and h_{14}. It will be noted, however, that this hypothesis is less than ten times more probable than H_8, another two-distribution hypothesis. Given the uncertainty of *a priori* probability assignments, we would tend to treat hypotheses within a factor of ten of each other in relative probability as virtually equally justified by the observations.

The assignment of anthropological meaning to the possible distributions is no longer a question in probability theory, but can often be done informally, sometimes implicitly through the choice of *a priori* probabilities. Thus, for example, the ratio of mean volumes for the two-distribution hypothesis H_9 is 69 percent, a ratio much smaller than that observed in intraspecies distributions; this hypothesis corresponds, anthropologically, essentially to a two-species hypothesis. However, we note that in hypothesis H_8, the ratio of mean volumes is

79 percent, a ratio that might just be consistent with a single-species interpretation in anthropological terms. If this anthropological interpretation is made, however, it must be noted that hypothesis H_8 is being modified to include the statements either that data 1–6 (from South Africa) are all females and data 7–9 (from East Africa) are all males, or that the two fossil populations being sampled are more different even than the most diverse of the thirty-seven living *Homo sapiens* populations (Martin and Saller 1959). These modifications of H_8 are inherently unlikely, so that the relative initial or *a priori* probability of H_8 and H_9, r_u (8,9), would be significantly less than unity. Of all the hypotheses considered here, H_9 is favored.

We conclude, therefore, that at least two distributions are being sampled, and that it is probable that these distributions are sufficiently distinct to justify the anthropological separation of the data into either distinct lineages or time-successive species, depending on the relative geological ages of the samples.

REFERENCES

ASHTON, E. H., T. F. SPENCE
  1958 Age changes in the cranial capacity and foramen magnum of hominoids. *Proceedings of the Zoological Society of London* 130: 169–181.
HOLLOWAY, R. L.
  1970 Australopithecine endocast (Taung specimen, 1924): a new volume determination. *Science* 168:966–968.
MARTIN, R., D. SALLER
  1959 *Lehrbuch der Anthropologie*, volume two. Stuttgart: Fischer.
PILBEAM, DAVID
  1969 Early Hominidae and cranial capacity, *Nature* 224:386.
  1970 Early Hominidae and cranial capacities (continued). *Nature* 227: 747–748.
  1972 *The ascent of man.* New York: Macmillan.
TOBIAS, P. V.
  1971 *The brain in hominid evolution.* New York: Columbia University Press.
TRIBUS, M.
  1969 *Rational descriptions, decisions and designs.* New York: Pergamon.
WOLPOFF, M. H.
  1969 Cranial capacity and taxonomy of Olduvai hominid 7. *Nature* 223:182–183.

Discussion

WOLPOFF: This is an extremely important topic because paleoanthropology IS hypothesis testing. If it is not hypothesis testing, I do not understand what it is.

SZALAY: It is an empirical science.

WOLPOFF: An empirical science is hypothesis testing. Data does not speak for itself. I have been in rooms with data and listened very carefully. The data never said a word. There are two very important aspects of hypothesis testing. Firstly a hypothesis has to be testable in the Popperian sense. It has to be, at least in principle, falsifiable, or it is not a hypothesis at all. Secondly, we must be very certain that the test that we propose for the hypothesis actually tests it. In Pilbeam and Vaišnys' paper (see Pilbeam and Vaišnys, this volume) we have an example in which the proposed test does not seem to test the hypothesis. It concerns the question of how many taxa of Lower Pleistocene hominids occurred. The test procedure that Pilbeam and Vaišnys propose is done in an ingenious manner. They suggest that we should look at the decisions in terms of probability statements. We could state, for instance, that one hypothesis indicates a single taxon, the second hypothesis is that there are two taxa, and so forth. They then propose a number of ways to determine which hypothesis is most probable. Unfortunately, they did not test a TAXONOMIC question. Instead they tested a SORTING question. This commonly confuses us. It is very important to realize that simply because we can sort samples, we have not at the same time shown that there are different taxa involved. Probably the best example of this is the fact that it is very easy to sort *H. erectus* in Java from *H. erectus* in China. We can do it on the basis of cranial capacity as Pilbeam and Vaišnys did. With a t-test we can show to a high probability that they are not the same samples. And they surely ARE NOT the same samples. They come from different time periods and they certainly are different morphologically. Yet most of us place them in the same taxon. Thus I suggest that in the process of hypothesis testing we should be very careful that our test in actuality tests the hypothesis.

ECKHARDT: Wolpoff's statement is well taken. In this sort of hypothesis testing, we face not one question but two. First is there a perceivable difference between the two samples? And second, what is the significance of that difference? Is the difference intraspecific or is it extraspecific? There are further questions having to do with whether these species are contemporary species or chronospecies, i.e. representing separate points in a single evolving line. Pilbeam and Vaišnys (see Pilbeam and Vaišnys, this volume) were testing a hypothesis about a species which may well have been merely a different species within the same evolving line by seeing if they could sort skulls which came from two contemporaneous hominoid species — so that the material used to test the hypothesis was by no means the same as the fossil material.

HOWELLS: The Pilbeam-Vaišnys paper is an abstruse, mathematical, logical one and might better be looked upon as a demonstration of method or suggestion of a new method. In addition to being an empirical science, we should remember that paleoanthropology is a non-experimental science. And we need these other methods of attack.

SZALAY: These points are all well taken. I would like to point out, however, that most debate in the literature revolves around mathematical, statistical questions. Few proponents of the single species, single lineage hypothesis, mainly Dr. Wolpoff and Dr. Brace, ever concern themselves with the kind of qualitative problems that systematists deal with daily. With mathematics you can easily prove that two samples may belong to the same species. The statistical methods used are not the usual overlying, authoritative tools that most paleo-systematists use to determine whether one is dealing with one biological sample or another. Unfortunately most of the arguments in the literature do not deal with the qualitative aspects of the fossils involved. What Pilbeam and Vaišnys are doing here is simply adding something from mathematical methodology to qualitative convictions that they do not discuss, because they take it for granted that the fossils have been described adequately and are well understood.

TOBIAS: One comment on what Wolpoff said a moment ago. There are obvious mosaic factors in evolution. His statement that sorting into two distinct populations does not necessarily connote sorting into two distinct taxa should be qualified by a comment on relevance. There are some parameters of populations for which sorting into two distinct populations will connote taxonomic relevance. And there are others where such sorting will not connote taxonomic relevance. So the general statement that he made should not be accepted as covering all cases and not necessarily the case chosen by Pilbeam and Vaišnys. If it is a point in time when brain evolution is of cardinal importance, it may well be that such sorting is of taxonomic relevance. In the devising of hypotheses for sorting, it has frequently happened — and Wolpoff has done this — that an attempt is made to see whether sorting into a two-peaked distribution exists at all by pooling what I would consider non-poolable data. Measurements on teeth of animals that lived as widely separated in time as two million years have been considered on a null hypothesis to represent a single population and peaks have been sought therefrom. In such cases data are confused which may come from taxonomically separated and sexually separated populations, and furthermore which may represent different phyletic sequences or sequential populations in the same sequence. Results of such analyses do not tell us very much about either taxonomy or phylogeny. Therefore I would sound a very strong warning that in devising hypotheses one must be very careful what material one chooses to erect one's hypotheses on.

WOLPOFF: This may surprise Tobias but I agree with him. I am not sure that at least in principle we are in disagreement. I believe that sorting samples is not necessarily the same as demonstrating taxa. Whether it is the same as demonstrating taxa in any particular case has to be determined for that case alone. There are no general criteria that we could apply to this problem. I am also glad that Szalay made the statement he did because it brought something else to mind. I think that he misunderstands the uses of statistics. Statistics cannot be used to determine whether or not two specimens belong in the same taxon. A statistic can only show whether certain types of data, namely those amenable to measurement, can be used to discriminate samples. Whether in the end those samples are then biologically discriminated or not depends entirely on the total morphological patterns of the samples, their placement in a phylogenetic scheme, and other criteria that are applied. Statistics cannot be used for anything beyond this.

SZALAY: That is what I believe in, Milford.

WOLPOFF: I am afraid that there is a lot of misunderstanding in the way statistics are used and I hope that as researchers test hypotheses about paleontological problems they will make sure that statistics are a tool and not an end result in themselves.

SZALAY: This is exactly what I and many other systematists do feel.

In the instance of the single species hypothesis qualitative differences were rudely set aside, ignored, for whatever reasons, and the statistical data were pushed to the forefront. It was maintained that if there were no bio-metrical differences that would warrant the separation of two lineages, there was only one lineage. And this might well be. Biometrically you might not be able to separate the several different samples of the African Plio-Pleistocene hominids. But qualitatively you can.

WOLPOFF: Our disagreement concerns which data are relevant to this problem and whether the approach of testing a null hypothesis is valid.

SECTION TWO

Neogene Hominoids and the Emergence of Hominidae

Observations on the Paleoecology of South Asian Tertiary Primates

K. N. PRASAD

A preliminary paper on the ecology of the fossil Hominoidea from the Siwaliks discussing *Ramapithecus* was published by me (Prasad 1971). Fossil records, especially of primates, though well documented, do not throw sufficient light on environment. A critical evaluation of the associated fauna is therefore important. The earliest record of higher primates is from the Oligocene of the Fayum, Egypt.

Propliopithecus and *Oligopithecus* already possessed two premolars characteristic of higher primates. A lower primate stage of three premolars, though yet to be discovered in Africa, already was present in *Amphipithecus* from the Upper Eocene of Burma. During early Tertiary, Africa was isolated. However, in the Lower Miocene, mastodonts and dinotheres invaded Europe and Asia. *Pliopithecus* followed by *Dryopithecus* evolved fully during the Miocene. Dryopithecines were widely distributed in Eurasia and various genera and species are known. Fauna earlier than Pliocene in Java (Tjidjulang) have not been recorded. A preliminary assessment of the ecology of South Asian Tertiary primates has been attempted on available evidence.

INDIA

Geological Setting

The geological succession is shown in Table 1. The Siwaliks extend in age from Middle Miocene to Lower Pleistocene. The earliest record of dryopithecine from the Siwaliks is a palate of *Sivapithecus sivalensis*

(Lydekker 1879). Pilgrim (1915), doubtfully assigned the material to Dhokpathan (Pliocene) which was subsequently rectified and assigned

Table 1.   Geological succession in India

Upper Siwaliks	Boulder conglomerates: conglomerates, sands, and grits
	Pinjor Stage: Variegated clays, sandstones and conglomerates
	Tatrot Stage: Hard brown sandstones and clays
Middle Siwaliks	Dhok Pathan Stage: Brown sandstones, orange clays with subordinate shales
	Nagri Stage: Massive grey sandstones and pink clays
Lower Siwaliks	Chinji Stage: Red clays and sandstones
	Kamlial Stage: Grey sandstones and pseudo conglomerates

to Nagri, as Indian dryopithecines are limited to the Miocene. The fossil Hominoidea have been adequately documented in a series of papers by Pilgrim (1927), Lewis (1937), Wadia and Aiyengar (1938), Simons and Pilbeam (1965) and Prasad (1962, 1964). The ecology of North Indian *Ramapithecus*, has been discussed by Tattersall (1969a, 1969b).

Faunal Associations

Detailed analyses of the fossils have shown that the dryopithecines are invariably associated with a well-developed *Hipparion* fauna and indicate a Miocene aspect. The Chinji-Nagri (Miocene) contains many primates, felids, a creodont *Dissopsalis*, primitive chalicotheres *Macrotherium*, dinotheres, mastodonts, anthracotherids, listriodonts and primitive suids. The associated fauna at Haritalyangar, where the largest number of dryopithecines and *Ramapithecus* have been recorded to date, reveal the percentage distribution shown in Table 2.

Ecology

No precise K/AR data are available but an age equivalent to about twelve million years is generally assigned for the primate-bearing beds on the basis of stratigraphy and fauna. Molarization of premolars, reduction of canines, bipedal posture and tool-using are yet to be critically evaluated. Premolars in *Ramapithecus* were partly molarized allowing a relatively large area for grinding suited probably for graminivorous diet. The transition from tropical forests to open woodlands coincided with the rise of the Himalayas further north at the end of the Miocene and partially altered the ecologic setting. The early part of Siwalik sedimentation was marked by heavy precipitation with a well-developed riverine system, studded with forests of angiospermous flora supporting a rich fauna (Prasad 1971).

Table 2. Faunal associations in India

Geological horizon	Locality	Total number	Groups	Percentage
Dhok Pathan (Pontian)	Dadhol Ladhyani Kiari Lehrisarail Tikri Ukhli	400	Carnivora Equidae Suidae Tragulidae Proboscidea	5 50 15 10 20
Nagri (Sarmatian)	Haritalyangar Jhol Chhajoli Dangar Dakhiot Danghota	850	Primates Carnivora Rodentia Equidae Rhinocerotidae Suidae Tragulidae Bovidae Proboscidea Crocodilia Chelonia Pisces	1.2 23.5 12.3 12.3 9.5 12.3 18.1 8.2 0.5 1.1 0.5 0.5

Evidence of Fauna from Chinji

A remarkable assemblage of dinotheres, primitive trilophodonts, forest-dwelling suids such as *Listriodon, Conohyus, Dicoryphochoerus, Propotamochoerus, Giraffokeryx,* and *Gazella,* innumerable crocodiles, and a plethora of pythons are noticed in Chinjis. The presence of gigantic turtles, monitor lizards and aquatic birds reminds us of a tropical humid climate with heavy precipitation.

Nagri Fauna

The Nagri fauna, in addition to the primates, contain many holdovers from Chinji. Innumerable bones, teeth, fragments of mandible and maxilla occur in the clay and sandstone formations. Diverse forms of higher mammals such as equids, tragulids, suids, rodents and rhinocerotids, in addition to crocodiles and fishes, form an important assemblage. One of the important fossil localities, Haritalyangar, where the most primates have been recovered, provides this interesting data.

There are more than fifty genera and as many species of mammals belonging to various groups (Prasad 1970). Evidence for the existence of inland lakes is forthcoming by the recovery of remains of reptiles, chelonians, crabs, and a wide variety of fishes along with other groups of mammals.

Fauna from Dhok Pathan and Tatrot

The Dhok Pathan (Pliocene-Pontian) Formation is the richest fossil-bearing horizon in the Siwaliks. Several of the giraffe family and short-jawed proboscideans (*Synconolophus*) and Bovidae make their appearance for the first time. The assemblage shows characteristic species of dry grass-land vegetation. Tatrot, which forms the transition stage between the Pliocene Dhok Pathan and Pleistocene Pinjor, was marked by heavy precipitation with no apparent stain of red color. The presence of semiaquatic animals such as hippopotamids, elephants, bovids, and suids indicates moist conditions of climate. Deposits of much eolian material and the pink color of the sediments in the Pinjor suggest drier conditions.

Climate and Fauna

The Siwalik deposits in general give evidence of a warm humid climate. Petrographic studies have revealed that the coarse sediments have been derived from a northerly mountain, rising probably during a wet season, and the finer clastic material from the south during a dry period. The Lower Siwaliks apparently passed through a wet period or, alternatively, sediments were deposited in shallow water. The Middle Siwaliks, chiefly Dhok Pathan, was characterized by less humidity. There was a reverse trend during Upper Tertiary, when wet conditions prevailed, and at the end of Tatrot the climate became much cooler. The rich mammalian fauna which inhabited the valleys under semimarshy conditions migrated or became extinct during the Pleistocene, as evidenced by the semiglacial characteristics of the deposits. Lewis (Krynine 1936), attempted to reconstruct the condition that prevailed during the Siwalik Period into three types viz. (1) river-bank aquatic fauna, (2) forest fauna, and (3) savanna, steppe, or veldt fauna.

The dinotheres and primitive trilophodonts with dentition suited for clipping succulent vegetation, probably preferred near-aquatic conditions in a warm humid lowland. Obviously, the higher proboscideans such as the short-jawed mastodonts *Synconolophus* and brevirostrines (*Anancus*) and stegolophodonts were fitted with dentition more suited for harsher vegetation in a rugged country. *Hipparion*, with broader hooves and well-developed lateral digits possibly preferred a savanna type of condition. Among the bovids, the presence of antelope suggests prairies or steppes, while *Capra* and *Bos* indicate a less arid environment.

The presence of *Orycteropus* (aardvark) indicates arid conditions. Tragulids inhabited river banks and hippopotamids river bottoms. The large majority of pigs, canids, and a few of the hominoids preferred partly forested environment during Chinji-Nagri (Sarmatian), though a few of the former adapted to drier conditions of Dhok Pathan. Cercopithecoids diversified during Dhok Pathan (Pliocene) with the concurrent decline of dryopithecines.

Early hominids such as *Ramapithecus* and primitive giraffids such as *Giraffokeryx* preferred a forest environment though giraffes are known to inhabit open grasslands with scattered trees. The Siwalik ecology seems to have been one of a wide belt of angiospermous forest interspersed with open woodlands and grassy plains with meandering streams and river banks.

Evidence of flora in the form of dicotyledonous woods preserved in the sediments along with the mammalian material indicate a forest type of habitat. Miocene flora of evergreen rain forest had a much wider distribution in India during mid-Tertiary. Fossil woods of *Dipterocarpaceae* originally distributed in the Malay Peninsula are also known from East Africa (Chowdhury 1966). *Gluta* confined to tropical evergreen forests where precipitation is over 3,000 millimeters was flourishing in West Bengal, Assam, and is now confined in India, to the extreme southwest coast and southern Burma. The moisture-loving *Dipterocarpaceae* and other fossil woods referable to *Mesua, Gluta, Cynometron* and *Callophyllum* in Southeast Asia (including the Siwaliks) and East Africa suggest that the climate during Mio-Pliocene was tropical with abundant rainfall supporting heavy forests. Fossil woods and other floral material are generally considered reliable indicators of past climate. The climate appears to have been synchronous and more or less uniform along the foothills of the Siwaliks from Assam to Punjab. Referring to the habitat of *Gigantopithecus bilaspurensis* from India, Simons and Ettel (1970) compare them to the Kwangsi assemblage. The Dhok Pathan fauna assigned to Pliocene has certain relatives of elephants and *Hipparion*, but is different from the Kwangsi assemblage containing *G. blacki* of Middle Pleistocene.

BURMA

Pondaung Stage

Mammalian fauna (see Table 3) containing some of the earliest known primates are assigned to Upper Eocene. The Pondaung sediments extend more or less northerly and attain a huge thickness (2,000 meters)

Table 3. Mammalian fauna from Pondaung (Modified after Colbert 1938)

Condylarthra	Perissodactyla	Artiodactyla
Pondaungia	Titanotheridae	*Anthracohyus*
	Sivatitanops	*Anthracothema*
	Metatelmatherium	*Anthracokeryx*
Primates	Rhinocerotoidea	Traguloidea
Amphipithecus	*Paramynodon*	*Indomeryx*
	Tapiroidea	
	Indolophus	
	Deperetella	

in the northern portion. They rest on Tabyin clays, a marine deposit, but in northerly sections are seen resting on Tilin sandstones (Colbert 1938). Important lithologic groups are beds of clay, purple, pale, or mottled, with a rich vertebrate fauna indicating their formation in freshwater lagoons.

Amphipithecus mogaungensis, probably a lemuroid, is the earliest-known form showing primate affinities. The Tertiary stratigraphy is one of completely interfingered marine and continental beds, the ecology of which is incompletely known. Predominance (95 percent) of anthracotheres in the mammalian assemblage is significant. The rest of the fauna comprise titanotheres, tapiroids and aquatic rhinoceros, *Metamynodon*.

CHINA

The Keiyuan formations in Yunan, China, containing fossil Hominoidea (Woo 1957, 1958) are generally correlated with the Chinji-Nagri formations of the Siwaliks. The Kwangsi caves have yielded a large number of mammalian remains including *Gigantopithecus* of Middle Pleistocene age. Remains of orangutan, rodents, porcupines and carnivores are known from the deposits. Simons and Ettel (1970) pointed out that the Kwangsi fauna could be divided into two groups. One group includes the orangutan, civet, badger, cat, tapir, and a canid all suited to a woodland or forest environment. The other assemblage of elephants, horse, rhinoceros, hyena, giant panda, goat and cattle are more adapted to a mixed savanna-woodland type of vegetation.

JAVA

Hooijer (1952) and von Koenigswald (1956) discussed in a series of suggestive papers the stratigraphy and correlation of mammalian faunas of Java. A correlation of Javanese faunas with those of India has been drawn up with a basal Tjidjulang-Dhok Pathan and Tatrot formation. The younger Trinil beds are equated with Narbadas beds of India (see Figure 1).

The Tjidjulang have an assemblage of *Hexaprotodon* and *Meryco-potamus*, indicating conditions of heavy precipitation. Vertebrate remains from Kali Glagah and Djetis beds indicate a close similarity with

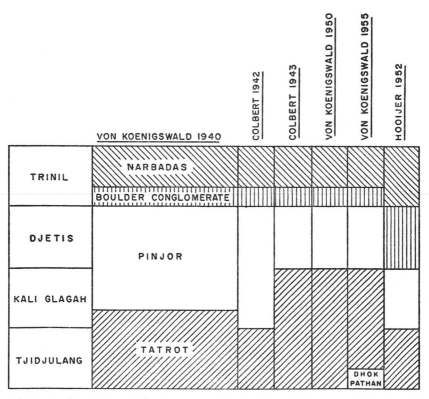

Figure 1.   Correlation of the Javanese and Indian Faunas (From von Koenigswald 1956)

Table 4.   Distribution of genera in Java and India (Modified after von Koenigswald 1956)

India	Dhokpathan	Tatrot	Pinjor
Pleistocene guide fossils:			
Hypselephas hysudricus		x	x
Equus		x	
Bos namadicus			x
Java			
Djetis:			
Leptobos			x
Nestoritherium			x
Hexaprotodon	x	x	x
Hypselephas		x	x
Kali Glagah:			
Hexaprotodon	x	x	x
Trilophodon	x		
Stegodon (11+)	x	x	
Hypselephas		x	
Tjidjulang:			
Hexaprotodon	x	x	x
Merycopotamus	x		x

Table 5.   Probable habitat distribution of hominoids and cercopithecoids

Group	Tropical forests	Open woodland	Savanna
Cercopithecoidea:			
Mandrillus	x		
Papio			
Theropithecus			x
Presbytis	x		x
Pongidae:			
Dryopithecus	x		
Sivapithecus	x		
Gorilla	x		
Pan	x		
Orang	x		
Incertae sedis:			
Gigantopithecus	x		
Early *Hominidae*			
Ramapithecus		x	
Australopithecus		x	
Homo erectus			x

the middle and upper Siwaliks (see Table 4). Von Koenigswald (personal communication) while reviewing the ecological setting of *Pithecanthropus* has made this interesting observation:

Java being so close to the equator, there cannot be much change in the tropical climate during Pleistocene. Pigs, deer, and crocodiles are abundant, also hippopotamus. There was slight deterioration of climate during Upper

Pleistocene. The water buffalo of the Trinil layers had relatively short horns whereas the buffalo of the Ngandong layers had two-meter horns which precludes its habitat in dense tropical jungles. The vegetation was more open as noticed in some islands east of Java like Sumba and Flores.

It is generally agreed that the Trinil fauna is post-Villafranchian and the Trinil beds are Middle Pleistocene corresponding to the second glaciation of the Ice Age in other parts of the world. Distribution (Table 5) of *Homo erectus* remains indicates their ability to cope with different types of climate; whereas the australopithecines were probably accustomed to a warmer climate, as evidenced by the fossil records.

REFERENCES

CHOWDHURY, K. A.
  1966   The Tertiary flora of India and probable disposition of continents. *The Palaeobotanist* 14(1):172–184.

COLBERT, E. H.
  1938   Fossil mammals from Burma in the American Museum of Natural History. *Bulletin of the American Museum of Natural History* 74:255–436.

HOOIJER, D. A.
  1952   Fossil mammals and the Plio-Pleistocene boundary in Java. *Proceedings of the Koninklijke Nederlandse Akademie van Wetenschappen, Amsterdam* 55:436—443.

KRYNINE, P. D.
  1936   Petrography and Genesis of Siwalik Series. *American Journal of Science* 34(5):422–446.

LEWIS, G. E.
  1937   Taxonomic syllabus of Siwalik fossil anthropoids. *American Journal of Science* 34:138–147.

LYDEKKER, R.
  1879   Further notices of Siwalik mammalia. *Records of the Geological Survey of India* 12:33–52.

PILGRIM, G. E.
  1915   New Siwalik Primates and their bearing on the questions of evolution of man and anthropoidea. *Records of the Geological Survey of India* 45(1):1–74.
  1927   A *Sivapithecus* palate and other primate fossils from India. *Palaeontologia Indica*, n.s. 14:1–24.

PRASAD, K. N.
  1962   Fossil primates from the Siwalik beds near Haritalyangar, Himachal Pradesh, India. *Journal of the Geological Society of India.* 3:86–96.
  1964   Upper Miocene anthropoids from the Siwalik beds of Haritalyangar, Himachal Pradesh, India. *Paleontology* 7:124–134.
  1970   The vertebrate fauna from the Siwalik beds of Haritalyangar, Himachal Pradesh, India. *Palaeontologia Indica*, n.s. 39:1–55.

1971   Ecology of the fossil Hominoidea from the Siwaliks of India. *Nature* 232:413–414.

SIMONS, E. L., P. C. ETTEL
1970   *Gigantopithecus. Scientific American* 222:76–84.

SIMONS, E. L., D. PILBEAM
1965   Preliminary revision of the Dryopithecinae (Pongidae and Anthropoidea). *Folia Primatologica* 3:89–152.

TATTERSALL, I.
1969a Ecology of North Indian *Ramapithecus. Nature* 221:451–452.
1969b More on the Ecology of North Indian *Ramapithecus. Nature* 224: 821–822.

VON KOENIGSWALD, G. H. R.
1956   Remarks on the correlation of mammalian faunas of Java and India and the Plio-Pleistocene boundary. *Proceedings of the Koninklijke Nederlandse Akademie van Wetenschappen, Amsterdam* 59(3):204–210.

WADIA, D. N., N. K. N. AIYENGAR
1938   Fossil anthropoids of India: a list of the fossil material hitherto discovered from the Tertiary deposits of India. *Records of the Geological Survey of India* 72:467–494.

WOO, J. K.
1957   *Dryopithecus* teeth from Keiyuan, Yunan Province. *Vertebrata Palasiatica* 1:25–32.
1958   New materials of *Dryopithecus* from Keiyuan, Yunan. *Vertebrata Palasiatica* 2:31–43.

The Early Fossil Hominids and Related Apes of the Siwalik Foothills of the Himalayas: Recent Discoveries and New Interpretations

A. P. KHATRI

INTRODUCTION

It is now generally agreed that the key to understanding the basic problems related to the ancestry of the Pleistocene hominids in Africa and Asia lies in pinpointing exactly how the separation between pongids and hominids took place in the Miocene/Pliocene period. To this age belong the Siwalik foothills of the Himalayas in India and the Rusinga Island and Fort Ternan deposits of Kenya. The first discovery of primate fossils in the Siwaliks dates back to the 1830's, while studies of the African dryopithecines began in the 1950's. Recent taxonomic assignments and re-evaluation of the old material from these two areas place most of it in the Dryopithecinae, while a few specimens in both areas belong to the genus *Ramapithecus*, established by Lewis in 1934. It is now generally agreed that *Ramapithecus* is the earliest human ancestor yet known: it lived fourteen to fifteen million years ago, in the late Miocene or early Pliocene period, in Africa and Asia. I shall review the present status of the Siwalik hominoids under the revised taxonomic regrouping and shall bring together material that has come to light during the past twenty-five years.

HISTORICAL REVIEW

The first mention of primate specimens from the Siwalik Hills of India goes back to 1837. A right astragalus of *Presbytis palaeindicus* (BMNH 1539) and a mandible of *Papio falconeri* (BMNH 15709) are the ear-

For Plates, see pp. ii–iii, between pp. 288–289

liest primate specimens of the Siwaliks of which we have a record.[1] The astragalus was mentioned in the *Transactions of the Geological Society, London* (1937) Series 2, 5: 499–502, and the mandible was recorded by H. Falconer and P. T. Cautley in the *Journal of the Asiatic Society of Bengal*, 6: 354–360. Falconer and Gautley's (1831–1868) and Richard Lydekker's (1876–1886) classic contributions and exhaustive monographs on the Siwalik vertebrate fauna described additional primate specimens. But all of these specimens were fossil monkeys (Cercopithecidae).

The real research on anthropoid apes commenced in 1910 with the publication of Pilgrim's classic paper "Notices of new mammalian genera and species from the Tertiaries of India." Here for the first time *Sivapithecus indicus*, *Dryopithecus punjabicus*, and *Semnopithecus asnoti* were mentioned. In 1915 Pilgrim established two additional species of *Dryopithecus* (*D. chinjiensis* and *D. giganteus*) and the new genus *Palaeosimia*, with the specific name of *rugosidens*. Almost all the primate specimens were discovered by M. Vinayak Rao, a subassistant of the Geological Survey of India, at several localities, particularly Chinji and Hasnot in the Salt Range and Haritalyangar in the Simla Hills. In 1927, Pilgrim described seven more hominoid specimens from the Siwaliks and established five new species: *Sivapithecus orientalis, Sivapithecus himalayensis, Sivapithecus middlemissi, Palaeopithecus* (?) *sylvaticus,* and *Hylopithecus hysudricus.* Of the seven Siwalik specimens he described in 1927, four (D. 196, 197, 199, and 200) were discovered by Pilgrim himself at Haritalyangar. Specimen D. 198 was collected by C. S. Middlemiss. The other two specimens, which were isolated molars, came from the Salt Range and were given to Pilgrim by C. Forester. Forester later deposited those specimens in the British Museum, London. The specimens collected by Falconer, Cautley, and Lydekker also went to the British Museum, while the collection made by Pilgrim and Rao became the property of the Indian Museum, Calcutta. In 1922, the American Museum of Natural History of New York sent out a Siwalik expedition under Dr. Barnum Brown. (Brown's collection of Siwalik vertebrate fauna was described

---

[1]   The following abbreviation are used in this paper:
1.   AMNH: American Museum of Natural History, New York
2.   BMNH: British Museum of Natural History, London
3.   NMNHP: National Museum of Natural History, Paris
4.   GSI: Geological Survey of India, Calcutta
5.   CMN: Coryndon Museum of Natural History, Nairobi
6.   YPM: Yale Peabody Museum of Natural History, New Haven
7.   NMK: National Museums of Kenya, Nairobi

by Colbert in 1935.) Brown found three primate specimens on which were established three new *Dryopithecus* species; these were named *D. pilgrimi* (AMNH 194111), *D. cautleyi* (AMNH 19412), and *D. frickae* (AMNH 19413), in honor of Pilgrim, Cautley, and Mrs. Henry Clay Frick, who provided funds to the American Museum for the Siwalik expedition. The *D. pilgrimi* specimen was collected from Ramnagar (Jammu), while the other two came from Hasnot in the Salt Range, West Punjab. These three specimens were described and discussed exhaustively by Brown, Gregory, and Hellman (1924) and by Gregory and Hellman (1926).

In 1931–1933 the Yale North India Expedition under G. Edward Lewis secured further collections of primate fossils from Hasnot and Haritalyangar and established four new genera and species: *Indraloris lulli* (1938), *Ramapithecus brevirostris* (1934), *Ramapithecus harien-sis* (1934), and *Sugrivapithecus salmontanus sivalensis*. Lewis named them after Indian gods, mythological heroes, and characters of the Indian epic *Ramayana*. The type specimens on which these new genera and species were established are in the Yale Peabody Museum, New Haven; their register numbers are YPM 13802, 13799, 13807, 13811, 13814, and 13806, respectively. The specimens of *Sugrivapithecus* and *Ramapithecus* (13811 and 13814) were obtained from Hasnot, in the Salt Range, while the other four specimens were collected from the Haritalyangar area in the Simla Hills.

In 1935, Helmut De Terra led the Yale-Cambridge India Expedition to the Siwalik Hills. The specimens were ultimately divided between the Yale Peabody Museum and Cambridge University, London. N. K. N. Aiyengar, a fossil collector with the Geological Survey of India, who was attached to the expedition, recovered seventeen new hominoid specimens from seven different localities. The localities were Kundan Nala near Chinji (two specimens), Chinji (four), Kanatti (one), Parrewali (one), Haritalyangar (four), Ramnagar (one), and Jammu (four). These finds were described by Gregory, Hellman, and Lewis (1938).

Prior to 1938, the total number of primate fossils from the Siwalik foothills was eighty-two, consisting mostly of maxillae, mandibular rami, molars, and other isolated teeth (Wadia and Aiyengar 1938). No long bones or other postcranial materials had been recovered, so that the locomotion of these creatures was unknown. Most of the specimens came from Chinji and Hasnot in the Salt Range (Pakistan) and from Haritalyangar and Ramnagar (India). They were collected by Theobald, Rao, Aiyengar, Lewis, Brown, De Terra (GSI D. 301),

Pilgrim, Lahiri (GSI D. 300), Middlemiss (GSI D. 198), Pascoe, Sen
(YPM 13835), and Bose. The greatest number of primate fossils was
found by Rao and Aiyengar, who held subordinate posts in the Geological Survey of India. Mr. B. K. Bose discovered a specimen of *Sivapithecus* at Dalsar, one mile north of Ramnagar, Jammu. This fossil is
now in the collection of the Prince of Wales College Museum at Jammu.

Between 1938 and 1950 there was a lull in research on the Siwalik
primate fauna. Meanwhile, Africa, particularly Rusinga Island and
the Fort Ternan beds of Kenya, yielded a rich crop of Miocene/Plio-
cene fauna. Thus the necessity arose for comparative work on the
Siwalik and African pre-Pleistocene hominoids in order to establish
their exact phylogenetic positions.

In 1951, 1954, and 1962, K. N. Prasad, of the Geological Survey
of India, explored the area around Haritalyangar while mapping its
geological formations. He discovered eleven specimens (Prasad 1962,
1964). He established the new species *Sivapithecus aiyengari* on the
basis of a left mandibular ramus (GSI 18039), naming it in honor of
N. K. N. Aiyengar, who had made a substantial addition to the Geological Survey of India primate collection in Calcutta.

In 1959 I explored the Haritalyangar area and found an almost complete primate mandible resembling that of the extant loris, but a little
larger (Khatri 1964). In September, 1970, I explored the area around
Ramnagar in Jammu for Miocene hominoids, and in May, 1971, I
visited Haritalyangar again.

In 1968 the Punjab-Yale University research team explored extensively around Haritalyangar and procured from a peasant an almost
complete mandible of a new species, *Gigantopithecus bilaspurensis*
(Simons and Chopra 1969a, 1969b). It is presumed to have come from
Pliocene Dhok Pathan beds of the Siwaliks.

In addition to this field research, the old material has been re-examined, particularly by Yale University scholars. Tattersall (1968) recognized a fragment of a left mandibular ramus of a large lorisid primate (YPM 19134) containing M_3, the roots of M_2, and the posterior
root of M_1. It has been assigned to *Indraloris lulli* (established by
Lewis in 1933). An upper right central incisor of *Dryopithecus* (YPM
16919) was also discovered in the old Siwalik collection at Yale. It fits
well in the alveolus of GSI 196 and may actually belong to it.

THE SIWALIK HILLS

The Siwalik foothills extend for more than 1,600 kilometers along the

Himalayas from Baluchistan to Assam (Map 1). They are sixteen to fifty-nine kilometers wide.[2] The sand gravels and conglomerates forming the Siwalik sediments are 4,570 to 6,100 meters (15,000 to 20,000 feet) thick and they rise to a height of 1,600 meters. Their strike is in a northwest-southeast direction. The word Siwalik is derived from a hill of the same name near Hardwar on a bank of the Ganga where the first mammalian fossils were recovered in the 1830's. Falconer, the first student of the Siwalik fauna, extended this name to the whole range. From Chandigarh, the Siwaliks look like small, pinkish hills at the base of a massive wall formed by the high Himalayas, which provide a dark background to the whole scene. The traverses from Jammu to Uddhampur, Pathankot to Dharamsala, and Chandigarh to Pinjor or Bilaspur give a sufficient idea of the physiography and composition of the Siwaliks. Gigantic escarpments, dipslopes, deep, meandering ravines, and huge gullies are the most common surface features of this area of sand and pebbles.

The Himalayas came into existence during the middle of the Eocene with the uplift of the Tethyan geosynclinal tract of sea deposits. The Siwaliks were formed during the mid-Miocene, a process that continued until the beginning of the Pleistocene. Thus the outermost Himalayan foothills, the Siwaliks, represent a late buckling of the erosional products of the Himalayas themselves and are not very dissimilar from the ones that are now being formed.

Pascoe (1919) and Pilgrim (1919) independently proposed a very ingenious and detailed hypothesis to explain the occurrence of the Siwalik deposits along the southern fringe of the Himalayas. It envisions Siwalik deposition taking place along a great longitudinal river — Pascoe's Indo-brahm and Pilgrim's Siwalik River — which flowed to the northwest. This great master stream was later disrupted by headward erosion of the left bank tributaries of its own lower course, equivalent to the lower Indus of today, and by the similar action of a proto-Ganga and a proto-Brahmaputra. De Terra (1936) and Krishanan and Aiyengar (1940) considered this hypothesis untenable in the light of their own research. De Terra considered the Siwaliks as a foredeep deposition on a littoral of almost continuous lagoons, with recently rejuvenated transverse streams forming the boulder beds.

Lithologically, the Siwalik deposits are subaerial waste from the

---

[2] Different authors cite different widths for the Siwalik belt. In Jammu it has been reported as twenty-four miles or thirty-eight kilometers (Wadia 1957: 366). Average width of the Siwaliks according to Colbert (1935: 6) is eight miles or thirteen kilometers.

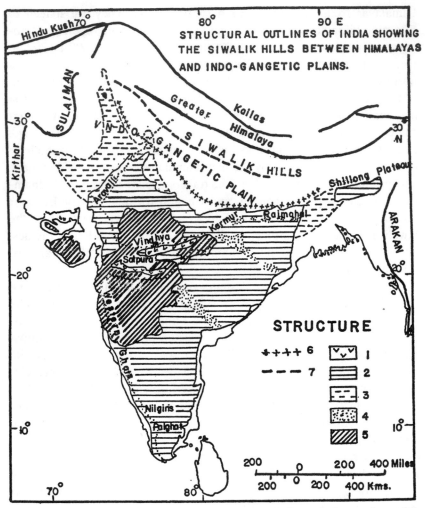

1 Narmada and Tapti troughs, 2 Peninsular Block, 3 Concealed extensions of 2,
4 Gondwana troughs, 5 Deccan lavas, 6 Boundary of Indo-Gangetic trough,
7 Siwalik Hills.

Map 1. View of India showing Siwalik Hills vis-à-vis Himalayas and Indo-
Gangetic Plain

Himalayas, consisting of alluvial detritus swept down by innumerable
streams and rivulets. In the fields, it is not possible to recognize the
Lower, Middle, and Upper Siwaliks because they form a continuous
deposition without any break. This classification is based on the three-
tier evolutionary succession of the vertebrate fauna which Pilgrim
established after his extensive paleontological studies, particularly of
fauna from Potwar and the Salt Range. Earlier, Falconer considered

the Siwaliks to be one continuous unit of Miocene age, and Lydekker divided it into upper and lower groups belonging to the Pliocene. Matthew (1924) considered lower, middle, and upper Siwalik faunas equivalent to Pontian, Middle Pliocene, and Lower Pleistocene age, respectively. Based on paleontological grounds, the Siwaliks are classified (Wadia 1957: 365) as in Table 1.

Table 1. Classification of Siwaliks

Upper Siwalik	Boulder Conglomerate zone	Lower Pleistocene to Lower Pliocene
	Pinjor zone	
	Tatrot zone	
Middle Siwalik	Dhok Pathan zone	Pontian to Middle Miocene
	Nagri zone	Middle Miocene
Lower Siwalik	Chinji stage	Tortonian
	Kamlial stage	Helvetian

For stratigraphy and fauna, the Potwar terrain north of the Salt Range, and the Kangra-Hardwar tract in Himachal and Uttar Pradesh are considered type areas. Different opinions regarding age and correlation of Siwalik beds are summarized in Figure 1.

The most important geotectonic features of the Siwalik system are its reversed overthrust faults, which are traceable for enormous distances (Wadia 1957: 388). In the extreme compression and stresses of tectonic, mountain-building processes, some of the folds became inverted or REVERSED. In such cases, the middle limb of the fold suffers the severest tension and gets into a highly inclined fracture or THRUST-PLANE, along which the dislocated portion of the fold slips as an entity over long distances, thus throwing the older pre-Siwalik rocks of the inner Himalayas over the younger ones of the Siwalik outer ranges (Figure 2).

IMPORTANT SIWALIK COLLECTIONS OF VERTEBRATE FAUNA

There are now five notable collections of Siwalik vertebrate fossils. They are located in the British Museum of Natural History, London; the Geological Survey of India Museum, Calcutta; the American Museum of Natural History, New York; Yale University Peabody Museum, New Haven; and the Department of Geology Museum,

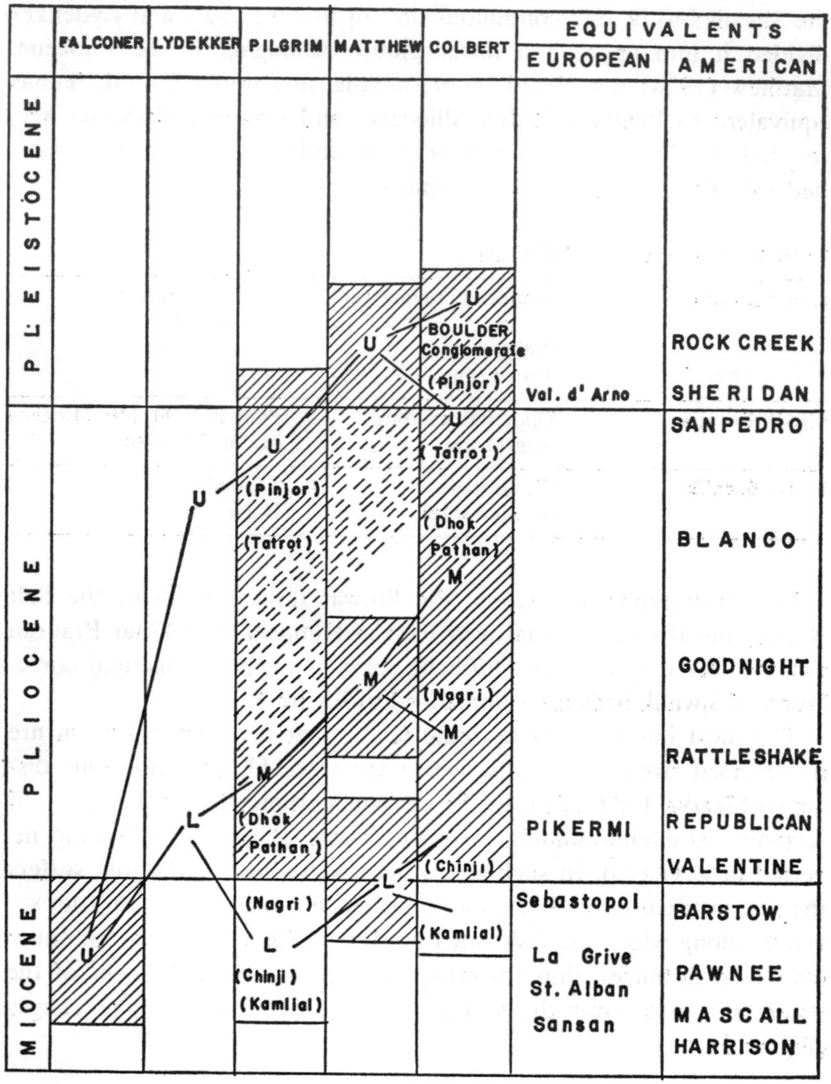

	FALCONER	LYDEKKER	PILGRIM	MATTHEW	COLBERT	EQUIVALENTS	
						EUROPEAN	AMERICAN
PLEISTOCENE					U		
				U	BOULDER Conglomerate (Pinjor)		ROCK CREEK
					(Pinjor)	Val. d' Arno	SHERIDAN
PLIOCENE		U	U (Pinjor) (Tatrot)		U (Tatrot)		SAN PEDRO
					(Dhok Pathan) M		BLANCO
			M	M	(Nagri) M		GOODNIGHT
			(Dhok Pathan)				RATTLESHAKE
		L			(Chinji)	PIKERMI	REPUBLICAN
				L			VALENTINE
MIOCENE	U		(Nagri) L (Chinji) (Kamlial)		(Kamlial)	Sebastopol	BARSTOW
						La Grive	PAWNEE
						St. Alban	MASCALL
						Sansan	HARRISON

Figure 1.   Comparative views of the correlation of different Siwalik horizons

Punjab University, Chandigarh. The earliest collections, made in the 1830's and later by Falconer and Cautley, are in the British Museum. The collection at Calcutta is the largest and most varied. It was built up mainly through the efforts of Lydekker and Pilgrim and later by several other officers of the Geological Survey of India. The American Museum of Natural History collection was assembled by Brown in 1922. The Siwalik fauna at the Yale Peabody Museum was acquired by

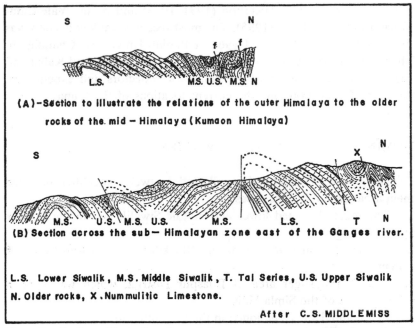

Figure 2. Sections illustrating the relationship of the outer Himalayas to the older rocks

Table 2. Important Siwalik collections of vertebrate fauna

Series numbers	Collectors	Museums
1.	Falconer and Cautley (1830–1850)	British Museum of Natural History, London
2.	Richard Lydekker (1876–1886) and Guy E. Pilgrim (1900–1930)	Geological Survey of India Museum, Calcutta
3.	Barnum Brown (1922–1923) — American Museum of Natural History Siwalik Expedition	American Museum of Natural History, New York
4.	G. Edward Lewis (1931–1933) — Yale North India Expedition	Yale University Peabody Museum, New Haven
5.	Helmut De Terra (1935) — Yale-Cambridge India Expedition	Yale University Peabody Museum, New Haven, and Cambridge University, Cambridge, England
6.	Exploration for the Remains of Early Man in India Research Project (Council of Scientific and Industrial Research, Government of India) (1958–1964)	Department of Geology Museum, Punjab University, Chandigarh

the Yale North India Expedition (1931–1933) and by the Yale-Cambridge India Expedition (1935). The most recent Siwalik collection was developed between 1958 and 1964 at Punjab University, Chandigarh. Most of the fossils have been discovered at locations around Kalka and Pinjor. Table 2 summarizes the names of collectors and expeditions, the year of collection, and the current locations of the fauna.

HOMINOID SITES OF THE SIWALIKS

Primate specimens have been collected at twelve localities in three main areas (Map 2). The areas are:
1.   The much-dissected lower and middle Siwalik belt in the Potwar synclinal basin.
2.   The country around Ramnagar, 103 kilometers east-northeast of Jammu.
3.   The Haritalyangar area of Bilaspur District, which was once a princely state of the Simla Hills.
   The hominoid sites mentioned in the literature are:
1.   India
   a.   Haritalyangar (31° 32′N; 76° 38′E); thirty kilometers northwest of Bilaspur town, Himachal Pradesh
   b.   Chakrana (31° 32′N; 76° 41′E); six kilometers east of Haritalyangar, Bilaspur District, Himachal Pradesh
   c.   Ramnagar (32° 49′N; 73° 22′E); at Kirmu and Dal Sar, five kilometers from Ramnagar, a small town 103 kilometers (by road) east of Jammu
2.   Pakistan (a-d in the Salt Range, Attock District, Punjab; e-i in the Salt Range, Jhelum District, Punjab)
   a.   Chinji (32° 41′N; 72° 22′E)
   b.   Kundal Nala (Southwest of Chinji)
   c.   Kanati (near Chinji)
   d.   Alipur
   e.   Hasnot (32° 49′N; 72° 19′ 30″E)
   f.   Bhandar
   g.   Jabi
   h.   Kotal Kund
   i.   Parrewali
   Of these sites, only the first three are now in India. Haritalyangar is the most productive, so it is searched repeatedly by investigators in India.

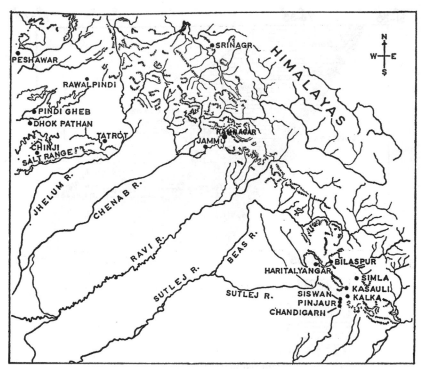

Map 2. Important fossiliferous sites of the Siwaliks

Haritalyangar (Plates 1–4) is named after the twin villages of Hari and Talyangar, one situated at the bottom of the valley and the other at the top. It is about thirty kilometers northwest of Bilaspur and about six kilometers from Dadhol, a bus stop, on the Bilaspur-Ladrol road.[3] On seeing the situation of Talyangar for the first time, one gets the impression that this area might once have been a large lake.

The Hari Temple Cuesta Scarp (Plate 3), locally called *Hari-Ka-Tibba*, is a treasure-house of primate fossils. It is only 200 meters north of Hari village and its horizon of red clay is fossiliferous (Plate 4).

The succession of geological horizons (Figure 3) in this area (Prasad 1964) is shown in Table 3.

NAHAN BEDS These are the earliest geological horizons exposed in

---

[3] A new road linking new Bilaspur township with Haritalyangar was constructed after the creation of Govindsagar Lake by the Bakhra dam on the Sutlej River. The old Bilaspur town, with its buildings and radiating roads, is now under this body of water. The road distances cited here are those before the creation of Govindsagar Lake.

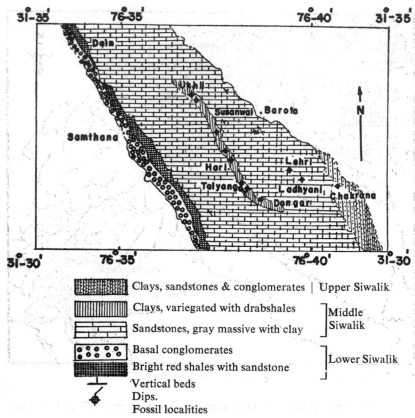

Figure 3.   Geological map of Haritalyangar area in Bilaspur, Himachal Pradesh

Table 3.   Succession of geological horizons in Haritalyangar area

Upper Siwalik	Pinjor Stage: variegated clay and sand- stones	Villafranchian Astian
	Tatrot Stage: hard brown sandstones with clays	
Middle Siwalik	Dhok Pathan Stage: brown sandstones, orange clays and dark shades	Pontian
	Nagri Stage: massive grey sandstones and pink clays	Sarmatian
Lower Siwalik	Nahan Stage: bright red shales and (Sutlej) sandstones	Upper Tortonian

this area. Their hallmark is sandstone interbedded with purple or greenish clay containing fossil wood.

NAGRI BEDS These beds consist of massive grey sandstones and pink clays. To the west of Haritalyangar, sandstones are overlaid by variegated clays containing *Hipparion theobaldi* and *Crocuta gigantea*. Four prominent ridges striking east-west, north-south, west-northwest–south-southeast, and northwest-southeast are exposed east of Haritalyangar and are rich in fossils.

DHOK PATHAN BEDS These beds are made up of drab clays and sandstones. Two fossiliferous exposures at Ladhyani (31° 32′N; 76° 40′E) and Lehri Serail (31° 32′N; 76° 30′E) yield fauna of Dhok Pathan stage.

PINJOR BEDS These are exposed at Chakrana (31° 32′N; 76° 42′E), about six kilometers southeast of Haritalyangar, and are comparable to Pinjor. The basal beds at Chakrana are of Tatrot stage (Astian) on paleontological evidence.

The Nagri zone (twelve to eight million years) has yielded the largest number of fossils.

Chakrana is six kilometers southeast of Haritalyangar. The type specimen YPM 13799 of *Ramapithecus brevirostris* was recovered one-fourth mile east of Chakrana.

Ramnagar is a small town 103 kilometers east-northeast of Jammu by road. Lower Siwalik (Chinji) fossiliferous beds are exposed at Kirmu and Dal Sar nearby. At least seven hominoid specimens have been recovered here. GSI D. 198 was collected by Middlemiss; and Pilgrim (1927) based the species *Sivapithecus middlemissi* on it. AMNH 19411 was collected by Brown in 1922, and Brown, Gregory, and Hellman (1924) established the species *Dryopithecus pilgrimi* on it.

Four specimens — numbers 600 (YPM 13822), 601, 602, and 603 (Gregory, Hellman, and Lewis 1938: 3–4) — collected by the Yale-Cambridge India Expedition of 1935 under De Terra were recovered from the Chinji beds southwest of Ramnagar. Specimen 600 is now in the Yale Peabody Museum, while the other three are in the Geological Survey of India Museum, Calcutta. All specimens are isolated molars.

The seventh find, which consists of an isolated left lower molar of *Dryopithecus* (previously assigned to *Sivapithecus darwini*), was collected by Bose from Dal Sar, a site two kilometers north of Ramnagar.

NATURE OF SIWALIK HOMINOID FINDS

These finds are generally in the form of isolated teeth and broken maxillary and mandibular fragments. The extreme rarity of upper dentition is difficult to explain. Postcranial material is totally absent. It has been suggested recently that the anthropoid apes of the Siwaliks were victims of hyaenodonts (Prasad 1964: 125). Hyaenodont bones are concentrated in the same localities and horizons in which primates are found. The fragmentary condition of the primate mandibles and maxillae may be due to mastication by hyenas and other carnivorous beasts.

NEW HOMINOID FOSSILS

Prasad (1962, 1964) collected primate fossils near Haritalyangar. His finds are now in the Geological Survey of India (GSI) Museum at Calcutta. Prasad described the following eleven specimens:

1.   GSI 18039. A left mandibular ramus with M_1, M_2, M_3, P_4, alveolus of the canine, and I_1, I_2. The molars and premolars are in position and show an advanced degree of wear. *Sivapithecus aiyengari*.

2.   GSI 18040. A fragment of a mandible of an old individual containing M_2 and M_3 with roots firmly in the base of the jaw. *Sivapithecus indicus*.

3.   GSI 18041. Single molar, M_1. *Sivapithecus salmontanus*.

4.   GSI 18042. Single molar, M_1. *Sivapithecus sivalensis*.

5.   GSI 18064. Fragment of a maxilla containing three molars. The M^1 and M^2 are partly worn, therefore details of cusps not clear. The M^3 is well preserved. *Sivapithecus sivalensis*.

6.   GSI 18065. An upper right premolar. This is of special importance because most of the other dental material recovered belongs to the lower portion. *Sivapithecus indicus*.

7.   GSI 18066. An upper canine from Nagri beds. *Sivapithecus indicus*.

8.   GSI 18067. Practically unworn lower right third molar from Nagri beds, east of Haritalyangar. *Sugrivapithecus gregoryi*.

9.   GSI 18068. Isolated upper third molar recovered from below the Hari escarpment. It is moderately worn but details are clear. *Dryopithecus punjabicus*.

10.   GSI 18069. Last lower premolar. *Sivapithecus sivalensis*.

11.   GSI 18070. Isolated molar. *Sivapithecus*.

The nearly complete mandible of a loris that I found in 1959 in the Haritalyangar area has not yet been described. The specimen belongs to the Geological Department, Punjab University, Chandigarh.

The almost complete mandible of *Gigantopithecus bilaspurensis* (Chandigarh — Yale Project Register Number 359/68) consists of both horizontal rami of the mandible joined at the symphysis. It contains the left C_1, P_3, and M_{1-3} and the right C_1, P_{3-4}, and M_{1-3}. The horizontal rami are broken off just posterior to the third molars. The specimen belongs to the Department of Anthropology, Punjab University, Chandigarh. It is claimed to be the most complete pre-Pleistocene hominoid mandible ever found in the Indian subcontinent (Simons and Chopra 1969a). It is supposed to have come from the upper levels of the Dhok Pathan beds northwest of Haritalyangar, and thus to be of Middle Pliocene age. But the circumstances of its discovery have not yet been fully described. During my visit to Haritalyangar in May, 1971, I was informed that this specimen had been discovered by a peasant who kept it in an obscure niche in his house and forgot it. When approached by members of the research team, he sold the specimen for a meager amount of money. If this is true, I wonder how one can be sure of its geological horizon.

In summary, there is a published record of thirteen new specimens of hominoid fossils from Haritalyangar discovered between 1951 and 1973. Before that, eighty-two primate specimens were recorded from the Siwalik beds (Wadia and Aiyengar 1938). To these we may add the two primate specimens that were discovered in the old Siwalik collection at the Yale Peabody Museum — YPM 19134 and YPM 16919. Therefore, we have a total of ninety-seven primate specimens from the Siwaliks on record.

REVISED CLASSIFICATION OF SIWALIK FINDS

Clearly, an excessive amount of splitting of Siwalik genera and species has occurred. The ninety-seven primate finds from the Siwaliks have been categorized into fourteen genera and thirty-one species (Table 4)[4] — one genus and one species of Lorisidae, four genera and five species of Cercopithecidae, and nine genera and twenty-five species of Pongidae. *Dryopithecus* was supposed to contain seven species; *Sivapithecus*, five species; *Ramapithecus*, two species; *Bramapithecus*, three species;

---

[4] Different authors have given different estimates of Siwalik primate genera and species. Colbert (1935) listed thirteen genera and twenty-nine species. Wadia and Aiyengar (1938) counted eleven genera and twenty-one species, and Wadia (1957: 370) mentioned fifteen genera of primates, including anthropoid apes.

and *Sugrivapithecus,* two species. Obviously, something was drastically wrong with the early nomenclature and taxonomy of Siwalik primates. It was long recognized that considerable synonymity exists among the forms, but the problems of correlating specimens and reducing the synonymity were left by earlier workers for a future time when more complete material might be available.

Gregory, Hellman, and Lewis (1938) began this task and reduced the Siwalik pongids to four genera and ten species. In 1965, Simons and Pilbeam suggested a revised classification of the African and Indian material. The African genera and species involved in this new taxonomic assignment were *Proconsul* species, *Sivapithecus africanus,* and *Kenyapithecus wickeri.* Most of the celebrated Siwalik genera and species disappear and are mainly amalgamated with *Dryopithecus.* *Sivapithecus* no longer has generic rank and is no longer considered to be near the line of human descent. It is now only a subgenus of *Dryopithecus.* Similarly, *Sugrivapithecus* is transferred to *Dryopithecus.* The genus *Bramapithecus* (with its three species — *B. thorpei, B. punjabicus,* and *B. sivalensis*), the African species *Kenyapithecus wickeri,* and *Dryopithecus punjabicus* are all considered hominid and are classified under *Ramapithecus* (Simons 1961). They are now junior synonyms of *Ramapithecus punjabicus* (the generic name comes from Lewis's *Ramapithecus brevirostris* and the specific name from Pilgrim's *Dryopithecus punjabicus*). *Sivapithecus aiyengari* (Prasad 1962) is also considered an invalid name. The specimen on which Prasad established this species belonged to an old individual; the canine is absent and the alveolus is filled in with cancellous bone. It belonged to *Dryopithecus aiyengari* (Simons 1967: 330). Thus Simons and Pilbeam (1965) classified all African and Siwalik material into two genera — *Dryopithecus* and *Ramapithecus. Dryopithecus* includes *Sugrivapithecus* and *Sivapithecus* and is considered to be an ape in the Pongidae. *Bramapithecus* is sunk into *Ramapithecus,* along with the African *Kenyapithecus wickeri. Ramapithecus* is considered to be the earliest known hominid, living twelve to eight million years ago in late Miocene or early Pliocene times in Africa and India.

RAMAPITHECUS — THE EARLIEST HOMINID

Before 1960, *Ramapithecus* was considered to be the most manlike of the Siwalik pongids, but no more than that. In 1961 and 1964, Simons began to rehabilitate this genus to its true position. In 1934, Lewis had

Table 4. Fossil primates of the Siwalik Hills (India)

	Lower Siwaliks		Middle Siwaliks		Upper Siwaliks		
	Kamlial	Chinji	Nagri	Dhok Patan	Tatrot	Pinjor	Boulder Conglomerate
LORISIDAE							
1. *Indraloris lulli* (Lewis), 1933			×				
CERCOPITHECIDAE							
2. *Papio falconeri* (Lydekker), 1886						×	
3. *Papio subhimalayanus* (V. Meyer), 1886						×	
4. *Cercopithecus hasnoti* (Pilgrim), 1910				×			
5. *Semonpithecus palaeindicus* (Lydekker), 1864							
6. *Macacus sivalensis* (Lydekker), 1878				×			
PONGIDAE							
7. *Simia of satyrus* (Linnaeus), 1866						×	
8. *Dryopithecus punjabicus* (Pilgrim), 1910		×	×				
9. *Dryopithecus pilgrimi* (Brown, Gregory, and Hellman), 1924		×					
10. *Dryopithecus cautleyi* (Brown, Gregory), 1924			×	×			
11. *Dryopithecus frickae* (Brown, Gregory, and Hellman), 1924							
12. *Dryopithecus chinjiensis* (Pilgrim),1915		×	×				
13. *Dryopithecus giganteus* (Pilgrim), 1915			×				
14. *Dryopithecus sivalensis* (Lewis), 1934			×				
15. *Sivapithecus orientalis* (Pilgrim), 1927			×				
16. *Sivapithecus himalayensis* (Pilgrim), 1927			×				
17. *Sivapithecus aiyengari* (Prasad), 1962		×					
18. *Sivapithecus indicus* (Pilgrim), 1910		×					
19. *Hylopithecus hysudricus* (Pilgrim), 1927			×				
20. *Palaeopithecus (?) sylvaticus* (Pilgrim), 1927			×				
21. *Palaeopithecus sivalensis* (Lydekker), 1879			×				
22. *Palaeopithecus sp.* (Pilgrim), 1913				×			
23. *Palaeosimia rugosidens* (Pilgrim), 1915		×					
24. *Ramapithecus brevirostris* (Lewis), 1934			×				
25. *Ramapithecus hariensis* (Lewis), 1934			×				
26. *Sugrivapithecus salmontanus* (Lewis), 1934			×				
27. *Sugrivapithecus gregoryi* (Lewis), 1936			×				
28. *Bramapithecus thorpei* (Lewis), 1934		×					
29. *Bramapithecus sivalensis* (Lewis), 1934				×			
30. *Bramapithecus punjabicus* (Lewis), 1934							
31. *Gigantopithecus bilaspurensis* (Simons and Chopra), 1968							

emphasized its hominid characters, but had classified it under the family Simidae, appending "(Hominidae?)" cautiously. Gregory, Hellman, and Lewis (1938) stated that "while the Siwalik genus *Ramapithecus* and the South African *Australopithecus* are still apes, by DEFINITION, they are almost on the human threshold in their known anatomical characters." Hrdlicka (1935), however, thought that *Ramapithecus* was a pongid. His opinion carried weight at that time, so that the importance of *Ramapithecus* was forgotten until Simons (1961) again called attention to its hominid features. Simons also discovered specimens that actually belonged to *Ramapithecus* but were wrongly assigned to other genera.

The specimens which have been said to belong to *Ramapithecus* are:
1.   YPM 13799. A right maxilla and premaxillae with dentition. This was a type specimen on which Lewis established the species *Ramapithecus brevirostris*. It was recovered in 1932 from the Nagri beds at Chakrana, four miles east of Haritalyangar, northwest of Bilaspur, Himachal Pradesh, India.
2.   YPM 13806; YPM 13814; YPM 13833. These three specimens in the Yale collection are mandibular fragments with molars intact. Lewis (1934) established *Bramapithecus* species on this material. They are now regarded as representing the lower jaws of *Ramapithecus*. The genus *Bramapithecus* is not considered valid and therefore is abolished.
3.   GSI D.118, D.119. The right and left mandibular rami of the same mandible recovered from Chinji beds. It was a type specimen on which Pilgrim in 1910 established the species *Dryopithecus punjabicus*.
4.   GSI D.185. A right maxilla recovered from Haritalyangar, Nagri beds, Bilaspur. It is a co-type of *Dryopithecus punjabicus*, established by Pilgrim in 1910. Simons (1964) diagnosed it as *Ramapithecus*.
5.   GSI 18068. Isolated upper third molar from Nagri beds from Haritalyangar. Discovered by Prasad and assigned to *Dryopithecus punjabicus* (Prasad 1962).
6.   NMK FT 1272. A left maxilla with canine, roots of P^3, and crown of P^4 to M^2.

NMK FT 1271. A right maxilla with M^1, M^2, and roots of M^3, and a right M_2.

These two maxillae were made the type specimens of the new genus and species *Kenyapithecus wickeri* established by Leakey (1962).

Based on the above material, particularly after the transfer of the type and co-type specimens of Pilgrim's *Dryopithecus punjabicus*, the new name *Ramapithecus punjabicus* Pilgrim 1910 was coined as a binomen of the new species. The following species are now considered

junior synonyms of *R. punjabicus*:
1. *Ramapithecus brevirostris*, Lewis (1934: 162)
2. *Bramapithecus thorpei*, Lewis (1934: 173)
3. *Bramapithecus sivalensis*, Lewis (1934: 173)
4. *Kenyapithecus wickeri*, Leakey (1962: 690)
5. *Dryopithecus punjabicus*, Pilgrim (1910: 63)

The specimens previously assigned to *Ramapithecus* but now considered not to belong to it are:
1. YPM 13807. Type specimen of the species *R. hariensis* Lewis (1934). It consists of a distorted maxillary fragment with worn M^1 and fractured and broken M^2. In 1937 Lewis transferred this specimen to *Sivapithecus sivalensis*, later regarded as *D.(S.) sivalensis* by Simons and Pilbeam (1965). It is a fragmentary specimen and therefore its exact position is difficult to determine (Pilbeam 1969: 100). Simons (1961) indicated the heteromorphic nature of its lower premolars, more characteristic of pongids than of hominids.
2. GSI D. 168 (YPM 13870 cast). A right horizontal mandibular ramus having crowns of P_3 to M_4 and the canine and incisor alveoli. Gregory, Hellman, and Lewis (1938) assigned it to *Ramapithecus*. Simons (1964) and Simons and Pilbeam (1965) consider it to be a pongid because of the presence of a simian shelf and heteromorphy in the lower premolars.

Lewis (1934) gave the following diagnostic features of *Ramapithecus*:
1. Dental arcade of the upper jaw that is parabolic, as in man, rather than U-shaped, as in apes.
2. Face slightly prognathous.
3. Absence of diastema in the dental series.
4. Small canine.
5. Antero-posteriorly compressed dentition.
6. Incisors approximately equal in size.
7. Canine ellipsoid with long axis normal to the curve of the dental arcade.
8. Third premolar and succeeding teeth progressive.

Simons and Pilbeam (1965) gave the following generic diagnosis of *Ramapithecus*, pointing out the main features in which it differs from *Australopithecus* and *Dryopithecus:*

Slightly smaller overall size [except *Proconsul africanus*, which they renamed *Dryopithecus africanus*], shallower mandible, less complex patterns of tooth crenulation, little or no evidence of cingula or Carabellis' cusps and shorter face. Incisors and canines reduced in relation to cheek-tooth size when compared to *Dryopithecus* but not as markedly as in *Australopithecus*;

incisor procumbancy intermediate. Differs from *Dryopithecus* and other apes in showing more widely spaced and much lower molar cusps, so that the central or occlusal fovea of the molars covers more of the crown surface of the tooth (even so these features show some variability in *Ramapithecus* and *Dryopithecus* as well as in modern *Homo* and *Pan*); sides of the upper molars, particularly, are more vertical; also differs from *Dryopithecus* in showing a larger and lower canine fossa, an arched palate, arcuate tooth row and a much shorter rostrum.

Leakey (1967) did not consider this generic definition to be satisfactory because body size, shallower palate, and shorter face are not taxonomically sound characters. He maintained that *Kenyapithecus wickeri* was a separate species and could not be sunk in *Ramapithecus*. He also transferred BMNH M-16649, the type specimen of his *Sivapithecus africanus*, to *Kenyapithecus* as *K. africanus*, a species that he regarded as ancestral to *K. wickeri*. To Leakey, *K. africanus* is the earliest hominid. Pilbeam (1969) considered Leakey's arguments to be "armchair juggling" and therefore dismissed them. Campbell (1966) and LeGros Clark (1964a) accepted the synonymy of *Kenyapithecus wickeri* and *Ramapithecus punjabicus* .

Ramapithecus occurred in Europe, China, Africa, and India. The right M^2 from the Pontian of Melchingen Württemberg in the Swabian Alps of Europe and attributed to *Dryopithecus fontani* by Branco (1898) shows features of *Ramapithecus* (Simons 1964). It occurs in late Miocene deposits. Woo (1958) described the type specimen of *Dryopithecus keiyuanensis* from deposits of uncertain age in Keiyuan, Yunan, China. But Chow (1958) believes that one of the two Chinese finds should be assigned to *Ramapithecus punjabicus*. However, until there is further detailed investigation, the allocation remains uncertain.

In summary, the following points emerge about *Ramapithecus*:

1.   It was a *Pan*-sized primate with a short face, arcuate palate, and an *Australopithecus*-like mandible. Dental and facial features resemble very closely those of *Australopithecus africanus*.

2.   Circumstantial evidence suggests that *Ramapithecus punjabicus* might have been a tool-using animal and a partial biped.

3.   It lived fourteen to fifteen million years ago, in the late Miocene/ early Pliocene period.

4.   *Ramapithecus* was a wide-ranging and mobile creature and was present in India, East Africa, Europe, and China.

GIGANTOPITHECUS — A NEW SPECIES FROM SWALIK

The mandible of *Gigantopithecus bilaspurensis* was obtained originally in three pieces. It was identified by G. W. Meyer, co-investigator of the Punjab-Yale University project.[5] Its main diagnostic features are:

1. Mandible is smaller in absolute size than available mandibles of *G. blacki*.

2. Anterior teeth are relatively smaller than those of *G. blacki*.

3. Teeth preserved (C through M_3) are little worn and do not show the polycuspidation that *G. blacki* teeth do.

4. In this simplicity of teeth, *G. bilaspurensis* resembles some *Dryopithecus* species, e.g. *D. sivalensis* and *D. indicus*.

5. Lower molar protoconids are smaller than metaconids and apexes of lower molar cusps are placed laterally. In this feature the molars are unlike those of *G. blacki* and *D. indicus* but resemble those of *Ramapithecus*.

6. Cheek-tooth occlusal faces show lingual and labial expansion, so that the sides of the teeth are oriented almost vertically. In this feature, too, they resemble *Ramapithecus*. In *Dryopithecus* and *G. blacki* the sides of the teeth are rounded.

7. Unlike *G. blacki* molars, those of *G. bilaspurensis* are not clearly divided into trigonid and talonid portions by a lingual indentation between the metaconid and entoconid.

There have been two main opinions regarding the phyletic relationship of *Gigantopithecus*. One school considers this genus to be an aberrant pongid with some changes in dental morphology as a result of either (1) adaptation to a new manner of feeding or (2) allometric changes to its large absolute size. According to the second school, the correct placement of the genus is in Hominidae as (1) ancestral to later hominids or (2) an extinct side branch of the Hominidae that lived in Southeast Asia contemporaneously with *Australopithecus* and/or *Homo*. Weidenreich (1946), von Koenigswald (1949, 1952, 1958), Heberer (1959), Dart (1960), and Woo (1962) advocated the placement of *Gigantopithecus* in Hominidae, while Pei and Woo (1956), Pei and Li (1959), Remane (1950, 1960), Ti-Cheng (1962), and Simons and Pilbeam (1965) thought that it belonged to the Pongidae.

Gigantopithecus bilaspurensis was undoubtedly a very large primate.

---

[5] This program has ceased to operate. I regret that this promising international collaboration has come to such a sorry end and that the jaw of an ape should have become a bone of contention, leading to acrimony and mistrust between two parties of rational men.

It is smaller than the Chinese Pleistocene species of *Gigantopithecus*, but it has larger premolars and molars than most other hominoids. In many characters this specimen bears more similarity to *Australopithecus, Ramapithecus,* and *Dryopithecus* than to *Gigantopithecus blacki*. It has been suggested (Simons and Chopra 1969b: 1) that although *Gigantopithecus* is far from the line of human ancestry, the biomechanics of its jaws and teeth are unquestionably human, and that this feature might have arisen in parallel with the similar mandibular and dental mechanics of *Ramapithecus*. Thus, *Gigantopithecus bilaspurensis* is thought to represent a side branch of Asian apes which achieved a dental mechanism closely approximating that of hominids. This ape lived in open country and its ancestor might have been a gorilla-like forest dweller similar to *Dryopithecus indicus* (Simons and Chopra 1969b).

SUMMARY

1. To date, ninety-seven primate specimens from the Siwalik foothills of the Himalayas have been discovered.
2. In age they extend from Lower Siwalik to Upper Siwalik, i.e. from Middle Miocene to early Pliocene.
3. In the literature these specimens have been classified in fourteen genera and thirty-one species.
4. The Siwalik primate fossils generally consist of mandibular and maxillary fragments, isolated teeth, and molars. Upper dentition is very rare. No cranial or limb bones have been recovered.
5. The family Pongidae includes such genera as *Dryopithecus, Sivapithecus, Bramapithecus, Ramapithecus,* and *Sugrivapithecus*.
6. In a revised classification (Simons and Pilbeam 1965), only two Siwalik genera are considered valid, viz., *Dryopithecus* and *Ramapithecus*.
7. *Sivapithecus* was once thought to be nearest to the line of human descent (Pilgrim 1910, 1915, 1927), and it held separate generic rank. Now it is reduced to a subgenus of *Dryopithecus* in the family Pongidae.
8. *Ramapithecus* is considered to be the only known late Miocene/early Pliocene hominid and the forerunner of man. It is a separate genus in the Hominidae. *Ramapithecus punjabicus* lived in India fourteen to eight million years ago, from upper Miocene to early Pliocene.
9. *Bramapithecus* (Lewis 1934), *Dryopithecus sivalensis* (Pilgrim 1910), and *Kenyapithecus wickeri* (Leakey 1962) are now considered

to be synonyms of *Ramapithecus punjabicus* in the Simons and Pilbeam classification.

10.   An almost complete mandible representing a new species, *Gigantopithecus bilaspurensis*, was discovered in 1968. It is thought to resemble species of *Australopithecus, Ramapithecus,* and *Dryopithecus* more than it does the Chinese Pleistocene species *Gigantopithecus blacki.*

11.   A future problem for investigators in the Siwalik Hills is to find cranial and postcranial bones of *Ramapithecus.* This will help to elucidate the evolution of erect posture, locomotion, behavior, and, most important, the capacity to make tools.

12.   An attempt should be made to fix the age of different Siwalik beds by radiometric methods so that their correlation could be done more confidently. Faunal correlations between mammals of Africa and India would then be more meaningful.

REFERENCES

BRANCO, W.
   1898   Die menschenänlichen Zähne aus dem Bohnerz der Schwäbischen Alp. *Jahreshefte des Vereins für Vaterländische Naturkunde in Württemberg* 54:1–144.

BROWN, BARNUM, W. K. GREGORY, MILO HELLMAN
   1924   On three incomplete anthropoid jaws from the Siwaliks, India. *American Museum Novitates* 130.

CAMPBELL, B.
   1966   *Human evolution.* Chicago: Aldine.

CAUTLEY, P. T., H. FALCONER
   1868   "Notice on the remains of a fossil monkey from the Tertiary strata of the Siwalik Hills," in *Palaeontological memoirs and notes of H. Falconer* 1. Edited by C. Murchison, 292–297. London: Hardwicke.

CHOW, M. C.
   1958   Mammalian faunas and correlations of Tertiary and early Pleistocene of South China. *Journal of the Paleontological Society of India* 3:123–130.

COLBERT, EDWIN H.
   1935   Siwalik mammals in the American Museum of Natural History. *Transactions of the American Philosophical Society,* n.s. 26:1–69, 378–396.

DART, R.
   1960   The status of *Gigantopithecus. Anthropologischer Anzeiger* 24: 139–145.

DE TERRA, H.
1936 Geological factors determining higher anthropoid evolution in India. *American Journal of Physical Anthropology* 21:8.

FALCONER, H.
1837 Note on the occurrence of fossil bones in the Siwalik range, eastward of Hardwar. *Journal of the Asiatic Society of Bengal* 6:233–234.
1859 *Descriptive catalogue of the fossil remains of vertebrates from the Siwalik Hills, the Nerbudda, Perim Island, etc. in the Museum of the Asiatic Society of Bengal.* Calcutta.
1868 *Palaeontological memoirs and notes of H. Falconer*, volumes one and two. Edited by C. Murchison. London: Hardwicke.

FALCONER, H., P. T. CAUTLEY
1836a *Sivatherium giganteum:* a new fossil ruminant genus from the valley of the Markanda in the Siwalik branch of the sub-Himalayan mountains. *Asiatic Researches* 19:1–24.
1836b Note on the fossil hippopotamus of the Siwalik Hills. *Asiatic Researches* 19:39–53.
1846–1849 *Fauna antiqua sivalensis*, parts one through nine. London: Smith and Elder.

GAUDRY, A.
1890 Le Dryopithèque. *Société Géologique de France. Memoranda* 1:5–11.

GREGORY, W. K., MILO HELLMAN
1926 The dentition of *Dryopithecus* and the origin of man. *Anthropological Papers of the American Museum of Natural History* 28:1–23.

GREGORY, W. K., MILO HELLMAN, G. E. LEWIS
1938 *Fossil anthropoids of the Yale-Cambridge India Expedition of 1935.* Carnegie Institution of Washington Publication 495:1–27.

HEBERER, G.
1959 The descent of man and the present fossil record. *Cold Spring Harbor Symposium on Quantitative Biology* 24:235–244.

HOOIJER, D. A.
1951 Questions relating to a new large anthropoid ape from the Mio-Pliocene of the Siwaliks. *American Journal of Physical Anthropology* 9:79–95.

HOPWOOD, A. T.
1933a Miocene primates from Kenya. *Journal of the Proceedings of the Linnaean Society of London* 38:437–464.
1933b Miocene primates from British East Africa. *Annals and Magazine of Natural History*, series 10, 11:96–98.

HRDLICKA, A.
1935 Yale fossils of anthropoid apes. *American Journal of Science*, series 5, 29:34–40.

KHATRI, A. P.
1964 Recent exploration of the remains of early man in India. *Asian Perspectives* 7:160–182.

KRISHANAN, M. S., N. K. N. AIYENGAR
    1940   Did the Indobrahm or Siwalik River exist? *Records of the Geological Survey of India* 75:1-24.

LEAKEY, L. S. B.
    1943   A Miocene anthropoid mandible from Rusinga, Kenya. *Nature* 152:319–320.
    1959   A new fossil skull from Olduvai. *Nature* 194:491–493.
    1960   *Adam's ancestors* (fourth edition). New York: Harper and Row.
    1962   A new Lower Pliocene fossil primate from Kenya. *Annals and Magazine of Natural History*, series 13, 4:689–969.
    1963   "East African fossil Hominoidea and the classification within this super-family," in *Classification and human evolution*. Edited by S. L. Washburn, 32–49. Chicago: Aldine.
    1966   *Homo habilis, Homo erectus* and the australopithecines. *Nature* 209:1279–1281.
    1967   An early Miocene member of Hominidae. *Nature* 213:155–163.
    1972   "*Homo sapiens* in the Middle Pleistocene and the evidence of *Homo sapiens* evolution," in *The origin of* Homo sapiens. United Nations Educational, Scientific and Cultural Organization, Ecology and Conservation Series 3:25–29. Paris.

LEAKEY, L. S. B., J. F. EVERNDEN, G. H. CURTIS
    1961   Age of Bed I, Olduvai Gorge, Tanganyika. *Nature* 191:478–479.

LEAKEY, L. S. B., M. D. LEAKEY
    1964   Recent discoveries of fossil hominids in Tanganyika at Olduvai and near Lake Natron. *Nature* 202:5–7.

LEAKEY, L. S. B., P. V. TOBIAS, J. R. NAPIER
    1964   A new species of genus *Homo* from Olduvai. *Nature* 202:7–9.

LEAKEY, M. D.
    1971   *Olduvai Gorge: excavations in Beds I and II (1960–1963)*. London: Cambridge University Press.

LE GROS CLARK, W. E.
    1964a   *The fossil evidence for human evolution*. Second edition. Chicago: University of Chicago Press.
    1964b   The evolution of man. *Discovery* (London) 25:49.
    1967   *Man-apes or ape-men? The story of discoveries in Africa*. New York: Holt, Rinehart and Winston.

LE GROS CLARK, W. E., L. S. B. LEAKEY
    1951   The Miocene Hominoidea of East Africa. *Fossil Mammals of Africa* 1:1–117. London: British Museum (Natural History).

LEWIS, G. E.
    1933   Preliminary notice of a new genus of lemuroid from the Siwaliks. *American Journal of Science*, series 5, 27:134–138.
    1934   Preliminary notice of new man-like apes from India. *American Journal of Science*, series 5, 27:161–179.
    1936   A new species of *Sugrivapithecus*. *American Journal of Science*, series 5, 31:450–452.
    1937   Taxonomic syllabus of Siwalik fossil anthropoids. *American Journal of Science*, series 5, 35:139–147.

LYDEKKER, R.
   1880   Siwalik and Narbada Proboscidia. *Palaeontologia Indica*, series 10, 1(5):182–292, plates 29–46.
   1882   Siwalik and Narbada Equidae. *Palaeontologia Indica*, series 10, 2(3):67–98, plates 11–15.
   1884a Siwalik and Narbada Carnivora. *Palaeontologia Indica*, series 10, 2(6):179–363, plates 26–45.
   1884b Siwalik and Narbada Bunodont Suina. *Palaeontologia Indica*, series 10, 3(2):35–104, plates 6–12.
   1886   The fauna of the Karnul caves. *Palaeontologia Indica*, series 10, 4(2): volumes 1–4 *passim*.

MAC INNES, D. G.
   1943   Notes on the East African Miocene primates. *East Africa and Uganda Natural History Society Journal* 17:141–181.

MATTHEW, W. D.
   1924   Fossil animals of India. *Natural History*, 208–214.

NAPIER, J. R.
   1963a Brachiation and brachiators. *Zoological Society of London Symposium* 10:183–195.
   1963b "The locomotor function of hominids," in *Classification and human evolution*. Edited by S. L. Washburn, 178–189. Chicago: Aldine.
   1967   Evolutionary aspects of primate locomotion. *American Journal of Physical Anthropology*, n.s. 27:333–343.

NAPIER, J. R., A. C. WALKER
   1967   Vertical clinging and leaping — a newly recognized category of locomotor behavior of primates. *Folia Primatologica* 6:204–219.

PASCOE, E. H.
   1919   The early history of the Indus, Brahmaputra, and Ganges. *Quarterly Journal of the Geological Society of London* 75:138–155.

PEI, W. C., Y. H. LI
   1959   Discovery of a third mandible of *Gigantopithecus* in Liu-Cheng, Kwangsi, South China. *Vertebrata Palasiatica* 2:193–200.

PEI, W. C., J. K. WOO
   1956   New materials of *Gigantopithecus* teeth from South China. *Acta Palaeontologica* 4:477–490.

PILBEAM, D. R.
   1966   Notes on *Ramapithecus*, the earliest known hominid, and *Dryopithecus*. *American Journal of Physical Anthropology* 25:1–25.
   1967   Man's earliest ancestors. *Science Journal* 3(2):47–53.
   1968   The earliest hominids. *Nature* 219:1335–1338.
   1969   Tertiary Pongidae of East Africa: evolutionary relationship and taxonomy. *Bulletin of the Peabody Museum* 31:1–185. New Haven: Yale University.

PILBEAM, D. R., E. L. SIMONS
   1965   Some problems of hominid classification. *American Scientist* 53 (2):237–259.

PILGRIM, G. E.
1910   Notices of new mammalian genera and species from the Tertiaries of India. *Records of the Geological Survey of India* 40: 53–71.
1915   New Siwalik primates and their bearing on the question of evolution of man and Anthropoidea. *Records of the Geological Survey of India* 45:1–74.
1919   The Siwalik River. *Journal of the Asiatic Society of Bengal*, n.s. 15:81–99.
1927   A *Sivapithecus* palate and other primate fossils from India. *Palaeontologia Indica*, n.s. 14:1–25.

PRASAD, K. N.
1962   Fossil primates from the Siwalik beds of Haritalyangar, Himachal Pradesh, India. *Journal of the Geological Society of India* 3:86–96.
1964   Upper Miocene anthropoids from the Siwalik beds of Haritalyangar, Himachal Pradesh, India. *Palaeontology* 7:124–134. London.

REMANE, A.
1950   "Bemerkungen über *Gigantopithecus blacki*," in *Über die neuen Vor- und Frühmenschenfunde aus Afrika, Java, China, und Frankreich*. Edited by H. Weinert, 113–148. *Zeitschrift für Morphologie und Anthropologie* 42.
1960   Die Stellung von *Gigantopithecus*. *Anthropologischer Anzeiger* 24(2–3):146–159.

ROBINSON, J. T.
1963a "Adaptive radiation in the australopithecines and the origin of man," in *African ecology and human evolution*. Edited by F. C. Howell and F. Bourlière, 385–416. Chicago: Aldine.
1963b Australopithecines, culture and phylogeny. *American Journal of Physical Anthropology* 21:595–605.

SIMONS, E. L.
1961   The phyletic position of *Ramapithecus*. *Postilla* 51:1–9.
1963   Some fallacies in the study of hominid phylogeny. *Science* 141: 879–889.
1964   On the mandible of *Ramapithecus*. *National Academy of Science Proceedings* 51:528–535.
1965   New fossil apes from Egypt and the initial differentiation of Hominoidea. *Nature* 205:135–139.
1967   The earliest apes. *Scientific American* 217:28–35.
1968   A source of dental comparison of *Ramapithecus* with *Australopithecus* and *Homo*. *South African Journal of Science* 64:92–112.

SIMONS, E. L., S. R. K. CHOPRA
1969a A preliminary announcement of a new *Gigantopithecus* species from India. *Proceedings of the Second International Congress of Primatology, Atlanta, Georgia, 1968* 2:135–142. Basel: Karger.
1969b *Gigantopithecus* (Pongidae, Hominoidea): a new species from North India. *Postilla* 138:1–8.

SIMONS, E. L., D. R. PILBEAM
1965   Preliminary revision of the Dryopithecinae (Pongidae, Anthropoidea). *Folia Primatologica* 3:81–152.

TATTERSALL, I. M.
1968   A mandible of Indraloris (Primates, Lorisidae) from the Miocene of India. *Postilla* 123:1–10.
TATTERSALL, I. M., E. L. SIMONS
1969   Notes on some little-known primate fossils from India. *Folia Primatologica* 10:146–153.
TI-CHENG, T.
1962   The taxonomic position of *Gigantopithecus* in Primates. *Vertebrata Palasiatica* 6:375–383.
VON KOENIGSWALD, G. H. R.
1949   Bemerkungen über *"Dryopithecus" giganteus* Pilgrim. *Eclogae Geologicae Helvetiae* 42:515–519..
1952   *Gigantopithecus blacki* von Koenigswald, a giant fossil hominoid from the Pleistocene of southern China. *Anthropological Papers of the American Museum of Natural History* 43:292–325.
1957   Remarks on *Gigantopithecus* and other hominoid remains from southern China. *Proceedings of the Koninklijke Akademie van Wetenschappen, Amsterdam,* series B, 60(3):153–159.
1958   *Gigantopithecus* and *Australopithecus. The Leech* 28:101–105.
WADIA, D. N.
1957   *Geology of India.* London: Macmillan.
WADIA, D. N., N. K. N. AIYENGAR
1938   Fossil anthropoids of India: a list of the fossil material hitherto discovered from the Tertiary deposits of India. *Records of the Geological Survey of India* 72(4):467–494.
WEIDENREICH, F.
1946   *Apes, giants and men.* Chicago: University of Chicago Press.
WOO, J. K.
1958   New materials of *Dryopithecus* from Keiyuan, Yunan. *Vertebrata Palasiatica* 2(1):38–42.
1962   The mandibles and dentition of *Gigantopithecus. Palaeontologia Sinica* 146:1–94.

Ramapithecus:
A Review of Its Hominid Status

GLENN C. CONROY and DAVID PILBEAM

GLENN C. CONROY and DAVID PILBEAM

Until the year 1910, only two fossil anthropoid specimens had been recovered from the Siwalik Hills of India although numerous other fossil mammals had been collected in the previous eighty years. The two specimens consisted of one isolated upper canine crown of a large ape, which was said by its describer (Falconer 1868) to resemble that of a male orang, and a fragmentary palate of a large ape, consisting of the greater portions of the left and right maxilla and most of the dentition (Lydekker 1879). The single upper canine was given the name *Pithecus cf. satyrus* by Falconer in 1868, but it has since been referred to *Dryopithecus indicus* (Pilgrim 1910a; Simons and Pilbeam 1965). The palate was originally designated *Palaeopithecus sivalensis* by Lydekker in 1879, but is now considered the type specimen of *D. sivalensis* (Simons and Pilbeam 1965). Unfortunately, Lydekker's genus *Palaeopithecus* had to be abandoned because it was a homonym of *Palaeopithecus* Voight 1865 (which, in turn, is a synonym of *Cheirotherium* Kaup 1835), a name applied to the Stegocephalian footprints of the Buntsandstein of Hildburghausen, Saxe-Meiningen, Germany (Lewis 1937a).

In 1910, Pilgrim (1910a) mentioned the discovery of a maxilla and mandible from "the Lower Siwaliks of Chinji." These he classified in a new species of *Dryopithecus*, *D. punjabicus*. In his brief discussion of the specimens, he remarked on their similarity to *D. rhenanus*, a species known only from isolated teeth in German Miocene deposits (Schlosser 1901). Although Gregory (1916) and Gregory and Hellman

(1926) mentioned the hominid features of certain of the teeth of *D. rhenanus*, it was not until 1963 that the implications of such hominid features for the status of *D. punjabicus* were recognized (Simons 1963).

In 1915, Pilgrim expanded his diagnosis of *D. punjabicus*. He took as the type specimen portions of the right and left horizontal ramus of the same mandible: the right side containing M_3 and the broken crown of M_2 while the left side preserved M_2 and the broken crown of M_3. The specimens were found near the village of Chinji (Pakistan) in a matrix of hard reddish clay, which suggested that they came from the top of the Chinji zone. Pilgrim included in the hypodigm a right maxilla, which had been found some years after the mandible in Haritalyangar, India, and contained the two premolars and the first two molars (GSI D. 185). Pilgrim (1913) had included this specimen in *Palaeopithecus*, but had realized his error two years later (Pilgrim 1915). The maxilla was considered to be from the Nagri zone.

Simons (1968) has thoroughly discussed the problems inherent in Pilgrim's diagnosis of *D. punjabicus*. As Simons points out, Pilgrim failed to make detailed comparisons of his new "species" with the type species of *Dryopithecus*, *D. fontani* from St. Gaudens, France (Lartet 1856). Pilgrim's comparisons were mostly with isolated teeth of *D. rhenanus* (Pohlig 1895) and *D. darwini* (Abel 1902).

Although Pilgrim considered *D. punjabicus* to be related to fossil pongids (and "*Sivapithecus*" *indicus* to be the ancestral hominid), many of the features he describes in the type specimen of *D. punjabicus* foreshadow the primitive hominid condition:
1. thick, shallow mandibular ramus posteriorly
2. steep-sided molars
3. relatively flat molar occlusal surfaces, even on unworn teeth
4. limited cingulum
5. high degree of interstitial wear, even in dentally young individuals.

Pilgrim was only able to compare the maxillary dentition of *D. punjabicus* (GSI D. 185) with two dryopithecine molars from the Swabian Bohnerz of Melchingen, figures of which were presented in Branco (1898) and Schlosser (1902). Pilgrim was certain that the maxilla belonged to the same species as the mandibular type specimens of *D. punjabicus*. His reasons centered upon the similar dimensions of the teeth, moderately low cusps, complexity of enamel folding, and the serrated edges of the buccal aspect of the molars. Interestingly enough, he considered that the differences between the upper molars of *D. punjabicus* and those of *D. rhenanus* lay in the fact that the former was broader, lower cusped, and had a less clear cingulum; all the distinguishing features are characteristic of later hominids. Pilgrim also included two isolated upper molars from Chinji in his hypodigm of *D. punjabicus* (GSI D. 186, GSI D. 187).

It must be remembered that Pilgrim's diagnosis was made a decade before the first description of an australopithecine (Dart 1925). It is no reflection on Pilgrim, then, that the hominid affinities of *D. punjabicus* went unnoticed for almost fifty years.

In 1934, Lewis described two genera, *Ramapithecus* and *Bramapithecus* (which contained three species), of hominid-like primates from the Siwaliks. These specimens had been collected by him during the 1932 Yale-North India Expedition.

Lewis based the genotype, *R. brevirostris*, on a right maxilla and premaxilla consisting of M^2, M^1, P^4, P^3, the alveolus of the canine, root of I^2, and the alveolus of I^1 (YPM 13799). The maxilla was found four miles east of Haritalyangar village in deposits of Nagri age. Lewis clearly recognized the hominid affinities of *Ramapithecus*; his systematic description reads:

Order Primates
Suborder Anthropoidea
Series Catarrhini
Family Simiidae (Hominidae?)
Genus *Ramapithecus*,[1] gen. nov.

In his diagnosis of the generic characters, Lewis (1934: 161) pointed out many features which suggested hominid affinities for *Ramapithecus*: parabolic dental arch, slight facial prognathism, lack of diastemata in dental series, small canine with transverse diameter exceeding anteroposterior dimension, relatively deep palate, and high interstitial wear. He concluded his discussion of *R. brevirostris* by remarking:

The high breadth indices, low and rounded cusps and simple structure of the molar crowns; the extremely bicuspid premolars, the man-like incisors and canine; and the divergent dental arcade and very slight prognathism are characteristic of *Ramapithecus*.

Lewis, in the same paper, also described a second species of *Ramapithecus*, *R. hariensis*.[2] He took as the holotype a fragment of a right maxilla containing the first and second molars (YPM 13807). This maxilla was recovered a quarter of a mile east of Haritalyangar village in deposits of the Middle Siwalik Nagri zone, from a horizon some

---

[1] *Ramapithecus* is named after Ráma, prince of Ayodhyà, deified protagonist of the Sanskrit epic *Rámàyana*, by the poet Valmiki.
[2] Named after the nearest village; Hari is one of the names of the Hindu deity of Vishnu.

2,000 feet below that of *R. brevirostris*. Lewis considered it to be more primitive than the genotype, particularly because of the small size of M¹ as compared to M² and the less pronounced interstitial wear. However, Lewis later (1937a) made this specimen a junior synonym of *D.* (*Sivapithecus*) *sivalensis*. Simons and Pilbeam (1965) followed this allocation with some misgivings, as they did with a similar specimen, GSI D. 191, which is also from Haritalyangar and preserves the left M² and M³. The taxonomic status of these specimens is, at present, uncertain; but they may belong to the *Ramapithecus* hypodigm.

The second hominidlike genus described by Lewis was that of *Bramapithecus thorpei*,[3] which had as its holotype a left mandibular ramus with M₃, M₂, M₁ alveolus and roots as well as a portion of the alveolus and root of P₄ (YPM 13814). The specimen was recovered about one and one-half miles from Hasnot in the Lower Siwalik Chinji zone. Although Lewis did not place this genus in the Hominidae, he saw that the marked differential wear, marked interstitial wear, and crown sculpture indicated that this form "may very well lie near the stem which led to the Hominidae proper" (1934: 161).

In 1937, Lewis (1937a, b) finished two works of significance, his taxonomic syllabus of Siwalik fossil anthropoids and his doctoral dissertation. In the former, he completed the first major attempt at synonymizing the plethora of generic and specific names given to the Siwalik primates. In the latter, he formally placed his genus, *Ramapithecus*, in Hominidae.

In the taxonomic syllabus, Lewis (1937a) retained three species of *Bramapithecus*: *B. thorpei* (Lewis 1934); *B. punjabicus* (Pilgrim 1910); and *B.? sivalensis* (Lewis 1934); he retained only one species of *Ramapithecus*, *R. brevirostris* (Lewis 1934). In his diagnosis of the latter genus, he remarked, "cheek teeth highly progressive, their size and proportions foreshadowing those of the Hominidae and *Australopithecus*..."

In a rather paradoxical paper, Hrdlička (1935: 34) refuted Lewis' claims concerning the hominid affinities of *Ramapithecus*. In spite of his critical tone, Hrdlička concluded his remarks by stating that *Ramapithecus* had "a greater general resemblance to the human than that of any other known fossil or living anthropoid ape..." and that the genus is "in general, nearer to man than are any of the Dryopitheci or the *Australopithecus*..."

Hrdlička's view seemed to be strengthened by the 1938 publication of Gregory, Hellman, and Lewis, in which they referred a right man-

---

[3] Named after Brahma, the creator and supreme soul of the universe, and first of the Hindu trinity.

dibular ramus with P₃-M₂ from Kundal Nala, Pakistan, to *R. brevirostris*. This jaw was characterized by narrow molar teeth and a sectorial P₃. Although Lewis had misgivings about this taxonomic placement, it was not until 1964 that Simons demonstrated that this jaw was probably that of a dryopithecine and not that of *Ramapithecus* (Simons 1964).

Beginning in the early 1960's Simons of Yale University began studying *Ramapithecus* (1961, 1963, 1964). Simons' 1961 study was a brief refutation of Hrdlička's rather polemical 1935 paper. Because the type maxilla of *R. brevirostris* reaches almost to the palatal intermaxillary suture, Simons was able to show that the dental arcade had to be somewhat parabolic in shape so that the intercanine breadth would not be excessively great (Simons 1961: Figure 2). He also determined that the length from the nasal aperture to the alveolar border of the incisors was reduced in *Ramapithecus*, contrary to Hrdlička's view; the length in *Ramapithecus* from the nasal aperture to I² was about 44 percent of the length from P³ to M², as opposed to ranges from 70 to 98 percent in *Pan*.

After Simons had studied the original dryopithecine material in Calcutta, he discovered that a second individual of the genus *Ramapithecus* was represented by Pilgrim's specimen GSI D. 185, the paratype maxilla of *D. punjabicus*.

Until 1963, then, *Ramapithecus* was represented only by upper dentitions. However, Simons' recognition of *D. punjabicus* as a junior synonym of *Ramapithecus* provided a necessary clue for recognizing the mandibles of *Ramapithecus*. Because it is usual to collect lower jaws in greater abundance than upper jaws, it became apparent that lower jaws of *Ramapithecus* must have been discovered, but not recognized as such. If Pilgrim (1915) had been correct in associating the maxilla GSI D. 185 with the type mandible of *D. punjabicus* (GSI D. 118/119) then it became necessary to consider these mandibular fragments as belonging to *Ramapithecus* in conjunction with Simons' referred maxilla (GSI D. 185). Although the generic name *Ramapithecus* is still valid, the species designation "*punjabicus*" has priority over "*brevirostris*." Thus, the correct binomen for the Indian forms, at least, becomes *Ramapithecus punjabicus*.

Because Lewis (1937a) had referred GSI D. 118/119 to his genus *Bramapithecus*, it became apparent that the specimens of that genus were in actuality the lower jaws of *R. punjabicus* (Simons 1964). Thus, the following became junior synonyms of *R. punjabicus*: *R. brevirostris*, *B. thorpei*, *B. punjabicus* and *B? sivalensis*. The mandibles previously assigned to *Bramapithecus* exhibit many hominid features, which distinguish them from the dryopithecines: posteriorly thick, robust mandibles; molars quadrate and crowded; individual cusps lacking high relief; marked interstitial wear; and horizontal ramus turning toward midline at about M_1.

The following list, based on Simons and Pilbeam (1965) and Simons (1968, 1972), is a complete list of specimens from the Indian subcontinent, which we feel can be considered as *Ramapithecus*:

1.   YPM 13799: type of *R. "brevirostris"* from Haritalyangar, India (Nagri zone).
2.   GSI D. 185: paratype maxilla of *R. punjabicus* from Haritalyangar.
3.   YPM 13806: right mandible from Haritalyangar (type of *Bramapithecus? sivalensis*)
4.   GSI D. 18068: left upper M^3 from Haritalyangar
5.   GSI D. 118/119: type of *R. punjabicus* from Chinji, Pakistan (Chinji zone)
6.   YPM 13814: mandible from Hasnot, India; type of *Bramapithecus thorpei* (Chinji zone)
7.   BMNH M. 13264: mandibular fragment from Attock, Pakistan (upper Chinji?)
8.   YPM 13833: M_3 and mandibular fragment from Kanatti, India (Chinji zone)
9.   BMNH M. 15243: left mandibular fragment with damaged P_4-M_3 from Domeli, Pakistan (Chinji zone)
10.   GSI D. 199: left mandibular ramus with P_4-M_3 from Haritalyangar, referred by Pilgrim (1927) to *Palaeopithecus? sylvaticus*
11.   GSI D. 18064: maxillary fragment with three molars from Haritalyangar (Prasad 1969)

In 1962, Leakey announced the discovery of a new genus and species of hominoid, *Kenyapithecus wickeri*, from Wicker's Farm, Fort Ternan, Kenya. Leakey's holotype of the genus consisted of a left maxillary fragment (Ft. 1272) preserving the P^4-M^2 with an associated canine; a right maxillary fragment (Ft. 1271) with M^1-M^2; a lower molar (M_2?); and a single central incisor found "several feet" from the other fragments. Although Leakey (1961) diagnosed the family as "incertae sedis," it is clear that he saw the hominid affinities of his specimen. Leakey mentioned these features in his diagnosis: low crowned molars and premolars; small, vertically placed upper canines; canine fossa; malar extending to level of M^1; marked interstitial wear and foreshortened face; relatively large cheek teeth. In all these features, *K. wickeri* clearly resembles the Indian *Ramapithecus* as well as the australopithecines. Because of these similarities, Simons (1963) considered *Kenyapithecus wickeri* a junior synonym of the previously named *R. punjabicus*. Leakey (1963: 32), on the other hand, considered *Kenyapithecus* material to be descended from the Lower Miocene form, which he and LeGros Clark had designated *Sivapithecus africanus* (1951). Consequently, Leakey maintained the generic distinction of the Ft. Ternan specimens from Indian *Ramapithecus*. In 1967 Leakey described further remains of this Lower Miocene material from Rusinga and Songhor, which he then designated as *K. africanus*, claiming that it represented the earliest hominid. Most, if not all, of Leakey's *K. africanus* material cannot be differentiated from other East African dryopithecines, and they most probably represent specimens of *D. nyanzae* or *D. africanus* (Pilbeam 1968, 1969a; Zwell 1972). Thus, they have no direct bearing on the question of hominid origins as discussed here. The generic synonymy of *Ramapithecus* and *Kenyapithecus* is now widely accepted (LeGros Clark 1964; Campbell 1966; Kurtén 1968; Andrews 1971).

In 1971, Andrews recognized that a portion of hominoid mandible found at Fort Ternan (KNM Ft. 45) was the lower jaw of the type maxilla of the Fort Ternan *Ramapithecus*. The specimen is a portion of the left body of the horizontal ramus, which includes the symphyseal region. The crowns of both premolars are preserved, as is the mesial root of the first molar and the root socket for the canine. The specimen is characterized by a strongly developed inferior transverse torus, low and robust mandibular body, small incisors and canines (evidence from root sockets), semisectoral and bicuspid P$_3$. Certain features of the Fort Ternan specimens differ from Indian *Ramapithecus*, particularly in the symphyseal region and anterior dentition. We feel that such differences should warrant a species distinction between the two forms, retaining *R. punjabicus* for the Indian form and *R. wickeri* for the African (Andrews 1971; Pilbeam 1972). It is important to note, however, that many of the differing features (i.e. P$_3$ morphology; relative canine size; canine morphology; symphyseal structure; incisor orientation), indicate that the Fort Ternan form is more primitive. This is to be expected in a species, which predates much of the Indian material by two to four million years (see section on dating). These differences, however, should not overshadow the basic hominid features shared by both species.

There are some finds outside the Indian subcontinent and Africa, which might plausibly be assigned to *Ramapithecus*. Branco (1897) described several isolated teeth from the Swabian Jura, which he

assigned to *D. fontani*. Simons and Pilbeam (1965) assigned a right
M^1 from this collection to *Ramapithecus*. Chow (1958) believes that
type material of *D.keiyuanensis* can be referred to *R. punjabicus*; the
associated fauna is equivalent to the Chinji and Nagri zones of the
Siwaliks. Also, some undescribed isolated teeth from Vallesian deposits
in Spain and Vindobonian deposits of Turkey might also be assignable
to *Ramapithecus*, but this is uncertain at the moment. A damaged
mandible from probable Turolian age sediments in Greece, at present
under study by von Koenigswald (1972), may well prove to be a *Ramapithecus* or a closely similar form.

STRATIGRAPHY AND DATING

Siwaliks

The Siwaliks of Pakistan and India represent a thick sequence of
Upper Cenozoic rocks, which are predominantly fluviatile deposits
derived from the rising Himalayan Mountains (Vondra and Johnson
1968). The nonmarine Cenozoic succession was called the "Nimadric
System". It is composed of the lower "Muree Series" and the upper
"Siwalik Series" (Anderson 1927). The Siwalik series, within which
all the fossil anthropoids were recovered, is divided into three "groups"
and six faunal zones as shown in Table 1 (Lewis 1937b).

Table 1.   Siwalik series

Siwaliks	Upper Group	Pinjor (?Middle Pleistocene) Tatrot (Early Pleistocene)
	Middle Group	Dhok Pathan (Turolian-"Plaisancian") Nagri (Vallesian-"Pontian")
	Lower Group	Chinji (Maremmian-"Sarmatian") Kamlial (Vindobonian)

At Haritalyangar, the Siwaliks are represented by over 1,500 feet of
mostly crossbedded, fine to coarse lithic sandstones, intercalated by

thin wedges of arenaceous siltstones, overlaid by over 3,600 feet of lenticular crossbedded, fine to medium arkosic sandstones, which interfinger with arenaceous siltstones. The units represent a channel floodplain complex deposited by meandering streams on an extensive alluvial plain. The deposition reflects the increasing uplift of the Himalayas (Vondra and Johnson 1968).

The Salt Range of Pakistan, which extends in a slight southwesterly direction along the northern side of the Jhelum River (Colbert 1935), is quite distinct from the Siwalik Hills of India (which are overthrust fault scarps). Immediately to the north of the Salt Range, forming a dissected peneplain lying between the Indus and Jhelum rivers, is the Potwar Plateau (Gill 1952). The type localities of Kamlial, Chinji, Nagri, Dhok Pathan, and Tatrot lie in this region. According to Anderson (1927: 665):

The Salt Range was gently elevated after the Eocene, and so remained up to some time in the Miocene; then subsided as part of the basis of deposition of the Siwalik beds, and finally rose during the later Tertiary and early Quaternary and transgressed for many miles southward by means of low-angle thrusting of Cambrian and later beds on the Tertiary.

It should be stressed that, at present, there is no way to correlate geologically the sediments in the Siwalik Hills of India and the Salt Range of Pakistan. Correlations, such as they are, can only be in biostratigraphical terms. Although lithology can be used in the Salt Range to map "zonal" boundaries, such is not the case with the Siwalik Hills of India (Gill 1952; Meyer, personal communication).

Because there is no way, at present, to date the Siwalik deposits radiometrically, the ages have been based on faunal correlations. There have been various correlations, as Table 2 illustrates. Lewis' correlation (1937b), based on the migrations and appearance of equid genera seems, with slight modification, the most probable.

Vertebrate paleontologists have traditionally defined the Miocene-Pliocene boundary by the first appearance of *Hipparion*, an equid genus, which had evolved in North America before 12.5 m.y. ago (Colbert 1935; Evernden et al. 1964). In a strict Lyellian sense, however, the boundary would be based on molluscan faunas. The earliest Pliocene microplankton occur between Berggren's (1969) zones 17 and 18. This would place the boundary at approximately 5.5 million years (Berggren 1969; Van Couvering 1972). It must be stressed, however, that this does not mean that Siwalik faunas, which have been traditionally labeled as Mio-Pliocene in age (Chinji-Nagri),

Table 2.   Comparative correlations of the Siwalik formations by various authors

Geologic time		Falconer 1868	Lydekker 1886	Pilgrim 1910b	Pilgrim 1913	Pilgrim 1934	Matthew 1929	Teilhard 1934	Colbert 1935	Lewis 1937b	Gill 1952	European Lewis 1937b	K-A dates of associated faunas VanCouvering 1972
Pleistocene	Upper												
	Middle									Break			
	Lower		Upper				Upper		Boulder conglomerate	Tawi / Break	Pinjor	Val d'Arno	
Pliocene	Upper			Upper	Boulder conglomerate	Boulder conglomerate		Boulder conglomerate	Pinjor	Tatrot / Break	Tatrot	Red Crag.	
	Middle		Lower		Pinjor	Pinjor	Middle		Tatrot	Break	Dhok Pathan	Roussillon Montpellier	4.0
	Lower				Tatrot	Tatrot		Boulder conglomerate	Dhok Pathan	Dhok Pathan	Nagri	Bohnerz Eppelsheim Maraga	12.5
Miocene	Upper			Middle	Bhandar / Dhok Pathan / Nagri	Dhok Pathan	Lower	Dhok Pathan	Nagri	Nagri	Chinji	St. Gaudens Lerida	13.5
	Middle			Lower	Upper Chinji / Lower Chinji / Lower Manchhar	Nagri / Chinji	Chinji	Chinji	Chinji	Chinji	Kamlial	La Grive Goriach Sansan	14.0 / 14.0 / 15.0
	Lower					Kamlial		Kamlial	Kamlial	Break			

are this young (as some have suggested). The faunal correlations of the Siwaliks are based on land mammal stages, not marine stages.

The date of appearance for *Hipparion* in the Siwaliks is still somewhat problematical. Earlier workers judged that *Hipparion* came from the Chinji as well as Nagri zones (Colbert 1935; Pilgrim 1913). More recent work, however, has thrown some doubt upon the presence of *Hipparion* in Chinji age deposits (Hussain 1969; Simons, Pilbeam, and Boyer 1971). Hussain (1969), for example, has argued that *Hipparion* first appeared in the Nagri zone (*H. nagriensis*), and then evolved into two forms, *H. antilopinum* and *H. theobaldi* in the upper Nagri or lowest Dhok Pathan zones. The question is still unresolved; *Hipparion* teeth have recently been recovered in Chinji age deposits of Pakistan (von Koenigswald, personal communication), from the lowest levels of the Siwalik section at Haritalyangar (Meyer, personal communication), and supposedly from the "Kamlial type locality" in Pakistan (Sarwar 1973). However, both Chinji and Nagri deposits have yielded *Ramapithecus* specimens. A summary of the paleoclimatic sequence, based on lithological and faunal analysis, is given in Table 3 (after Krynine 1937). It should be mentioned, however, that climate cannot be used as a primary basis for any stratigraphic scheme (Flint 1959).

Analyses of the Nagri fauna with paleoecological reconstructions have been published by several authors (Lewis 1937b; Tattersall 1969a, b). These studies have emphasized the macrofaunal elements, which are not as ideally suited to ecological reconstructions as the microfauna. However, until the numerous rodent specimens collected recently by Yale expeditions to Haritalyangar are complete, such must be the case. Macrofaunal studies do increase in significance, however, if they can be augmented by lithological analyses of the faunal sites. Such is the case for the Siwaliks (Tattersall 1969a; Lewis 1937b; Krynine 1937).

The Nagri zone contains several primate genera (*Ramapithecus, Dryopithecus, Indraloris*). The most common remains of other mammals are those of suids, followed by *Hipparion*, rhinocerotids, tragulids, and rodents. Proboscideans are rare. The Chinji zone differs from the Nagri in that it has a relative abundance of carnivores, proboscideans, and anthracotheres as well as the other forms that are also common in Nagri beds (Lewis 1937b).

The dinotheres and primitive trilophodonts, which characterize the Chinji, have teeth adapted to eating lush, succulent herbage. Other forms in the Chinji that suggest warm, humid climates are the forest-

Table 3.   Siwalik series of northwest India (after Krynine 1937)

Zone	Petrography and lithology	Dominant fauna	Climate and paleogeography
Kamlial	About 20 percent of red siltstones, mudstones, and shales; 80 percent of grey dark grey greywackes; mix-schist arenites including ture of fresh and weathered material; some authigenic hematitic concretions; intraformational conglomerates	Very poor fauna: general aspect forecasts Chinji; distribution somewhat like Nagri (?); abundant fossil wood	Tropical humid climate with seasonally distributed, fairly heavy rainfall; region of deposition forms a well-drained savanna with prairie and forest spaces about equally distributed; probably moderate relief in source area
Chinji	Over 75 percent of red siltstones, mudstones, and chales; 25 percent of grey channel schist arenites; mixture of fresh and weathered material; notable subaerial postdepositional decay; numerous authigenic hematitic concretions; intraformational conglomerates	Dinotheres and primitive trilophodonts; forest-dwelling pigs; *Giraffokeryx*; crocodiles; pythons; turtles; aquatic birds	Numerous watercourses bordered by rainforest cover; few open spaces in between; flat relief but good drainage in basin of deposition; tropical humid climate with high rainfall and high temperature
Nagri	Over 50 percent of grey schist arenites; red and orange siltstones and clays subordinate; mixture of fresh and weathered detritus; moderate to marked subaerial postdepositional decay; some authigenic hematitic concretions; intraformational conglomerates abundant	Fauna similar to Chinji but with a less marked predominance of river and forest dwellers plethora of suids; abundant palm trees	Numerous watercourses although humidity less marked than during Chinji; savanna with forest and open prairie, with the latter predominating toward the top of the section; seasonal rainfall decreasing; moderate relief
Dhok Pathan	From 50–90 percent of grey or buff schist arenites; 10 to 50 percent of orange siltstones; paler colors near top; moderate or slight indications of subaerial decay; allogenic hematic concretions; desert wind-borne silt at top	Primitive elephantids; antelopes; *Hipparion*; general influx of dry grassland types; *Orycteropus* at very top	Savanna passes into prairie, then steppe and finally (at least locally) into desert; scant rainfall; probable high temperatures; rivers dwindle

dwelling suids, tragulids, the okapi-like *Giraffokeryx*, numerous crocodiles, pythons, and turtles. In the Nagri zone, there is an influx of more
savannah-dwelling types — *Hipparion*, antelopes, primitive elephantids,
some suids, *Giraffa*, etc.

In summary, the dominant Chinji forms indicate humid, tropical
lowlands, with heavy forest and some grasslands. The Nagri fauna
suggests less humid conditions, although an abundance of palm trees
and dicotyledonous woods, such as *Dipterocarpoxylon*, indicates a
continuance of tropical climates (Lewis 1937b; Prasad 1971).

Fort Ternan

Fortunately, the tuffaceous deposits at Fort Ternan can be dated by
the potassium-argon [K/A] method. Two biotite fractions from a tuff
immediately underlying the fossil mammal horizon were dated at
14.7 ± 0.7 and 14.0 ± 0.2 m.y. (Bishop, Miller and Fitch 1969). These
dates are in agreement with earlier dates on large biotites from the
same sequence (Evernden et al 1964; Evernden and Curtis 1965).

A further K/A age determination was made on finegrained phonolites from an outcrop some seventy feet above the fossil mammal
site. Ages of 11.80 ± 0.2 m.y. and 11.0 ± 0.3 m.y. were obtained. The
phonolites were tested again by $^{40}AR/^{39}Ar$ and six-point whole rock
$^{40}Ar/^{39}Ar$ isochron analysis, giving ages of 12.6 ± 0.7 and 12.5 ± 0.4
m.y. (Bishop, Miller, and Fitch 1969). Thus, the *Ramapithecus* material from Fort Ternan can be dated between 14.0 and 12.5 m.y.

At present, the most thorough study of the Fort Ternan fauna is
Gentry's analysis of the Bovidae (1970), which forms the basis of the
following paleoecological survey. The two bovid genera, *Oioceros* and
Protragocerus, form the bulk (86 percent) of the bovid fauna. The
cursorial features in the limb bones of *O. tanyceras* resemble those
in such plains-living antelopes as Alcelaphini and Antilopini, rather
than those of bush or woodland antelope such as Tragelaphini or
Cephalophini. The hypsodont teeth of *Pseudotragus* are not those of
a forest-living antelope. Thus, the ecological picture deduced from
the bovids (at least) is one of open woodland. However, it bears
noting, as Gentry points out, that both Schlosser (1903) and Kurtén
(1952) were able to find two broad faunal divisions in lower Pliocene
sites in China, woodland and steppe. That this might also be the case
at Fort Ternan is suggested by some of the other faunal elements
(e.g. *Pliopithecus*).

On the basis of radiometric, geophysical, and paleontological evidence, it is clear that faunal exchange between Eurasia and Africa was possible during Maremmian times although the two continents had previously been separated for fifteen million years (from the early Oligocene to the early Miocene — see references in Van Couvering (1972). Berggren and Phillips (1970) analyzed the fossil foraminifera before and after closure of the Tethys; these indicate that the Afro-Arabian plate moved against Eurasia about the time of evolution of *Borelis melo*, i.e. between eighteen and fourteen million years ago. This would correlate with the migration of proboscideans from Africa to Eurasia during the early or middle Burdigalian land mammal age around eighteen m.y. (Savage 1967; Van Couvering 1972). By comparison, the northeast part of the Indian block collided with Asia at the end of the Eocene (Veevers, Jones, and Talent 1971). Thus, the radiometric, paleogeographic, and paleontological evidence would lend support to the suggestion that *R. wickeri* could have been ancestral to *R. punjabicus*.

STRUCTURE AND FUNCTION

Information is available on the crown or root structure of almost all upper and lower teeth, on mandibular morphology (except the ascending ramus), and on the form of the lower face. Cheek teeth have relatively steep buccal and lingual sides and broad, flat occlusal surfaces showing relatively less relief than in *Dryopithecus*. Certain features of the cheek teeth are primitive. For example, P_3 morphology is midway between that in *Dryopithecus* and *Australopithecus*; molars in *Ramapithecus* are low crowned while in later hominids they are higher crowned with much thicker enamel. Yet, the total morphological pattern of the *Ramapithecus* dentition can quite plausibly be interpreted as intermediate between a hypothetical pongid ancestor and known Pliocene Hominidae. If all those specimens tentatively identified as *R. punjabicus* are truly to be included in the hypodigm, an interesting pattern of occlusal wear can be observed. The difference in the amount of wear on adjacent molars appears to be more marked than in *Dryopithecus* from India. If this is a constant difference between the genera, it would imply either that tooth wear proceeds faster in *Ramapithecus* or that tooth eruption is delayed compared to *Dryopithecus*. The cheek teeth of *R. punjabicus* are more closely packed mesiodistally than in *Dryopithecus* of equivalent dental age, and this mesial shifting of cheek teeth in *Ramapithecus* may well be due to masticatory stresses. Both the wear and the mesial shifting probably imply heavy tooth use and powerful chewing.

A feature of the canine structure in *Ramapithecus*, mentioned only briefly in the past, deserves emphasis. The upper canine alveolus of YPM 13799 is oriented so that its long axis is set at an angle of some sixty degrees to the mesiodistal axis of the tooth row; this feature is not found in the Pongidae, but is characteristic of the Hominidae. Presumably, this correlates with a mesiodistally shortened canine crown (and a somewhat foreshortened face). Such a canine crown would probably resemble the hominid incisorlike canine rather than the more tusklike pongid type. The relative canine sizes for a variety of extant and fossil hominoids are given in Conroy (1972). The information derived from both the canine root and the crown size indicates that the canines of *R. punjabicus* are relatively small. This is also true for *R. wickeri* (Conroy 1972). Some workers have suggested that *Ramapithecus* had small canines because it was a female ape. However, compared even to female (or supposedly female) living and extinct apes of similar facial and dental size, *Ramapithecus* still has relatively small canines. The only known canine crown of *Ramapithecus*, preserved in the specimen from Fort Ternan, is more primitive than that of any Pliocene or Pleistocene hominid. It broadly resembles that of the pygmy chimpanzee, *Pan paniscus*. When allowances are made for allometric differences (changes in proportion due to changes in size), *Ramapithecus* has a canine somewhat larger (relative to cheek tooth size) than that of *Australopithecus* and smaller than that of Pongidae. This might be expected from a very early hominid. So here we have a small but apelike canine, exactly what might be expected if hominids evolved from pongids. Three maxillae, Ft. 1272, YPM 13799, and GSI D. 185, provide evidence that canine roots are oriented in the sagittal plane between seventy-five and ninety degrees to the occlusal plane of the cheek teeth. This is probably correlated with the small size of the canine root and perhaps with a more orthognathous face than can be found in apes, even in the female pygmy chimpanzee. However the evidence is interpreted, it does appear quite clear that *Ramapithecus* canines were relatively and absolutely reduced compared to pongids; this reduction implies that the behavior of this creature was already different in some significant ways from that of penecontemporary pongids.

The lateral incisor is known only in YPM 13799 and then only from the root. The root is relatively tiny in cross-sectional area (at the alveolar margin) and would have carried a correspondingly small crown. It measures 3.5 millimeters mesiodistally by 5.5 millimeters labiolingually; equivalent dimensions in female pygmy chimpanzees with smaller cheek teeth are five to six millimeters and six to seven millimeters. The root was oriented some ten degrees more vertically in YPM 13799 than in the pygmy chimpanzee, and presumably the crown was also more nearly vertical. The distal half of the central incisor root was diminutive, some 13.5 millimeters long from tip to alveolar margin. In female pygmy chimpanzees, roots are at least 16.5 millimeters long, and in normal-size chimpanzees (which have cheek teeth in the same size range as *Ramapithecus*) values of the order of twenty millimeters are more typical. The incisor root of this specimen of *Ramapithecus* was curved, and it seems highly probable that the central incisor crown would have been more vertically oriented with respect to the occlusal plane of the rest of the dentition than in any living ape. Leakey (1967) has described an isolated upper central incisor from Fort Ternan, which he believes to be part of the same individual as the maxilla Ft. 1271 and Ft. 1272; this incisor is probably *R. wickeri*, although the possibility that it represents some other primate cannot be entirely ruled out. As Simons (1969) has pointed out, this tooth, when compared to cheek teeth, is smaller — particularly in crown height — than the condition typical of modern apes and *Dryopithecus*. However, this reduction in size may not have been as marked in the Fort Ternan form as in the Indian form. This could be explained if the Indian specimens were of younger geological age, which seems probable. A small, isolated upper central incisor of what may well be a *Ramapithecus* has been recovered from Dhok Pathan horizons in Pakistan (von Koenigswald, personal communication).

There is an alveolar diastema between C and I^2 (also between I^2 and I^1) in YPM 13799. However, by analogy with the female pygmy chimpanzee, the gap between canine crown and incisor crown would probably have been closed. It would seem more likely, therefore, that the canine and incisor crowns would have formed a more or less vertically oriented cutting blade anteriorly. The shape of the upper dental arcade cannot be determined exactly, but it is most probable that the incisors were set approximately in a straight line while the cheek teeth diverged somewhat posteriorly. The dental arcade would have been much shorter from front to back than in a chimpanzee of approximately comparable cheek tooth size.

A number of important anatomical features of the lower facial region can also be seen in the various *Ramapithecus* specimens. The maxillary zygomatic process originates above the first molar, as in some *Dryopithecus, Oreopithecus,* the pygmy chimpanzee, and Pleistocene hominids. This feature may be a function of facial shortness, as in the small chimpanzee, although such an anterior position in *Ramapithecus* is unusual in animals of equivalent cheek tooth size. All three specimens of *Ramapithecus,* which preserve this region, show this character; it may well therefore be typical of the genus. A canine fossa is also consistently present. The palate, at least in the Indian forms, is deeply arched. This indicates that the maxillary alveolar processes were elongated, and shows that the face of *Ramapithecus punjabicus,* although short, was deep. The zygomatic arch serves a number of functions, among which are the resolution of chewing forces produced during mastication and the origin of certain masticatory muscles, i.e. the masseter. The more anterior the origin of the zygomatic process, the more anteriorly can the masseter muscle originate; this probably increases its power. There is evidence to suggest that the zygomatic arches were widely flaring (Andrews, personal communication). This would have the effect of increasing the area for a large temporal muscle, as well as allowing the masseters to exercise a more horizontal pull on the mandible, a further adaptation to rotary chewing. Subnasal prognathism was much less marked in *Ramapithecus* than in living apes. The length of the naso-alveolar clivus of YPM 13799 from the inferior nasal margin to the interdental septum between I^1 and I^2 is 14.5 millimeters. In a chimpanzee of equivalent dental size a normal value for this measurement would be around thirty millimeters and even a small female pygmy chimpanzee yields a value of twenty-one millimeters. *R. punjabicus* shows none of the anterior alveolar prognathism typical of modern pongids.

Thus a complex of maxillary features in *Ramapithecus* indicates a shortened, deep face which was probably adapted to relatively more powerful chewing than is normal for pongids of similar size. The expanded cheek tooth occlusal surfaces, heavy tooth wear, and crowded tooth rows similarly support this conclusion.

Until recently the lower jaws and teeth of *Ramapithecus* have been less well-known than associated upper parts have been (see Andrews 1971; Pilbeam 1969b). The Domeli mandible (Pilbeam 1969b), BMNH 15423, although queried by some (Leakey 1970), is considered by us to be clearly a *R. punjabicus.* It is one of the smallest known and is probably a female. It confirms the interpretations derived from the maxillae. This specimen represents a hominid that was short-faced and had a crowded tooth row with heavily worn teeth. The P₃ roots are oriented at an angle of some fifty-five degrees to the mesiodistal axis of the rest of the cheek teeth. The crown would have been only slightly longer mesiodistally than the crown of P₄ (X-ray photographs show that the roots of P₃ and P₄ are subequal in mesiodistal length). As in the mandibular specimen from Fort Ternan, there is a relatively well-developed inferior transverse torus; in BMNH 15423 the symphysis is relatively deep, but the mandibular body shallows and thickens posteriorly as in YPM 13806 and 13814. All of these features are probably adaptations for resisting lateral stress (Andrews 1971).

Evidence from the type specimen of *R. punjabicus* would indicate that the gonial angles were everted, again suggesting powerful masseter muscles. The inferior portion of the ascending ramus of *R. punjabicus* originates at the M₂–M₃ border and appears to rise steeply, suggesting a relatively vertical ramus (Jolly 1970). If the face of *Ramapithecus* was deep, as evidence from the upper jaws suggests, the ascending ramus would have been high. The probable *Ramapithecus* from the Dhok Pathan of Pakistan (von Koenigswald, personal communication) preserves a left mandibular fragment resembling BMNH 15423 quite closely, a small isolated upper molar similar to M¹ of YPM 13799, as well as the incisor mentioned previously.

In several quite specific ways the adaptations listed above resemble those to be seen in Pliocene and early Pleistocene Hominidae. The cranium of *A. boisei*, for example, was clearly adapted to extremely powerful mastication (Tobias 1967; Pilbeam 1972). The face is anteroposteriorly short and very deep, the molars show considerable wear, and the masseter was powerful and originated more anteriorly than in any ape. Of course, *Ramapithecus* is more primitive than *Australopithecus* in a number of features. Anterior teeth were probably less vertically oriented, incisors relatively larger, canines still to some extent morphologically apelike (at least in *R. wickeri*), and cheek teeth more primitive. However, *Ramapithecus* does make an excellent ancestor for *Australopithecus*, and it exhibits in developed or incipient form the characteristic dental and facial adaptations of later Hominidae.

DISCUSSION

That hominids did not become digitigrade quadrupeds like *Erythrocebus* or *Theropithecus* indicates that their immediate ancestors (presumably members of the genus *Dryopithecus*) were not cercopithecoid-like quadrupeds, but instead resembled in significant features the living African pongids (Conroy and Fleagle 1972; Zwell and Conroy 1973). *Ramapithecus* might well have been an arboreal form, which was beginning to spend increasing amounts of time foraging on the forest floor, perhaps at forest margins or in open woodland.

It has become rather widely accepted that the presence of large projecting canines in adult male nonhominid primates is due to differences between males and females in social behavior. The loss of large canines in hominids, it is said, was due to certain profound changes, which occurred in social behavior rather than to changes in feeding patterns. For example, Washburn (1960) expresses what can perhaps be described as the "consensus" view in associating male canine reduction with weapon use, and it has long been argued that the small canines of *Australopithecus* indicate a prolonged pre-Pleistocene tool-using history for the Hominidae. In this view hominid male canines are small because their aggressive functions have been replaced by tools.

There are some objections that can be made to this thesis. First, at least three lineages of Tertiary hominoids evolved small canines: *Ramapithecus*, *Oreopithecus*, and *Gigantopithecus* (as well as the subfossil, lemur, *Hadropithecus*). It is improbable that their implemental activities would have been more developed than those of living chimpanzees, the males of which have large canines. Stone tool-making to a set and regular pattern appears in the geological record only some 2.6 million years ago (Isaac, Leakey, and Behrensmeyer 1971), long after the hominoids listed above appeared. Holloway (1967) has suggested that reduction in male canine size is part of a general reduction in sexual dimorphism, male aggressiveness and so on, correlated with changes in hormonal systems. Jolly (1970) has also discussed this problem in detail and has proposed plausible models linking anterior tooth reduction to dietary changes during hominid phylogeny.

It is an oversimplification to state that the evolution of the hominid dentition has involved simply a reduction in male canine size. The canines of both males and females have become reduced in the Hominidae. Perhaps more importantly, their morphology has changed as well. Canines have become incisiform, they have been incorporated functionally (and morphogenetically) into the incisor complex, and anterior diastemata have been eliminated to form a continuous cutting battery of sharp-edged, vertically oriented anterior tooth crowns. Any theory attempting to explain the evolution of the hominid dentition must take these changes in morphology and organization into account.

Recently, a number of objections have been raised to the hominid status of *Ramapithecus*. Eckhardt (1972) and Robinson (1972), for example, have proposed that *Gigantopithecus* would form a more plausible pre-*Australopithecus* form than *Ramapithecus*. *Gigantopithecus bilaspurensis* comes from the Dhok Pathan zone of the Siwalik Hills (5-9 m.y.), and consists of one large mandible with most of the dentition preserved (Simons 1972). *G. blacki* is known from three mandibles and numerous isolated teeth from deposits in China that probably span the range of time equivalent to the European late Villafranchian and early post-Villafranchian (Cromerian, Biharian, or early Middle Pleistocene; Simons 1972). Age ranges on such deposits would be perhaps 1-2.5 m.y. *G. bilaspurensis* can plausibly be seen as ancestral to *G. blacki*, and can in turn be readily derived from the Siwalik form, *D. indicus* (Pilbeam 1970).

Although similar to the hominids in tooth proportions (the anterior teeth are somewhat reduced), *Gigantopithecus* only superficially resembles Hominidae (Pilbeam 1970; Simons 1972). Thus canines have low crowns, but are still conical, pointed teeth; they become rapidly worn to a flat surface, and resemble thereby the premolars. Morphologically and functionally, *Gigantopithecus* canines are very different from those of hominids; they are clearly not incisiform.

Stratigraphic considerations also rule out *Gigantopithecus* as a hominid. A relatively small-toothed and small-jawed *Australopithecus* is known from deposits 5.5 m.y. old in Kenya (Patterson, Behrensmeyer, and Sill 1970). A mandible from Turolian age deposits (5-9 m.y.) in Greece (von Koenigswald 1972) is clearly hominidlike (it resembles *Ramapithecus*) and differs markedly from *G. bilaspurensis*; the same can be said of the probable hominid tooth from the Ngorora Formation in the Baringo Basin (Bishop and Chapman 1970).

Gigantopithecus spans the wrong range of time to be acceptable as a hominid ancestor. Had it lived contemporaneously with, or earlier than, *Ramapithecus*, it might more sensibly have been viewed as a hominid precursor.

One other, more theoretical, objection has been raised to the hominid status of *Ramapithecus*, and indeed of all forms older than eight million years. Sarich and Wilson (1967a, b) have, in a variety of publications, maintained that primate albumins (serum proteins) have evolved at a constant rate; that is, amino acid replacements have occurred at a regular rate with respect to time alone. Albumins have not yet been sequenced; the similarities between albumins of different species are therefore assessed according to their degree of immuno-logical correspondence. "Immunological distance" is a measure of similarities and differences between species, and is $100 \times \log$ ID, where ID is an "index of dissimilarity." Sarich and Wilson note that for paired comparisons of primates, ID increases in a way that parallels classical taxonomy. Thus man and chimpanzee have a very low ID, man and macaque a higher one, man and capuchin higher still, and so forth. This is what might have been expected.

However, Sarich and Wilson go further. They argue that the rate of change of ID has been regular through time, and that changing ID can be related to time through the function:

$$\log ID = kt$$

where k is a constant, and t the time since the divergence of the two species under consideration.

Supporting evidence for such an exponential relationship comes from certain uniformities in the albumin data. Thus if closely related primate taxa A, B, and C are compared with a less closely related so-called "reference" taxon D, the ID values of AD, BD, and CD are generally found to be subequal, or sufficiently similar for any departures from equality to be accounted for by invoking Poisson random sampling explanations (Sarich 1968: 94). Such uniformity can only be explained, it is argued, by assuming regularity of mechanism. The mechanism proposed is a constant rate of "neutral" amino acid fixations, which is due to random mutations that should accumulate at relatively constant rates over long enough time periods (Kimura 1968; King and Jukes 1969).

The neutral fixation-random mutation theory has been attacked by a number of workers (Clarke 1970; Corbin and Uzzell 1970; Richmond 1970). Uzzell and Corbin showed that, by phyletic analysis of sequenced proteins over a wide array of species of known phylogeny (branching sequence), it was unlikely that amino acid differences had accumulated by chance alone; that is, selection had clearly played a major role.

Why then the uniformity in albumin data? Uzzell and Pilbeam (1971) suggested that uniform comparisons with respect to reference albumins were due to at least two factors. First, comparisons were phenetic (comparing proteins as they are today) rather than phyletic (attempting to compensate for changes that must have occurred in the past); therefore, they were inherently more uniform. Second, comparisons between a reference albumin, D, and more closely related taxa A and B will inevitably be similar because so much of the pathways from D to A and D to B will have been shared in common.

If regularity is not the answer, why should man, chimpanzee, and other apes be so similar genetically to each other? At least two explanations may be invoked. Goodman and his colleagues (1971) have argued that the evolution of hemochorial placentas in higher primates has slowed down protein evolution because potential maternal-fetal incompatibilities will tend to reduce heterozygosity. Kohne (1970) and others have further proposed that protein evolution, especially those parts of proteins that are subject to low or mainly stabilizing selection pressures, is generation dependent, and that the increasing generation length in higher primates slowed the rate of change of such proteins.

Sarich's claim that the albumin-derived date for the hominid-chimpanzee dichotomy is only 3 to 5 m.y. ago seems increasingly improbable in the light of new and well-dated *Australopithecus* finds from East Africa. His statement (1971: 123) that "one no longer has the option of considering a fossil specimen older than about eight million years as a hominid *no matter what it looks like*" is best interpreted as overenthusiasm for a new technique.

CONCLUSIONS

Ramapithecus is the form most plausibly interpreted as the late Cenozoic ancestor of *Australopithecus*. However, it is likely that not all *Ramapithecus* are ancestral to *Australopithecus*; rather, late *Ramapithecus* and early *Australopithecus* may have been contemporaries, if not sympatric. If *Ramapithecus* is the earliest hominid, the Hominidae evolved from Pongidae, probably of the genus *Dryopithecus*, around fifteen m.y. ago. Early hominids lived in forest or forest fringe habitats and were probably basically ground feeders. Canine and incisor reduction, which began early, was unlikely to have been linked with tool or weapon use, but rather with shifting diets and changes in masticatory function. Much more material on *Ramapithecus* is urgently needed before more definite statements can be made about other important aspects of hominid evolution, such as those involving the brain and postcranial skeleton.

REFERENCES

ABEL, O.
1902 Zwei neue Menschenaffen aus den Leithakalkbildungen des Wiener Beckens. *Sitzungsberichte der Akademie der Wissenschaften, Wien* Kl 3, Abteil 1:1171.

ANDERSON, R. VAN V.
1927 Tertiary stratigraphy and orogeny of the Northern Punjab. *Bulletin of the Geological Society of America* 38:665.

ANDREWS, P.
1971 *Ramapithecus wickeri* mandible from Fort Ternan, Kenya. *Nature* 231:192.

BERGGREN, W.
1969 Cenozoic chronostratigraphy, planktonic foraminiferal zonation and the radiometric time scale. *Nature* 224:1072.

BERGGREN, W., J. PHILLIPS
1970 "Influence of continental drift on the distribution of Tertiary benthonic foraminifera in the Caribbean and Mediterranean region." Woods Hole Contribution 2376, Symposium on the geology of Libya, 1969.

BISHOP, W., G. CHAPMAN
1970 Early Pliocene sediments and fossils from the northern Kenyan Rift Valley. *Nature* 226:914.

BISHOP, W., J. MILLER, F. FITCH
1969 New potassiumargon age determinations relevant to the Miocene fossil mammal sequence in East Africa. *American Journal of Science* 267:669.

BRANCO, W.
1897 Die menschenähnlichen Zähne aus dem Bohnerz der schwäbischen Alb. *Jahreshefte des Vereins für Vaterländische Naturkunde in Württemberg* 1(54):1.
1898 Die menschenähnlichen Zähne aus dem Bohnerz der schwäbischen Alb. *Jahreshefte des Vereins für Vaterländische Naturkunde in Württemberg* 1(2):1.

CAMPBELL, B.
1966 *Human evolution.* Chicago: Aldine.

CHOW, M.
1958 Mammalian faunas and correlation of Tertiary and early Pleistocene of South China. *Journal of the Paleontological Society of India* 3:123.

CLARKE, B.
1970 Darwinian evolution of proteins. *Science* 168:1009.

COLBERT, E.
1935 *Siwalik mammals in the American Museum of Natural History.* Transactions of the American Philosophical Society, n.s. 26:1–69, 378–396.

CONROY, G.
   1972   Problems in the interpretation of *Ramapithecus:* with special reference to anterior tooth reduction. *American Journal of Physical Anthropology* 37:41.
CONROY, G., J. FLEAGLE
   1972   Locomotor behavior in living and fossil Pongids. *Nature* 237:103.
CORBIN, K., T. UZZELL
   1970   Natural selection and mutation rates in mammals. *American Naturalist* 104:37.
DART, R.,
   1925   *Australopithecus africanus:* the man-ape of South Africa. *Nature* 115:195.
ECKHARDT, R.
   1972   Population genetics and human origins. *Scientific American* 226: 94.
EVERNDEN, J., D. SAVAGE, G. CURTIS, G. JAMES
   1964   Potassium-argon dates and the Cenozoic mammalian chronology of North America. *American Journal of Science* 262:145.
EVERNDEN, J., G. CURTIS
   1965   The potassium-argon dating of late Cenozoic rocks in East Africa and Italy. *Current Anthropology* 6:343.
FALCONER, H.
   1868   *Palaeontological memoirs and notes of H. Falconer*, volume two. London: Hardwicke.
FLINT, R.
   1959   Pleistocene climate in eastern and southern Africa. *Bulletin of the Geological Society of America* 70:343.
GENTRY, A.
   1970   "The Bovidae (Mammalia) of the Fort Ternan fossil fauna," in *Fossil vertebrates of Africa 2.* Edited by L. S. B. Leakey and R J. G. Savage, 243–324. New York: Academic Press.
GILL, W.
   1952   The stratigraphy of the Siwalik Series in the Northern Potwar, Punjab, Pakistan. *Journal of the Geological Society of London* 108, part 4:375.
GOODMAN, M., J. BARRABAS, G. MATSUDA, G. MOORE
   1971   Molecular evolution in the descent of man. *Nature* 233:604.
GREGORY, W.
   1916   Studies on the evolution of the primates. *Bulletin of the American Museum of Natural History* 35(19):239.
GREGORY, W., M. HELLMAN
   1926   The dentition of *Dryopithecus* and the origin of man. *Anthropological Papers of the American Museum of Natural History* 28(1): 1–27.
GREGORY, W., M. HELLMAN, G. LEWIS
   1938   *Fossil anthropoids of the Yale-Cambridge India Expedition of 1935.* Washington: Carnegie Institute Publication 495.

HOLLOWAY, R.
    1967   Tools and teeth: some speculations regarding canine reduction. *American Anthropologist* 69:63.

HRDLIČKA, A.
    1935   The Yale fossils of anthropoid apes. *American Journal of Science,* series 5, 29:34.

HUSSAIN, S.
    1969   "Revision of *Hipparion* (Equidae, Mammalia) from the Siwalik Hills of Pakistan and India." Unpublished doctoral dissertation, Rijksuniversiteit Utrecht, Utrecht, the Netherlands.

ISAAC, G., R. LEAKEY, A. BEHRENSMEYER
    1971   Archaeological traces of early hominid activities east of Lake Rudolf, Kenya. *Science* 173:1129.

JOLLY, C.
    1970   The seed-eaters: a new model of hominid differentiation based on a baboon analogy. *Man: Journal of the Royal Anthropological Institute* 5:5.

KIMURA, M.
    1968   Evolutionary rates at the molecular level. *Nature* 217:624.

KING, J., T. JUKES
    1969   Non-Darwinian evolution. *Science* 164:788.

KOHNE, D.
    1970   Evolution of higher-organism DNA. *Quarterly Review of Biophysics* 3:327.

KRYNINE, P.
    1937   Petrography and genesis of the Siwalik Series. *American Journal of Science* 34:432.

KURTÉN, B.
    1952   The Chinese *Hipparion* fauna. *Commentationes Biologicae* 13(4):1.
    1968   "Dating the early stages of Hominid evolution," in *Evolution und Hominisation* (second edition). Edited by G. Kurth. Stuttgart: Gustav Fischer Verlag.

LARTET, E.
    1856   Note sur un grand singe fossile qui se rattache au groupe des singes supérieurs. *Comptes Rendus de l'Académie des Sciences* 43:219.

LEAKEY, L. S. B.
    1961   A new Lower Pliocene fossil primate from Kenya. *Annals of the Magazine of Natural History*, series 13, 4:689.
    1963   "East African fossil Hominoidea and the classification within this super-family," in *Classification and human evolution*, 32–49. Edited by S. L. Washburn. Chicago: Aldine.
    1967   An early Miocene member of Hominidae. *Nature* 213:155.
    1970   "Newly" recognized mandible of *Ramapithecus. Nature* 225:199.

LE GROS CLARK, W.
    1964   *The fossil evidence for human evolution* (second edition). Chicago: University of Chicago Press.

LE GROS CLARK, W., L. S. B. LEAKEY
    1951   *The Miocene Hominoidea of East Africa.* Fossil Mammals of Africa 1. British Museum (Natural History).
LEWIS, G.
    1934   Preliminary notice of new man-like apes from India. *American Journal of Science* 27:161.
    1937a   Taxonomic syllabus of Siwalik fossil anthropoids. *American Journal of Science* 34:139.
    1937b   "Siwalik fossil anthropoids." in Unpublished doctoral dissertation, Yale University, New Haven.
LYDEKKER, R.
    1879   Further notices of Siwalik mammals. *Records of the Geological Survey of India* 12:33.
    1886   Siwalik Mammalia, supplement one. *Memoirs of the Geological Survey of India* 10(4):1.
MATTHEW, W.
    1929   Critical observations upon Siwalik mammals. *Bulletin of the American Museum of Natural History*, 56(7):437.
PATTERSON, B., A. BEHRENSMEYER, W. SILL
    1970   Geology and fauna of a new Pliocene locality in north-western Kenya. *Nature* 226:918.
PILBEAM, D.
    1968   The earliest hominids. *Nature* 219:1335.
    1969a   *Tertiary Pongidae of East Africa.* Bulletin of Yale Peabody Museum 31.
    1969b   Newly recognized mandible of *Ramapithecus: Nature* 222:1093.
    1970   *Gigantopithecus* and the origins of Hominidae. *Nature* 225:516.
    1972   *The ascent of man.* New York: Macmillan.
PILGRIM, G.
    1910a   Notices of new mammalian genera and species from the Tertiaries of India. *Records of the Geological Survey of India* 40(1):63.
    1910b   Preliminary note on a revised classification of Tertiary freshwater deposits of India. *Records of the Geological Survey of India* 40(3):185.
    1913   Correlation of the Siwaliks with mammalian horizons of Europe. *Records of the Geological Survey of India* 43(4):264.
    1915   New Siwalik primates and their bearing on the question of the evolution of man and the Anthropoidea. *Records of the Geological Survey of India* 45:1.
    1927   A *Sivapithecus* palate and other primate fossils from India. *Paleontologica Indica*, n.s. 14:1.
    1934   *Correlation of ossiferous sections in the Upper Cenozoic of India.* American Museum Novitates 704.
POHLIG, H.
    1895   *Paidopithex rhenanus* n.g., n. sp., le singe anthropomorphe du Pliocène rhenan. *Bulletin de la Société belge de géologie* 9:149.
PRASAD, K.
    1969   Critical observations on the fossil anthropoids from the Siwaliks of India. *Folia Primatologica* 10:288.

1971   Ecology of the fossil Hominoidea from the Siwaliks of India.
        Nature 232:413.

RICHMOND, R.
1970   Non-Darwinian evolution: a critique. *Nature* 225:1025.

ROBINSON, J.
1972   *Early Hominid posture and locomotion.* Chicago: University of
        Chicago Press.

SARICH, V.
1968   "The origins of the hominids: an immunological approach," in
        Perspective on human evolution. Edited by S. L. Washburn and
        P. C. Jay, 94–121. New York: Holt, Rinehart and Winston.
1971   "A molecular approach to the question of human origins," in
        Background for man. Edited by P. Dolhinow and V. Sarich,
        60–81. Boston: Little, Brown.

SARICH, V., A. WILSON
1967a   Immunological time scale for human evolution. *Science* 158:1200.
1967b   Rates of albumin evolution in primates. *Proceedings of the Na-
        tional Academy of Science* 58:142.

SARWAR, M.
1973   Society of Vertebrate Paleontology News Bulletin 97.

SAVAGE, R.
1967   "Early Miocene mammal fauna of the Tethyan region," in *Aspects
        of Tethyan biogeography.* Edited by C. Adams and D. Aser.
        Systematics Association Publication 7. London.

SCHLOSSER, M.
1901   Die menschenähnlichen Zähne aus dem Bohnerz der schwäbischen
        Alb. *Zoologischer Anzeiger* 24(643):261.
1902   Beiträge zur Kenntnis der Säugetierreste aus den süddeutschen
        Bohnerzen. *Geologische u. paläontologische Abhandlungen* 5:117.
1903   Die fossilen Säugetiere Chinas, nebst einer Odontographie der re-
        zenten Antilopen. *Abhandlungen der Kgl. Bayerischen Akademie
        der Wissenschaften* 22:1.

SIMONS, E.
1961   The phyletic position of *Ramapithecus. Postilla* 57.
1963   Some fallacies in the study of hominid phylogeny. *Science* 141:879.
1964   On the mandible of *Ramapithecus. Proceedings of the National
        Academy of Science* 51:528.
1968   A source for dental comparison of *Ramapithecus, Australopithe-
        cus,* and *Homo. South African Journal of Science* 64:92.
1969   Late Miocene Hominid from Fort Ternan, Kenya. *Nature* 221:
        448.
1972   *Primate evolution.* New York: Macmillan

SIMONS, E., D. PILBEAM
1965   Preliminary revision of the Dryopithecinae (Pongidae, Anthro-
        poidea). *Folia Primatologica* 3:81.

SIMONS, E., D. PILBEAM, S. BOYER
1971   Appearance of *Hipparion* in the Tertiary of the Siwalik Hills of
        North India, Kashmir and West Pakistan. *Nature* 229:408

TATTERSALL, I.
1969a Ecology of North Indian *Ramapithecus*. *Nature* 221:451.
1969b More on the ecology of North Indian *Ramapithecus*. *Nature* 224: 821.

TEILHARD DE CHARDIN, P., R. STIRTON
1934 A correlation of some Miocene and Pliocene mammalian assemblages in North America and Asia with a discussion of the Mio-Pliocene boundary. *Bulletin of the Department of Geological Sciences* 23(8):277. University of California.

TOBIAS, P.
1967 *Olduvai Gorge*, Volume two. Cambridge: Cambridge University Press.

UZZELL, T., D. PILBEAM
1971 Phyletic divergence dates of hominoid primates: a comparison of fossil and molecular data. *Evolution* 25:615.

VAN COUVERING, J.
1972 "Radiometric calibration of the European Neogene," in *Calibration of hominoid evolution*. Edited by W. Bishop and J. Miller, 247–271. Scottish Academic Press.

VEEVERS, J., J. JONES, J. TALENT
1971 Indo-Australian stratigraphy and the configuration and dispersal of Gondwanaland. *Nature* 229:383.

VONDRA, C., G. JOHNSON
1968 Stratigraphy of the Siwalik deposits of the Sub-Himalayan Gumbar Sakarghat fault block in Himachal Pradesh, India. *Geological Survey of America Annual Meeting* (abstracts).

VON KOENIGSWALD, G.
1972 Ein Unterkiefer eines Fossilen Hominoiden aus dem Unterpliozän Griechenlands. *Proceedings of the Koninklijke Nederlandse Akademie van Wetenschappen, Amsterdam* series B, 75(5):385.

WASHBURN, S. L.
1960 Tools and human evolution. *Scientific American* 203:63.

ZWELL, M.
1972 On the supposed *Kenyapithecus africanus* mandible. *Nature* 240: 236.

ZWELL, M., G. CONROY
1973 Multivariate analysis of the forelimb of *Dryopithecus africanus*. *Nature* 244–373.

Remarks on the Reconstruction of the Dental Arcade of Ramapithecus

CHRISTIAN VOGEL

Since the discovery and the original description of the famous maxillary fragment YPM 13799 of *Ramapithecus brevirostris* from the Siwaliks in northern India by Lewis (1934), its systematic classification within the family of Hominidae and its significance for the origins of the hominids have become focal points of phylogenetic studies, primarily in the works of Simons (1961, 1963, 1964a, 1964b, 1967, 1968, 1969), Simons and Pilbeam (1965), and Pilbeam (1966, 1967, 1969). Simons (1964a) renamed this fossil *Ramapithecus punjabicus* (Pilgrim 1910) and placed it with other fossil fragments of jaws, as well as teeth, from different sites in northern India, East Africa, China, and Europe for several reasons (see Simons and Pilbeam 1965). This identification of *Ramapithecus* with other fragments and its placement among the hominids are certainly topics deserving further investigation and discussion (see, for instance, Andrews 1971; Conroy 1972; Frisch 1962, 1967; Genet-Varcin 1969; von Koenigswald 1972; Leakey 1963, 1967; Skaryd 1971, and Yulish 1970).

Currently, there is a general tendency to classify *Ramapithecus* with the hominids, because, it is usually asserted, the maxillary dental arcade of *Ramapithecus*, unlike the typical U-shaped dental arcade of the Pongidae and other non-human primates, is parabolic, and therefore similar to that of the hominids. This statement is primarily based on hypothetical attempts to reconstruct the dental arcade using the right maxillary fragment YPM 13799, described by Lewis (1934) under the name of *Ramapithecus brevirostris*. In his original description, Lewis remarked: "The dental arcade of the upper jaw is parabolic, rather than U-shaped as in recent Simiidae, and hence the palate broadens pos-

For Plates, see p. iv, between pp. 288–289

teriorly" (1934: 162).

In 1961, Simons, for the first time, published a reconstruction draw-ing of the dental arcade on the basis of the maxillary fragment YPM 13799, which showed a nearly parabolic form with the postcanine rows of teeth strongly diverging posteriorly (see Figure 1a). This reconstruc-tion was accepted and reproduced unchanged by numerous authors as proof of the similarity of *Ramapithecus* to the hominids.

Finally, in 1969, Genet-Varcin, using the same outline drawing of YPM 13799 produced by Simons in his reconstruction, demonstrated that a completely different reconstruction indicating similarity with the typical U-shaped dental arcade of the pongids and other non-human primates was also possible (see Figure 1b). Let us disregard for the moment that the original drawing by Simons, which was also used by Genet-Varcin, gives an outline of the maxillary fragment as seen at an

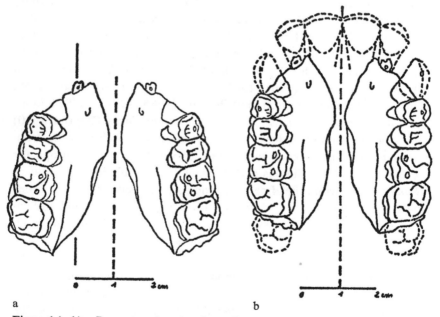

a   b

Figure 1 (a, b). Reconstruction drawings of the upper dental arcade of *Rama-pithecus punjabicus* from the maxillary fragment YPM 13799 according to Simons (1961) and Genet-Varcin (1969)

angle not perpendicular to the level of dental occlusion. This outline must have been the result of observing the original fragment at a slightly oblique angle from the back, after the real vertical axis of the maxillary fragment had been tipped to a buccally inclined position, causing the fragment to be seen at a slightly oblique angle from the lingual side. These operations considerably influence the possibilities of reconstruction, especially since the buccally tipped vertical axis of the maxillary fragment presents the I^2 in a position which is not representative of the original, thus falsifying one of the most outstanding characteristics of the YPM 13799 maxilla, hitherto overlooked in all description and discussion of this famous fossil.

Because both Simons and Genet-Varcin made use of the same outline drawing of the fragment, which had been somewhat falsified in its original configuration, we first were interested in determining which of the reconstructions, that of Simons or that of Genet-Varcin, represents a more realistic picture of the actual form of the dental arcade of *Ramapithecus*, i.e. of the maxilla YPM 13799. This question is pertinent to the determination of the systematic and phylogenetic position of *Ramapithecus*, because the dental arcade was either U-shaped, as in the non-human Simiae and in the reconstruction of Genet-Varcin (which would necessitate other convincing arguments for the hominid nature of *Ramapithecus*), or it was more parabolic with definite posterior divergence of the postcanine teeth rows, thus preserving the claim that this characteristic indicates the membership of *Ramapithecus* among the Hominidae.

For the purpose of a closer examination of both reconstructions, my student Wegner (1972) was assigned the task of examining the angles of certain connecting lines between molar cusps of both maxillary halves in recent Pongidae and Hylobatidae, and in modern man. For this study 102 complete upper dental arcades from *Pan troglodytes*, *Gorilla gorilla*, *Pongo pygmaeus*, *Hylobates* (various species), and *Homo sapiens* were employed.

The dental arcades were photographed at an angle perpendicular to the occlusion level, the tips of the molar cusps having been marked previously with a pencil. On the photographs the diagonal connections of protoconus and metaconus, as well as those of paraconus and hypoconus of M^1 and M^2 (both molars are in situ in the original fragment YPM 13799), were drawn on both sides. The respective points of intersection of these lines in the single molar teeth M^1 and M^2 then were connected to one another on each half of the dental arcade, and these connecting lines were extended forward (or backward, respectively[1]) up to the point of intersection of the lines of both halves of the dental arcade (Figure 2). The angle (x) at this point of intersection serves as

---

[1] In approximately half of the maxillae of *Pan* and *Pongo* (above all, among the males) points of intersection occurred which lay not in front of, but behind the dental arcade (indicated in the tables by a negative suffix).

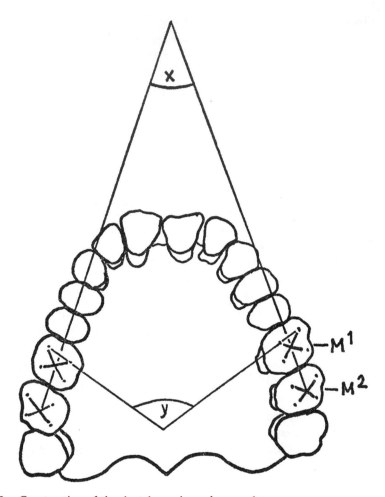

Figure 2.   Construction of the dental arcade angles x and y

an indication of the relative position of the horizontal axis of both molar rows, i.e. the shape of the dental arcade (angle of molar rows).

Then, paraconus and protoconus of M^1 on both sides were connected, the lines being extended lingually until they intersected in the middle of the palate at an obtuse angle (y, see Figure 2). This angle y should characterize the mutual position of the first molar teeth of both sides to each other (angle of molar position). For comparison, both angles (x and y) were also determined in both reconstructions of the dental arcade of YPM 13799.

Assuming a stable configuration for the molar cusp pattern, it was expected that a relative broadening of the posterior part of the dental arcade (a process occurring, for example, during hominid evolution) results in an increase of the angle of molar rows (x) correlated with a corresponding decrease of the angle of molar position (y). This hypothetical expectation is significantly verified by our data on recent pongids, hylobatids, and hominids; the respective coefficients of correlation (r) are given in Table 1.

Table 1.   Coefficients of correlation between angle x and angle y

genera	r-values
Hylobates	-0.82**
Pongo	-0.67*
Gorilla	-0.71**
Pan	-0.87**
Homo	-0.69**

* $\alpha = 0.05$.
** $\alpha = 0.01$.

For a more detailed comparison, we calculated the regression lines of angle y against angle x and of angle x against angle y for each genus separately. The results (see Table 2 and Figure 3) clearly indicate that each genus has its own typical regression lines, which as a whole demonstrate the expected general trend that the larger the angle x, the smaller the angle y.

Table 2.   Equation formulas of regression lines

Hylobates:	$y = -1.61 x + 158.9$	$x = -0.41$	$y + 70.3$
Pongo:	$y = -0.96 x + 159.5$	$x = -0.46$	$y + 74.1$
Gorilla:	$y = -1.24 x + 160.2$	$x = -0.41$	$y + 69.0$
Pan:	$y = -0.62 x + 163.8$	$x = -1.22$	$y + 199.3$
Homo (sapiens):	$y = -0.88 x + 145.8$	$x = -0.54$	$y + 93.9$

In order to demonstrate the genus-specific correlations, as well as the distribution of the individual values forming typical point clusters in the system of coordinates for each genus, we calculated the 95 percent-ellipses of distribution on the basis of a computer program from Rempe (see Lewin, Rempe, and Jürgens 1969). These ellipses (Figure 4) present us with an excellent survey of the average differences, the variability, and the limits of distribution, as well as the degree of correlations of both angles in all genera under observation. *Homo sapiens* offers the greatest variability, followed by *Pongo*. The ellipse of *Hylobates* overlaps with the ellipse of *Homo sapiens*, as well as with the ellipses of all

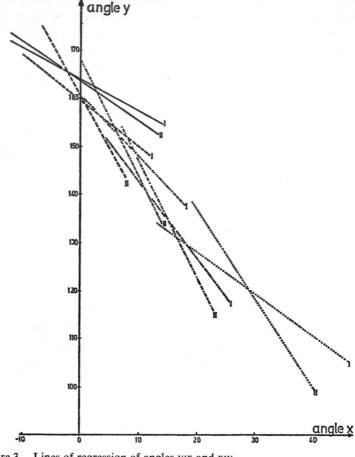

Figure 3.   Lines of regression of angles y:x and x:y
　　　　　　─────── = *Pan*　　　　　　I = y to x
　　　　　　─..─.. = *Gorilla*　　　　II = x to y
　　　　　　───── = *Pongo*
　　　　　　─.─.─ = *Hylobates*
　　　　　　.......... = *Homo*
　　　　　　Given for both axes in degrees

pongid genera, approximately to the same extent on both sides. The ellipses of *Homo* on the one side and of the Pongidae on the other are clearly distinguished by their position within the system of coordinates.

For control and comparison, the points of both reconstructions of the dental arcade of *Ramapithecus* (YPM 13799) were then plotted onto the same system of coordinates. Figure 4 demonstrates that the reconstruction of Simons falls well within the range of the 95 percent-ellipse of *Homo sapiens*, while the reconstruction of Genet-Varcin falls within the range cf the Pongidae (remarkably not within the range of Hylobatidae); however, of the genera of recent pongids, it is included here only in the ellipse of *Pongo*.

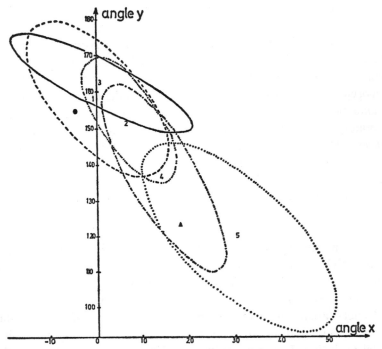

Figure 4.   Ninety-five percent ellipses of distribution (positions of *Ramapithecus*, according to reconstructions of Genet-Varcin and Simons)

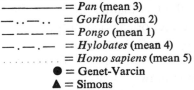

──────── = *Pan* (mean 3)
—..—.. = *Gorilla* (mean 2)
——— = *Pongo* (mean 1)
—.—.— = *Hylobates* (mean 4)
.... = *Homo sapiens* (mean 5)
● = Genet-Varcin
▲ = Simons

These results allow the following conclusions: There is a general negative correlation between the size of the angle x, which is formed by the molar row axes (M^1–M^2) of both sides of the upper dental arcade, and the size of the angle y, which is formed by the connecting lines of the M^1-cusps paraconus and protoconus of both sides of the dental arcade. This general correlation among all genera of living hominoids is a strong indication that the molar cusp pattern has not been influenced by the broadening of the posterior part of the dental arcade during hominid evolution. The 95 percent-ellipses of distribution are different and yet, typical for each genus within the living hominoids. However, there is a distinct distance between *Homo sapiens* on the one side and the recent Pongidae on the other. Because, for this correlation, neither of the reconstructions falls outside of the range of either the hominids or the pongids in general, and because the reconstruction of Simons falls within the range of distribution of *Homo sapiens*, and that of Genet-Varcin within the range of Pongidae (as both experimental reconstructions were intended to do on the basis of the differing presupposed opinions of the two authors), our results do not produce any definite proof as to which of these reconstructions represents more accurately the actual shape of the maxillary dental arcade of *Ramapithecus*. The remarkable fact remains, however, that the reconstruction of Genet-Varcin is exceptionally included among the recent pongids in the 95 percent-ellipse of the genus *Pongo*.

According to our comparative study, both reconstructions may represent valid possibilities for the shape of the dental arcade, hence serving as the basis for differing interpretations of *Ramapithecus* in respect to its hominid status. Therefore, a solution to this problem must be sought elsewhere.

As already mentioned, the original reconstruction drawing of the dental arcade of YPM 13799 from Simons (1961), which was also used by Genet-Varcin and many others, gives an outline of the maxillary fragment as seen at an angle not perpendicular to the original level of dental occlusion. It is remarkable that Simons himself did not realize the falsifying and misleading effect of the buccally inclined position in his reconstruction, in spite of the fact that he presents a photograph of the original fragment in the correct orientation in the same publication (1961). In comparing both figures (Figure 1 and Plate 1), the main difference in the position of the lateral incisor (I^2) becomes clearly evident. When a straight line is drawn connecting the lingual walls of the teeth M^2–P^3, and this line is extended forward, the alveolus and root of I^2 in the outline drawing of Simons' reconstruction fall well to the medial, i.e. lingual, side of this line, whereas in the correctly oriented photograph of the original the position of the I^2-alveolus is lateral, i.e. buccal, to this line. This difference has important consequences for the possibilities of reconstructing the dental arcade. Therefore, both the reconstructions by Simons and Genet-Varcin are based on slightly inaccurate conditions.

The lateral, i.e. buccal, position of I^2 just in front of the canine, and in line with the postcanine teeth-row can be considered an outstanding feature of the *Ramapithecus* maxillary fragment YPM 13799. In all pongids and other recent catarrhine primates, as well as in the dryopithecines and all fossil hominids known to the present author, the alveolus of I^2 falls clearly to the medial, i.e. lingual, side of the line connecting the lingual walls of the molar and premolar teeth. The same is true in general for maxillae of recent *Homo sapiens*; there are only a few individual exceptions where the position of I^2 is similar to YPM 13799. But even these exceptions do not prove indisputably that YPM 13799 had a parabolic dental arcade similar to *Homo sapiens*. There are at least two primitive fossil hominoids which present similar positions of I^2 as YPM 13799 without possessing parabolic upper dental arcades: *Aegyptopithecus* (early Oligocene, Fayum, Egypt) and *Pliopithecus* (Miocene, Europe). These two fossils and the above-mentioned individual exceptions in modern man have only straight and posteriorly diverging postcanine tooth-rows in common. Therefore, the one conclusion which definitely can be drawn from the position of I^2 in the maxillary fragment YPM 13799 is that it had posteriorly diverging post-canine tooth-rows. We must wait for more fossil material of *Ramapithecus* to decide whether the extraordinary position of I^2 should be considered as an individual variation of the YPM 13799 fragment or whether it is a typical characteristic of *Ramapithecus punjabicus*.

As we have seen, there is no compelling reason to conclude from the maxillary fragment YPM 13799 that *Ramapithecus* had a hominidlike parabolic maxillary dental arcade. Therefore, we must look for further evidence for classifying *Ramapithecus* with the hominids.

Simons and Pilbeam (1965) have pointed out that YPM 13799 presents an unusually deep canine fossa typical for later hominids but atypical for apes. Indeed, YPM 13799 shows a distinct and deeply grooved canine fossa just above the tips of the roots of P^4, which is not visible in adult gorillas, seldom in adult orangs (here the position is somewhat different), and only as a smooth impression in some adult chimpanzees. However, a clearly circumscribed and deeply imprinted groove is frequently present in hylobatids (in both *Hylobates* and *Symphalangus*). The position of this canine fossa is nearly identical with that of YPM 13799. The same is true for many skulls of *Presbytis* (especially of *Presbytis* [*Trachypithecus*] *geei*), juvenile chimpanzees, and, in a somewhat higher position, for *Cercopithecus* and juvenile *Pongo pygmaeus* (for further details, see Vogel, 1966; Seiler 1971). In general, a well-marked groove imprinted by the origin of the musculus caninus (the so-called fossa canina) seems to be typical for relatively short muzzled catarrhine primates, as, of course, *Ramapithecus* was. This groove is not a specific characteristic of the hominids.

Another characteristic which Simons (e.g. 1968) claims as a hominid feature may also be the consequence of the shortening of the maxillae in *Ramapithecus*: the forward position of the anterior insertion of the jugal arch lying above M^1. The same position is to be found in most recent colobines, especially in the genera *Presbytis* and *Colobus*, which also possess relatively short muzzles.

All hitherto discussed features of the maxillary fragment YPM 13799, whether taken as single characteristics or taken as a "total character complex," are not sufficient to warrant the inclusion of *Ramapithecus* in the Hominidae.

Furthermore, it should not be overlooked that there are some features in the dentition of YPM 13799 which are far from being typically hominid, e.g. the sharp crests of the buccal cusps of the molar and premolar teeth and the outward curvature of the anterior crista of the paraconus of P^3. Referring to Welsch (1967), the tooth wear facets of YPM 13799 are similar to those of recent pongids and fossil dryopithecines. The root of I^1, as can be judged from the alveolus, shows an extensive backward curvature of the apex, which is not a typical hominid characteristic.

These critical remarks on the evaluation of some characteristics of the maxillary fragment YPM 13799, treated by many modern authors as typical hominid traits, do not deny the possibility that *Ramapithecus* should be classified with the hominids; rather, they demonstrate that the phylogenetic position of *Ramapithecus* as judged from the maxillary fragment YPM 13799 is far from being indisputably hominid. The thorough examination of the individual characteristics, as well as the total character complexes, necessary for a valid evaluation leaves us with insufficient evidence for proving the hominid status of this fossil. The ideal resolution of our dilemma, of course, would lie in the discovery of a number of new and better preserved fossil remains of *Ramapithecus*.

REFERENCES

ANDREWS, P.
1971   *Ramapithecus wickeri* mandible from Fort Kenya. *Nature* 231:
192–194.

CONROY, G. C.
1972   Problems in the interpretation of *Ramapithecus:* with special reference to anterior tooth reduction. *American Journal of Physical
Anthropology* 37:41–48.

FRISCH, J. E.
1962   Neuer Fund eines fossilen Hominoiden in Kenya. *Anthropologischer Anzeiger* 25:298–301.
1967   Remarks on the phyletic position of *Kenyapithecus*. *Primates* 8:
121–126.

GENET-VARCIN, E.
1969   *À la recherche du primate ancêtre de l'homme*. Paris: Edit. Bou-
bée et Cie.

LEAKEY, L. S. B.
1963   "East African fossil Hominoidea and the classification within this
super-family," in *Classification and human evolution*. Edited by
S. L. Washburn, 32–49. Chicago: Aldine.
1967   An early Miocene member of Hominidae. *Nature* 213:155–163.

LEWIN, T., U. REMPE, H. W. JÜRGENS
1969   Beziehungen zwischen Gesichtsmaßen und Berufen bei Schwedin-
nen aus Göteborg. *Zeitschrift für Morphologie und Anthropologie*
61:245–257.

LEWIS, G. E.
1934   Preliminary notice of new man-like apes from India. *American
Journal of Science* 27:161–181.

PILBEAM, D. R.
1966   Notes on *Ramapithecus*, the earliest known hominid, and *Dryopithecus*. *American Journal of Physical Anthropology* 25:1–5.
1967   Man's earliest ancestors. *Science Journal* (reprint): 47–53.
1969   Tertiary Pongidae of East Africa. *Bulletin of the Peabody Museum*
31:1–185.

PILGRIM, G. E.
1910   Notices of new mammalian genera and species from the tertiaries
of India. *Records of the Geological Survey of India* 40:63–71.

SEILER, R.
1971   Die Gesichtsmuskulatur und ihr Einfluß auf das Gesichtsskelett
bei catarrhinen Primaten Teil II. *Gegenbaurs Morphologisches
Jahrbuch* 116:147–185.

SIMONS, E. L.
1961   The phyletic position of *Ramapithecus*. *Postilla* 57:1–10.
1963   Some fallacies in the study of hominid phylogeny. *Science* 141:
879–889.
1964a On the mandible of *Ramapithecus*. *Proceedings of the National
Academy of Sciences* 51:528–535.

1964b Old World higher primates classification and taxonomy. *Science* 144:709–710.

1967 The significance of primate paleontology for anthropological studies. *American Journal of Physical Anthropology* 27:307–332.

1968 A source for dental comparison of *Ramapithecus* with *Australopithecus* and *Homo*. *South African Journal of Science* 64:92–112.

1969 Late Miocene hominid from Fort Ternan, Kenya. *Nature* 221: 448–451.

SIMONS, E. L., D. R. PILBEAM

1965 Preliminary revision of the Dryopithecinae (Pongidae, Anthropoidea). *Folia Primatologica* 3:81–152.

SKARYD, S. M.

1971 Trends in the evolution of the pongid dentition. *American Journal of Physical Anthropology* 35:223–240.

VON KOENIGSWALD, G. H. R.

1972 Was ist *Ramapithecus? Natur und Museum* 102:173–183.

VOGEL C.

1966 Morphologische Studien am Gesichtsschädel catarrhiner Primaten. *Bibliotheca Primatologica,* Fasc. 4. Basel: Karger.

WEGNER, J.

1972 "Untersuchungen zur phylogenetischen Stellung von *Ramapithecus brevirostris* anhand von Zahnbögen rezenter Hominoidea." Dissertation. Kiel.

WELSCH, U.

1967 Die Altersveränderungen an Primatengebissen. *Gegenbaurs Morphologisches Jahrbuch* 110:1–181.

YULISH, S. M.

1970 Anterior tooth reduction in *Ramapithecus. Primates* 11:255–263.

Kenyapithecus *and* Ramapithecus:

EMILIANO AGUIRRE

The arguments on the origin of man, at a suprageneric level, have long been focused on the antiquity of the branching of man's ancestry from that of the closest group of Hominoidea, the Pongidae. Opinions have been widely divergent: there has been support for a very modern branching, namely Pleistocene, and for an individualization of the human line as old as Eocene, or even older (Hürzeler 1962).

Recent discoveries in very early Pleistocene and Upper Pliocene sites in the East African Rift Valley — Olduvai Gorge, and Lake Baringo to Lake Rudolf areas — have displayed a view of well-diversified representatives of the family Hominidae in the Late Neogene. On the other hand, notwithstanding the relevant work of the Yale expeditions in El Fayum, conducted by Simons, it is difficult, in the present state of knowledge, to extrapolate backwards to the Oligocene a vertical classification of the Hominoidea, because of the lack of evidence from any country and from any age in the vicinity of the fertile strata of Jebel Qatrani. Consequently the arguments are concentrated on the possibility of identifying either a member of the family Hominidae or, at least, a representative of the ancestry of the human family, among the Hominoidea known from different Miocene sites in Eurasia and East Africa.

Several candidates have been proposed as such representatives because they exhibit trends which diverge from pongids or resemble hominids. First we have to discard *Oreopithecus*: its adaptive features to both brachiation and bipedal posture or "verticalization," have proved to be a case of convergence or isomerism, while its dentition separates this taxon definitely from Cercopithecoidea, Pongidae, and

Hominidae. There is no indication of human ancestry in any of the fossil Hominoidea from the "Upper Vindobonian" and "Vallesian" mammal stages of Cataluña (Crusafont 1958, 1965).

Two collections of fossil material stand out with special claims in this matter, constituting a subject for arguments in recent literature: one from the Siwaliks, including individual fossils which were described by different authors under a variety of well-known denominations, and joined under a single generic and specific name, *Ramapithecus punjabicus* (Pilgrim) by Simons and Pilbeam (1965); the other from the Lower-Middle to Middle Miocene of Kenya, well-dated radiometrically, partially described originally as *Sivapithecus africanus* by LeGros Clark and Leakey (1951), and later generically separated by Leakey as a new genus, *Kenyapithecus*, with two species, *K. africanus* (Clark and Leakey) from the Burdigalian sites in the Kavirondo Gulf, and *K. wickeri* (L. Leakey), the type species, from the Vindobonian site of Fort Ternan.

This African material is currently referred to in recent literature, after Simons and Pilbeam (1965), as *Ramapithecus*, the name *Kenyapithecus* being rejected as a synonym. This procedure is inconvenient for the following reasons:

1. Assuming all this material under the single name "*Ramapithecus*," many peculiarities of the African fossils — whatever their taxonomic meaning — are ignored or set aside in scientific discussions or comparative studies. When the same is done in didactic or popular science books or papers, ignorance is generated about the valuable contributions which can be derived from those African fossils and from their descriptions by Leakey.

2. With this procedure, not only an important span of time and geographic distance are telescoped, but a serious risk is taken of absorbing more than one taxon, at least at a specific level.

Specific differences can be anticipated between populations so distant geographically, and ranging through a geologic time of more than six million years. In fact such differences do occur, and the problem is to evaluate them and their importance for taxonomic and phylogenetic problems, instead of ignoring and veiling them. Any solution to the question of the evolution of the Hominoidea in the period considered, which discounts or minimizes these differences may be right accidentally, but will stay scientifically inconsistent.

3. Notwithstanding several, or even many, traits similar or shared in common by the two groups of fossils, differences exist, so that equivocation cannot be avoided when the affinities of *Ramapithecus* are

questioned. Even if, as in several papers, a distinction is made between Asiatic and African *Ramapithecus*, or if each particular fossil is designated by its collection label, traits which differ significantly are mixed, so that one cannot realize which particular animal resembles or differs from either dryopithecines or man: we seem to be trying to trace the phylogeny of a chimaera.

4. Even worse, *Ramapithecus* is often illustrated by means of composite illustrations or reconstructions, such as the one generously divulged by Simons (1968), which, moreover, is apparently deficient in other respects, such as in the orientation of the maxillary branches relative to the unpreserved sagittal plane.

Let me emphasize once more the opinion I have expressed elsewhere (Aguirre 1972) that the many similarities between Asiatic *Ramapithecus* and African *Kenyapithecus* are by no means, in the present state of knowledge, sufficient either to convince us of generic identity, or to minimize the existing differences.

These differences must be taken into account and separately considered when phylogeny and possible relations to either dryopithecines or man are discussed. These are of course of different and uncertain phylogenetic and/or taxonomic significance: but IT IS URGENT, AS A MATTER OF METHOD, to discuss them widely before assuming a generic identity, and, if such identity is seriously agreed upon, let us decide or try to get to a decision on specific diversity, and then refer to the African fossils honestly as *R. wickeri* (L. Leakey) and *R. africanus* (Clark and L. Leakey), distinctly, without intermixing the traits particularly shared by these African forms and the Asiatic form or forms.

I do not think it necessary to explain once more in detail these differences (see Aguirre 1972), nor quote particularly every work or author dealing with them. Let me stress, however, one trait, among others, which impressed me when I first saw the materials together (some were in casts, but later I examined the originals). The molar crowns of Asiatic *Ramapithecus* are, in their occlusal shape, more rectangular than parallelogramic, or even square, and the crests and fossettes in their crowns tend to be more transverse than oblique, while in *Kenyapithecus* none of these traits are observed, the crests being oblique, the fossettes not transversally elongated, and the outlines of the crowns are parallelogramic. On the other hand, the cusps of the molars are, in *Kenyapithecus*, large in their base, rounded in their section, convex in their slopes, tending to touch each other and closing the central valleys, as in true bunodont teeth, while in *Ramapithecus* — I mean the Asiatic form — the molar crowns are widely excavated, the cusps marginal and less developed with acute ridges in their descending slopes that are not precisely bunodont.

This last trait also allows an inference related to the diet, which very likely was different in these two groups of fossils, and consequently may have an effect on the phylogenetic question. The kind of molar cusps exhibited by the Asiatic specimens classified as *Ramapithecus* clearly differ from those of other Eurasian dryopithecines and those of *Kenyapithecus* or of Plio-Pleistocene hominids, and could be interpreted, alternatively, as either primitive or secondarily specialized. If the first interpretation is right, Asiatic *Ramapithecus* could hypothetically represent the status of an ancestor to either *Kenyapithecus* or man. Now, this is difficult for *Kenyapithecus* if we are right in attributing to the Asiatic fossils an age record from very Upper Vindobonian to Vallesian mammal stages. On the other hand, there are indications which suggest that the molar crowns of *Ramapithecus* — I mean the Asiatic form — are specialized and divergent from most of the Eurasiatic dryopithecines, from the strong bunodont trend of *Gigantopithecus*, from recent pongids and from recognized hominids: these indications are the overall rectangular shape in upper molars and the pattern of crests and valleys. The interpretation of these molar crowns as specialized is therefore more probable, and such specialization could be related to an adaptation to a softer diet (frugivorous?). If this was so, the Asiatic *Ramapithecus* is best discarded as man's ancestor, and should represent a side branch of the dryopithecine or proconsuline stock. The parallelogramic and bunodont crowns of *Kenyapithecus*, on the contrary, could more easily be imagined as related to those of an ancestor of man.

This African group also seems to be more linked to man's line of evolution by the shapes and features of the symphyseal and premaxillary region as far as we can know them presently.

Finally, two more controversial features are: the roots of the upper P3 and the crown of the lower P3. Triradiculate first upper premolars occur not only in *Kenyapithecus*, but also in the Asiatic *Ramapithecus*, namely in the specimen GSI-D.185, and I suspect it in YPM 13799; this trait is also observed in several samples of *Proconsul* and *Hispanopithecus*, and I have the impression that it is normal to all these genera. But the structure of the observed crowns of upper P3 in *Kenyapithecus* is peculiar, with a marked labial cingulum, a triangular basal shape, mesiodistally elongated, and one is tempted to interpret its shape as primitive, related to either *Ramapithecus* or Plio-Pleistocene Hominidae.

Hürzeler was first to emphasize the significance of the bicuspidate lower P3 as distinctive of the human family, as a feature impossible to derive from the sectorial elongate, unicuspidate lower P3 of the pongids either living or fossil. Many scholars have criticized this interpretation, opposing the evidence of a bicuspidate trend or mutation in living chimpanzees. Let us consider that this feature has played a role in the identification of the human evolutionary branch, that is the origin of Hominidae, notwithstanding an isomeric reappraisal of this trend in *Oreopithecus* and in chimps, independently. On the other hand, the presence of this trend in the Upper Miocene *Dryopithecus*, does not imply a great antiquity of this trait in the ancestry of man. A bicuspidate lower P3, as well as bipedalism and brachiation can appear in separate families in different times. Briefly, I do not think this trait irrelevant because of its repetition, nor do I think that it must be supposed to be extremely old in human ancestry. As a consequence, the lower P3 of *Kenyapithecus* being distinctively short relates to *Proconsul*, to *Ramapithecus*, and to *Dryopithecus*; even its being unicuspidate, and its mesial wall being more vertical, is of interest.

In summary, I have the strong feeling that the name *Kenyapithecus*, may represent a taxon of generic integrity sufficiently defined by available fossil material, and its absorption as a synonym of *Ramapithecus* — which has recently become popular — is inappropriate. Moreover, the known differences between these two taxa may be interpreted from the point of view of both phylogeny and ecology as being significant, and give more weight of probability for the ancestry of man on the side of *Kenyapithecus*.

REFERENCES

AGUIRRE, E.
   1972   Les rapports phylétiques de *Ramapithecus* et *Kenyapithecus* et l'origine des Hominidés. *L'Anthropologie* 76:501–523.

CRUSAFONT, M.
   1958   Nuevo hallazgo del Póngido vallesiense *Hispanopithecus. Boletín Informativo de Actividades Europeas en Paleontología de Vertebrados,* nn. 13–14. Sabadell, Spain.
   1965   El desarrollo de los caninos en algunos *Driopitécidos* del Vallesiense de Cataluña. *Notas y Comuns. Inst. Geol. y Minero de España* 80.

HÜRZELER, J.
   1962   Quelques réflexions sur l'histoire des Anthromorphes. *Colloq. Internat. C.N.R.S., Paris, 1961,* 441–450.

LE GROS CLARK, W. E., L. S. B. LEAKEY
  1951   The Miocene Hominoidea of East Africa. *Fossil Mammals of Africa* 1. London: British Museum (Natural History).
SIMONS, E. L.
  1968   A source for dental comparison of *Ramapithecus* with *Australopithecus* and *Homo*. *South African Journal of Science* 64:92–112.
SIMONS, E. L., D. PILBEAM
  1965   A preliminary revision of Dryopithecinae (Pongidae, Anthropoidea). *Folia Primatologica* 3:81–152.

Gigantopithecus *as a Hominid*

R. B. ECKHARDT

In several earlier works (Eckhardt 1971, 1972, 1973) I played the role of a devil's advocate in the discussion of hominid origins. That is, I contended that if, on the average, only exceedingly slight heritable changes occurred in a number of linear dental dimensions over even a very short period of geological time, then teeth the size of those which characterize gigantopithecine populations could be reduced to those found in australopithecines. Because the only fossil material presently assigned to *Gigantopithecus* consists of numerous large teeth and a few proportionately large jaws, this demonstration could be considered to have removed one of the major obstacles to the consideration of a direct ancestral-descendant phylogenetic relationship between these two hominoid forms. But even this rather modest proposal seems to have disturbed several well-known scientists and their associates (Dobzhansky et. al. 1972) because it challenged some current dogmas about human ancestry.

At present most anthropologists and paleontologists do not seem to think that *Gigantopithecus* should be accorded hominid status. Indeed, the consensus among most of those who have recently expressed their opinions on the subject (Pilbeam 1970; Simons and Ettel 1970) seems to indicate the converse. However, it is only fair to point out that since the initial discovery of several of its teeth in 1935 by von Koenigswald, *Gigantopithecus* has also had a number of supporters of its hominid status.

The first of these was Weidenreich, who in 1945 altered his earlier view (1937: 145) that these teeth belonged to a giant orangutan. But although Weidenreich changed his opinion on the taxonomic status of *Gigantopithecus* from ape to hominid, he still believed that it had been enormous in size. As mentioned by Dart (1960), Broom and Schepers

(1946) were the next to point out its resemblances to the australopithecines. Then, in 1952, von Koenigswald, who like Weidenreich had originally believed *Gigantopithecus* to be a large anthropoid, also modified
his view to allow recognition of this primate as a hominid, although one
which only paralleled the human line and was not ancestral to later
Asian hominids. Dart (1960) considered *Gigantopithecus* to be a
"variant on the Australopithecine theme," and Woo (1962) likewise
saw it as a primitive hominid form.

Those who make up this array of scholars base their views on a body
of data which over the years has increased in amount, diversity, and diag-
nosticity, from just one tooth of vaguely known spatial and temporal pro-
venance to over a thousand teeth and several nearly complete mandibles
excavated under the supervision of qualified paleontologists. Despite
this increase in evidence which has lent considerable support to their conclusions, those who would place *Gigantopithecus* in the hominid line
have been unable to persuade other members of the field that their position has more merit in it than alternative explanations which account
for the similarities of its dental characteristics to those of later hominids
in terms of parallels or convergences (Pilbeam 1970). The present lack
of consensus on this issue may indicate that the idea that *Gigantopithecus* is a hominid is wrong. But if the idea is not wrong, then at least it
might be termed premature. Here I use the term premature in the very
lucid and useful way that it was recently defined by Stent (1972: 84): "a
discovery is premature if its implications cannot be connected by a series
of simple logical steps to canonical, or generally accepted, knowledge."
Such a definition allows us to avoid the purely temporal connotations
of the term "premature" — connotations which are largely irrelevant
to the basic problem. The remains of *Gigantopithecus* have been known
for nearly four decades. The controversy about their interpretation goes
back just as far — and it has endured despite the fact that the amount
of fossil evidence has increased vastly, and despite good evidence that
at least some, if not all, members of this genus existed several million
years earlier in time than was thought possible only a few years ago.
These are but a few of the developments which should have led to a
unified conclusion about the taxonomic status of this primate. That
they apparently have not suggests that the disparity in interpretation
arises not from the nature and amount of evidence but from the conceptual frameworks into which this evidence is placed. For this reason I
do not propose to advocate here the position that *Gigantopithecus* is a
hominid. Instead, I will attempt to clarify the basic issues which must

be resolved before this taxon can be related in a less ambiguous manner to later stages in hominid evolution.

For the moment, I will consider the australopithecines to represent the earliest level of primate evolution to which hominid status is generally accorded. There are a few who might still exclude the australopithecines from a position ancestral to the genus *Homo*. These would include Zuckerman (1950), von Koenigswald (1962), and R. Leakey (1972). The respected position of these dissenters indicates that their views have not been taken lightly by their colleagues. It also emphasizes at the outset the difficulty in deciding just what does comprise canonical knowledge in the field of human evolution. Perhaps the major reply that can be made to their various objections is that excluding australopithecine populations represented by known fossil remains from a position ancestral to later members of the genus *Homo* leaves us in a somewhat difficult position. Members of the genus *Homo* would then have to be derived from fossil populations which are presently unknown, but which would in all probability be extraordinarily similar to the australopithecines which have already been discovered. The known postcranial remains of these indicate upright posture, and members of some populations have been found acompanied by evidence of material culture. These characteristics may not be necessary criteria for hominid status, but to many they do seem sufficient.

If *Gigantopithecus* occupied a position in our ancestry, it would most plausibly be as an ancestor of the australopithecines. But there is a difference between plausibility and certainty. In recognition of this, I have listed the major objections to such a phylogenetic position for *Gigantopithecus*.

1.   There are other (and better) candidates for hominid ancestry than *Gigantopithecus*.

2.   Some morphological features of *Gigantopithecus* are too much like those of pongids to allow its inclusion among the Hominidae.

3.   The features in which *Gigantopithecus* resembles the hominids can be explained in ways other than its occupying a position ancestral to the australopithecines.

4.   No suitable selective mechanism has been proposed to explain how *Gigantopithecus* populations might have been transformed in the course of evolution into those which are now accepted as hominids.

5.   *Gigantopithecus* populations existed too late in time to be ancestral to the australopithecines.

For analytical purposes I will deal with each of these separately; however, it should be recognized that these issues are all interrelated.

OTHER CANDIDATES FOR HOMINID ANCESTRY

Before we analyze the evidence favoring other candidates for hominid ancestry it would be well to resolve a basic question: What is a hominid? Reasonable definitions of this taxonomic category have been given. Perhaps the one most frequently cited is that originally given by LeGros Clark (1964: 119). Definitions, particularly clear ones like Clark's, are quite desirable because they supply a precise focus for discussion. But they also have one drawback: they may convey a deceptive air of certainty. Our ability to formulate or cite a precise definition of any category may foster the impression that we can recognize the members of that category with a corresponding degree of assurance. The recurrent disagreement about hominid origins should indicate that this impression is not warranted.

This is a problem not unique to students of human evolution. In an analogous endeavor, the attempt to discover the origin of life itself, the astronomer Sagan (Schlovskii and Sagan 1966: 184) remarked "Any child can tell the difference between a live puppy, a dead puppy, and a toy puppy." Yet the boundary between life and nonliving matter remains an elusive one to the scientist. Why is this? The child's criteria have been arrived at inductively, perhaps on the basis of his experiences with examples of all three categories. The real question for us is: would this type of experience enable him to recognize the FIRST puppy? I do not think that this necessarily follows.

Recognition of the earliest members of any category is not based on a process of observation alone. This can easily be seen by examining an extreme case. Even if that observation could include substantially all of the intermediate populations (e.g. between dog and non-dog or predog), then demarcation of the transition point would not involve just observation, but also definition. And definition and recognition are logically two different types of intellectual activity (although in practice they may influence each other).

Need definitions of taxonomic categories such as the Hominidae be arbitrary? Some have answered this question in the affirmative. For example, Simons (1968: 95) has said:

The point in time past when everyone would agree that such animals had reached definite hominid status would always have to be agreed on arbitrarily, no matter how much scholars do eventually come to know about skeletons of Miocene, Pliocene, and Pleistocene human ancestors. It should not be forgotten that in the purely hypothetical case that skeletons representing each and every generation of our forerunners were known, the separating line would have to be drawn between parents and their own offspring.

Such a statement is puzzling to a population biologist. It is likely to be a misleading guide to discovering the earliest hominids because it focuses on individuals — parents and offspring — rather than on populations, and speciation is an event which occurs at the population level. Furthermore, it emphasizes morphological change rather than reproductive isolation; while both changes are commonly involved in speciation, the latter is an indispensable element while the former is an incidental although routine consequence.

Both of these features of Simons' approach indicate a misunderstanding (or misstatement) of the ecological and genetic events involved in the process of speciation. This, in turn, seems to be related to a failure to distinguish clearly between two rather different types of evolutionary events: anagenesis and cladogenesis.

In anagenesis (upward or progressive evolution), slight gradual genetic changes can accumulate generation by generation even in one continuous, non-branching phyletic line, giving rise to time-successive populations which differ from each other in appearance. When two such populations are separated by a long period of time — as they might be if sampled before and after a substantial gap in the geological record — they might be as distinct from each other as two different contemporaneous species of the same genus. The extent of this difference in appearance between ancestors and their direct descendants is sometimes recognized by giving them different formal taxonomic names, e.g. *Homo erectus* and *Homo sapiens,* and the evolutionary process involved here is sometimes referred to as phyletic speciation. But it should be recognized that the distinction between one "species" and the next in such a case is quite arbitrary. Indeed, as I have argued elsewhere (Eckhardt 1970), it is really a celebration of our current lack of knowledge, and we should expect that any distinction which can temporarily be made between the two evolutionary stages may disappear as additional specimens filling the present void are discovered.

The second type of event, cladogenesis (branching evolution), is a much more appropriate model for the origins of the Hominidae. It is generally agreed that present-day great apes are descended from the dryopithecines which lived during the Miocene and Pliocene, and occupy substantially the same broad ecological niche that dryopithecines did. Over the same period of time our line has branched from the dryopithecine stem into a new ecological zone.

Among population biologists the most generally accepted explanation of how cladogenesis occurs is provided by the theory of geographic speciation (Mayr 1942). This holds that in sexually reproducing animals a new species develops when a population first becomes geographically isolated from its parental species, then during this period of isolation it acquires characteristics which promote or guarantee reproductive isolation when the external barriers break down.

Geographic speciation is not the only model which has been advanced to account for cladogenesis, but as Mayr (1965: 480) has more recently observed, the essential component of speciation, that of the genetic repatterning of populations, can take place only if these populations are temporarily protected from any disturbing inflow of alien genes. This can be done best by extrinsic factors, namely, spatial isolation. It appears that such spatial isolation is always maintained by geographic barriers. The possibility is not yet entirely ruled out that forms with exceedingly specialized ecological requirements may diverge genetically without benefit of geographic isolation; the burden of proof rests, however, on supporters of this alternative mode of speciation.

Recognition that cladogenesis as well as anagenesis is likely to have played an important role in the origin of hominids allows us to differentiate clearly among several categories of earlier primates.

1.   Nonhominid primate populations which were ancestral only to other nonhominid primate populations. Examples here might include populations of the Miocene lorisid *Progalago dorae* (MacInnes 1943; Simons 1972: 169), as well as populations of Pleistocene orangutans (Hooijer 1948).

2.   Nonhominid primate populations which were ancestral to both hominid and nonhominid populations. For the last half century, following the work of W. K. Gregory, most anthropologists have agreed that some populations of *Dryopithecus* would belong here.

3.   All primate populations in modern man's own exclusive evolutionary line. *Homo erectus* would be a late and relatively noncontroversial instance of this.

In cladogenetic terms, the word hominid should logically be reserved for the members of the third category. How can we distinguish this category from the others? Traditionally, morphological evidence has been the predominant, if not exclusive, basis for distinguishing species. But it is not the morphological characteristics of individuals which evolve; it is the gene pool of the population which undergoes evolutionary changes. There are shifts in the frequencies of alleles at various loci in the gene pool of the population and in the expression of these genes as they become coadapted to each other. The phenotypic characteristics of individuals in the population will then reflect these factors to a greater or lesser extent.

Even in living populations where we have a great wealth of data to work with, phenotypic characteristics are a very imperfect guide to the presence or absence of isolating mechanisms which could restrict gene flow. On the one hand we have sibling species (morphologically similar or even identical populations that are nevertheless reproductively isolated), and on the other hand, populations as different in appearance as *Papio hamadryas* and *Theropithecus gelada* which can still produce viable, fertile offspring when mated (Newth 1956). But at least in populations of living organisms, even in problematical cases such as the ones mentioned above, the inferred existence of population boundaries can be checked against observations of the actual breeding behavior of the animals. This is, of course, not possible when we are dealing with fossil material.

Perhaps it was the limitations of the fossil record that Simons had in mind when he said that the transition point between nonhominids and hominids would have to be agreed on arbitrarily, even if we had skeletons representing each and every generation of our forerunners. But it would have been very much more acurate to say that by itself the morphological evidence provided by primate fossil remains is likely to be of limited value in detecting the point at which speciation (in a cladogenic or branching sense) occurred in the origin of a hominid line. I realize that this opinion is less optimistic than that generally expressed in the field today. Most scholars would probably agree with LeGros Clark's (1964: 120) statement that

it should be possible even in relatively early stages of their initial segregation and divergence from one another, to determine whether ... a fossil is representative of the evolutionary sequence already committed by incipient changes to the developmental trends characteristic of the Hominidae, or to those characteristic of the Pongidae.

But LeGros Clark also recognized that such a determination would be possible only through an analysis of the total morphological pattern of a fossil hominoid, "PROVIDED THAT SUFFICIENT DATA ARE AVAILABLE" (emphasis mine). Unfortunately, such data are often not forthcoming for most Miocene and Pliocene hominoids. Instead of skeletons representing each and every generation as in Simons' hypothetical case, in reality we typically have only occasional, fragmentary fossils sprinkled over thousands or millions of years. Furthermore, the specimens usually found are jaws and teeth. The morphological characteristics represented in this material furnish a most uncertain basis for the discrimination of early hominids from early pongids. Many traits, such as a semisectorial P₃ (one with a small lingual eminence in addition to the usual large buccal cusp), canines smaller than the average found in adult pongids, and the presence of interstitial wear, which are used as evidence for the hominid status of certain Tertiary hominoid specimens still exist as occasional variants in nonhominid populations even today. They very probably did as well at and prior to the time that a hominid line diverged from the pongid line. Since this is the case, the occurrence of one or even a few of them together in occasional INDIVIDUAL Miocene or Pliocene hominoid fossils cannot be taken as persuasive evidence for the existence of hominid POPULATIONS (contra Simons 1968). And when we are working with fragmentary, unassociated material, it is misleading to imply that a total morphological pattern can be perceived. The pattern which emerges, like that in a mosaic, may be one of our own *de novo* construction rather than a reconstruction of a pattern which once existed in nature and has come to us as a jigsaw puzzle.

This statement is easy to support. I have found semisectorial third lower premolars in approximately one-third of the individuals in a relatively large sample of living chimpanzees, as well as in jaws contained in museum collections. Gregory and Hellman (1926: 93) illustrate the lower jaw of a female gorilla with a canine which does not project above the plane formed by the tips of the other teeth. Interstitial wear is routinely found in the dentition of numerous nonhominids, including *Dryopithecus indicus,* the chimpanzee, and even the rhinoceros (Simons 1972: 240); and the further contention that interstitial wear occurs earlier in life in hominids than in nonhominids (Simons 1972: 45) has not been adequately documented. Support for or disproof of the idea that early interstitial wear is a hominid characteristic will probably be difficult to obtain because of the paucity of specimens (modern or fossil) of known age, and because the rate of interstitial wear is dependent not only on age but on other factors such as diet, which are also generally unknown for most specimens. This list of hominid-like characteristics also found in members of nonhominid populations could easily be expanded.

In fact, some characteristics which have been used to support assignment to the Hominidae rather than to the Pongidae of some Miocene and Pliocene hominoids are utterly useless for this purpose. Perhaps the clearest example of this appeared in the "Preliminary Revision of the Dryopithecinae (Pongidae, Anthropoidea)" (Simons and Pilbeam 1965: 138), where the following statement was made:

In known parts *Ramapithecus* resembles later *Australopithecus* from the Pleistocene, and the total morphological pattern makes its assignment to the Hominidae entirely reasonable. By the early Pliocene at the latest, facial and dental features characteristic of later hominids were well established. These are: relatively small incisors and canines, homomorphic upper AND BY INFERENCE, LOWER PREMOLARS . . . (emphasis added).

The inference that if upper premolars of a Pliocene hominoid are homomorphic the lower ones will be as well simply does not follow. The upper premolars of ALL living hominoids, from gibbons through man, are typically bicuspid, while, as noted above, the third lower premolars of apes usually, although not invariably, bear a single cusp.

Because of the small numbers of fragmentary remains presently at hand, in attempting to distinguish the earliest hominids we should concentrate not merely on the differences between individual associated specimens, but on the distictiveness of populations.

The model of geographic speciation can provide us with some useful guidance here. By itself it cannot indicate which Tertiary hominoids were hominids, but there is some likelihood that it can help us to eliminate some present candidates from lack of persuasive evidence for including them in a distinct hominid population. This would allow us to scrutinize those remaining somewhat more closely using additional criteria.

According to this model, in the process of speciation there are two important points (which could be regarded as the ends of a genetic continuum): (1) that at which geographic isolation initially occurs, and (2) that at which reproductive isolation is completed.

Both of these would be quite difficult, if not impossible, to detect with any degree of precision in the fossil record. But this does not completely vitiate the predictive value of this model when we confront the fossil record. By the time that populations are held to have reached the stage where they are recognizable as hominids even on the basis of a few incomplete fossils, it is reasonable to assume that the gene pools of these populations have been distinct for a considerable period of time. And it is not unreasonable to expect to find some indication of the separate existence of these populations. Convincing positive evidence of this would be furnished by the discovery of reasonably complete and diagnostic specimens of several individuals together in an appropriate ecological setting. When such evidence is not available, we should recognize that the "hominid" characteristics of the specimens in question can be explained in some of the other ways discussed above.

When this approach is taken, the case for most supposed mid-Tertiary "hominids" breaks down. This statement applies to several candidates for which hominid status has been suggested in the recent past: *Propliopithecus haeckli* (Kurtén 1972; Kinzey 1971), *Ramapithecus punjabicus* (Simons 1961), *Kenyapithecus wickeri* (which L. S. B. Leakey considers to be distinct from *Ramapithecus)*, and *Kenyapithecus africanus*. The specimens assigned to each of these taxa typically are found either associated with other primates that are generally agreed to be nonhominids, or as isolated individual specimens.

If any such association represents a true biocenosis (in the sense of Shotwell 1955), so that the representatives of supposedly hominid and nonhominid primate taxa were part of the same community during life, then it presents a strong argument against any significant ecological divergence of those proposed as early hominids from synchronic and sympatric nonhominids. To circumvent this difficulty it could be suggested alternatively that these associations of hominid and nonhominid primates represent not biocenoses but thanatocenoses (different communities whose members are brought together only after death). But each additional discovery necessitating this explanation makes that explanation less convincing, as it requires a concatenation of improbabilities.

Since *Ramapithecus* is widely believed to be the best candidate for hominid ancestry at present, I will consider the evidence supporting this belief in detail. As yet we have fewer than a dozen dental and gnathic fragments representing this genus, despite the general belief that its members are thought to have been distributed over Eurasia and Africa for about ten million years. The opinion that *Ramapithecus* represents the earliest hominid is debatable on morphological grounds alone (as pointed out by Wolpoff 1971; Eckhardt 1971, 1972; and Robinson 1972; as well as others going back to Hrdlička 1935). Disregarding this basis for skepticism, *Ramapithecus* was again proposed as a hominid by Simons, whereupon inferences were made that its known morphological characteristics implied tool use and upright posture (Simons 1961), as well as terrestrial bipedalism, scavenging, and possibly hunting on the savanna (Pfeiffer 1969).

Nevertheless there has been a growing body of evidence which indicates that these speculations about the behavior of *Ramapithecus* were not warranted to begin with. Tattersall's (1969a, 1969b) studies of the ecology of *Ramapithecus* indicate that it lived in a forest environment rather than on the savanna. Fossil remains attributed to it are consistently found associated with those of dryopithecine apes. The persistent failure to find any tools associated with the fossil remains attributed

to *Ramapithecus* finally led Jolly (1970) to suggest an alternative explanation for its short face: that it represented an adaptation not to
eating meat but to eating seeds, like *Theropithecus gelada*. But a
savanna-living monkey is an inappropriate model to explain morphological features found in a forest-dwelling hominoid. Presumably in
recognition of this, Pilbeam (1972: 99) now tells us that

Ramapithecus was a predominantly forest-living, arboreal animal, capable
of arm-swinging and suspension in the trees, yet coming to the ground for
food. (However, the possibility should be borne in mind that *Ramapithecus*
was a knuckle walker).

Given present evidence it is quite unlikely that *Ramapithecus* represents the beginning of a separate hominid line. It is probable that the
specimens which comprise the hypodigm of this genus represent an artificial collection — neither distinct genetically from associated dryopithecines nor related to each other in any closer degree than to this
associated material. This will remain the most likely explanation until
there is some indication that a recognizably separate and distinct population of these organisms existed, as evidenced by the finding of several specimens together and unassociated with the remains of other apes.

This is not an unreasonable criterion to set. It has already been met
by two other Tertiary taxa, *Oreopithecus bambolii* and *Gigantopithecus
blacki*. Both of these are represented by abundant finds from well-defined
sites at which they do not appear to be associated with other hominoids.

Of course, existence as a distinct taxon does not by itself establish
hominid status. In this regard it is worth noting that after a recent re-
study of *Oreopithecus*, Szalay (1973) concluded that this catarrhine primate may have no close phylogenetic ties with either pongids or hominids. Among the evidence cited by Szalay as a basis for this conclusion is his estimate of the approximate brain size of *Oreopithecus* as
about 200 cubic centimeters. Szalay's rejection of hominid status for
Oreopithecus is also supported by the ecological evidence, which indicates that like *Ramapithecus* it was a forest-dweller.

Although even more abundant (over a thousand specimens known),
the remains of *Gigantopithecus* are limited to jaws and teeth. By themselves these remains may allow no certain determination of taxonomic
status at the present time. They give us no direct indication of its posture,
mode of locomotion, or cranial capacity. But the occurrence of its fossil remains in savanna areas (Pilbeam 1970) implies both ecological and
genetic isolation from other dryopithecines and occupation of a teres-
trial niche similar in at least some aspects to that of later hominids.

SIGNIFICANCE OF PONGID-LIKE FEATURES OF
GIGANTOPITHECUS

Members of *Gigantopithecus* populations typically show a number of morphological features (discussed in the next section) which are also typically found in australopithecines. But fossil remains of *Gigantopithecus* are also marked by some traits, such as posteriorly diverging mandibular rami, which occur as well in members of pongid populations. Does this automatically bar *Gigantopithecus* from membership in the Hominidae? Before making a specific decision in this situation it would be well to examine the general case.

If we accept the idea that the hominid line came into existence by diverging from that of the pongids, then it should be expected that populations sampled from the base of the hominid phylogenetic sequence would show some evidence of their pongid heritage. Of course, this point could be acknowledged but membership in the Hominidae could be further restricted to those populations most of whose members showed a predominance of hominid morphological traits. This would amount to superimposing a second set of criteria — those of grade — on populations which on independent grounds, such as ecological evidence, appear to belong in the hominid clade. Such a decision would be arbitrary, and there would seem to be room for disagreement here (but if this arbitrariness is realized, divergences of opinion based on these secondary criteria should not affect conclusions about the phylogenetic sequence).

One further point should be made with respect to those traits in which *Gigantopithecus* appears to differ from generally accepted hominids; that is, in many of these same traits *Gigantopithecus* also differs from the pongids. Dart (1960) and Broom and Robinson (1952: 101) are among the few to have stressed this. Broom's statement is repeated here.

Gigantopithecus, which Weidenreich held to be a giant human being, and which we have regarded as a giant ape-man, is in an awkward position when studied by "adequate biometric methods." The length and breadth of the "upper molar," according to Ashton and Zuckerman, "do not differ from the upper second molar of the male gorilla." So if this tooth is to decide the affinity, it is an anthropoid ape. But the third lower molars are larger, much larger indeed, than those of the gorilla, and these teeth would lead to the conclusion that it cannot be placed with the gorilla and is not an anthropoid ape.

But these differences from other known pongids and hominids present a problem in determining the phyletic position of *Gigantopithecus* only if there is an insistence on the narrowest application of the doctrine of irreversibility of evolution. Otherwise, this hominoid provides a plausible morphological intermediate between earlier dryopithecines and the australopithecines. A similar conclusion has recently been reached by Robinson (1972: 255).

ALTERNATIVE EXPLANATIONS FOR THE HOMINID-LIKE FEATURES OF *GIGANTOPITHECUS*

The hominid-like features of *Gigantopithecus* include small incisors and canines, bicuspid front lower premolars, and a mandibular morphology strikingly similar to that found in early robust australopithecines. The usual explanation for these traits in the dentition of *Gigantopithecus* is that they represent parallels to similar features found in the Hominidae but do not imply membership in that taxonomic category.

The most recent explication of this point of view is given by Pilbeam (1970). He provides functional interpretations for the dental features of *Gigantopithecus*, and sees this functional complex as having evolved to enable the animal to process a diet which was like that reported by Jolly (1966) for the gelada baboon. The gelada's diet is said to consist of large quantities of small items such as seeds, grass, and corms. Mastication of these is thought to have caused heavy wear on the anterior dentition and to have led to the selection for genes controlling characters which would increase the area of chewing surface in that region in both primates.

There are several problems with this explanation for the dental characteristics of *Gigantopithecus*. First, it is circular. We are told that *Gigantopithecus* must have had a diet like that of the gelada because of the dental resemblances between these two forms. Then we are told that the dental characteristics of *Gigantopithecus* existed because they were evolved in response to the demands placed on them by such a diet. In point of fact, there is no independent evidence to support the contention that *Gigantopithecus* subsisted on a diet like that of the gelada. Certainly food sources other than seeds and corms exist on savannas and might have been available to *Gigantopithecus*.

Other objections to Pilbeam's interpretation remain. He states that dental characteristics found in *Gigantopithecus* are shared with *Ramapithecus* and *Australopithecus* as well as with the gelada; but no reason is given for what is apparently an assumption: that the similarity of *Ramapithecus* to *Australopithecus* must be due to phylogenetic relationship, while the resemblance of *Gigantopithecus* to *Australopithecus* must be due to parallel evolution. If both *Ramapithecus* and *Giganto-pithecus* subsisted on the same diet, as Pilbeam contends, then the survival of the line thought to be represented by *Ramapithecus* and the extinction of the one represented by *Gigantopithecus* cannot be explained logically in terms of this common factor. This is an inherent weakness in the application of the seed-eating hypothesis to hominid evolution.

The hominid-like features of *Gigantopithecus* may represent parallels rather than evidence of phylogenetic relationship with the australopithecines, but at present there appears to be no objective independent evidence to support this interpretation. The explanation of the hominid-like dental traits of *Gigantopithecus* via analogy with a distantly related and ecologically dissimilar primate (*Gigantopithecus* was several times the size of the gelada monkey — size is an extremely important factor influencing a species' ecology) is less economical than one which recognizes the greater likelihood of homology between two forms both more closely related (both gigantopithecines and the australopithecines are hominoids) and more similar ecologically.

SELECTIVE MECHANISMS WHICH MAY HAVE SHAPED *GIGANTOPITHECUS* POPULATIONS

Pilbeam (1970) was led to the suggestion that *Gigantopithecus* must have consumed a diet like that of the gelada after realizing that *Gigantopithecus* was at least ecologically distinct from other apes, as indicated in his statement:

G. *bilaspurensis* is found associated with an open country fauna, and one can probably infer a similar non-forested habitat for G. *blacki*. It is likely therefore that *Gigantopithecus* species were adapted to foraging in relatively open country. None of the extant apes are so adapted ecologically, and for analogies among living primates it is necessary to turn to the ground-living Old World monkeys.

But while none of the extant apes usually occupy such a niche there can be little doubt that they are preadapted to do so. Chimpanzees living in the wild have been known to range into savanna areas and to defend themselves from predators found there by wielding hand-held clubs and by hurling objects. And by now over a hundred instances of attempted predation by chimpanzees have been observed, with a significant number of the attempts culminating in successful capture of prey (Teleki 1973).

There is little basis for believing that a large hominoid like *Giganto-*

pithecus would have been any less capable of predation if forced to adapt to terrestrial life in open areas where game was abundant, and what may have begun as a necessary shift from the predominantly herbivorous diet of pongids to the more omnivorous one of hominids could have triggered an ever-widening series of behavioral and morphological alterations.

The most evident changes are observable in the dentition. Robinson (1972: 255) has suggested that reduction in the anterior teeth indicates that the new diet did not cause heavy wear there. This is certainly a possibility. Yet, conversely, some specimens do seem to show considerable wear on the front teeth. Moreover, while some of the changes seen, e.g. in height of the canines, are reductions, others, such as the transformation of the anterior lower premolars into bicuspid teeth, would have increased the area of chewing surface, as correctly perceived by Pilbeam (1970).

What we see here could be interpreted as the direct result of conversion of a former herbivore into at least an omnivore. Unlike mammals with a longer phylogenetic history of eating mainly meat, the cheek teeth of pongids were not suited for slicing flesh and gnawing raw meat from bones. If required by a change in diet, in time, selection might have modified the cheek teeth to serve this function. But this does not seem to have been necessary. The incisors of pongids were already blade-like teeth and could have immediately been turned to slicing meat instead of fruit and other vegetation.

It might seem paradoxical at first that the projecting canine (such a prominent feature of the dentition of one common group of carnivores, the Canidae, that it is identified etymologically with them) should be reduced under such circumstances. But this tooth is used in typical carnivores mainly for piercing and holding prey as well as in agonistic displays. In pongids, killing and carrying are performed with much greater frequency and facility by the hands (Teleki 1973). The same is true for agonistic display (Schaller 1965). There would thus have been little obstacle to the conversion of the canine into a useful additional incisiform tooth, as is found in the australopithecines. In *Gigantopithecus*, this stage has not been reached, but there has already been a reduction in the crown height of the canine. In itself such a reduction could have conferred a selective advantage under the hypothetical conditions outlined above, since it would have made this tooth less subject to breakage, with consequent exposure of the root canal and increased likelihood of debilitating infections.

These anterior dental modifications could have left most of the cheek teeth virtually unchanged, not surprising since these present good general-purpose grinding surfaces. The only really notable alteration here was the conversion of the typically single-cuspid anterior lower premolar of pongids into the bicuspid tooth found in gigantopithecine and australopithecine populations. This could have occurred quite easily. As the canine became part of the slicing and gnawing functional complex, the anterior lower premolar against which it formerly sheared would have been freed to assume new shapes and functions. Developmentally, it might have come under the influence of the morphological field of the adjacent cheek teeth; functionally, it would have increased the surface area available for mastication; and evolutionarily, it could have required no more than an increase in the frequency of genes which control the expression of the small lingual cusp (which already occurs as a not infrequent variant in pongid populations).

Beyond the dentition we must rely even more heavily on inference. It does seem that in overall body size gigantopithecines were larger than australopithecines, but I suspect strongly that the difference has been consistently overstated from the time of Weidenreich (1945) to the present (Simons and Ettel 1970). As Garn and Lewis (1958) and others have pointed out, the dentition is a poor guide to the overall size of an animal. On the present evidence there is no necessity to assume that *Gigantopithecus* greatly exceeded the gorilla in stature or bulk. Significantly, the earliest reasonably well-dated australopithecine specimens are quite consistently more robust (although like *Gigantopithecus* they were probably sexually dimorphic) than later ones.

If there is a phylogenetic connection between *Gigantopithecus* and the australopithecines, any necessary reduction in body size from one to the other can be explained with little difficulty. If *Gigantopithecus* hunted, it could have dispatched its prey readily without using any implements. But the initially fortuitous use of any hand-held weapon, whether rock or club, might have enhanced killing power. Any behavioral tendencies in this direction would thus have been selected for. Once more prevalent and effective, such abilities would have permitted a reduction in body bulk without any effective loss in the ability to kill. Any such decrease in size would have conferred at least two potential advantages: a reduction in energy requirements (which would have been selected for particularly during periods of food scarcity) and a gain in speed and agility. These developments could have culminated in the evolution of a smaller, swifter, tool-using biped — a hominid recognizable on structural and cultural as well as ecological grounds.

TEMPORAL RELATIONSHIPS OF GIGANTOPITHECINE AND AUSTRALOPITHECINE POPULATIONS

As there are no chronometric dates available for material associated with any *Gigantopithecus* fossils, the basic problem is one of determining the relative chronological positions of these with respect to representatives of australopithecine populations.

Trying to pinpoint the date of the earliest australopithecine populations is at best a hazardous undertaking. Only a generation ago the best estimate of their age was about half a million to a million years ago (Howells 1952). This estimate has undergone a series of successive revisions. One of the first steps in this process was the dating by the potassium-argon technique of the remains of a robust hominid ("Zinjanthropus") to 1.7 million years ago. Another major step resulted from the series of finds made during the late 1960's in the Omo River Valley of Ethiopia (Howell 1969). Remains found there consist of jaws and teeth that are thought to represent both large and small australopithecines. Although no postcranial elements have as yet been discovered, there is close correspondence between known parts from Omo and those found at other sites from nearby regions with about the same approximate date. For example, at East Rudolf, Kenya, jaws and teeth closely resembling those at Omo are associated with skulls and limb bones which are clearly those of australopithecines (R. Leakey 1972).

At Omo, hominid finds range as far back as about 3.1 million years; those from strata at East Rudolf to something less than 2.6 million years ago. If the Pleistocene is accepted as having begun about 2.5 to 3.0 million years ago (Howell 1968: 568), then these discoveries at Omo and East Rudolf would push the known history of the australopithecines back into the latest stages of the Pliocene.

Still more recently, two more discoveries have been made which are thought by some investigators to establish the existence of even earlier hominid populations. One of these is a mandibular fragment bearing one molar tooth, found at Lothagam Hill in northwestern Kenya (Patterson et al. 1970). The date originally given by these authors for this fossil was around 5.0 to 5.5 million years. This has since been repeated in a number of secondary sources (Pilbeam 1972: 150; Edey 1972: 50; Lasker 1973: 258). Some caution should be exercised here, however. The fossil was not itself dated directly. What information do we have bearing on its age? To begin with, we know that it is contained in a specific stratum (designated as unit 1) of the Lothagam succession, and it is this stratum as a whole for which we have dates. An overlying sill of basalt has given a whole-rock K-Ar date of 3.71 ± 0.23 million years; thus we know that the fossil must at least be older than this. Similarly, Pliocene volcanic rocks underlying unit 1 have a whole-rock K-Ar age of 8.31 ± 0.25 million years; this would set a probable maximum age for the jaw fragment. But we would make an error in judgment to infer from the precision of these K-Ar dates that a high degree of accuracy is indicated for the conventionally cited age of 5.0 to 5.5 million years. This age is the approximate midpoint between the two K-Ar determinations and was possibly arrived at by noting the position of the fossil within its bed. It should be noted, however, that the authors themselves remarked that within this layer "deposition was continuous, although at varying rates" (Patterson et al. 1970).

The morphological characteristics of the Lothagam specimen leave us in about as uncertain a position as did the dating evidence. It consists of but one molar tooth set in a small section of horizontal ramus. This is an anatomical region which is known to show great variation within and overlap between several different hominoid taxa which are recognizable as distinct only on the basis of other evidence. We can safely conclude that the Lothagam specimen represents a Middle to Late Pliocene hominoid of medium to large size; anything beyond this is conjecture.

The other fossil sometimes mentioned as evidence for the existence of hominids antedating those found at Omo is a second upper molar tooth crown from the Ngorora Beds of the Baringo Basin in the Northern Rift Valley of Kenya. It has been known for a generation that molar tooth crowns of hominoids as different as modern man and the chimpanzee resemble each other quite closely (Schuman and Brace 1954). Clearly, even less ample and less diagnostic fossil evidence is available from Baringo than from Lothagam to support the hypothesis that australopithecine populations existed before those found at Omo.

From the preceding discussion, several points emerge:
1.   The oldest securely dated australopithecine remains have been found at Omo; they are from about 3.1 million years ago.
2.   These remains consist of isolated teeth and several mandibles and mandibular fragments.
3.   The mandibles are extremely large and robust, and the teeth span a considerable range in size.
The age of *Gigantopithecus* should be considered against this background.

The Chinese hominoid populations referred to as *Gigantopithecus blacki* are usually said to be of Middle Pleistocene age (e.g. von Koenigswald 1952; Kahlke 1961a, 1961b, 1961c, 1968; Day 1965; Pilbeam 1970; Brace, Nelson, and Korn 1971; Simons 1972). As the references indicate, this opinion has been repeated for two decades, long enough for it to attain the status of dogma, and long enough for a new generation of workers to enter the field unaware that this dogma rests on an extremely tenuous chain of associations. The evidence bearing on this point has been reviewed extensively elsewhere (Eckhardt 1971, 1972, unpublished material), so I will cover only the main points here.

Von Koenigswald was told that the first teeth of *Gigantopithecus* which he purchased in Hong Kong were obtained from the provinces of Kwangsi and Kwangtung in South China. Yellow earth in the pulp cavities of these teeth provided further support for the belief that they belonged to the "orang fauna" previously found in the cave and fissure deposits of those provinces. Von Koenigswald also observed that the collections of fossils obtained from different drugstores were all similar in composition and state of preservation, but noted with appropriate caution that the question of whether they formed a naturally occurring unit with components of uniform age should be left open.

However, in the same year that von Koenigswald acquired the first *Gigantopithecus* teeth, Teilhard the Chardin et al. (1935) stated that all over China south of Tsinling there would eventually be recognized a perfectly homogeneous Lower Pleistocene "Stegodon fauna." They recognized that this South China fauna was rather sharply distinct from that of North China associated with the remains of *Homo erectus* at Peking, but held this difference to be due to the fact that the southern and northern sites were located in different faunal provinces rather than to differences in geological age. This point of view gained currency with the passage of time (e.g. Bien and Chia 1938; Colbert 1940; von Koenigswald 1952; and Colbert and Hooijer 1953). If substantiated by factual evidence, it would make untenable the hypothesis that the Chinese gigantopithecine populations represent possible ancestors of the australopithecines, it being a sound tenet of evolutionary biology that ancestors not appear exclusively later than their supposed descendants.

But the contemporaneity of *Gigantopithecus blacki* with *Homo erectus* has never been demonstrated by direct association. Nor has it been accepted by all anthropologists and paleontologists. For one, Weidenreich (1945) had expressed his reservations about equating temporally the fauna of Choukoutien with that of the South China caves, which he believed to be earlier. More recently, Weidenreich's point of view has been supported by Chow (1958) for several reasons.

1. Over the course of many years, more than twenty localities with

abundant remains typical of the *Stegodon- Ailuropoda* faunas have been discovered and a number of them have been more or less systematically excavated; at none of these has any trace of *Gigantopithecus* been found.

2.   The age of nearly all of the mammalian genera listed by Pei (1957) as actually accompanying the Chinese *Gigantopithecus* mandibles can be anywhere from Middle Pleistocene back to latest Middle Pliocene.

3.   Some of the faunal elements directly associated with *Gigantopithecus* specifically imply dates in the early end of this range. *Mastodon* is generally known from Pliocene horizons in China, and the small size of the teeth of deer and tapirs which occur at the *Gigantopithecus* sites lends additional support to the earlier dates.

4.   Stratigraphically, the deposits which have yielded *Gigantopithecus* fossils are found at a height of over ninety meters above local ground level, while caves containing components of the *Stegodon-Ailuropoda* faunas are generally found only a few meters above the local ground level.

5.   The cave deposits bearing fossils of *Gigantopithecus* are hard reddish travertine beds rather than the yellowish sediments of silt or clay generally found accompanying the *Stegodon-Ailuropoda* faunas. Based on these observations, Chow (1958: 126) concluded:

Gigantopithecus is probably not a component element of [the] *Stegodon-Ailuropoda* fauna as it is generally thought to be. Rather it belongs to a distant fauna to which the name "*Gigantopithecus* fauna" may be applied, and the age is in all probability older than that of the *Stegodon-Ailuropoda* faunas, namely, Early Pleistocene (Villafranchian) or even earlier.

Chow's views, based on the Chinese discoveries alone, gained some indirect confirmation about ten years later when a fourth mandible of *Gigantopithecus* was discovered in the Dhok Pathan zone of Himachal Pradesh in northern India (Simons and Chopra 1969). The sediments in which it was found were estimated to be between five and nine million years old (Simons and Ettel 1970). Then, as now, India and South China belonged to the same (Sino-Malayan) faunal province, and it is unlikely that the spread of a terrestrial hominoid like *Gigantopithecus* from one area to another within this region would take very long. In their classic paper Bartholomew and Birdsell (1953) estimated that protohominids must have expanded throughout the continental tropics and subtropics of the Old World so rapidly that their dispersal would have appeared instantaneous in geological time.

Based on the preceding discussion, a few general points may be made.

Because of the uncertainties inherent in reasoning from faunal correlations to chronological ages, the Middle Pleistocene date usually given for the Chinese populations of *Gigantopithecus* remains a possibility — but only that. As Chow has emphasized, a whole range of earlier dates, from Villafranchian back into the Pliocene, remain evident possibilities as well.

Of course, it could be argued that the date of the Indian specimen, which has been assigned to a different species (*G. bilaspurensis*), is not at all relevant to the problem of dating the Chinese members of this genus. But, at the very least, it does establish the existence of *Gigantopithecus* in a time range which precedes all known australopithecine specimens save extremely incomplete finds like Baringo and Lothagam. And thus it quite definitely makes the debate over the precise date of the Chinese gigantopithecine populations essentially irrelevant to the general question of whether some members of this genus existed earlier than the earliest known australopithecines.

SUMMARY

Is *Gigantopithecus* a hominid? As I have indicated here, the answer to that question depends in part on how that taxonomic category is defined, whether on morphological grounds or on the basis of probable ecological niche and inferred behavior. The issue can be clarified somewhat by inquiring instead whether *Gigantopithecus* could have been ancestral to the australopithecines, whose hominid status appears to be in the realm of canonical knowledge. But even then, many separate areas of evidence and theory must be considered, and the discoveries which could prove to be most persuasive still remain to be made.

Any conclusion reached on the basis of the present incomplete evidence could, of course, prove to be wrong in the light of later discoveries. Premature certainty, in either direction, is likely to remain the greatest barrier to the objective assessment of additional developments.

But, at the very least, the evidence as it now stands no longer allows us to rule *Gigantopithecus* out of a position ancestral to the australopithecines with any degree of assurance. Moreover, there is much better evidence than for any other known Miocene or Pliocene hominoid that *Gigantopithecus* is a hominid.

REFERENCES

BARTHOLOMEW, G. A., J. B. BIRDSELL
  1953   Ecology and the Protohominids. *American Anthropologist* 55: 481–498.
BIEN, M. N., L. P. CHIA
  1938   Cave and rock-shelter deposits in Yunnan. *Bulletin of the Geological Society of China* 18:325–347.
BRACE, C. L., H. NELSON, N. KORN
  1971   *Atlas of fossil man.* New York: Holt, Rinehart and Winston.
BROOM, R., J. T. ROBINSON
  1952   *Swartkrans ape-man:* Paranthropus crassidens. Transvaal Museum Memoir 6. Pretoria.
BROOM, R., G. W. H. SCHEPERS
  1946   *The South African fossil ape-men: the Australopithecinae.* Transvaal Museum Memoir 2. Pretoria.
CHOW, M. M.
  1958   Mammalian faunas and correlation of Tertiary and Early Pleistocene of South China. *Journal of the Paleontological Society of India* 3:123–130.
COLBERT, E. H.
  1940   Pleistocene mammals from the MaKai Valley of northern Yunnan, China. *American Museum Novitates* 1099:1–10.
COLBERT, E. H., D. A. HOOIJER
  1953   Pleistocene mammals from the limestone fissures of Szechwan, China. *American Museum of Natural History Bulletin* 102:5–134.
DART, R.
  1960   The status of *Gigantopithecus. Anthropologischer Anzeiger* 24(2-3):139–145.
DAY, M.
  1965   *Guide to fossil man.* Cleveland: World.
DOBZHANSKY, T., W. G. KINZEY, E. MAYR, D. PILBEAM, B. PATTERSON, E. L. SIMONS
  1972   Letter to the editor of *Scientific American,* later retracted.
ECKHARDT, R. B.
  1970   Bigeneric nomina: an historical and evolutionary perspective. *American Journal of Physical Anthropology* 33(3):337–339.
  1971   "Hominoid dental variation and Hominid origins." Unpublished doctoral dissertation. University of Michigan, Ann Arbor.
  1972   Population genetics and human origins. *Scientific American* 226(1):94–103.
  1973   *Gigantopithecus* as a hominid ancestor. *Anthropologischer Anzeiger* 34:1–8.
EDEY, M. A.
  1972   *The missing link.* New York: Time-Life Books.
GARN, S. M., A. B. LEWIS
  1958   Tooth size, body size, and "giant" fossil man. *American Anthropologist* 60:874–880.

GREGORY, W. K., M. HELLMAN
1926   The dentition of *Dryopithecus* and the origin of man. *Anthropological Papers of the American Museum of Natural History* 28:1–123.

HOOIJER, D. A.
1948   Evolution of the dentition of the orang-utan. *Nature* 162:306.

HOWELL, F. C.
1968   Omo research expedition. *Nature* 219:567–572.
1969   Remains of Hominidae from Pliocene/Pleistocene formations in the Lower Omo Basin, Ethiopia. *Nature* 223:1234–1239.

HOWELLS, W. W.
1952   *Mankind so far*. Garden City, New York: Doubleday.

HRDLIČKA, A.
1935   The Yale fossils of anthropoid apes. *American Journal of Science* 229:34–40.

JOLLY, C. J.
1966   "Evolution of baboons," in *The Baboon in medical research*, volume two. Edited by H. Vagtborg, 323–338. Austin, Texas: Texas University Press.
1970   The seed-eaters: a new model of hominid differentiation based on a baboon analogy. *Man* 5:5–26.

KAHLKE, H. D.
1961a On the complex of the *Stegodon-Ailuropoda*-fauna of South China and the chronological position of *Gigantopithecus blacki* v. Koenigswald. *Vertebrata Palasiatica* 2:83–108.
1961b Wo und wann lebte *Gigantopithecus? Natur und Volk* (Bericht der Senckenbergischen Naturforschenden Gesellschaft), 91:277–287.
1961c Zur chronologischen Stellung der südchinesischen *Gigantopithecus*-Funde. *Zeitschrift für Wissenschaftliche Zoologie* 165:47–80.
1968   "Zur relativen Chronologie ostasiatischer Mittelpleistozän-Faunen und Hominoidea-Funde," in *Evolution und Hominisation*. Edited by G. Kurth, 91–118. Stuttgart: Gustav Fischer Verlag.

KINZEY, W. G.
1971   Evolution of the human canine tooth. *American Anthropologist* 73:680–694.

KURTÉN, B.
1972   *Not from the apes*. New York: Random House.

LASKER, G. W.
1973   *Physical anthropology*. New York: Holt, Rinehart and Winston.

LEAKEY, L. S. B.
1959   A new fossil skull from Olduvai. *Nature* 184:491.

LEAKEY, R. E. F.
1972   Further evidence of Lower Pleistocene hominids from East Rudolf, North Kenya 1971. *Nature* 237:264–269.

LE GROS CLARK, W. E.
1964   *The fossil evidence for human evolution*. Chicago: University of Chicago Press.

Mac INNES, D. G.
   1943   Notes on the East African Miocene primates. *Journal of East African and Uganda Natural History Society* 17:141–181.
MAYR, E.
   1942   *Systematics and the origin of species.* New York: Columbia University Press.
   1965   *Animal species and evolution.* Cambridge, Massachussetts: Harvard University Press.
NEWTH, D. R.
   1956   Soviet embryology. *Science News* 40:7–18.
PATTERSON, B., A. K. BEHRENSMEYER, W. D. SILL
   1970   Geology and fauna of a new Pliocene locality in North-western Kenya. *Nature* 226:918–921.
PEI, W. C.
   1957   Discovery of *Gigantopithecus* mandibles and other material in Liu-Cheng district of central Kwangsi in South China. *Vertebrata Palasiatica* 1:65–72.
PFEIFFER, J. E.
   1969   *The emergence of man.* New York: Harper and Row.
PILBEAM, D. R.
   1970   *Gigantopithecus* and the origins of Hominidae. *Nature* 225(5232): 516–519.
   1972   *The ascent of man.* New York: Macmillan.
ROBINSON, J. T.
   1972   *Early hominid posture and locomotion.* Chicago: University of Chicago Press.
SCHALLER, G. B.
   1965   "The behavior of the mountain gorilla," in *Primate Behavior.* Edited by I. DeVore, 324–367. New York: Holt, Rinehart and Winston.
SCHLOVSKII, I. S., C. SAGAN
   1966   *Intelligent life in the universe.* New York: Dell.
SCHUMAN, E. L., C. L. BRACE
   1954   Metric and morphologic variations in the dentition of the Liberian chimpanzee: comparisons with anthropoid and human dentitions. *Human Biology* 26:239–268.
SHOTWELL, J. A.
   1955   An approach to the paleoecology of mammals. *Ecology* 36:327–337.
SIMONS, E. L.
   1961   The phyletic position of *Ramapithecus. Postilla* 57:1–10.
   1968   A source for dental comparison of *Ramapithecus* with *Australopithecus* and *Homo. South African Journal of Science* 64:92–112.
   1972   *Primate evolution.* New York: Macmillan.
SIMONS, E. L., S. R. K. CHOPRA
   1969   *Gigantopithecus* (Pongidae, Hominoidea), a new species from North India. *Postilla* 138:1–18.
SIMONS, E. L., P. C. ETTEL
   1970   *Gigantopithecus. Scientific American* 222:76–85.

SIMONS, E. L., D. R. PILBEAM
   1965   Preliminary revision of the Dryopithecinae (Pongidae, Anthropoidea). *Folia Primatologica* 3:81–152.
STENT, G.
   1972   Prematurity and uniqueness in scientific discovery. *Scientific American* 227:84–93.
SZALAY, F.
   1973   Cranial anatomy of *Oreopithecus*. *Science* 180:183–185.
TATTERSALL, I. M.
   1969a Ecology of North Indian *Ramapithecus*. *Nature* 221:451–452.
   1969b More on the ecology of North Indian *Ramapithecus*. *Nature* 224: 821–822.
TEILHARD DE CHARDIN, P., C. C. YOUNG, W. C. PEI, H. C. CHANG
   1935   On the Cenozoic formations of Kwangsi and Kwangtung. *Bulletin of the Geological Society of China* 14:179–205.
TELEKI, G.
   1973   The omnivorous Chimpanzee. *Scientific American* 228:32–42.
VON KOENIGSWALD, G. H. R.
   1952   *Gigantopithecus blacki* von Koenigswald, a giant fossil hominoid from the Pleistocene of Southern China. *Anthropological Papers of the American Museum of Natural History* 43:293–325.
   1962   General remarks on the absolute length and relations in size of the premolars in early and modern hominids. *Bibliotheca Primatologica* 1:120–130.
WEIDENREICH, F.
   1937   The dentition of *Sinanthropus pekinensis*. *Paleontologia Sinica*, n.s. D, 1:1–180.
   1945   Giant early man from Java and South China. *Anthropological Papers of the American Museum of Natural History* 40:1–134.
WOLPOFF, M. H.
   1971   *Metric trends in hominoid dental evolution*. Cleveland: Case Western Reserve University Press.
WOO, J. K.
   1962   The mandibles and dentition of *Gigantopithecus*. *Paleontologia Sinica* 146:1–94.
ZUCKERMAN, S.
   1950   South African Anthropoids. *Nature* 166:188.

The Double Descent of Man

GROVER S. KRANTZ

There is a marked difference of opinion today regarding how long ago man's ancestors separated from those of the African apes. In recent years studies of biochemical characteristics of higher primates have led several investigators to the conclusion that man's lineage has been distinct for only four or five million years. In contrast to this, the generally accepted phylogeny based on the fossil record seems clearly to indicate a separation for twenty million years or more. There would appear to be no room for compromise between these two views with a five-fold difference in the times proposed. They are not just two ways of interpreting the data — they represent two quite different kinds of data. If one view is correct, the other is basically in error.

If the fossil record is being correctly read, the "evolutionary clock" must be wrong in some way. The observed chemical differences are certainly there, but just how they relate to times of separation must be re-examined. On the other hand, if the "evolutionary clock" is even approximately correct, our usual interpretation of the fossil record is in error in some major way. In this paper it will be shown how this fossil record might be quite differently interpreted to conform with the shorter chronology.

A detailed presentation of the biochemical investigations is not pertinent here. It is practical to give only a general outline of the various conclusions that have been reached by recent studies.

The assumption can be made that nonadaptive differences in protein molecules occur randomly, and will become fixed in a species by chance. These changes will gradually accumulate, and over sufficiently long periods of time this will average out at a fairly regular rate. The differences in the proteins between any two living animals represent an accumulation of random variations in both of the separate lines of descent since their last common ancestor. The longer the time since that ancestral population lived, the greater the number or quantity of differences between the two living forms.

Wilson and Sarich (1969) summarized the findings on albumin, hemoglobin, DNA, and transferrin in terms of the distinctions found among man, the apes, and various kinds of monkeys. In all cases they found that catarrhine monkeys differed far more from the human condition than did the apes. Of the apes, the gorilla and chimpanzee were much more like man than they were like the orangutan or gibbon.

Albumin was considered the most useful, and from it they concluded that if monkeys separated from the ape line thirty million years ago, then four or five million years would be quite enough to account for the far smaller differences between man and the African apes. The other substances gave slightly different results, but were close enough to support the general conclusion that this last phylogenetic split could not have occurred more than ten million years ago at most (see also Sarich, Wilson 1966, 1967a, 1967b; Sarich 1968, 1970, 1971).

Doolittle and Mross (1970) support this conclusion in their finding that fibrinopeptides in man and chimpanzee are identical. Sheep, goat, and ibex are also identical in their fibrinopeptides as are llama and vicuna. Other pairs of animals which have one amino acid difference in their fibrinopeptides are horse — donkey, water buffalo — cape buffalo, cat — lion, and dog — fox. The indication is that man and chimpanzee can be no more distantly related than any of this last-named group of animal pairs.

Nonno, Herschman, and Levine (1969) compared carbonic anhydrases of the erythrocytes in various primates and came to essentially the same conclusion: the difference between man and chimpanzee is almost trivial compared with the difference between man and monkey. Myoglobin comparisons by Hudgins, et al. (1966) pointed in the same direction by showing that hominoids were all similar to one another and quite different from either cercopithecoids or ceboids.

These conclusions have been challenged by Read and Lestrel (1970) on the basis of the mathematical model used to translate biochemical differences into phylogenetic years. Specifically they questioned Sarich and Wilson's use of albumin data with an exponential model and suggest a power function model instead. This permits a much longer separation between man and apes but must remain an unproven, although interesting, possibility. Uzzell and Pilbeam (1971), however, show reason to reject this interpretation.

Some have suggested that there has been a deceleration of molecular evolution in the higher primates, which may be related to their larger size and longer gestation periods and generations. This would reconcile the minimal biochemical differences with long phylogenetic separations (e.g. Goodman, et al. 1971). From this it would follow that hominoids have had slower protein evolution than the smaller cercopithecoids and ceboids. If this were true, the larger hominoids should show fewer differences from New World monkeys than should the Old World monkeys. That this is demonstrably not the case indicates that molecular evolution is approximately constant regardless of body size, gestation time, or generation length (Sarich, Wilson 1967a).

Strong objections have also been raised by Buettner-Janusch (1969) on several grounds. He notes that various kinds of hemoglobin exist which appear to have changed at quite different rates over time, and he raises the question of which rate is most pertinent. He brings up the possibility of parallel selection and also objects that if these changes were truly random, strictly lineal rates of changes over time might not result. Most strongly, he emphasizes that it is the fossil evidence that contradicts the biochemical conclusions.

An excellent review of both sides of the matter by Uzzell and Pilbeam (1971) concludes with an acceptance of the fossil interpretation. They argue only for a fifteen to twenty million year separation of man's lineage. A careful reading of this work, however, seems to indicate as much support for the five million year separation as for the longer one. Mainly they emphasize the various uncertainties in the whole biochemical approach, even though they accept its conclusions on certain nonprimate phylogenies.

Simons (1969) rejects the short separation of man and apes by stressing the K/A dates of fossils, which he identifies as ancestors of the various living hominoids. Leakey (1967) reads the fossil record similarly, giving man a long and separate lineage. Almost all recent textbooks on physical anthropology present the same interpretations.

The idea that man and apes parted company very recently is not original with Sarich and Wilson, but they have produced new evidence for it. Weinert (1932), basing his judgment on their anatomical similarities, proposed that man and chimpanzee shared a common ancestor as recently as the late Pliocene. Washburn and Hamburg (1965), noting especially the brachiating or arm-swinging characteristics shared by man and apes, concluded that their last common ancestor had fully developed this form of locomotion. Such an ancestor, they said, does not have to be dated any earlier than two to four million years ago.

(It might also be noted that in 1925, while Keith located the division between hominids and pongids in the Middle Oligocene, the time scale he was using placed that event at only 1,200,000 years ago.)

That man and all of the apes had a single, brachiating, common ancestor in fairly recent times appears to have been impossible because of geographic considerations. Consequently I propose parallel developments of the brachiating mode of locomotion in a manner which will still permit a very close relationship. My solution may not be correct in every detail, but it appears to be more consistent with known facts than any alternative. Should any of these "facts" turn out to be incorrect, my conclusions would certainly have to be re-examined.

Brachiating apes (gorilla, chimpanzee, orangutan, and gibbon) are, or were, arboreal specialists whose major form of locomotion WHEN MOVING IN TREES is to swing hand over hand underneath branches. Complex anatomical adjustments in the bones and muscles of the arms, shoulders, and chest, which are necessary in order to accomplish these movements, are found in all the brachiators. Even the gorilla, who has recently adapted largely to quadrupedal ground living on the forest floor, shows all these modifications. Man, who has changed his locomotor adaptation entirely, still retains virtually all of these same anatomical peculiarities which are found in apes (Washburn 1971).

It must be remembered that absolute body size affects a brachiator's manner of locomotion. Only the gibbon and siamang are light enough to be fully dependent on their arms for most of their arboreal travel. As body sizes become larger, the weight increases faster than does the ability of the arms to suspend it. While climbing, a large ape will use its arms for overhead support, but it will generally also use its legs for additional weight-bearing. Regardless of body size and consequent locomotion differences, the brachiating modifications of the arms and thorax are essentially the same.

The so-called monkey brachiators, like *Ateles*, require the same modifications for arm mobility as do the apes. Because of their small size, other modifications that correspond to the high ratios of weight to strength are absent. The fact that gibbons parallel the larger apes in these traits is an anomaly which might be explained by their having had a far larger ancestor at some time in the past.

The original brachiator — the postulated common ancestor of man and all the apes — would have been fully committed to a life in and around trees. Any extensive movements on the ground would, after many generations, eventually have led to some new set of terrestrial locomotor adaptations. The problem with brachiating apes is that they are presently located in two forested areas widely separated by grasslands and deserts in which trees are few and far between. The gorilla and chimpanzee are found in the central African forest areas, while the orangutan and gibbon live in the forested part of southeast Asia. Between these two forest zones there is today a gap of about 3,000 miles of grasslands (savannas), through which brachiating apes cannot travel and still remain active brachiators.

This grassland barrier has apparently been there since the beginning of the Miocene Epoch, at least twenty-five million years ago (Axelrod 1952). If the African and Asian apes had a common brachiating ancestor, it must have dated back to twenty-five million years ago when a continuous forest MAY have existed. Otherwise, one group could not have reached its present location from the forest where both originated. Not only is this antiquity contradicted by Sarich's data, but the fossil record strongly indicates that full brachiation had not evolved at such an early date. Because certain protein molecules argue for a common ancestor of ALL apes at about ten million years ago, there would appear to be no way to account for their present separation.

(One suggestion is that brachiation evolved in Asia and the ancestors of the African apes and man then knuckle-walked to Africa. No fossils of such a knuckle-walking exbrachiator have been reported from the area between the two forested zones where other fossils are common. Yet, such a form must have been highly successful to have spread over this whole region. It must also be explained why they are not in this area today. One might ask, if man's postbrachiating ancestor was a knuckle-walker, why did he become bipedal? Erect posture is easier to explain if it was adopted before a different terrestrial adaptation developed.)

The solution to this dilemma becomes possible if two things are considered. First, the definition of ape and monkey should be understood in terms of locomotor adaptations as well as in terms of dentition. Second, the fossil evidence of locomotor adaptations in early primates should be accepted as it is and not forced into any preconceived notions of what constitutes an ape or monkey by definitions based only on living primates.

Monkeys are basically quadrupeds. They normally walk and run on all fours, whether on branches or on the ground, with their spinal columns parallel to the surface over which they are moving. Monkeys also usually have tails. In contrast, apes will suspend themselves below branches with the body commonly held in a vertical position while moving. They have long mobile arms and broad shoulders — a specialization which is farther removed from the primitive mammalian condition than is the monkey's body design. Apes also have lost their external tails because the stub and its muscles have been incorporated into closing off the pelvic opening from below. At some time in their ancestry, the apes must have had typically monkeylike bodies.

In respect to teeth the situation is reversed. Ape molars have a simple design, with five blunt cusps on the lower and four cusps on the not-quite-square upper molars. Old World monkeys have just four cusps, above and below, arranged in a square. On each monkey molar the forward pair of cusps are connected to each other by a strong cross ridge, and the rear cusps are similarly connected. These so-called bilophodont molars are considered to be quite superior in their ability to chew vegetation, thus giving the monkeys a wider range of adaptability and certain additional ecological possibilities (Van Valen 1969); most monkeys also have a broadened fifth cusp on the lower third molars making these teeth "trilophodont". Because the ape (and human) molars are closer to the original mammalian condition, they represent a stage through which monkey molars probably passed in evolving to their present superior adaptation (von Koenigswald 1969: 40).

Considering just these two characteristics, it is evident that monkeys have the less specialized locomotor design while apes have the less specialized molar pattern. (In most other respects monkeys and apes are quite similar.) The common ancestor of these two kinds of primates would necessarily have had the more primitive traits of each. Thus a monkeylike body with apelike teeth, and of considerable antiquity, would be neither a monkey nor an ape, but would likely be the common ancestor of both.

A fossil primate fitting this description was recently discovered by Simons in Oligocene deposits of Egypt's Fayum Basin (1967). In terms of dentition, this *Aegyptopithecus zeuxis* was very much an ape, and so Simons called it. In terms of body design, however, the limb and tail bones mentioned by Simons show that it was clearly a monkey. It is an ideal representation of what the common ancestor of apes and monkeys must have been like, and it is dated just about when such an ancestor might have lived. (For several years I have used the term "ape-toothed monkey" for this kind of primate — a cumbersome name, but descriptive.) Since the time of *Aegyptopithecus*, some of its descendants could have evolved bilophodont molars (and a few other improvements) and become monkeys, while others developed brachiation and ultimately became apes as we know them today.

The subsequent history of the monkey line will be dealt with later, but is not important at this point. What concerns us more is what happened to the evolving ape line because it included our ancestors as well. It is suggested here that it was this group of ancestral "apes" who were the first primates to leave the trees and to adopt a mainly terrestrial, or ground-living, way of life when the great grasslands opened up.

The world's grassland environment, which is so conspicuous today, did not exist in the Oligocene Epoch (Stirton 1959: 327). It has developed only since the Early Miocene — plants have been evolving in ways just as spectacular as animals. In the Miocene, many mammalian orders rapidly evolved new forms adapted to living in grasslands, and largely adapted to eating the grasses themselves (Colbert 1961: 361). The same opportunity was open to primates as well, and they availed themselves of it — although possibly somewhat later in time than was the case with some other orders of mammals.

From the paleontological record it is possible to conclude that primates expanded into and adapted to grassland living not just once, but on at least three occasions. Each time the newcomers left the trees, they must have all but eliminated the preceding group of primate ground dwellers. The first descent was made in the Early or Middle Miocene by the ancestors of the apes, and incidentally, of ourselves. This was the first step in the "double descent" of man. (My apologies to students of kinship who have long used this term in a different context.)

Fossil remains of this first wave of terrestrial primates are fairly abundant, especially jaws and teeth. They are commonly referred to as "Miocene apes" although their distribution through time may not include the Early Miocene (this is still being argued) and does include some of the Early Pliocene. This gives them a time span from perhaps as much as twenty-five million years ago up to about ten million years ago. The term "ape" is even more of a misnomer because these were not fully apes in the sense of their locomotor adaptations.

Current opinion would include all Miocene "apes" in three genera: *Dryopithecus*, *Pliopithecus*, and *Ramapithecus*. They are collectively called the dryopithecines, which used to be described by as many as twenty different generic names. *Dryopithecus* (= *Sivapithecus* = *Proconsul*, etc.) is thought to include the ancestors of the larger apes; *Pliopithecus* (= *Limnopithecus* = *Epipliopithecus*) has been claimed as a gibbon ancestor; and *Ramapithecus* (= *Kenyapithecus*) is considered by many to be on man's line of evolution (Simons 1964; Simons and Pilbeam 1965). Some questions will be raised later as to the reality of this last-named genus.

The evidence that these Miocene "apes" were actually tailed, terrestrial quadrupeds comes from several sources, primarily from the fossil bones themselves. It has been curiously difficult for most authorities to accept this fossil evidence on face value. This may have been because they are called "apes," and everyone knows that apes are tailless brachiators (see Patterson 1955: 28).

LeGros Clark and Leakey (1951) have published detailed descriptions of the then known postcranial bones of all East African Miocene "apes." Their analysis clearly pointed to four-footed locomotion on the ground, much as in modern baboons or macaques. Subsequent discoveries have repeatedly confirmed this interpretation, yet each time the describers seem reluctant to accept what the bones indicate.

One study of the sacrum of *Pliopithecus* has shown that it had a respectable tail (Ankel 1965), and this might also have been the case for the other types. Not being brachiators, they did not need to incorporate the tail into closing off the pelvic opening. However, the tailless condition may have begun at this time. Coon (1962: 161) has noted the diminution or virtual loss of the tail by some terrestrial monkeys who have no function for it, and he concludes from this that the brachiators lost their tails during an earlier, terrestrial adaptation. This may have been true, at least to some degree, but it was only with the development of large-bodied brachiators that the external tail was irrevocably lost through the new function of its remnants.

There are numerous characteristics in the arms of brachiators which are evident from the bones. Known fossils of Miocene "apes" show a mixture of brachiating and quadrupedal traits. The relative elongation of the forelimb over the hindlimb is absent in both *Dryopithecus* and *Pliopithecus*. Elongated fingers, making the hand hooklike, are not evident in the African *Dryopithecus* (*Proconsul*) specimen. These are probably the two most consistent traits of brachiators' arms. Their absence leads to the conclusion that these Miocene forms had a basically quadrupedal orientation.

Clear data on the largest dryopithecines is lacking so it is largely a presumption on my part that they had arms like the medium and small-sized Miocene "apes." In these larger forms, evidence from several foot bones argues for a weight-bearing design as in baboons rather than for a mainly grasping foot as in arboreal primates (LeGros Clark, Leakey 1951).

The characteristic design of the brachiator wrist, as found in all the apes, man, and australopithecines, is also found in the one Miocene specimen *Dryopithecus (Proconsul) africanus* (Lewis 1969, 1971). It is a fair presumption that all Miocene "apes" had the same kind of wrist inherited from their ultimate common ancestor. By itself, and in view of hand and arm lengths, this wrist is not enough to prove brachiation. It does, however, indicate a close relationship of all the hominoids to each other as opposed to the cercopithecoids.

Certainly the Miocene "apes," however terrestrial, would have done considerable tree climbing on various occasions. Given the considerable body size of most of them, this tree climbing could be expected to emphasize vertical body position with pulling by the arms. An incipient form of partial brachiation is thus expectable. Only later, when a fuller return to arboreal life occurred, would this proclivity be elaborated into complete brachiation.

Pilbeam and Simons (1971) described several arm bones of European dryopithecines as chimpanzeelike, as opposed to orangutan, and suggested they were already knuckle-walkers. Fully arboreal habits can be ruled out by the limited forest cover and seasonal availability of tree food in their environment. The possibility of monkeylike terrestrial quadrupedalism was not seriously considered.

The environments in which Miocene "ape" fossils occur strongly indicate terrestrial habits, if only by elimination. These finds are often in areas that are sparsely forested or fully grassland today, and which have had a similar vegetative cover since the Miocene. There were clearly not enough trees to provide large tracts of arboreal environments in some instances. Associated fossils of other mammalian types support this because they are, in part, of types adapted to savannas or open grasslands (LeGros Clark, Leakey 1951). A possible exception is the Nagri zone in northern India, which was then mainly tropical forest with only a few savanna-adapted animals (Tattersall 1969). Still, the Nagri hominoids may have been part of the minority savanna fauna.

Another reason to suspect that living apes once had a terrestrial ancestor is the great difference in body size between the sexes in several species. This sexual dimorphism varies considerably. In gibbons, males and females are almost exactly the same size; in man and chimpanzee, males outweigh females by about 20 percent; and in gorillas and orangutans, the males average twice the bulk of the females. Relative lengths of the canine teeth differ between the sexes to about the same degree as does body weight.

In most arboreal primates, both sexes of which are of about the same size, rapid flight is the major means of avoiding predators. Whatever the basic orientation of the species, there is a certain body size for it that permits maximum speed of escape, regardless of sex. In contrast, terrestrial primates are often forced to engage in active combat with potential predators. This fighting is normally done only by the males in order to protect the rest of the social group. Reproductive efficiency is assured by having small females, which can raise as many offspring as possible on the given food resources. The males, on the other hand, are as large and powerful as possible for maximum fighting effectiveness. Sexual dimorphism in baboons is the greatest among living primates; adult male baboons outweigh females by two and one-half to one (DeVore, Washburn 1963, see Figure 3).

If an arboreal primate shows great sexual dimorphism, it is a reasonable presumption that its ancestors once lived on the ground, and that since then there has been no selective pressure to erase the difference. In the case of the gibbon, its aerial acrobatics are so precise that recent selection might well have favored a return to sexual equality. In man and chimpanzee some leveling off has occurred, while in the gorilla and orangutan the ancient sexual dimorphism is retained for lack of any good reason to lose it. If the apes did not have a terrestrial period in their ancestry, we would be hard pressed to explain the sexual differences which do occur. A similar dimorphism among certain arboreal monkeys will be used later to argue for a temporary terrestrial background for them too.

There is one more line of evidence pointing to a grassland ancestry for the apes, which Adriaan Kortland discovered in his studies of weapons use. He found that most arboreal and terrestrial primates have quite different practices which follow from their contrasting environments. In throwing a missile, the arboreal monkey executes an aimed drop, while the terrestrial monkey attempts a horizontal throw. In wielding a long stick, the arboreal primate will jab with it, as if between branches, whereas the terrestrial one will swing it back and forth like a club because he has the space to do so.

Kortlandt reports that whenever brachiating apes throw missiles or wield sticks, they usually use the grassland procedures instead of the arboreal ones. This alone convinced him that ape ancestors in the Miocene must have been terrestrial, and since then they have not been under great pressure to change their weapons habits (Kortlandt, Kooij 1963).

The exploitation of terrestrial environments by Miocene "apes" was apparently quite successful. Many of their habits can be guessed at by analogy with baboons, which have recently inherited the same environmental niche. Thus we may assume for them an omnivorous diet, consisting, to a significant degree, of grass seeds and roots. They most likely would also have used the occasional trees and rocky cliffs as sleeping places and as refuges from some predators. Their inferred sexual dimorphism may be taken to indicate a division of labor in which males did most of the fighting. Anything else along the line of social organization would be pure speculation at this point.

Ground "apes" came to an end as they were replaced by a new wave of terrestrial primates in the early Pliocene. This time the newcomers from the trees were cercopithecoid monkeys whose success was most likely based on their bilophodont molars, which were evolving during the Miocene (von Koenigswald 1969; Simons 1970). The replacement was not immediate; this is indicated by the fact that Lower Pliocene deposits include fossils of dryopithecine ground "apes" as well as *Mesopithecus*, the major genus of monkey invaders.

There are very few remains of fossil monkeys from the entire Miocene Epoch, from their possible Oligocene ancestor, *Aegyptopithecus*, up to their impressive appearance on the ground in the Pliocene. During this time their evolution must have proceeded mainly in the African tropical forest region where fossil evidence of all kinds is scarce. (see Napier 1970 for a very different geographical interpretation.)

By ten million years ago monkeys had achieved their present general anatomy and had already separated into two major divisions. The first groundliving true monkey, *Mesopithecus*, has been identified as a member of the colobines, a subfamily of Old World monkeys (LeGros Clark 1959: 59; Genet-Varcin 1969: 73). The other subfamily of cercopithecine monkeys apparently remained entirely confined to the African forests for the time being.

Mesopithecus evidently outcompeted the ground "apes" and eventually usurped almost their entire environment. Only a few of these "apes" survived; they did so by perfecting the ecological niche of arboreal brachiation for which they already had some adaptation. Most of the ground "apes" could not have survived because there were no forests close enough for them to adapt to. Only those located on the fringes of the African and Asian forests were in a position to be able to make this new adjustment. At this point they disappear from the fossil record until recent times because they were restricted to forest habitats.

Avis made a classic study of brachiation in which she showed how apes can occupy a niche not available to monkeys. Contrary to what one might expect from their great size, it is the ape rather than the monkey that can most easily reach the tips of small branches for feeding. They will hold onto one or more small branches with one hand and also with each foot, then reach the other long arm out to where a branch would not carry the weight of even a small monkey. In fact, tests show they even prefer to climb on yielding branches rather than the rigid ones that monkeys seek (Avis 1962). Thus an ecological niche for giant brachiators was at least available when these "apes" lost out in the competition on the ground.

Gibbons are rather different from the other apes, and are in some ways monkeylike as in their small size, sexual equality, and incipient bilophodonty of the molars (von Koenigswald 1969: 47). It may be no coincidence that they developed only in the Asian forests where there was no monkey competition at that time.

Before terrestrial monkeys appeared, ground "apes" evidently occupied the whole range of Afro-Asiatic grasslands and much of Europe as well. These large and highly mobile animals showed few differences from one end of their range to the other. Those "apes" on the edges of the African forests were probably no more than a species apart from the "apes" living on the edges of the Asiatic forests. This observation applies to the ancestors of gorilla, chimpanzee, and orangutan; gibbon ancestors at this time were already possibly a separate genus.

What is being indicated here is a parallel evolution of the brachiating modifications in the African and Asian great apes, rather than the previous existence of an already brachiating common ancestor. Given closely related species of ground "apes" in Africa and Asia, with both of them under the same ecological pressure and adapting to similar new environments, the resulting specializations ought to have been very nearly the same. That the gibbon is more divergent is not surprising because it probably had experienced a period of separate evolution on the ground before returning to the trees. (Why the gibbon developed the same brachiating modifications is not at all clear if it was, in fact, always a small primate.)

Such arguments for parallel evolution should not be pushed too far, but in this case the requisite parallel conditions are so clear-cut, it seems unavoidable. This then solves the dilemma of how the brachiators might have had so recent a common ancestor as Sarich's conclusions call for and yet be located where they are. This last common ancestor was a ground "ape" rather than a brachiator. About ten million years ago this ancestral "ape" became divided into two groups, which independently began to exploit new and widely separated environments of the same kind. The fact that Sarich suggests a date of only eight million years ago for this African-Asian split between the giant brachiators is a minor difference. His figures are subject to some possible error and mine are based on geological dates, which are also imprecise.

There is more to this theory of terrestrial primates. Today, the colobine descendants of *Mesopithecus* no longer dominate the grasslands. They met the same fate which they had dealt to the earlier ground "apes." About five million years ago a new wave of monkeys moved out of the African forest to occupy the grasslands and displace their predecessors. The colobine survivors followed a similar path to that taken by the apes before them by returning to the forests, both in Africa and Asia. The African group, genus *Colobus*, adopted a semibrachiating way of life and is now fully arboreal again. Only their sexual dimorphism and fossil ancestors remain as evidence of their terrestrial past. In Asia there are several genera of colobines collectively referred to as langurs. They are also returning to arboreal life, but are under less pressure to do so; many af them, in fact, still compete quite well on the ground in certain areas. The present distribution of colobines is difficult to explain by any other theory than a common terrestrial ancestry.

The second wave of true monkeys to adapt to the ground is from the cercopithecine branch of the family. These are the baboons and macaques, which today continue to be the dominant nonhuman primate group in the grasslands. The reason for their success compared with the preceding colobines is difficult to pin down in anatomical terms — cheek pouches do not seem inherently superior to sacculated stomachs. Perhaps the difference lies in behavior. Anyone who has known and handled a gentle colobus monkey is appalled by the aggressive, if not downright obnoxious, behavior of macaques. If this behavioral contrast has sufficient antiquity, it could perhaps account for the colobines' losing out to such determined competitors. There may be any number of other reasons.

Returning to the history of the apes, there is one more environmental shift yet to be described. Some five million years ago a group of African apes, already good brachiators, separated from the rest and returned to the grasslands for the second time. On this occasion the posture adopted on the ground was bipedal — walking and running on the hind limbs only. For a medium-sized brachiator, already adjusted to erect posture from hanging underneath branches, erect bipedal locomotion on the ground would be, at least, a reasonable possibility. The various advantages of bipedalism in terms of a better viewpoint and freedom of the hands will not be dealt with here. The evolution of man from this point onward is subject to only minor disagreements. It is much more of a problem to understand how our ancestors reached the condition described here.

Why a brachiator should have abandoned tree life may not be obvious, especially when the ground was well occupied by quadrupedal primates. Several theories have been advanced, most notably a supposed deforestation of certain areas. This may well have been the case but, even without it, population pressure should have been at work, pushing some members of the species into attempting new ecological adaptations.

The recent suggestion by Washburn (1971) that man's ancestors were knuckle-walkers like the great apes just prior to assuming bipedal locomotion deserves some mention here. Tuttle (1967) has shown that man's hands do not appear to be derived from recent knuckle-walkers. Likewise, Oxnard's (1969) study of the shoulder indicates man's most closely resembles that of the orangutan, a total arborealist, while those of the gorilla and chimpanzee are modified for weight support on the ground. Oxnard finds that the common ancestor of man and the African apes must have been totally arboreal.

Of course it may well be that man's ancestors were knuckle-walkers in the Miocene after their first descent from the trees. The fact that *Dryopithecus (Proconsul) africanus* had the hominoid type of wrist strongly suggests this possibility for the terrestrial ancestors of all apes. Full development of arboreal brachiation came later in the Pliocene and evidently erased whatever knuckle-walking adaptations may have evolved prior to that time. Only in the African apes did knuckle-walking appear (or reappear) when they too returned to living, at least partially, on the ground for the second time.

The apparent coincidence in time of the second monkey invasion of the ground with the second descent of man's ancestors raises interesting possibilities. Did the same event drive both groups out of the trees? No such event is obvious unless it is deforestation again.

Another possibility depends on colobine monkey evolution. When the surviving colobines in Africa, under pressure from early macaques, readapted to the trees, they could have in turn pressured some of the ape-toothed brachiators out of their recently established arboreal niche. These apes then returned to the ground, but this time with such a novel adaptation as to be able to compete successfully with any ground monkey.

The proposed sequence of events in primate evolution is diagrammatically illustrated in Figure 1 as a series of adaptations from forests to grasslands to forests and yet again to grasslands. In Figure 2 these same events are illustrated again with somewhat more realistic geographical referents.

One major problem remains with this scheme of higher primate evolution. This is the question of how to interpret the fossils now called

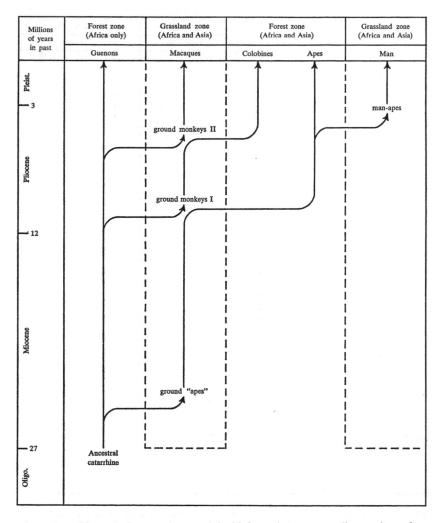

Figure 1. This evolutionary picture of the higher primates according to the author is drawn in such a way as to emphasize adaptative shifts between forests and grasslands. Only five major types of living primates are shown for the sake of simplicity. Both the forest and the grassland zones are shown twice to avoid lines of evolution crossing one another geographically, which in fact they did. Only in the African forests has there been an unbroken line of arboreal primate occupancy, and this has been the source of repeated invasions of the grasslands. Dates of separations in this scheme are closely comparable to those calculated by Sarich on quite different grounds

Ramapithecus. Because Simons, Leakey, and many others consider these as human ancestors, which had already separated from the apes, they require another explanation to fit the present picture. *Ramapithecus* fossils are limited to jaws and teeth. Compared with other Miocene

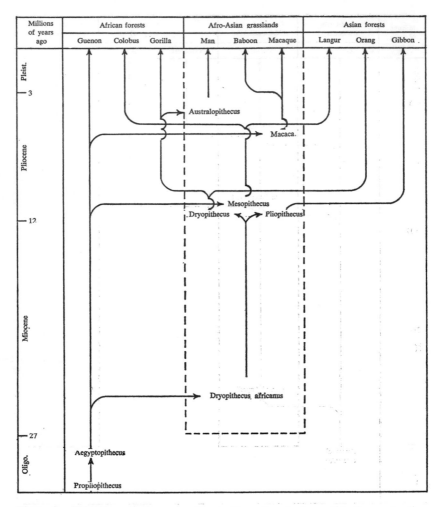

Figure 2.   Primate evolution according to the author is drawn this time according to actual geographical regions and includes more living and fossil types. This chart has the drawback of several lines crossing one another on the African forest-grassland boundary, but it also shows separations between African and Asian developments, which were combined on the previous chart. The line of man's ancestry can be followed from the African forests to the grasslands, back into the forests, and finally onto the grasslands again with man's second descent

"apes," they are short muzzled and their canine teeth do not project very far. Claims of a rounded, humanlike palate are based on a dubious reconstruction. Because no complete palate has been reported, one could just as easily orient the maxillary fragments with parallel molar rows. Such a reconstruction would also allow for larger, more apelike incisors (see Figure 4).

A precanine diastema is evident in the photographs of two Indian specimens of *Ramapithecus* (Simons 1969: 329), yet this is ignored in the published reconstructions. The notable interstitial (interproximal) wear thus is not a hominid trait following from a closed tooth row; chimpanzees show at least as much interstitial wear as does man (Wolpoff 1971). The very diagnostic lower anterior premolar has not been reported in any descriptions to date, although a bicuspid form of this tooth, if it existed, would go far to support the hominid interpretation. Clear evidence of the actual form of this premolar can be seen in the Wenner-Gren cast of *"Kenyapithecus,"* in which the upper canine has been worn by a long, pointed, sectorial lower anterior premolar. Other supposedly hominid traits of *Ramapithecus* are questioned by Genet-Varcin (1969: 95–97), and she tentatively reconstructs the palate very much as I have done.

Some have argued that man is not descended from *Dryopithecus* because our ancestors never had projecting canines (Kinzey 1971). This is untenable because *Ramapithecus* and *Propliopithecus* did in fact have some canine projection. If a small amount of canine reduction occurred in our ancestry, then a greater amount of such reduction is simply a matter of degree and not of kind.

There are several possible interpretations of these fossils other than the one that takes them as early representatives of the strictly human line. They could be either an extinct group, or else they alone could be the ancestors of all apes and man while the other fossil types became extinct. Because neither of these choices is easily demonstrable, a third alternative will be suggested, which is not likely to be well received in certain quarters: *Ramapithecus* fossils are merely female specimens of a type whose males have been variously called *Proconsul major* and *Dryopithecus* (= *Sivapithecus*) *indicus*. This idea requires some explanation.

The Miocene "apes," having been successful quadrupedal ground livers for perhaps as long as fifteen million years, were faced with many of the same problems as are the most recent terrestrial monkeys. Defense against carnivores would have been just as important then as now. With three times as long to adapt to these circumstances, it is quite possible that these "apes" developed sexual dimorphism further than any other primate.

The kinds of differences, including length of canines, between *Ramapithecus* jaws and those of *Dryopithecus indicus* are about the same as between female and male baboons (see Figure 3); only they are carried to a somewhat greater extent. The degree of sexual dimorphism in-

Figure 3.   Upper canines of baboons show extreme sexual dimorphism. The female canine (A) projects only moderately beyond the other teeth, while the male canine (B) is more than twice as long and is an effective fighting weapon. This dimorphism is accompanied by a corresponding difference in body weight and is characteristic of terrestrial primates (redrawn from Eimerl and DeVore 1965)

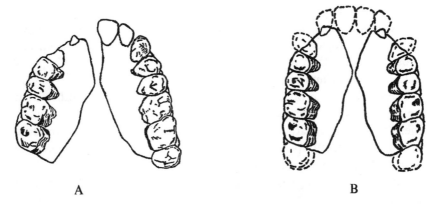

Figure 4.   *Ramapithecus* jaw fragments permit at least two kinds of reconstructions. Simons has placed a right palate fragment from India with a row of teeth from Africa to form a diverging, humanlike dental arch (A). The same Indian fragment can be placed against a mirror image of itself and oriented to produce a typically apelike dental arch (B). With no difficulty, the anterior teeth can be drawn in with apelike proportions and with a generous diastema. If *Ramapithecus* consists of female specimens of a terrestrial "ape," the short canines are just what would be expected

dicated could have been on the order of three to one in terms of body weight. As might be expected according to this idea, the two types have been found in the same deposits in East Africa, India, and China (Simons 1968). They are also among the latest in time of the ground "apes," hence, expectably, the most fully evolved. A species with such dimorphism would have contained the genetic potential to give rise to subsequent populations of either large or small body sizes as well as to populations retaining this dimorphism. Simons and Pilbeam (1971) have taken strong exception to this idea, but they have not described what a female *Dryopithecus indicus* would look like except to say it has smaller canines.

The valuable efforts of Simons and Pilbeam (1965) in simplifying the terminological confusion of the dryopithecines might now be carried a step further. Leaving aside *Pliopithecus* as a distinct type, all other late Miocene/early Pliocene ground "ape" fossils might be lumped into a single, wide-ranging group. Observed differences would then be of two kinds: sexual and geographical. The major distinctions, such as palate size, mandible robustness, and canine projection simply separate males from females. Geographic differences, which can also shift locations over time, may be of species level or only subspecific. These would include differences in the sizes of each sex, various degrees of sexual dimorphism, and such details as amount of enamel wrinkling, cingulum development, relative cusp sizes, etc.

This widespread population of ground "apes" became extinct sometime in the early Pliocene, some without issue and others, as indicated here, by adapting as giant brachiators in two widely separated tropical forest environments. Until more fossils are found and described, geographical location is about the only indication of which of the known forms might be the ancestor of man during this, his first, adaptation to terrestrial life.

The above scheme is quite hypothetical, and as noted, is in major disagreement with most authoritative opinions on fossil primates. Certainly there are weak points in it, and in places I postulate a great deal where there is little or no evidence currently available. Still, the picture is reasonably consistent with known facts, and it would take more than nit-picking to demonstrate that it is totally in error. If this presentation stimulates enough research and/or original thinking to prove it false, then it will have served its purpose almost as well as if it is proven correct.

REFERENCES

ANKEL, FRIDERUN
  1965 Der Canalis Sacralis als Indikator für die Länge der Caudal-region der Primaten. *Folia Primatologica* 3:263–276.
AVIS, VIRGINIA
  1962 Brachiation: the crucial issue for man's ancestry. *Southwestern Journal of Anthropology* 18:119–148.

AXELROD, DANIEL I.
1952   A theory of angiosperm evolution. *Evolution* 6:26–60.
BUETTNER-JANUSCH, JOHN
1969   The nature and future of physical anthropology. *Transactions of the New York Academy of Sciences*, series II, 31:128–138.
COLBERT, EDWIN H.
1961   *Evolution of the vertebrates.* New York: Science Editions.
COON, CARLTON S.
1962   *The origin of races.* New York: Alfred A. Knopf.
DE VORE IRVEN, S. L. WASHBURN
1963   "Baboon ecology and human evolution," in *African ecology and human evolution.* Edited by F. Clark Howell and Francois Bourlière, 335–367. Chicago: Aldine.
DOOLITTLE, R. F., G. A. MROSS
1970   Identity of chimpanzee with human fibrinopeptides. *Nature* 225: 643–644.
EIMERL, SAREL, IRVEN DE VORE
1965   *The primates* (Life Nature Library). New York: Time.
GENET-VARCIN, E.
1969   *A la recherche du primate ancêtre de l'homme.* Paris: Boubee.
GOODMAN, MORRIS, JOHN BARNABAS, GENJI MATSUDA, G. W. MOORE
1971   Molecular evolution in the descent of man. *Nature* 233:604–613.
HUDGINS, P. C., C. M. WHORTON, T. TOMOYOSHI, A. J. RIOPELLE
1966   Comparison of the molecular structure of myoglobin or fourteen primate species. *Nature* 212:693–695.
KEITH, SIR ARTHUR
1925   *The antiquity of man.* London: Williams and Northgate.
KINZEY, WARREN G.
1971   Evolution of the human canine tooth. *American Anthropologist* 73(3):680–694.
KORTLANDT, ADRIAAN, M. KOOIJ
1963   "Protohominid behavior in primates," in *The primates.* Symposia of the Zoological Society of London 10:61–88.
LEAKEY, L. S. B.
1967   An early Miocene member of Hominidae. *Nature* 213:155–163.
LE GROS CLARK, W. E.
1959   *The antecedents of man.* New York: Harper and Row.
LE GROS CLARK, W. E., L. S. B. LEAKEY
1951   The Miocene Hominoidea of East Africa. *Fossil Mammals of Africa* 1:1–117 London: British Museum (Natural History).
LEWIS, O. J.
1969   The hominid wrist joint. *American Journal of Physical Anthropology* 30:251–268.
1971   Osteological features characterizing the wrists of monkeys and apes, with a reconsideration of this region in *Dryopithecus (Proconsul) africanus. American Journal of Physical Anthropology* 36:45–48.

NAPIER, JOHN R.
  1970   "Paleoecology and catarrhine evolution," in *Old World monkeys.*
         Edited by J. R. and P. H. Napier, 55–95. New York: Academic
         Press.
NONNO, L., H. HERSCHMAN, L. LEVINE
  1969   Serologic comparisons of the carbonic anhydrases of primate
         erythrocytes. *Archives of Biochemistry and Biophysics* 136:361–
         367.
OXNARD, CHARLES E.
  1969   Evolution of the human shoulder. *American Journal of Physical
         Anthropology* 30:319–332.
PATTERSON, BRYAN
  1955   "The geologic history of non-hominid primates in the Old World,"
         in *The non-human primates and human evolution.* Edited by
         James A. Gavian, 13–31. Detroit: Wayne State University Press.
PILBEAM, D. R., E. L. SIMONS
  1971   Humerus of *Dryopithecus* from Saint Gaudens, France. *Nature*
         229:406–407.
READ, D. W., P. E. LESTREL
  1970   Hominid phylogeny and immunology: a critical appraisal. *Science*
         168:578–580.
SARICH, VINCENT M.
  1968   "The origin of the hominids: an immunological approach," in
         Perspectives on human evolution 1. Edited by S. L. Washburn
         and Phyllis Jay, 94–121. New York: Holt, Rinehart and Winston.
  1970   "Primate systematics with special reference to Old World mon-
         keys," in *Old World monkeys.* Edited by J. R. and P. H. Napier,
         177–226. New York: Academic Press.
  1971   "A molecular approach to the question of human origins," in
         Background for man. Edited by Phyllis Dolhinow and Vincent
         Sarich, 60–81. Boston: Little, Brown.
SARICH, VINCENT, A. C. WILSON
  1966   Quantitative immunochemistry and the evolution of primate albu-
         mins: micro-complement fixation. *Science* 154:1563–1566.
  1967a Rates of albumen evolution in primates. *Proceedings of the Na-
         tional Academy of Sciences* 58:142–148.
  1967b Immunological time scale for hominid evolution. *Science* 158:
         1200–1203.
SIMONS, ELWYN L.
  1964   The early relatives of man. *Scientific American* 211:50–62.
  1967   The earliest apes. *Scientific American* 217:28–35.
  1968   "New fossil primates: a review," in *Perspectives on human evolu-
         tion* 1. Edited by S. L. Washburn and Phyllis Jay, 41–60. New
         York: Holt, Rinehart and Winston.
  1969   The origin and radiation of the primates. *Annals of the New
         York Academy of Sciences* 167:319–331.
  1970   "The deployment and history of Old World monkeys (Cercopith-
         ecidae, Primates)," in *Old World monkeys.* Edited by J. R. and
         P. H. Napier, 99–137. New York: Academic Press.

SIMONS, ELWYN L., D. R. PILBEAM
  1965   Preliminary revision of the Dryopithecinae (Pongidae, Anthropoidea). *Folia Primatologica* 3:81–152.
  1971   A gorilla-sized ape from the Miocene of India. *Science* 173:23–27.
STIRTON, R. A.
  1959   *Time, life and man.* New York: John Wiley.
TATTERSALL, IAN
  1969   Ecology of north Indian *Ramapithecus*. *Nature* 221:451–452.
TUTTLE, R. H.
  1967   Knuckle-walking and the evolution of hominoid hands. *American Journal of Physical Anthropology* 26:171–206.
UZZELL, T., D. PILBEAM
  1971   Phyletic divergence dates of hominoid primates: a comparison of fossil and molecular data. *Evolution* 25:615–635.
VAN VALEN, LEIGH
  1969   A classification of the primates. *American Journal of Physical Anthropology* 30:295–296.
VON KOENIGSWALD, G. H. R.
  1969   "Miocene Cercopithecoidea and Oreopithecoidea from the Miocene of East Africa," in *Fossil vertebrates of Africa*, volume one. Edited by L. S. B. Leakey, 39–52. New York: Academic Press.
WASHBURN, S. L.
  1971   "The study of human evolution," in *Background for man*. Edited by Phyllis Dolhinow and Vincent Sarich, 82–117. Boston: Little, Brown.
WASHBURN, S. L., D. A. HAMBURG
  1965   "The study of primate behavior," in *Primate behavior*. Edited by I. DeVore, 1-15. New York: Holt, Rinehart and Winston.
WEINERT, HANS
  1932   *Ursprung der Menschheit.* Stuttgart: Ferdinand Enke.
WILSON, A. C., V. M. SARICH
  1969   A molecular time scale for human evolution. *Proceedings of the National Academy of Sciences* 63:1088–1093.
WOLPOFF, M. H.
  1971   Interstitial wear. *American Journal of Physical Anthropology* 34:205–228.

Hominoid-Hominid Heterography and Evolutionary Patterns

KATHARINE W. HULBERT

This essay briefly reports concepts derived from a continuing study of conditions and adaptations which may have promoted some ancestral dryopithecine stock to the hominid condition. I have been attempting to test a hypothetical model for hominization previously presented (Hulbert 1971) which suggested that adaptation to the shorelines of the tropical and subtropical Old World by some protohominid basal stock may have been the critical factor in that process. The marine environment has been seriously considered as a possible niche for evolving man by a number of other writers (Sauer 1952, 1966; Hewes 1968; Sopher 1965; Morgan 1972) although there is at present no fossil evidence to support this thesis. Other empirical evidence, however, along with theoretical considerations, tends to be supportive to the extent that, as it seems to me, this is a plausible and viable approach toward clarification of that still little understood process.

I originally based my argument upon the following premises: (1) the greater the degree of adaptation to a discrete ecological environment by local demes of a species, the greater the reluctance of members to move beyond the range to which they are accustomed (Hulse 1967: 393), and (2) primate species do not migrate as a unit from one region to another (Simons 1969: 139). Gene-flow by means of mating between adjacent groups is the more ordinary means for spreading hereditary characteristics (Hulse 1967: 394; Garn 1969: 191).

I am indebted to the National Institute of General Medical Sciences, The National Institutes of Health, for a Special Fellowship (#5–F3–GM–33, 134–01 to 03) for the opportunity to do field work for my dissertation (Hulbert 1970). This work aroused my interest in the differential rates and directions of gene-flow between local groups as related to marine vs. inland adaptive patterns.

We cannot say, on the basis of the evidence presently available, from precisely what period of time protohominids occupied the range generally accepted as that of the australopithecines (Simons 1969: 139), from Africa to Southeast Asia, accepting *Meganthropus* as an australopithecine (Robinson 1955). The relationship between *Ramapithecus* in North India, and *Kenyapithecus* in Africa (Simons 1964) provides further evidence that some, possibly bipedal, dryopithecine ancestral stock must have been widespread in the tropical Old World (e.g. Birdsell 1972: 209). It is now common knowledge that some australopithecines living close to the Pliocene-Pleistocene border were already habitually bipedal toolmakers, and that the transition to the hominid condition had already taken place at some earlier time. There may be evidence from Kenya that hominids evolved prior to the production of stone tools (Leakey 1968; Harris 1972: 25).

Hominization was going on at some time in the Neogene in Africa, Asia, and/or perhaps Europe. There is no certainty that one area was more important than another as the nursery of modern man. If the ancestral stock from which man evolved was so widespread it is not necessary to postulate a single area of origin. It is sufficient to demonstrate that demes of the ancestral type were within cruising range of each other, and that relatively uniform selection pressures were brought to bear upon the majority of them throughout the range. It is recognized that characters can recur in more than one geographical area (Wilson and Brown 1953: 100).

Various adaptations required by differing habitats within the range would have differed to a greater degree between contrasting ecological zones than within a constant continuous zone. Rates of gene-flow would surely have differed as the habitats themselves differed, keeping our premises in mind, and local gene-pools would themselves have differed proportionately according to their location. Some demes with overlapping gene-pools must have stretched across the range of the protohominids if the end result was a single species throughout the range. This condition would have been more likely to occur in a constant environment occupied by demes having similar adaptive patterns, than in environments occupied by demes having different adaptive patterns. The coastal zone is the only continuous zone, fairly constant in nature, and stretches, however deviously, throughout the range here postulated for protohominids.

I have suggested (Hulbert 1971) that there may have been a significant difference between rates of gene-flow along coasts as compared with rates of gene-flow between inland demes because of the constancy of that environment. Gene-flow between inland demes would have been more often deterred by geographical barriers. Interruption of the coastal zone by river deltas, etc., would not have entailed any radical change in environment or types of foods available. These differential rates of gene-flow are seen as a gene-flow system channeled by relative degrees of adaptation to various ecological niches in a manner consonant with the initial premises, the time-span involved, the geographical range, and modified by demographic factors.

We should consider the possibility that protohominid gene-pools were not isolated, but constituted genetic clines with gene-flow throughout the range at a rate sufficient to maintain the integrity of some ancestral species to have resulted in man evolving as a single species. This argues for a large, widespread population divided into overlapping gene-pools.

Theoretically, there is strong selection either for or against partial intrinsic barriers (Dobzhansky 1952: 208, cited in Wilson and Brown 1953: 98). During the hominoid-hominid shift we would expect intrinsic barriers to have been selected against, again because a single species resulted.

We would expect the ancestral species of protohominids, if they were so widespread, to be highly heterogeneous. Man is the most widespread primate geographically, and a highly variable species. This too would be expected because of the theoretical proposition that "the greater the geographical area encompassed, the less homogeneous will be the population..." (Wilson and Brown 1953: 104). It may also be significant that increased rates of gene-flow along continuous ecological zones exploited by genetically overlapping demes of a single species would tend to increase variability and by so doing increase evolutionary rates (Fisher 1930, cited in Weiss 1972: 41).

It is generally agreed that man is less specialized than other living primates (Brace and Ashley Montagu, 1965). It follows that his ancestral stock inhabited areas which selected for nonspecialization. This argues not only for "open" habitats, but also for seasonally changing and challenging environments which require adaptability rather than adaptation. Demanding environments probably increase capabilities (Jolly 1972: 350). While fairly constant in nature (temperature ranges, foods, etc.) the tropical marine shores are also seasonally changing and challenging.

The uniqueness of man is being re-evaluated (e.g. Count 1972). Man is unique in degree only (Eisenberg 1972). He is not unique because he is bipedal (Hewes 1961, 1964; Napier and Napier 1967: Plate 70), but because he is HABITUALLY bipedal. He is not unique because he has culture defined as learned behavior, but because of the degree to which he is dependent upon learned behaviors, and the degree to which he is able to transmit them not only from individual to individual, but from group to group. I define the "cultural niche" as progressively greater dependence upon an accumulating repertoire of innovative and learned behaviors transmitted from generation to generation through time, and from group to group through space, gradually replacing dependence upon genetically controlled behaviors.

Approaching the problem of hominization from the level of living nonhominid primates may be the more productive approach at the present time (Burton and Bick 1972: 53; Pilbeam 1972: 1101; Harrison 1967). Working primatologists are exploring the mechanisms for diffusion of protocultural traits in and between groups of living primates (e.g. van Lawick-Goodall 1972; Frisch 1968; Tsumori 1967). Some primate groups might be described as "protocultural isolates" (cf. Marias 1969).

In comparing the various ecological niches in which wild primates are found today, ranging from montane, rain, and gallery forests, and mangrove swamps, to grassy savannas, virtually treeless semidesert and fringe areas (Tappen 1960; Napier 1962), we would expect the environment in which hominization occurred to have been of the "open" or "fringe" variety. *Ramapithecus* fossils are found in deposits which are described as forest fringe (Jolly 1972: 63). More terrestrial primates have adapted to open and variable environments, covered wider geographical ranges, and are more omnivorous in their diets (Washburn 1962: 159–160). The adaptability of Old World macaques and baboons has made it possible for them to occupy almost all of the tropical and subtropical regions of the Old World with little speciation (DeVore and Hall 1965: 21). In contrast, factors for speciation seem to be more prevalent among forest monkeys (Tappen 1960: 110; Jolly 1972: 271).

There is evidence from geology and the distribution of living wild primates that Africa and Asia have been virtually separated since the Miocene epoch (Tappen 1960: 113; Napier 1970: 74). It appears that only such adaptable, fringe area species as the macaques have maintained genetic interchange between these continental areas since that time because only they are related taxonomically below the family level. I would suggest that protohominids were at least as adaptable and also maintained genetic interchance between Africa and Asia, and that dry, sandy, "open" land bridges, or even narrow water barriers, were no deterrent to that exchange.

Evidence that narrow water channels cannot have been ecological barriers for some living nonhominid primates and/or early man is found in Southeast Asia. In the distribution of *Macaca fascicularis* (Medway 1970) it is evident that crossings have not resulted in speciation which would imply genetic interchange on a continuous basis in both directions. Great intraspecies variation is indicated by the fact that twenty-one subspecies are listed for this macaque (Napier and Napier 1967: 207). The greatest deviation is represented by *Macaca maurus,* the Celebes black ape, found across the Wallace Line.

Numerous authors have attempted to explain the presence of primates on the Philippine Islands, as well as on Celebes and neighboring islands, by resorting to hypothetical land bridges which are believed to have existed at times of low sea levels during glacial periods (e.g. Napier 1970; Oakley 1964). A thorough study of ocean depths as recorded on thirteen United States Naval Oceanographic charts which ranged in scale from 1.37 to 50 miles per inch,[1] has convinced me that even if the seas were one hundred fathoms lower than at present, which is twice the estimated lowering reported for the Würm glacial period (Napier 1970), water channels remained between the Palawan land extension of Borneo and the Philippines, between the Sulu Archipelago extension of Mindanao and Borneo, and that a proposed land bridge from Taiwan to Luzon, or from the Philippine land mass (Mindanao region) to Celebes (Oakley 1964; Napier 1970), could not have existed. The latter would have spanned the Wallace Line. That primates found on Celebes, or in the Philippines, got to their present locations by crossing water channels one way or another is indicated by this study. The channels remaining at low sea levels must have been more treacherous than they are today due to the fact that the South China and Sulu Seas were virtually landlocked — climatological conditions, tides and winds considered (United States Naval Oceanographic Office Publication 236, 1945). Nevertheless, they were crossed.

In the case of early man, *Meganthropus* is found in the Djitis level in Java the lower part of which has been recently dated 1.9 million years ± 0.4 million years B.P. (Birdsell 1972: 256). This was a warm period (Birdsell 1972: figure 8–1). If no land bridges existed between Java and mainland China at the time, how did this presumed hominid reach Java without crossing water?

There are very few coastal sites known for early man (Vallonet, Ein Hanech, Sidi Abderahman) and so far as I am aware, we have no fossil evidence for protohominids in marine environments at present. There is ample evidence that middle Pleistocene man occupied a wide variety of habitats, seemed to favor river and lake shores, and avoided mountainous

---

[1] I wish to express my gratitude to two of my students, Michael Berry and George Rogers. Jr., who assisted with this project. The short report which resulted is listed in the references as Hulbert, n.d.

areas. "Since all of our evidence is from interior regions, there may have been considerable exploitation of sea coasts of which we know nothing" (Chard 1969: 98–99). Harrison, reporting upon his work in Borneo, makes the statement that artifacts which presumably date from early or middle Pleistocene times are found only near the coast (Harrison 1972). The recent report on skeletal material from Kow Swamp, South Australia, which claims that this material, though dated only nine to ten thousand years old, bears a close resemblance morphologically to *Homo erectus* forms from Java rather than to modern Australian aborigines (Thorne and Macumber 1972: 316–319), raises another question. If this resemblance should be confirmed this may provide further evidence that pre-*sapiens* man was capable of crossing thirty miles of water (at the least) which separated the Sahul and Sunda shelves during low-water periods. If this material is representative of pre-*sapiens* or transitional forms of *Homo sapiens,* it may also demonstrate the irregularity of the time level at which "sapienization" took place.

In line with this model one would expect that eventually evidence of extinct branches of the hominoid-hominid line will be found in isolated pockets bordering the mainline gene-flow routes. The living great apes, so physiologically close to man (cf. Chiarelli 1972), may represent such branches diverging at various time periods and in various parts of the range.

Time and space do not permit discussion of the possible effects of marine adaptation by protohominids upon physiological changes which that environment might account for, such as those which might have been influenced by increase of protein in the diet (cf. Stini 1971), or of salt, or iodine or other factors.

Man has long since usurped most of the shorelines of the world, and it may be no wonder that other primates are seldom found in that environment except as permitted by man. If the shorelines were earlier inhabited by some stock of dryopithecines ancestral to man it might well be that the more progressive and adaptable species or genera eliminated any other primate competitors for that niche. Just as man is his own worst enemy today, primates, particularly protohominids, may have always been the major predators on other primates.

Concepts from evolutionary theory, from primatology, geology, archaeology, and oceanography have been presented which tend to support the viability of a model for hominization based upon the adaptation of some protohominid species to the shorelines of the tropical and subtropical Old World during the Neogene. This ecological adaptation by a widespread population of protohominids, linked deme to deme by a network of gene-flow synchronous with diffusion of protocultural traits, is postulated to have been a critical factor in the evolutionary diversion of the hominids from an ancestral hominoid basal stock.

REFERENCES

BIRDSELL, J. B.
  1972 *Human evolution* (first edition). Chicago: Rand McNally.
BRACE, C. L. and M. F. ASHLEY MONTAGU
  1965 *Man's evolution.* New York: Macmillan.
BURTON, FRANCES D. and J. A. BICK
  1972 A drift in time can define a deme: the implications of tradition drift in primate societies for hominid evolution. *Journal of Human Evolution* 1:53–59.
CHARD, CHESTER S.
  1969 *Man in prehistory.* New York: McGraw-Hill.
CHIARELLI, B. A.
  1972 Comparative chromosome analysis between man and chimpanzee. *Journal of Human Evolution* 1:389–393.
COUNT, E. W.
  1972 On the uniqueness (?) of man. *Abstract book.* Portland: Fourth International Congress of Primatology, August 15–18.
DE VORE, IRVEN and K. R. L. HALL
  1965 "Baboon ecology," in *Field studies of monkeys and apes.* Edited by Irven DeVore, 20–52. New York: Holt, Rinehart and Winston.
EISENBERG, J. F.
  1972 Mammalian social systems. *Abstract book.* Portland: Fourth International Congress of Primatology, August 15–18.
FRISCH, JOHN E.
  1968 "Individual behavior and intertroop variability in Japanese macaques," in *Primates.* Edited by Phyllis C. Jay, 243–252. New York: Holt, Rinehart and Winston.
GARN, STANLEY
  1969 "Geographical, local and micro-races," in *Evolutionary anthropology.* Edited by Hermann K. Bleibtreu, 187–197. Boston: Allyn and Bacon.
HARDY, SIR ALISTER
  1969 Was man more aquatic in the past? *The New Scientist* March 17:642–645.
HARRIS, MARVIN
  1972 The human strategy: you are what they ate. *Natural History* 81,F: 24–25.
HARRISON, TOM
  1967 A primate special symposium 2 of the 1966 Pacific Science Congress. *Asian Perspectives* 10:19–21.
  1972 The prehistory of Borneo. *Asian Perspectives* 13:17–45.

HEWES, GORDON W.
1961 Food transport and the origin of hominid bipedalism. *American Anthropologist* 63:687–709.
1964 Hominid bipedalism: independent evidence for the food-carrying theory. *Science* 146:416–418.
1968 A new ecological model for hominization. *Proceedings of the Eighth International Congress of Anthropological and Ethnological Sciences, Tokyo* 3:276–278.

HULBERT, KATHARINE W.
1970 A study in human ecology: the sea-fishing people of the southwest coast of India. *Dissertation Abstracts International* 31(3):1030–B.
1971 "A hypothetical model of gene-flow patterns between proto-hominid demes." Paper at the 70th Annual Meeting of the American Anthropological Association, New York, November 19.
n.d. A reconsideration of Southeast Asian migration routes for man and animals during low sea-level periods of the Pleistocene.

HULSE, FREDERICK S.
1967 "Race as an evolutionary episode," in *Human evolution*. Edited by Noel Korn and Fred Thompson, 385–401. New York: Holt, Rinehart and Winston.

JOLLY, ALISON
1972 *The evolution of primate behavior*. New York: Macmillan.

LEAKEY, L. S. B.
1968 Bone smashing by late Miocene hominidae. *Nature* 218:528–530.

MARIAS, EUGENE
1969 *The soul of the ape*. New York: Atheneum.

MEDWAY, LORD
1970 "The monkeys of Sundaland: ecology and systematics of Cercopithecids of a humid equatorial environment," in *Old World monkeys: evolution systematics and behavior*. Edited by J. K. Napier and P. H. Napier, 513–553. New York: Academic Press.

MORGAN, ELAINE
1972 *The descent of woman*, New York: Stein and Day.

NAPIER, JOHN
1962 Monkeys and their habitats. *The New Scientist* (295):88–92.
1970 *The roots of mankind*. Washington, D.C.: Smithsonian.

NAPIER, JOHN and PRUE H. NAPIER
1967 *A handbook of living primates*. London: Academic Press.

OAKLEY, KENNETH P.
1964 *Frameworks for dating fossil man*. Chicago: Aldine.

PILBEAM, D. R.
1972 Evolutionary anthropology. *Science* 175:1101.

ROBINSON, J. T.
1955 Further remarks on the relationship between "Meganthropus" and Australopithecines. *American Journal of Physical Anthropology* 13:429–446.

SAUER, C. O.
1952 *Agricultural origins and dispersals*. New York: The American Geographical Society.

1966   "Sedentary and mobile bents in early societies," in *The social life of early man.* Edited by S. L. Washburn. Chicago: Aldine.

SIMONS, ELWIN L.
1964   The early relations of man. *Scientific American* 211:50–62.
1969   "Some fallacies in the study of hominid phylogeny," in *Evolutionary anthropology.* Edited by Hermann K. Bleibtreu. Boston: Allyn and Bacon.

SOPHER, DAVID
1965   *The sea nomads.* Singapore: Lim Bian Han.

STINI, WILLIAM
1971   Evolutionary implications of changing nutritional patterns in human populations. *American Anthropologist* 73:1019–1030.

STRAUSS, WILLIAM L. JR.
1963   "The classification of *Oreopithecus,*" in *Classification and human evolution.* Edited by S. Washburn. New York: Wenner-Gren Foundation for Anthropological Research.

TAPPEN, N. C.
1960   Problems of distribution and adaptation of the African monkeys. *Current Anthropology* 1:91–120.

THORNE, A. G. and P. G. MACUMBER
1972   Discoveries of Late Pleistocene man at Kow Swamp, Australia. *Nature* 238:316–319.

TSUMORI, ATSUO
1967   "Newly acquired behavior and social interactions of Japanese monkeys," in *Social communication among primates.* Edited by Stuart A. Altmann, 207–219. Chicago: University of Chicago.

VAN LAWICK–GOODALL, J.
1972   Observational learning among the Gombe Stream chimpanzees. *Abstract book.* Portland: Fourth International Congress of Primatology.

WASHBURN, S. L.
1962   "The analysis of primate evolution with particular reference to the origin of man," in *Ideas on human evolution.* Edited by W. W. Howells, 154–171. Cambridge, Mass.: Harvard University Press.

WEISS, MARK L.
1972   Frequency and maintenance of genetic variability in natural populations of *Macaca fascicularis. Journal of Human Evolution* 1:41–48.

WILSON, E. O., W. L. BROWN, JR.
1953   The subspecies concept and its taxonomic application. *Systematic Zoology* 2:97–111.

Traits of Discontinuity in Human Evolution

V. P. YAKIMOV

The evolution of man seems to be a continuous process of development of hominization features, of accumulation of species properties in the morphological structures, ecology and ethology of fossil higher primates and hominids. In this respect it seems hardly different from the evolutionary formation of any other biological species. If it were possible to consider each successive link of the entire phylogenetic chain of species formation, or even analyze the intraspecies interpopulation variability at each stage of human evolution without exception, then the process of hominization doubtless would be proved to be continuous. However, to obtain such data would imply the need to fix each point of the process in its dynamics, which is hardly feasible at all, much less with respect to the past. Discrimination of two genetically interrelated phenomena is possible only after a newly emergent property has become sufficiently pronounced and, hence, discernible.

Human evolution is a specific process, inasmuch as the major hominization features, as they evolved and were fixed by evolution, would dramatically upset the existing biological relations and cause their qualitative transformation, reflecting the discontinuous nature of the process itself.

This paper is an attempt to discuss the evolution of man from the above-described standpoint, with special reference to some of the most important features acquired by man's nearest ancestors.

Most researchers today agree that the transition of some fossil species of higher primates to bipedal walking was a turning point in their evolution along the hominid line (Khrisanfova 1967: 3–21;

Uryson 1965: 27–38; Napier 1967), thereby supporting the well-known idea that that was a decisive step towards *Homo sapiens*.

The acquisition of bipedalism by ancient hominoids such as *Australopithecus*, implied a substantial reorganization of the entire system of gravity forces in the physiques of these primates (Brovar 1960; Kummer 1965: 227–248, 1969: 316–321). This process was associated with morphological and biomechanical changes in the structure of the body.

Zenkevich, studying the evolution of the locomotor apparatus of animals, noted that the formation of such an apparatus that would provide for a high speed of locomotion, maneuverability and efficiency of the process of movement, constituted an essential feature in the progressive evolution of animals (1944: 129–171). This process, however, entails quite formidable discrepancies between the locomotor apparatus in the process of evolutionary development on the one hand, and the rest of the organs, on the other.

Hominoids and hominids managed to overcome these discrepancies in their evolution, and although some authors (Quigley 1971: 519–541) regard the acquisition by the hominids of a unique bipedal locomotion as a "biological error," such an abrupt discontinuity in the evolution of quadruped primates paved the way for the emergence of man. The center of gravity, or rather the "sphere" of its movement (Brovar 1960) was fixed by evolution in man's ancestors by a parallel formation of the load bearing organ of locomotion — the foot — as well as by the development of the whole system of bones, muscles, and ligaments, by a complex reconstruction of the equilibrium organs, and by other similar processes, all of which proceeded in a sufficiently rigorous system of coordinations and correlations of different orders (Shmalgauzen 1938, 1940).

The improvement of bipedal locomotion and the transition from "shuffling" to "striding" gait were also made possible by a well-known factor: the non-uniform development of different groups of muscles of the hip joint and of the free lower limb itself. Some of these muscles played a special role. As far back as the 1930's, Deshin (1938) demonstrated the importance of m. iliopsoas for the weight bearing limb in walking, while Kotsitadze (1972), through a combined use of electromyography and ichnography discovered the obvious part played by the adductors in the single limb bearing phase of walking, that is to say at the moment equilibrium is maintained on one leg. Both authors have contributed largely to our understanding of the biomechanics of the "striding" gait.

The change in nutritional pattern was an essential factor behind the growing importance of bipedal walking. After man's ancestor had turned omnivorous with a marked taste for animal food, the pattern of gravity forces of his body underwent a drastic alteration following the reduction in the digestive tract capacity. One would be hard put to defend the thesis that purely herbivorous primates, such as the gorilla with its enormous, constantly filled belly, might have turned bipedal.

The change of nutritional pattern, however, played another far more important role, as it secured for the hominids a special position in biocenosis. The broadening of the scope of edible foods by inclusion of the flesh of medium-size and relatively large mammals, obtained actively (not by corpse eating, as maintained by some authors [Padberg 1967: 1–14]) marked a rupture of the nutritional chains typical for the primates. The "super"-primate link narrowed, accompanied by a corresponding increase in the number of links on the lower rungs of the ecological pyramid; man's ancestors came to share with carnivores the niche of the consumers of the final link of the food chain. Subsequently man occupied the upper link of that chain and phased out carnivorous animals, though the latter did not become the next to last link of the food chain.

One should also note the effect of the new nutritional pattern of man's ancestors on their intraherd relationships. The entire process hardly lends itself to detailed analysis without the problem being developed more extensively, but some aspects of the process will be just mentioned, those which in our view merit closer attention.

Van Lawick-Goodall's observations (1971) of wild chimpanzees have shown that sometimes several of them take part in catching their prey — young or adult monkeys. Apparently, though not necessarily, several members of the group concert their efforts temporarily, in something like the chase pacticed by gregarious carnivores as well as by ancient primitive hunters, though in a different way and on a different developmental level.

The process of eating the prey is also one that largely contributes to the fusion of the group. The same author observed chimpanzees to gather round a lucky "hunter" and beg for pieces, mostly without success. Undoubtedly, the crowding of the chimpanzees around the prey depends to a considerable extent on such a "factor" as the size of the object of eating. The very same "factor" apparently caused individuals to get together for eating their prey in man's ancestoral groups — fossil hominoids. Naturally enough, herbivorous forms seeking and eating their food over considerable territories and relatively independently of one another could not be subject to the effect of such an additional uniting "factor."

Another important point connected with the transition of higher primates to animal food concerns the possible effect of this event on the structure of the group or herd. Here again Goodall's observations are of value. The researcher has noted that the hierarchical relationships among chimpanzee males can be violated only where live prey is concerned. In such a case, the dominant male as often as not finds himself begging and rudely turned down by the prey owner who otherwise would have unquestioningly surrendered to the dominant male any vegetable food, no matter how attractive. As applied to human evolution this interesting fact may serve as a basis for extremely valuable theoretical conclusions.

Thus, a discontinuity in the evolution of man's ancestors brought about by an essential qualitative change of their mode of nutrition, was bound to entail serious upheavals in their ecology and ethology and lead to a substantial restructuring of herd relations. This factor was likewise among the major prerequisites for new relationships in the emergent human society.

The bipedal mode of locomotion brought to life essentially new behavior patterns of terrestrial higher primates, among which a higher level of "implemental" activity was particularly important inasmuch as it was associated with a step forward in the psychic development of these primates as well as with an advance of their system of visual and kinesthetic analyzers. With the forelimbs emancipated from locomotor functions, accidental sporadic usage of natural objects as tools gave way to their systematic application for obtaining food, for defense or attack. In consequence, objects came to be regarded in their "implemental" sense and their handling was becoming increasingly purposeful. The higher primates' constant "implemental" usage of various natural objects became an indispensable condition of their existence. Several groups of hominoid primates took precisely such an adaptive path of evolution. Some of them, including the ancestors of the hominids, attained a level of tool-using performance conductive to a qualitatively new phenomenon — acting on the objects used with a view to imparting to them a required size or shape.

Out of this long and rather consistent process one should single out certain points which help assess the changes in the primates' activities and their attitude toward the objects they used. The numerous recent finds of skeletal remains of *Australopithecus* and chopped pebbles in East Africa are weighty evidence that as far back as two-and-a-half to three million years ago these hominoids not only were able to handle natural objects, but also to modify them (Arambourg 1967: 562–566; Howell 1969: 1234–1329; Leakey 1971: 241–249). Stone became the object treated — a material with as yet unknown properties which was, moreover, too hard for natural organs such as teeth or upper limbs. So, for the working of pebble to be successful, a qualitatively new mediating element was to be included in the operation — an object with which to work another object.

Ethnologically, this constituted an essential change in the behavior of the primates. In his series of experiments with chimpanzees Khroustov (1964: 503–509) has shown that various forms of tool-handling activity of modern anthropoids, even to the extent of treating the objects with natural organs, never go beyond a certain psycho-physiological barrier to achieve the use of mediators.

An equally important consideration is that while using a mediator the primate's attention should be fixed on the object being acted upon and not on that with which the primate is acting. Yet, according to Fabri (1958: 23–31; Jerison 1963), apes manipulating objects concentrate their attention precisely on the changes in the object serving as a "tool" while the other object, that being acted upon, remains merely a background, a substrate of action. On the contrary, man, while making a tool, that is to say while actually in the process of work, rivets his attention on the object being worked. It follows that in order to master the art of using a mediator to work hard objects, such as a pebble, fossil hominoids were to undergo a considerable change of their neurofunctional processes, above all reorientation of the flow of kinesthetic and visual perceptions. So, here again is an important turning-point in the evolution of higher primates, a symptom of discontinuity of the process.

Another important problem is that of progressive development of the hominoid brain caused by ever more complicated forms of implemental activity as a condition of their existence and transition to some treatment of natural objects.

Many researchers, when comparing various forms of hominoids or hominids which they place at different but sequential stages of evolutionary development, take into consideration the size and complexity of the brain. Even adversaries of the so-called "brain Rubicon" (Tobias 1964: 3–4, 1968: 81–92) do not fail to consider the endocranial capacity (both absolute and relative) to be a criterion of the degree of hominization. Thus, the capacity of Olduvai Hominid 7 has long been "a bone of contention": twenty or thirty cubic centimeters this or that way could tip the scale toward a greater or smaller degree of "humanness" of this primate (Campbell 1964: 33–38; Holloway 1966: 103–121; Wolpoff 1969: 223).

I am inclined to side with those who hold that the difference between the *Australopithecus*-like ancestors of man and their descendants — true hominids — manifested itself morphologically in the cranial capacity and, in particular, in the brain structure. This viewpoint, though somewhat conservative, has recently been supported by a good deal of factual evidence. Thus, a study of intergroup variability of endocranial capacity in Australopithecidae (including *A. habilis*) and *H. erectus*, the most ancient true hominid known to date, has shown no transgression to exist between them (Kochetkova 1970: 3–19). Transgression appears only if the top value of intragroup variability (± 3) is used, but this approach is bound to cause grave doubts as to the applicability of such a comparison.

The gap between these two groups in terms of the brain becomes even more sizable in the light of structural data obtained by a detailed comparative endocranial study.

Kochetkova has performed quite a few endocranial studies on fossil australopithecines and man's earliest ancestors (Kochetkova 1966: 457–496, 1967: 22–40) with the result that she has found essential differences in the endocranial structure of the groups compared, which are ascribed by her to the qualitative difference in the neurofunctional activities of the two groups. For Australopithecidae, the distinguishing features can be listed as follows: a relatively small absolute size of the brain (endocranium); a small frontal lobe with a beak-like pole; a solid contact of the frontal and temporal lobes at a very obtuse angle; a negligibly small lower parietal lobule, etc. The hemispheres have a fairly smooth spherical surface free from any marked protrusions or depressions characteristic of the endocrania of *H. erectus* and associated with the emergence of specifically human fields in the cortex. A similar type of brain characterizes the modern pongids. *A. habilis* has likewise not been found to differ from the rest of Australopithecidae by the ratio of brain parts (Kochetkova 1969a: 29–42, 1969b: 102–104).

If these data are interpreted in psychophysiological terms, one is led to assume that the functional systems of the cortex of Australopithecidae, incuding *A. habilis*, and those of the modern pongids are fairly close by the levels of their development. The inadequate development of important regions of the brain in Australopithecidae suggests that they thought, similarly to modern pongids, at the level of images and notions, but not of concepts as man does (Kochetkova 1966: 457–496, 1967: 22–40). This was the neurofunctional basis for the pebble-treatment activity of Australopithecidae which reflected no qualitative change in the ethology of these primates, but was merely a manifestation of a higher level of implemental activity of the early Quaternary hominoids.

Australopithecidae and their chronological successors — the earliest true hominids (*H. erectus*) — are separated by a qualitative gap which manifests itself in two interrelated areas: the morphology of the brain (endocranium) and the nature of tools. *H. erectus*, as distinct from his predecessor, had an endocranium with marked foci of a more intensive growth in the lower lobe and the parietal-temporal region (Kochetkova 1966: 457–496, 1967: 22–40). Cytoarchitectonically, these are the regions of formation of cortical areas 37, 39, and 40 in the parietal lobe, and 44 and 45 in the frontal lobe. In psychophysiological terms, these areas in the parietal-temporal and frontal lobes are closely associated with labor activity and speech communication, i.e., specifically human features.

It is well known that the main tools of the Abbevillean or Chellean cultures associated with various representatives of the earliest man (*H. erectus ssp.*), for all their outward primitiveness, exhibit above all clear-cut geometrical features and constancy of shape. This fact coupled with the data on the endocranial surface structure, suggests that the earliest man evolved conceptual thinking and acquired an ability to make tools in keeping with abstract concepts of their shape and utilitarian purpose. This assumption is affirmed by the structural analysis of endocrania together with tool development at the subsequent stages of human evolution (Kochetkova 1966: 457–496, 1967: 22–40).

The point of discontinuity in human evolution marked by transition from systematic use of natural objects and their partial treatment to the making of tools of a fixed configuration is of special importance, inasmuch as the labor process itself turned into a precondition of man's subsequent biological progress. The process of labor aimed at making a tool (an artifact) called for systematic and consistent actions, for concentrated attention on the actions which were to lead to a desired and sufficiently clearly conceived goal. Labor operations required special body and head postures, convenient for work, a greater degree of coordination of movement of both hands, a higher precision of holding an object with the fingers; in short, labor was associated with a progressive development of tactile, kinesthetic, and visual perceptions This sort of activity required not only purposefulness, but also will-power needed to see a job to the desired end result. Tool-making exerted a formative effect on the nervous processes as well.

Man acquired a special place in biocenosis largely through his progressively developing purposeful making of tools. This process gained enormous momentum when man became a social being; this was based on man's communal tool-making activity and on speech as a means of communication among the members of a primitive collective, both tremendously important for the latter's progressive development.

When man became aware of the practicability of a specific tool, and individual experience could be shared by the whole collective through communication by speech, the process of improvement of labor activity received an additional impetus. The progress of labor activity, the step-by-step development of speech, and the growing complexity of social relations, all gradually pushed man beyond the realm of purely biocenological relations. At that stage, discontinuity in human evolution played a particularly significant role, because it engendered new social laws specific to man and his society (Roginsky 1947: 5–23).

REFERENCES

ARAMBOURG, C.
1967   La deuxième mission scientifique de l'Omo. *L'Anthropologie* 71: 562–566.
BROVAR, B.
1960   *Sily tyazhesti i morfologiya zhivotnykh* [The forces of gravity and the morphology of animals]. Moscow.
CAMPBELL, B.
1964   Just another "man-ape?" *Discovery* 25:37–38.
DESHIN, A. A.
1938   Mekhanizm vrashcheniya taza vokrug vertikalnoy osi tazobedrennogo sustava opornoy nogi pri khodbe [The mechanism of pelvic rotation around the vertical axis of the hip joint of the bearing leg in walking]. *Arkhiv anatomicheskoy gistologii* [Archive of Anatomical Histology] 18.
FABRI, K.
1958   Obrashchenie s predmetami u nizshikh obezyan i problema zarozhdeniya trudovoy deyatelnosti [Tool manipulating by apes and the problem of the origin of labor activity]. *Sovetskaya antropologiya* [Soviet Anthropology] 1.
HOLLOWAY, R.
1966   Cranial capacity, neural re-organization and hominid evolution: a search for more suitable parameters. *American Anthropologist* 68:103–121.

HOWELL, F. C.
1969 Remains of Hominidae from Pliocene/Pleistocene formations in the Lower Omo Basin, Ethiopia. *Nature* 223:1234–1239.

JERISON, H. J.
1963 Tool-using performances. *Current Anthropology* 4:491.

KHRISANFOVA, E.
1967 O neravnomernosti morfologicheskoy evolyutsii gominid [On the irregularity of the evolution of hominids]. *Voprosy antropologii* [Problems of Anthropology] 26.

KHROUSTOV, H.
1964 Formation and highest frontier of the implemental activity of anthropoids. *Proceedings of the VII International Congress of Anthropological and Ethnological Sciences, Moscow, 1963,* volume three, 503–509.

KOCHETKOVA, V.
1966 Sraynitelnaya kharakteristika endokranov iskopaemykh gominid v paleonevrologicheskom aspekte — Iskopaemye gominidy i proiskhozhdenie cheloveka [Comparative endocranial characteristics of fossil hominids in paleoneurological aspects — Fossil hominids and the origin of man]. *Trudy Instituta etnogafii AN SSSR* [Transactions of the Institute of Ethnography AN SSSR] 92. Moscow.

1967 Osnovnye etapy evolyutsii mozga i materialnoy kultury drevnykh lyudey [Basic stages of brain evolution and of material culture of ancient man]. *Voprosy antropologii* [Problems of Anthropology] 26.

1969a Reconstruction de l'endocrâne de l'*Atlanthropus mauritanicus* et de l'*Homo habilis*. *Proceedings of the VIII International Congress of Anthropological and Ethnological Sciences, Tokyo, 1968,* volume one, 102–104.

1969b Vozmozhnye varianty makrostruktury mozga Homo habilis [Possible variants of the macrostructure of the brain of *Homo habilis*]. *Voprosy antropologii* [*Problems of Anthropology*].

1970 Novye dannye o makrostrukture mozga gominid i ikh interpretatsiya [New data on the macrostructure of the brain of hominids and their interpretation]. *Voprosy antropologii* [Problems of Anthropology] 34.

KOTSITADZE, Z.
1972 *Anatomobiomekhanicheskie osnovy evolyutsii vertikalnoy khodby* [Anatomobiomechanic foundations of the evolution of vertical walking].

KUMMER, B.
1965 "Das mechanische Problem der Aufrichtung auf die Hinterextremität in Hinblick auf die Evolution der Bipedie des Menschen," in *Menschliche Abstammungslehre.* Edited by G. Heberer. Stuttgart.

1969 General problems in biomechanics of the upright posture and gait. *Proceedings of the VIII International Congress of Anthropological and Ethnological Sciences, Tokyo, 1968,* volume one, 316–322.

LEAKEY, R.
1971   Futher evidence of Lower Pleistocene hominids from East Rudolf,
        North Kenya. *Nature* 231:241–245.
NAPIER, J.
1967   The antiquity of human walking. *Scientific American* 216:56–66.
OAKLEY, K.
1963   *Man, the tool-maker*. London: British Museum (Natural History).
PADBERG, W.
1967   Annidation und Hominisation. *Ethnographisch-archäologische
        Zeitschrift* 8(1):1–14.
QUIGLEY, C.
1971   Assumption and inference on human origin. *Current Anthr.* 12
ROGINSKY, YA.
1947   Nekotorye problemy pozdneyshego etapa evolyutsii cheloveka v
        sovremennoy antropologii [Some problems of the latest stage of
        evolution of man in contemporary anthropology]. *Trudy Instituta
        etnografiyi AN SSSR* [Tansactions of the Institute of Ethno-
        graphy AN SSSR] 2.
SHMALGAUZEN, I.
1938   *Organizm kak tseloe v individualnom i istoricheskom razvitii* [The
        organism as a whole in individual and historical development].
        Moscow.
1940   *Puti i zakonomernosti evolutsionnaga processa* [Ways and regu-
        larities of the evolutionary process]. Leningrad.
TOBIAS, P.
1964   The Olduvai Bed I Hominine with special reference to its cranial
        capacity. *Nature* 202.
1968   Cranial capacity in anthropoids, apes, *Australopithecus* and
        Homo habilis, with comments on skewed samples. *South African
        Journal of Science* 64:81–91.
URYSON, M.
1965   Nekotorye teoreticheskie problemy sovremennogo ucheniya ob
        antropogeneze [Some theoretical problems of contemporary doc-
        trines about anthropogenesis]. *Voprosy antropologii* [Problems of
        Anthropology] 19.
VAN LAWICK-GOODALL, J.
1971   *In the shadow of man*. Boston: Houghton-Mifflin.
WASHBURN, S.
1960   Tools and human evolution. *Scientific American* 203:3–15.
WOLPOFF, M.
1969   Cranial capacity and taxonomy of Olduvai Hominid 7. *Nature*
        223:182–183.
ZENKEVICH, L.
1944   Ocherki po evolyutsii dvigatelnogo apparata zhivotnykh [Notes
        on the evolution of the locomotor apparatus of animals]. *Zhurnal
        obshchey biologii* [Journal of General Biology] 5(3).

Discussion

[Professor Prasad showed slides of the Siwalik region and hominoid fossils therefrom].

ECKHARDT: Dr. Prasad, in your paper (see Prasad, this volume) you remark that *Ramapithecus* preferred forest environments. But in your chart on "Probable distribution of hominoids and habitat" you placed *Ramapithecus* in "open woodland" habitat. Would you please clarify this?

PRASAD: The geological setting is different in the Siwaliks, East Africa, and other places. For example, there were three stages of mountain building activity in the Himalayas. With each period of uplift the ecological setting changed. We have hominoid material from the Chinji, i.e. Middle Miocene, extending right up to the Upper Miocene. There is a difference in the forest fauna depending on the climate. During the rising of the Himalayas there was heavy precipitation especially at the late stage, i.e. Upper Miocene, whereas in the earlier stage, the Chinji, the Himalayas were still part of the Alpine arc and still at the infant stage. *Ramapithecus*, which we consider hominid, were already used to near forest type conditions. They were just beginning the stage in which the distinction between open and forest type came into existence.

ECKHARDT: This is not quite a hominid distinction since present day chimpanzees are known to range into the same types of environmental settings reconstructed here.

PRASAD: The point here is that we should not base our conclusions only on climates. And we should never make any statement on the basis of a single primate fossil. We should study the associated fauna. For example, the *Ramapithecus* association is a very characteristic Miocene fauna much of which indicates a near forest environment. But we have very few samples of *Ramapithecus* and we are not able to say definitely what they are. Nevertheless they are important finds. Now we can only say that the associated fauna, especially of the Miocene, may indicate forest habitat for some of these animals.

SZALAY: Dr. Prasad, what numerical value would you accept for the Chinji in millions of years?

PRASAD: We have not dated the Siwaliks but from a stratigraphic point of view I think that we can probably consider it to be fifteen million years.

TUTTLE: If we must search for superlatives, which is the first hominid?

WOLPOFF: This question becomes more interesting by the moment. At this point we might be witnessing the rise and fall of *Ramapithecus* as a hominid. Certainly, new information available indicates that *Ramapithecus* is much less hominid-like than previously thought. Yet *Ramapithecus* is a very interesting primate. In the papers we are discussing (Prasad, Khatri, Conroy and Pilbeam, Vogel, Aguirre, Eckhardt, this volume) we have about the full gamut of views about *Ramapithecus*. Conroy and Pilbeam (see Conroy and Pilbeam, this volume) present the traditional view of *Ramapithecus*; it is a hominid because it had a parabolic dental arcade, more or less bicuspid P_3, the lower part of the face is reduced in size, and the canine is relatively small by comparison with the other teeth. *Per contra* information in Dr. Vogel's paper (see Vogel, this volume) and a report in 1973 by Walker and Andrews indicate that most of these criteria are incorrect. Dr. Vogel showed very effectively that the dental arcade of *Ramapithecus* is unlikely to be parabolic. Instead there is a parallel, or at least a straight line relationship, for the tooth rows of the palate. Alan Walker's re-reconstruction of the Fort Ternan mandible (FT 45) clearly shows that the snout of this creature was very small and that there was very great reduction of the incisors, particularly the central incisors. Thus the total picture that we have is a dental arcade that is V-shaped. The earlier dryopithecines are also known to have V-shaped snouts. The canine is not of hominid type. Instead it is a pongid-type canine that articulates with the premolar which is no more semi-sectorial than that of the chimpanzee. If we term the Fort Ternan premolar semi-sectorial, we must also term the chimpanzee premolar semi-sectorial. It articulates with that canine in a shearing manner. There was no lateral grinding, wearing the back of the canine flat, as in *Gigantopithecus*. Instead the posterior edge of the canine is worn to a sharp edge in *Ramapithecus*.

[Dr. Vogel summarized and illustrated his paper with slides].

VOGEL: Now we cannot say that *Ramapithecus* is not a hominid. But the whole set of characters claimed for the hominid status of *Ramapithecus* is not convincing by itself. We should bear in mind that convergences in morphological characteristics may exist because of similar functional demands.

TUTTLE: Is there further discussion on *Ramapithecus?*

PRASAD: *Ramapithecus* is represented by half a dozen maxillary and mandibular specimens. When viewed together they indicate a hominid more than a pongid. The premolars are molarized, the incisors are small, the lingual cusps on the molars are very prominent and cingula are absent. The second and third molars are equal in size and provide more grinding surface area. I favor a parabolic shape for the reconstructed dental arcade.

ECKHARDT: The very fact that we have few specimens is one of the best reasons not to consider *Ramapithecus* a separate early hominid taxon. Further, the presence of the bicuspid or semi-sectorial premolars which has been proffered in support of hominid status for *Ramapithecus* are found in about one chimpanzee out of three in relatively large samples.

PRASAD: I am not sure that you should compare *Ramapithecus* with chimpanzee specimens because *Ramapithecus* shows very advanced features by comparison with Asian *Dryopithecus* and *Sivapithecus*.

WOLPOFF: In my earlier remarks I was not arguing against *Ramapithecus* being a hominid *per se*. But I would argue against applying the criteria which were originally advanced for its hominid status. On the basis of the new Walker and Andrews reconstruction we can no longer claim that it has a parabolic dental arcade. It certainly has a pongid type canine in the way it functioned with the lower premolar. I have compared the lower third premolar with lower third premolars of *Sivapithecus*. They are identical to small detail. Because of Darwin's hypothesis that canine reduction occurred early in hominid evolution, we may have been looking at the wrong end of the dental arcade in order to show that it is a hominid. The anterior end is very dryopithecine-like, especially in comparison with the African dryopithecines. However, there are other features that should be re-examined carefully now that we know more about the anterior end of the snout. The molars are square and are packed together, the maxilla is short, and judging from the position of the maxillary sinus, the face is very deep, by which I mean that the distance from the orbit to the tooth row is very great. These are features that we would expect to find in a primate adapted to a heavily masticated diet. Hominid divergence is closely connected to reliance on a very heavily masticated diet. In sum, we should re-examine *Ramapithecus* and perhaps view it in a new and different light.

SZALAY: The Andrews and Walker reconstruction shows that it is a primitive pongid-like arch. But the only point of fact that you were emphasizing against its hominid status is the upper canine of the *wickerii* palate. It is an incisiform mediolaterally constricted tooth which is very different from the pongid canine. It is small and aligned with the remaining cutting edges as pointed out long ago by Every and now Conroy and Pilbeam also very astutely show it (see Conroy and Pilbeam, this volume).

WOLPOFF: I disagree with this description of the Fort Ternan canine.

TUTTLE: Another possible primitive hominid is *Gigantopithecus*. Dr. Eckhardt, would you comment on *Gigantopithecus* in this regard.

[Professor Eckhardt summarized his paper].

AUDIENCE: What is the date of *Gigantopithecus?*

ECKHARDT: Dating is all over the place. There are two main bodies of material, one from China and one from India. The Indian specimen is assigned to Middle Pliocene by Simons and Chopra. The Chinese material is usually said to be Middle Pleistocene although the evidence for that date is rather shaky.

TOBIAS: We seem to have two kinds of problem here that apply to both the *Ramapithecus* and *Gigantopithecus* theories. The first question is, could the population represented by available fossils be ancestral to later well-testified hominids? If the answer is affirmative, the second question is, does this necessarily make them members of the family Hominidae? Could they be ancestral? Are they hominids? There are ancestors that have not yet become hominids way back in the Oligocene if you like. Now to answer the question, "Are they ancestral?" We require an answer which is compatible on two grounds. They must be morphologically suitable candidates for ancestry. And they must be temporally suitable candidates for ancestry. Bob Eckhardt, I am perplexed by your statement (see Eckhardt, this volume) "And there is much better evidence that it [*Gigantopithecus*] is a hominid than any other Miocene or Pliocene hominoid now known". Do you really feel that the evidence for *Gigantopithecus* is much better, not just numerically, but morphologically and chronologically, than is that for *Ramapithecus* to have been a hominid?

ECKHARDT: Dr. Vogel and others have shown that the evidence for *Ramapithecus* being a hominid is extraordinarily equivocal. Dr. Prasad presented evidence that remains of *Ramapithecus* are typically found in a forested environment. This is not a hominid niche. I would accept the idea that *Ramapithecus* had something to do with hominid ancestry in the same way that other dryopithecine primates did. Whether it is itself a separate hominid taxon seems at present to be highly doubtful. With regard to the dating, one of the largest questions to be resolved now has to do with the dating of the Chinese *Gigantopithecus* specimens. I reviewed the evidence on their dating (see Eckhardt, this volume). The Middle Pleistocene date for these specimens which is now part of virtually every textbook that discusses the subject is based on a series of tenuous associations which goes through seven or eight points. There is no direct association between undoubted Chinese Middle Pleistocene hominids and *Gigantopithecus*. They are only inferred to be connected by a scheme of faunal correlations, each component of which is quite tenuous. We could usefully leave the dating question in limbo in relation to the Chinese specimens.

TOBIAS: Would you accept that the Chinese specimens, though not necessarily the Indian specimen, could be ruled out from any possible claim to hominid ancestry?

ECKHARDT: No, I would not accept that because the evidence at hand indicates that the date of the Chinese specimens may be anywhere from Middle Pliocene to Middle Pleistocene. The fact that you find an Indian *Gigantopithecus* specimen from the Middle Pliocene in the same faunal province as the South Chinese specimens seems to confirm that the Chinese specimens may be earlier than has commonly been accepted.

SZALAY: Even the oldest possible date for the Chinese specimens is the Middle Pliocene. Although it is very unlikely they could be as old as 3.5 million years. Still this is considerably younger than the Indian material, which in many ways is also more primitive. Thus the Chinese material is not relevant to the systematic questions that should be answered here.

VON KOENIGSWALD: According to new discoveries of *Hipparion* (the three-toed horse which is the guide fossil for the Pliocene), the Kamlial, Chinji, and Nagri, are all of Lower Pliocene age. The Dhok Pathan is Middle Pliocene. During the Pliocene, the Himalayas and Alps were uplifted with concomitant change of climate. Savanna conditions developed. In the Chinji, wet forest conditions prevailed. But by the time of the Dhok Pathan there were steppe conditions in the same area. There was a completely new biotope, a complete change of the fauna. Hominization was begun during these transitions. Despite what several critics have said, *Ramapithecus* is still the most suitable form for the hominid ancestor. A difficulty to non-geologists is that the Pontian, with the first *Hipparion*, in Germany and America is called the Pliocene, in France and Switzerland is often included in the Miocene. *Kenyapithecus* really comes from the Miocene. It is at least two or three million years older than *Ramapithecus*.

If you compare these two forms you will see that they have nothing to do with each other. *Kenyapithecus* is not a *Ramapithecus*. The lower jaw described by Andrews is the jaw of a pongid. The inclination of the symphysis is of a sort that would never be expected in a hominid — the higher primates came from Africa. Like the elephants they did not leave Africa until the beginning of the Miocene. It is impossible that pongids could occur in the Old World before the Lower Miocene. This rules out that *Amphipithecus* had anything to do with the pongids — *Gigantopithecus* could never be a forerunner of man because it occurs together with *Sinanthropus*. *Gigantopithecus blacki* is of Middle and partly perhaps of Lower Pleistocene age. It is a different species from the *Gigantopithecus* found in the Siwaliks. Without doubt the Siwalik form is of Middle Pliocene age. It is smaller and less hypsodont and there are other differences.

TOBIAS: Professor von Koenigswald, please tell us about the new Greek mandible which may be *Ramapithecus?*

VON KOENIGSWALD: The Miocene was a period of wet forests that formed lignite beds. All the European remains of *Dryopithecus* come out of these layers. Now in Greece for the first time a mandible has been found with the steppe fauna of Pikermi. The specimen is not very well preserved. But it shows a few characteristics which we also find in *Ramapithecus*. We are not sure because we have only one specimen and the teeth are very worn. That is all we can say now. It indicates that by that time the higher primates had begun to infiltrate into a new environment. This is very important. The same situation existed in India where in the Chinji there were forest conditions. Then it became drier and drier. The various faunas in India, termed Kamlial, Chinji, Nagri, and Dhok Pathan, do not have many species in common. Therefore, it is doubtful to me that the same species of *Ramapithecus* occurred in several stages.

ECKHARDT: Pilbeam has stated that *D. fontani*, one of the type specimens of *Dryopithecus*, was living under savanna conditions. Furthermore, chimpanzees are found on savannas. Hence the significance of this as an absolutely telling feature that (a) the new mandible is *Ramapithecus*, and (b) that it was a hominid are open to question. Dr. von Koenigswald, you said that *Gigantopithecus* and *Sinanthropus* are found together. Would you please tell us at what site?

VON KOENIGSWALD: We found a great amount of material in Chinese drugstores. In many cases we do not know the actual sites. Most importantly certain species of *Stegedon* and elephants in the fauna evidence that they are of Middle Pleistocene age and not older.

ECKHARDT: Then I would be correct to summarize what you said as follows: there are no known sites in which *Gigantopithecus* and *Sinanthropus* are found together.

VON KOENIGSWALD: Not in a site. But they have been found together in associations which were collected by drugstores. According to what has been found together several times and according to the preservation of the specimens there can be absolutely no doubt for a paleontologist that these species occur together.

GOODMAN: The key to the question of the earliest hominid is when the most recent common ancestor of man and chimpanzee existed. If the fossils discussed here occur more recently in time than when we think the most recent common ancestor of chimpanzee and man existed and their characteristics tend to place them more toward the phyletic line going to *Homo* or *Australopithecus* than in the phyletic line going to *Pan* then from a phylogenetic or cladistic point of view we would say that they are on the hominid or hominine line. The fact that some features of *Ramapithecus* are somewhat more chimpanzee-like than human-like does not destroy the possibility that it still could have been on the line going to *Australopithecus* and *Homo* rather than on the line going to *Pan*. One would expect the common ancestor of man and chimpanzee in its dental and face morphology to be more *Pan*-like than *Homo*-like. However the new evidence seems to counteract the thought that we have to go all the way back to the Oligocene to derive a separate line for man as Kurtén would like us to do. The most recent common ancestor of man and chimp would be about twelve to fourteen million years ago if we accept *Ramapithecus* to be on the line to *Homo*.

TUTTLE: Now we must draw the curtain on *Ramapithecus*. Fred Szalay will now show slides of *Oreopithecus*.

SZALAY: In brief, *Oreopithecus* possesses no significant shared advanced dental similarities to hominids or other hominoids. Except for a few features indicating that *Oreopithecus* was a highly arboreal form which brachiated in some fashion, there are no good points of evidence to relate it to any of the hominoids. It is a late Miocene representative of an independent offshoot from a very early cercopithecoid level of organization as often stated in the past.

ECKHARDT: Some material, at least one tooth that I know of, from East Africa has been related to *Oreopithecus*. Have you seen it and what is your opinion of it?

SZALAY: It is one M_3. It was named *Mabokopithecus* by Professor von Koenigswald. It has a central cuspule in the talonid basin and a crest closing the posterior fovea. It looks something like an *Oreopithecus* M_3 but the mesoconid is the only solid piece of evidence that would relate it to *Oreopithecus*. Now I am not saying that it is not an oreopithecid or another sort of primate but this feature also exists in a variety of other groups, e.g. some pigs.

TUTTLE: Is there anyone on the panel or in the audience who would like to take the stance that *Oreopithecus* is a hominid?

[No one responded to this request].

SECTION THREE

New Perspectives on Australopithecus
and Other Early Hominidae

A New View of Speciation in Australopithecus

SUSAN CACHEL

The existence of two morphologically distinct forms of australopithecine, gracile and robust, has been recognized since fossil discoveries first established the unequivocal presence of early Pleistocene hominids in Africa. This article will argue that the dimorphism shown by the known australopithecines is not a result of simple evolutionary change, sexual characteristics, or extreme dietary specializations, but is a result of selective pressures operating on sympatric predators. After this idea has been advanced, predatory behavior in the australopithecines and its possible evolution through time will be discussed in the light of recent studies on modern social carnivores, as an attempt is made to achieve an integrated picture of hominid evolution up to the appearance of *Homo*.

ALTERNATIVE EXPLANATIONS OF AUSTRALOPITHECINE DIMORPHISM, AND OPPOSING ARGUMENTS

The most rational explanation of the existence of two australopithecine forms, given a paucity of stratigraphic data, is that a phylogenetic progression is represented, one form being ancestral to the other. Recent discoveries in East Africa have negated this phylogenetic explanation by demonstrating the coexistence of these morphologically distinct forms through a long span of time. Confronted with such evidence, any

I wish to thank Dr. K. W. Butzer and Mr. R. Susman for discussing various aspects of arguments elaborated here; and I especially wish to thank my advisor, Dr. R. H. Tuttle, for reading the rough draft of this paper. I am currently receiving financial support from a National Science Foundation Graduate Fellowship.

simple explanation of evolution of one type into the other becomes untenable.

The presence of a gracile and robust australopithecine can also be interpreted by sexual dimorphism, but this explanation fails because of the distribution of these forms through the sites, and because a careful survey of the material within a single site often yields remains of both sexes. Tobias (1972) has compiled a preliminary demographic analysis of the fossil material, and has concluded that neither evolutionary change nor sexual dimorphism alone can explain the presence of the two known australopithecine forms. Instead, the phenomenon of coexistence through a notable span of geologic time — stretching back to at least five million years B.P. — must demonstrate marked ecological divergence between these forms.

The most prominent explanation of australopithecine dimorphism now holding sway is Robinson's dietary hypothesis, which is predicated upon just such an ecological divergence. This hypothesis recognizes two distinct hominid lineages (different even to the generic level) separated on the basis of subsistence (Robinson 1954). At some time in the Tertiary, a differentiation of woodland- as opposed to savannah-exploiting hominids is thought to have taken place, a dichotomy eventually yielding robust and gracile australopithecines respectively. The robust forms were primarily vegetarians in forested areas, but the gracile forms, developed through movement into open country, were more omnivorous, having teeth adapted for chewing herbaceous food but also capable of tearing or rending meat. Thus, the two main tenets of the dietary hypothesis are that morphological differences between the known australopithecine forms are capable of being explained by an omnivorous/herbivorous dichotomy; and that paleoecological reconstructions of the hominid sites bear out anatomical inferences by providing evidence of dry climatic regimes during occupation by the gracile type and relatively wet regimes during occupation by the robust type. Acknowledgment of these principal claims is necessary for the dietary hypothesis to be fully acceptable, yet neither one stands firmly.

The morphology of australopithecine dentitions does not demonstrate the clear distinction between omnivorousness and herbivority seen in other mammalian groups. The teeth of *A. robustus*, presumed to be adapted to an herbivorous diet, show none of the specializations, such as hypsodonty and cresting, which would characterize herbivority in other forms. The teeth of the robust australopithecine remain good bunodont teeth, capable of processing both vegetation and animal protein. The only consistent features in which they differ from the teeth of the gracile *A. africanus* are the development of the post-canine teeth relative to the anterior dentition, and the great absolute size of individual cheek teeth.

Robinson (1956: 149) elaborates the idea that these features are the result of selection for an extensive post-canine occlusal surface. The implied evolutionary history of the robust australopithecine is a progression from a large vegetarian with expansive jaws to a large vegetarian experiencing selective pressure for reduction of jaw size and achieving this at the cost of the anterior dentition. Consideration of *A. robustus* features as primitive tends to obscure the underlying cause of size and proportion differences along the dental arcade — that such differences are a direct result of allometric changes, rather than being mere retentions undergoing alteration. Increasing body size expands the size of the body volumetrically; food intake to accommodate this body mass must also expand by volume. The tooth row, however, expands in a linear fashion. The allometric factors contrasting cubic and areal increase can then cause the advance of posterior dental surface over anterior. This is so because, given the basic mammalian divergence between the anterior dentition — which prepares food for processing (stabbing, cropping, biting-off) — and the posterior dentition — which actually processes the food passed backward (slicing, grinding, crushing) — increasing size will lead to an emphasis of that part of the dentition which processes food, the posterior part. Of two similar forms, the larger will have a more greatly emphasized posterior dentition. Allometric factors, then, can result in proportional differences along the dental arcade and absolute differences between individual cheek teeth.

Other dental features distinct between the two australopithecine types can also be linked to allometric factors. Occlusal differences, for example, which cause the mandibular cheek teeth of *A. robustus* to wear more on the lingual surface and those of *A. africanus* to wear more on the buccal surface can be explained by an increase of lower arch width in *A. robustus* which results in the maxillary arch meeting the opposing tooth rows in a more lingual position (Robinson 1956: 19). Such width in the *A. robustus* dental arcade is a direct effect of the larger size of the post-canine teeth — which causes the buccal margins of the arcades to diverge. Even the celebrated distinction in the first lower deciduous premolars rests not on structural criteria *per se,* but on the degree of molarization which is present. Assuming that *A. robustus* needed to extend its posterior occlusal surface on allometric grounds, the appearance of the first deciduous premolar can be explained in terms of the influence of advancing molar fields.

As has long been recognized, morphological characters other than those of the dentition — such as strength of mandible and development of a sagittal crest — can also be explained by allometry operating in the robust form of australopithecine. It therefore appears as though many of the traits differentiating the two forms of australopithecine are allometric in origin and are not the result of entirely new genetic structures. Furthermore, size increases in *A. robustus* do not form an automatic link with herbivorous diet. In a warm climate, safety from predators and not efficiency (with greater volume to surface area for heat retention) seems to be the only selective factor affecting the evolution of large herbivores. At any rate, no herbivorous specialization*s per se* can be found in *A. robustus,* only allometric changes initiated by a cause to be discussed later.

The second tenet of the dietary hypothesis, that paleoecological reconstructions support an omnivorous/herbivorous dichotomy among the australopithecines, also cannot be proven. Major ecological differences were supported by paleoenvironmental reconstructions which posited the existence of robust australopithecines in areas of lush plant growth, and gracile australopithecines in arid or semi-arid regions of relatively meager growth. The principal basis for these paleoenvironmental reconstructions, however, Brain's projected rainfall curve, established by analysis of South African cave sediments, has been questioned by Butzer (1971a). A more intensive investigation of the Taung site (Butzer 1974) has further shown the falsity of previous ecologic reconstructions. Although the site is on the edge of the Kalahari, the gracile Taung hominid is thought to have inhabited the region during a time of humid or sub-humid climate — conditions classically postulated for the occurrence of the robust form. The downfall of environmental support for the gracile/robust ecologic dichotomy signifies that this dichotomy, as now considered (an omnivorous/herbivorous distinction), has completely fallen through.

The situation thus stands that gracile and robust australopithecines appear together throughout late Pliocene-early Pleistocene times. Their contrasting traits cannot be explained in terms of simple evolution, sexual dimorphism, or dietary differences, but are explained most reasonably by allometric factors. Both forms lived under identical climatic regimes and were probably coexistent through most of their ranges, being sympatric as well as synchronic (Tobias 1972: 67) since the deposition of the Lower Omo Basin sediments and continuing so until about one million years B.P. (and much later if Butzer's unpublished investigation of the Taung hominid correctly positions this find in time).

Surely special ecological factors were operating to allow the long coexistence and sympatry of these forms; and observed distributions through time and space cannot be explained by invoking extreme adaptations in diet, because the morphology of preserved material does not bear this out. The answer to this quandary of ecological divergence lies in the allometric differences between the gracile and robust types.

ALLOMETRY AMONG SYMPATRIC PREDATORS

Looking at allometric differences between the gracile and robust australopithecines as though simply another mammalian group and not the Hominidae were under consideration — and leaving aside, for the moment, questions of cultural capacity — it appears as though size differences between the hominids can best be explained by viewing them as sympatric predators selecting different sized prey. The problem is how the resources of a common area were divided. It seems certain that the answer lies in the allometric factors which established morphological differences. If one considers the animal group which best develops sympatry on allometric grounds, a logical basis for australopithecine dimorphism would lie in the division of prey resources by hunting hominids according to size.

It is a recognized fact that predator size is correlated with size of prey taken, thus ensuring a continuum of predators varying with prey. Being most intensively studied among *Anolis* lizards (Schoener 1968), this phenomenon also holds true for some other reptile groups (Arnold 1972) and for mammal populations (Rosenzweig 1968; Schaller 1972). These allometric factors are probably a reflection of hazards being reduced to an acceptable limit by narrowing the gap in size between predator and prey. Herbivores of course are not subject to this kind of selection, because no struggle is involved in cropping vegetation. Size differences among the australopithecines would therefore mean sympatry was possible through preferential prey choice. When the gracile/robust dichotomy was established, tool-use and manufacture could not have played a significant role in affecting morphological evolution. It is probably true that, unless weapons are made for long-distance use, the physical size of a predator is important; and tools made for preparing a kill could not have changed the necessity for certain physical standards among the hominids.

With all this, it is important to remember that major physical objections to australopithecine hunting have been removed by virtue of re-

cent investigations into the functional anatomy of australopithecine bipedalism (Lovejoy and Heiple 1970; Heiple and Lovejoy 1971; Lovejoy et al. 1973). The traditional view held that while these hominids
were truly bipedal, they were rather inefficiently so, resulting in creatures that could run well enough, but were incapable of erect long-
distance striding. Lovejoy and his colleagues, on the other hand, have
recently interpreted the same post-cranial specimens to reveal the australopithecines as hominids fully capable of bipedal activity and, in
some respects, more developed bipeds than modern man. The total configuration of the bipedal complex is foreign, but fully efficient, and this
final impression of australopithecine locomotor adaptations is enlarged
by considering the two forms similarly adapted, therefore being part of
a single radiation on locomotor specializations. The two types show
their descent from a common bipedal ancestor, because it is unlikely
that parallel evolution could give rise to such similar morphologies.

Interpretation of the great similarity between gracile and robust australopithecine, and the therefore common origin of both, is accentuated
by recent studies of the hominid brain (Tobias 1971) which purport to
show no marked difference in the cranial capacity of the two forms.
Given that cranial capacity is a poor substitute for knowledge of actual
cultural activities, it may still tell something about capacity for culture.
Presumably this capacity was rather similar in the two forms.

LATE TERTIARY PREDATOR/PREY RELATIONS

The interrelationships of mammalian carnivores through the later Cenozoic can be analyzed through known phylogeny and biogeography,
although a definitive analysis must wait until Tedford of the American
Museum publishes results of his investigations. Still, it seems clear that
felids, hyaenids, and canids must be considered, with some special relation existing between felids and hyaenids. The purpose of undertaking
such an analysis is that it will reveal possible empty niches capable of
being filled by hunting hominids.

A niche for sabre-toothed carnivores has existed through the Tertiary, because the felids have evolved machairodont forms at least three
times during the history of the family (Thenius 1967), and the marsu-
pial borhyaenids of South America, as well as the North American Eocene creodont *Apataelurus* also have independently filled the niche of
long-canined carnivores. It has long been thought that the existence of
megaherbivores is a necessary prerequisite for the development of these

carnivores, which would presumably use stealth to bring down prey, leaping from ambush to stab thick-skinned ungulates (Simpson 1941). A long-canined form gave rise to the modern genera *Panthera* and *Felis* at a late date. These "normal" felids did not appear until the Pliocene, and did not really expand until the extinction of the machairodont cats, triggered by the loss of megaherbivores. These early "normal" felids probably behaved very much like their machairodont ancestors.

Matthew (1930) and Ewer (1967) remark that the sabre-toothed carnivores would open a niche for a bone-crushing form, because none of the long-canined animals seem to have been capable of processing the bony remains of their prey. Since the major dental adaptation of the hyaenids is the existence of great crushing premolars, this presupposes an elaborate interaction of felids and hyaenids through time, an interaction which is confirmed in North America (where hyaenids, with the exception of one rare Pleistocene genus, never penetrated) by the development of bone-crushing dogs (Dalquest 1968; Webb 1969). Although scavenging hyaenids occur in the Old World with machairodont cats and presumably fill the basic adaptation of the family, predatory hyaenids may have evolved from a scavenging form to occupy niches left open before the development of "normal" felids. (Ewer 1967). The two surviving hyaenid genera show this scavenging/predatory dichotomy on dental (Ewer 1954) and craniological features (Buckland-Wright 1969), and adaptive differences between these genera only serve to point out the possibilities of the Miocene hyaenid radiation (Thenius 1966). The true nature of this radiation is yet unknown, but it seems certain that divergences were emphasized along the lines of predation and more pure scavenging (Ewer 1967).

To reconstruct the felid-hyaenid predatory interaction, late Cenozoic sabre-toothed felids would be carnivores specialized for preying upon contemporary megaherbivores, a niche which "normal" felids, descended from machairodont cats, fill today. Because such specialization would leave untouched medium- to small-sized herbivores, these animals would fall prey to hunting hyaenids and large canids. Small canids, such as fox and jackal, are ignored in the present analysis. Although they may have entered the Old World long before large canids, they are not primarily ungulate predators. (The same objection allows one to ignore small felids, ursids, procyonids, mustelids, and viverrids.) According to present evidence, the canids entered Africa at a late date. As a family whose evolution has been almost entirely in North America with the exception of aberrant sub-groups, such as the Oligocene Amphicyoninae, which survived into the Pontian of Europe (Matthew 1930;

Gregory and Hellman 1939), the Canidae reached Africa during the Plio/Pleistocene. A canid of undetermined genus and species is found in Quarry E of the Varswater Formation dated at four million years B.P. at Langebaanweg in the South African Cape (Klein 1974). An undoubted large canid — *Lycaon*, in fact — occurs in the somewhat younger (?) Lower Omo Shungura Formation (Butzer 1971b). The biogeographic accident which restricted canids to the New World until a late date would dictate that small- and medium-sized African ungulates would become the prey of hyaenids, present in marked diversity. Yet, if hyaenid predation is thought of as a principally nocturnal activity, a niche for diurnal predators on small- and medium-sized animals would remain open. The canid-like cheetah, which partly fills this niche today, only reached Africa in the Pleistocene from a Eurasian point of origin (Thenius 1967). The niche of diurnal predator on small- to medium-sized ungulates which it now partly occupies with the Cape hunting dog would have been vacant in Africa during earlier periods. It is possible that the emergence of hunting activities among hominids was conditioned by the lack of such predators to fill an available niche. Instead of postulating as yet unknown environmental crises which would drive proto-hominids to hunting — such as the spread of grasslands with concomitant decrease of forest — one may instead discuss the emergence of hominid hunting activities as a positive response to available resources which were not being exploited.

Ungulate species existing during the Plio/Pleistocene of Africa which would offer a resource for exploitation by predators were concentrated among the bovids and suids. The bovid and suid expansion, in fact, coincided with the hyaenid radiation and the supposed time of hominid orientation to hunting activities. Bovid-suid exploitation would therefore be a major feature of both hyaenid and hominid predation, and would be the basis for evolution of intricate predator/prey relations.

The bovids of Africa are known to have undergone diversification before the Pleistocene. Wells (1957, 1967) considers the Alcelaphini, Cephalophini, and Neotragini to be indigenous to Africa — these groups form an earlier stratum of Villafranchian antelopes, while the Hippotragini, Strepsicerotini, and Reduncini of the African Villafranchian represent a later element of Afro-Eurasian origin. The Antilopini, while not differentiated in Africa, may have arrived at an earlier date, for a variety of gazelles were present, not all of which need to have been confined to markedly dry areas. Wells (1967) believes that the alcelaphines and antilopines account for most of the early African antelope fauna; the alcelaphines (comprising the damaliscine-wildebeest-hartebeest group) would provide large antelope forms, the gazelles would provide small antelope forms.

The African suids would also offer a spectrum of available small- to medium-sized ungulates. Freeman (1973), discussing hominid hunting adaptations in Paleolithic Cantabrian Spain, characterizes the European wild boar as an animal nearly impossible to kill without benefit of long-range weapons, nets, or well-organized hunting groups, since *Sus* appears to have been utilized only in the Upper Palaeolithic, although certainly available before. Yet, many suids were present in the African Plio/Pleistocene, and it is possible that several of these fossil forms may have been more vulnerable to contemporary hominid hunters than is the present *Sus scrofa*. Cooke (1963) demonstrates that at least three divergences among the African fossil suids occur in the early Pleistocene. Strange-tusked forms are present whose adaptations are unknown, although Thenius (1970) argues that social behavior is a more adequate explanation for the extreme tusk morphology of certain pigs than any anatomical functional explanation. A second group of extinct pigs had bunodont dentitions similar to that of the modern *Sus* and presumably corresponding adaptations. The hypsodont dentitions of the third group of fossil pigs (as, *Notochoerus*) lead to speculations that they may have been open-country grazers, and perhaps more vulnerable to attack by hominid predators.

Investigation of australopithecine/prey interaction — as opposed to the elucidation of possible interaction — is hindered by the presence of a second distinct hominid form to whom stone artifacts and evidence of well developed hunting can be attributed. If hunting by this second hominid or carnivore predation could be discounted, the South African cave sites and the occupation surfaces at Olduvai Gorge might yield significant information.

Rejection of the South African cave breccias and the Olduvai living sites as presently equivocal sources of information on australopithecine /prey interactions leaves only the Omo Basin deposits as potential sources of information on such relations. Thus, the Shungura and Usno formations, containing approximately twenty hominid locales, and dating from 3.75 to 1.93 million years B.P., offer an unrivaled source of information on possible australopithecine activity. The modern vegetation of the region has been examined by Claudia Carr (Butzer 1971b), and discovered to be a combination of tree shrub savannah with much grassland, semi-deciduous wooded savannah, seasonally wet lowland plains, and grassland/shrub steppe. Bonnefille's analysis of pollen samples (Butzer 1971b) reveals the same mosaic picture of grasslands, tree savannahs, and riverine forests during the late Pliocene.

Huntable elements of the Omo Basin fauna (Butzer 1971b), leaving out the megaherbivores, were *Camelus, Stylohipparion,* four genera of pigs (including *Notochoerus,* the possible open-country grazer), giraffids, and a variety of antelope — three genera of reduncines, a bushbuck (*Tragelaphus*), and an undetermined number of alcelaphine species. Impala and gazelle were also present, as were huntable primates: the open-country forms *Papio* and *Simopithecus,* and the arboreal *Colobus* and *Cercopithecus.* A variety of carnivores were present — hyaenids (including the definitely predatory *Crocuta*), sabre-toothed cats, a possible true lion, *Canis,* and *Lycaon.*

An undisputed hominid kill site (?), FxJj3, occurs in the contemporary East Rudolf Kenyan region, at Koobi Fora (Isaac et al. 1971). Here the evidence rests within a depression in an abandoned stream channel. Hippo limb bones occur with undisputed stone artifacts, and a date from the associated KBS tuff yields a time of 2.61 million years B.P. It is possible that hominids encountered a mired hippo — certainly hippopotamus seems rather large game to attack at this date without benefit of miring chance. FxJjl, a site from another stream channel at the same level, also provides evidence of an occupation and cultural activities. Furthermore, a recent work reports the existence of both a number of stone artifact associations in derived contexts and an *in situ* concentration of artifacts (FtJi2) in Member F of the Omo Basin Shungura Formation, dated at approximately two million years B.P. (Merrick et al. 1973). These cultural occurrences at Koobi Fora and at the younger Shungura Member F are presumed to be the result of australopithecine activity.

PREDATOR/PREY RELATIONS AND THE EMERGENCE OF THE HOMINIDAE

The foregoing sections have dealt with morphologic adaptations of the australopithecines, the possible carnivore niche which they would have filled, and the ungulates upon which they would have preyed. Now a discussion of hominid hunting itself, and particularly the evolution of hunting behavior through time, is in order.

Treatments of the rise of hominid hunting often assume the existence of proto-hominids which were behaviorally (and sometimes anatomically) very similar to the modern chimpanzee. These primates are subjected to a rather sudden environmental crisis which leads to the expansion of grasslands at the expense of woodlands. Attempting to survive under new conditions, these primates begin to emphasize meat-eating, because prey species are so abundant in the open lands. Bipedal locomotion arises in response to open-country orientation, group cooperation is accentuated, and the hunting career of the hominids is underway.

In opposition to this classical picture of hominid origins and late hunting, however, one can instead posit an entirely different and perhaps more plausible sequence of events. Basic to this sequence is the idea that no pronounced environmental change was necessary for the emergence of hunting hominids. Evidence from the Omo Basin and from Olduvai — where the most strenuous efforts have been made to reconstruct past climates and geography — indicates that hominids lived in environmental mosaics, and not exclusively in a single, completely open-country environment. From this it is possible to extrapolate back to a point where proto-hominids also lived in such mosaics and would not need an environmental crisis to drive them to other regions. In corroboration of this assumption, the dryopithecine apes, which almost certainly gave rise to the Hominidae, apparently also lived in environmental mosaics. The advantages of living in a patchy environment are obvious. If an animal is capable of opportunistic resource exploitation, the conjunction of forest, open-country, the interface between these regions, and riverine or lacustrine habitats is an optimal living area.

Living in an environmental mosaic, the dryopithecine ape giving rise to the hominids would suddenly be confronted with a wealth of huntable small- to medium-sized ungulates, as the great bovid-suid expansion occurred. During the Tertiary, it is assumed that any predatory hyaenas (apparently evolved from a basic scavenging type) would be specialized for preying upon these Old World ungulate forms; "normal" felids do not occur until late in the Tertiary. Both predatory hyaenas and "normal" felids would hunt nocturnally, however, leaving open a niche for a diurnal small- to medium-sized ungulate predator. Hence the dryopithecine ape ancestral to the hominids and living in an environmental mosaic would continually come into contact with huntable ungulates having no specialized diurnal predators. The existence of an environmental mosaic would yield a hominoid with opportunistic resource exploitation strategies, continually being confronted with an unexploited resource.

In this analysis, the dryopithecine ancestral to the Hominidae is presumed to act very much like other omnivorous animals (proto-carnivores) placed in a similar situation. This is an assumption which would be questioned by investigators who take the modern chimpanzee or gorilla as a model for the dryopithecine proto-hominid, reconstructing this proto-hominid as an essentially herbivorous animal only gradually turning to hunting. While it is true that the African apes are the closest living relatives of man, this does not necessarily make them the logical choice for an evolutionary model. One has to have some idea of the behavioral and anatomic range of the Miocene apes and build evolutionary models on this basis. The variability in functional anatomy and behavior shown by the surviving hominoids leads one to suspect that the dryopithecines need not have been confined to any one behavioral or locomotor type. Behaviorally, the dryopithecine ancestral to the hominids may have been capable of filling an open carnivore niche from the beginning.

Recent analysis of a partial hominid humerus from Ileret, dating between one and two million years B.P. (McHenry 1973), is thought to yield evidence for the existence of a hominid in East Rudolf at this time capable of forms of locomotion involving the forelimb. Basically, however, the anatomical evidence does not conflict with Oxnard's canonical analysis of australopithecine shoulder material (Oxnard 1968), the end result of which was that Oxnard postulated the descent of the australopithecines from a form capable of arboreal suspension. Given this evidence it is possible to say that the dryopithecine ancestral to the Hominidae was an arboreal animal capable of suspensory locomotion. Recent work on the ground locomotion of orang-utans indicates that a truly arboreal animal can easily adopt sophisticated postures for ground movement. The implications of this statement are that *Pan* and *Gorilla,* while very close to the Hominidae, need have nothing to offer for the development of hominid bipedalism. The dryopithecine ancestral to man may have separated from the African ape stock at a relatively late date without having to evolve knuckle-walking. If knuckle-walking can be developed in a comparatively short period, this would explain both the similarity of man to the African apes and his wide anatomic divergence from them. Also it would imply that ground-dwelling orientations in these two groups evolved independently.

The origins of hominid bipedalism are therefore still obscure, and it is uncertain whether major elements of this adaptation need to have developed on the ground rather than in the trees. The gracile and robust australopithecine display the same adaptations to bipedal locomotion and thus are descended from the same proto-hominid form. This proto-hominid, living in an environmental mosaic, and possibly developing aspects of bipedalism while still arboreal, would respond to the opportunity of new food resources offered by unexploited ungulate groups within the same patchwork of environments. There would be no necessity to emerge from deep forest to completely open savannahs, because the native environment itself would be a mosaic. Hunting would occur at a very early point in hominid history, and would not necessarily be the culmination of general foraging activities.

Size differences between the australopithecines are the result of an adjustment to the size of prey taken by each species. Although group hunting would influence the necessity of correlating size of hunter to prey, the necessity for evolving predator size grades would still exist, since killing of prey would have taken place by body-to-body contact. Stone tools were used for food preparation (flensing, cutting meat, smashing bone) rather than for killing prey, because, in its earliest stages, this is assumed to have been solely a matter of physical contact and force exerted by the predator.

Williams (1972) speaks of size divergence as a result of interspecies competition among *Anolis* lizards. Whenever two species are widely dispersed and intermixed they show a marked difference in size, both species changing to accomplish this. Increasingly complex faunas show lesser or no divergence. Instead, the phenomenon which Williams graphically describes as the "crowded middle" occurs. If a great number of species exist, an animal in the middle size range cannot readily adapt by changing size — ecological coadjustment must involve another dimension. Species intermediate in size are therefore ecologically diverse, but the largest and smallest species retain their original ecology. They are sympatric because their coadjustment has been made on absolute size. This analysis holds possibilities for australopithecine evolution. Certain intriguing hominid discoveries in the Lower Omo Basin show that some form of australopithecine radiation is recorded here (Howell 1969). Ecological orientations — at least as revealed by isolated teeth — must have been rather diverse. Could the Omo remains represent the "crowded middle" of hominid evolution? During the deposition of the Omo Succession, an ecologically diverse group of middle-sized hominids, evolving away from the original hominid predatory orientation, might have coexisted with the pre-eminently successful predators, gracile and robust australopithecines. At the Plio-Pleistocene boundary, some minor ecological crisis would have driven the middle range of hominids to extinction, leaving only the gracile and robust extremes which retained the original hominid ecology. This may explain the apparent change through time of the larger hominid, from hyper-robusticity to a slightly more gracile form (Tobias 1972). Without the existence of many intermediate species to drive the size extremes apart, gracile and robust australopithecine could have approached each other in size, as happens in Williams' analysis.

Whatever processes selected for the origins of bipedality in hominids would have been accentuated by an active hunting life. The bipedal hominid would have enjoyed an advantage not otherwise available to non-canid carnivores—the ability to share large amounts of food, especially with the young and non-hunting guardians of the young. Food-carrying is thus the functional equivalent of canid regurgitation, and would also have allowed the cohesive type of group life fostered among wolves and the Cape hunting dog (Mech 1970; Kühme 1965a, 1965b).

The existence of a self-perpetuating closed group with a continued identification through time characterizes all the social carnivores. Group life is established through a number of cohesive behaviors. Submission among wolves is a cohesive behavior (Schenkel 1967), as is food begging and sharing among Cape hunting dogs (Kühme 1965a, 1965b). Cohesive behaviors in the lion (Schaller 1972) are by no means as pronounced as in the canids. This is reflected in the less integrated nature of lion groups and the presence of intense antagonism and aggression within the group. It is possible, however, that social grooming and contact is more important to harmony in lion groups than among the canids mentioned. The spotted hyaena (Kruuk 1972), while more of a social animal than the lion, is not as advanced as the canids toward the creation of a cohesive group. Integrative behavior in *Crocuta* probably rests on the group versus non-group dichotomy seen in elaborate scent-marking and defense of clan territory against intrusion. Probably also important is the mobbing behavior which hyaenas employ against lions, and sometimes against a group member in "baiting." The life of the pack is emphasized in this aggressive activity toward outsiders.

Hominid cohesive behaviors are most likely to have resided in social grooming and feeding. The expression of hominid social cohesiveness through grooming and greeting is a logical outgrowth from a general primate base. In social feeding, however, the hominid group is assumed to have achieved its most harmonic integration. Only hominids among all other primates possess elaborate social mechanisms for food sharing. Furthermore, in all existing hunting and gathering groups, generosity, as expressed in the sharing of food, is of intense importance. Early hominids are therefore assumed to have resembled the Cape hunting dog in their extreme emphasis on food sharing to achieve integration, and it is possible that the social structure of these hominids also resembled that of *Lycaon* in its lack of ranking and division of labor between hunters and guardians of the young.

The question of intragroup ranking is also important in discussing hunting. Ranking in *Lycaon* has not been detected, and probably does not occur in *Crocuta* either (females equal or larger in size than males would tend to diminish pre-existing sexual ranking). The wolf, while possessing a hierarchy, has separate ranking for each sex and an emphasis on personal relationships which creates great flexibility. While ranking also occurs in the lion, the aggression of group members is such that a constant challenge to dominance is always present. A lack of ranking yields a lack of leadership during hunting, which is functionally important in that, far from a single prey animal being selected by the group leader and followed to the end, pack members will be able to test various prey animals individually for weakness or disease before the group as a whole turns to that animal. For this reason, it is safer to have no hunting leader. A lack of ranking or a diminished hierarchical system is therefore functional for survival at a certain level of group huntint activity, and can be assumed in the australopithecine groups.

The expansion of the neocortex is another convergent development in hominids to the canid condition. Radinsky (1969), discussing the evolution of the brain in felids and canids, holds that the development of social carnivore life among Miocene canids paralleled the development of an expanded neocortex and was perhaps responsible for it. The same argument can apply to hominids. Yet major expansion of the hominid brain beyond that of modern great apes does not seem to have occurred until the *A. africanus*-"Homo habilis" transition (Tobias 1971). Perhaps this expansion after a long period of stability was initiated by competition with large canids like *Lycaon* reaching Africa. The apparent failure of the robust australopithecine to achieve a similar expansion might be attributed to the primary orientation of this hominid toward hunting larger ungulates. Competition with canids would not have been so severe. Can one date the beginning of true cooperative hunting from this point of brain expansion? Of course the australopithecines, like all other higher primates, can be expected to have possessed group life and behaviors, but such behaviors would become accentuated in "Homo habilis." If the australopithecines hunted like other social carnivores, "Homo habilis" perhaps evolved more elaborate hunting activities, with division of labor in the hunt itself necessitated by an actual hunting strategy adopted beforehand. Of all the social carnivores, only the wolf has been reported to show such cooperative hunting, and even the wolf ordinarily adopts the coursing method — each pack member first setting out after a different animal, and then all turning to the slowest and most feeble ungulate. Because the wolf also demonstrates a flexible hierarchy, perhaps the australopithecine emphasis on lack of intragroup ranking was lost at the *Homo habilis* transition. The presence of leaders would facilitate planned hunting.

Throughout this evolutionary span, it is assumed that food resources, and not predation, had the greatest effect on hominid development. Hominids living in an environmental mosaic could head for trees or sleeping cliffs at night when nocturnal predators began hunting. Emancipation from nocturnal danger came only with the control of fire or the ability to construct good shelters. Such technological advances would also enable hominids to utilize large meat sources fully — carcasses would not have to be abandoned at night to lions and hyaenas.

SUMMARY

Morphological differences between the gracile and robust australopithecine can be analyzed in terms of allometry. This enables one to speculate that size differences were established on the basis of preferential prey selection, as these hominids turned to hunting at a very early period to fill a vacant diurnal carnivore niche when small- to medium-sized ungulates were expanding. Orientation toward hunting would have been facilitated by the mosaic environments in which proto-hominids lived. Stone tools made by the autralopithecines were used for food processing, rather than as weapons to subdue prey. It is possible to speculate about the existence of a "crowded middle" in hominid evolution, and the destruction of this range of species might explain the decreasing size of the robust australopithecine with time.

The social behavior of these hominids is thought to be convergent to that of other social carnivores, especially canids and hyaenids. Food-sharing and a lack of intragroup ranking which would facilitate hunting at this level of hominid evolution are elements of social organization most closely approaching those of modern social carnivores. The expansion of brain size seen at the *A. africanus*-"Homo habilis" transition parallels that thought to have taken place in canids when social hunting arose. This expansion may have been stimulated by competition with *Lycaon*. The robust australopithecine, concentrating on larger ungulates than either *Lycaon* or *A. africanus* would not have felt this competition. *Homo* is thought to have been capable of strategic hunting, in contrast to the australopithecines, where members of a hunting group would set out after prey independently, all members then turning to the slowest individual prey animal.

REFERENCES

ARNOLD, S. J.
 1972   Species densities of predators and their prey. *American Naturalist* 106:220–236.

BUCKLAND-WRIGHT, J. C.
 1969   Craniological observations on *Hyaena* and *Crocuta* (Mammalia). *Journal of Zoology, London* 159:17–29.

BUTZER, K. W.
 1971a *Environment and archeology* (second edition). Chicago: Aldine.
 1971b The Lower Omo Basin: geology, fauna and hominids of Plio-Pleistocene formations. *Naturwissenschaften* 58:7–16.
 1974   "Paleoecology of South African australopithecines: Taung revisited." Current Anthropology 15:367–382, 398–426.

COOKE, H. B. S.
 1963   "Pleistocene mammal faunas of Africa, with particular reference to southern Africa," in *African ecology and human evolution.* Edited by F. C. Howell and F. Bourlière, 65–116. Chicago: Aldine.

DALQUEST, W. W.
 1968   The bone-eating dog, *Borophagus diversidens* Cope. *Quarterly Journal of the Florida Academy of Science* 31:115–129.

EWER, R. F.
 1954   Some adaptive features in the dentition of hyaenas. *Annals of the Magazine of Natural History* 7:188–194.
 1967   "The fossil hyaenids of Africa — a reappraisal," in *Background to evolution in Africa.* Edited by W. W. Bishop and J. D. Clark, 109–123. Chicago: University of Chicago Press.

FREEMAN, L. G.
 1973   The significance of mammalian faunas from Paleolithic occupations in Cantabrian Spain. *American Antiquity* 38:3–44.

GREGORY, WM. K., M. HELLMAN
 1939   On the evolution and major classification of the civets (Viverridae) and allied fossil and recent Carnivora: a phylogenetic study of the skull and dentition. *Proceedings of the American Philosophical Society* 81:309–392.

HEIPLE, K. G., C. O. LOVEJOY
 1971   The distal femoral anatomy of *Australopithecus. American Journal of Physical Anthropology* 35:75–84.

HOWELL, F. C.
 1969   Remains of Hominidae from Pliocene/Pleistocene formations in the Lower Omo Basin, Ethiopia. *Nature* 223:1234–1239.

ISAAC, G., *et al.*
 1971   Archeological traces of early hominid activities, east of Lake Rudolf, Kenya. *Science* 173:1129–1134.

KLEIN, R. G.
 1974   Environment and subsistence of prehistoric man in the southern Cape Province, South Africa. *World Archaeology* 5:249–284.

KRUUK, H.
1972   *The spotted hyena.* Chicago: University of Chicago Press.

KÜHME, W.
1965a Communal food distribution and division of labour in African hunting dogs. *Nature* 205:443–444.
1965b Freilandstudien zur Soziologie des Hyänenhundes (*Lycaon pictus lupinus* Thomas 1902). *Zeitschrift für Tierpsychologie* 22:495–541.

LOVEJOY, C. O., K. G. HEIPLE
1970   A reconstruction of the femur of *Australopithecus africanus. American Journal of Physical Anthropology* 32:33–40.

LOVEJOY, C. O., K. G. HEIPLE, A. H. BURSTEIN
1973   The gait of *Australopithecus. American Journal of Physical Anthropology* 38:757–780.

MATTHEW, W. D.
1930   The phylogeny of dogs. *Journal of Mammalogy* 11:117–138.

MC HENRY, H. M.
1973   Early hominid humerus from East Rudolf, Kenya. *Science* 180: 739–741.

MECH, L. D.
1970   *The wolf.* New York: Natural History Press.

MERRICK, H. V., *et al.*
1973   Archaeological occurrences of early Pleistocene age from the Shungura Formation, Lower Omo Valley, Ethiopia. *Nature* 242: 572–575.

OXNARD, C. E.
1968   A note on the fragmentary Sterkfontein scapula. *American Journal of Physical Anthropology* 28:213–217.

RADINSKY, L. B.
1969   Outlines of canid and felid brain evolution. *Annals of the New York Academy of Sciences* 167:277–288.

ROBINSON, J. T.
1954   The genera and species of the Australopithecinae. *American Journal of Physical Anthropology* 12:181–200.
1956   *The Dentition of the Australopithecinae.* Transvaal Museum Memoir 9.

ROSENZWEIG, M. L.
1968   The strategy of body size in mammalian carnivores. *American Midland Naturalist* 80:299–315.

SCHALLER, G. B.
1972   *The Serengeti lion.* Chicago: University of Chicago Press.

SCHENKEL, R.
1967   Submission: its features and function in the wolf and dog. *American Zoologist* 7:319–329.

SCHOENER, T. W.
1968   The *Anolis* lizards of Bimini: resource partitioning in a complex fauna. *Ecology* 49:704–726.

SIMPSON, G. G.
  1941   The function of saber-like canines in carnivorous mammals. *American Museum Novitates* 1130.
THENIUS, E.
  1966   Zur Stammesgeschichte der Hyänen (Carnivora, Mammalia). *Zeitschrift für Säugetierkunde* 31:293–300.
  1967   Zur Phylogenie der Feliden (Carnivora, Mammalia). *Zeitschrift für zoologische Systematik und Evolutionsforschung* 5:129–143.
  1970   Zur Evolution und Verbreitungsgeschichte der Suidae (Artiodactyla, Mammalia). *Zeitschrift für Säugetierkunde* 35:321–342.
TOBIAS, P. V.
  1971   *The brain in hominid evolution.* New York: Columbia University Press.
  1972   "Progress and problems in the study of early man in sub-Saharan Africa," in *The functional and evolutionary biology of primates.* Edited by R. H. Tuttle, 63–93. Chicago: Aldine.
WEBB, S. D.
  1969   The Pliocene Canidae of Florida. *Bulletin of the Florida State Museum* 14:273–308.
WELLS, L. H.
  1957   Speculations on the Palaeogeographic distribution of antelopes. *South African Journal of Science* 53:423–424.
  1967   "Antelopes in the Pleistocene of southern Africa," in *Background to evolution in Africa.* Edited by W. W. Bishop and J. D. Clark, 99–107. Chicago: University of Chicago Press.
WILLIAMS, E. E.
  1972   "The origin of faunas. Evolution of lizard congeners in a complex island fauna: a trial analysis," in *Evolutionary biology,* volume six. Edited by Th. Dobzhansky et al., 47–89. New York: Appleton-Century-Crofts.

Dietary Adaptations of
Australopithecus *and Early* Homo

JOHN A. WALLACE

What did the australopithecines eat? Around this question revolves one of the most contended issues in present-day human paleontology. Almost twenty years have passed since Robinson (1954) first published his dietary hypothesis, a tripartite thesis of hominid behavior, causation, and classification. Robinson claimed that (1) the robust australopithecines were vegetarians, whereas the gracile australopithecines were omnivores; (2) occupation of these niches was the most important cause of their dental differences; and (3) the two australopithecines belonged to separate lineages and they were generically distinct: the robust forms were called *Paranthropus*; the gracile forms, *Australopithecus*.[1]

Most students of early hominid evolution — Dart, LeGros Clark, von Koenigswald, Mayr, Campbell, Brace, Wolpoff, Tobias, and others — have rejected the dietary hypothesis. But these critics seemingly have overlooked the fact that the dietary hypothesis subsumes three hypotheses. To deny, as did Tobias (1967), the generic distinction of *Paranthropus* is not to deny that robust and gracile australopithecines (even if only specifically distinct) belonged to different lineages, or that they ate different foods, or that they had different dental adaptations.

This paper is based on part of the author's unpublished doctoral dissertation submitted to the University of the Witwatersrand. I thank C. K. Brain, P. V. Tobias, R. E. Leakey, and F. T. Masao for permission to examine the fossil hominids in their care. This work was supported by the Wenner-Gren Foundation for Anthropological Research.

[1] Recently, Robinson (1967; 1972a; 1972b) suggested sinking *Australopithecus* and transferring the gracile australopithecus from Taung, Sterkfontein, and Makapansgat to *Homo*, with the new nomen *H. africanus*.

Though Tobias rejected the generic separation of robust and gracile australopithecines, he was propelled by the strength of his anatomical observations to the same conclusion as Robinson: the robust and gracile australopithecines (*A. robustus/boisei* and *A. africanus* in Tobias' nomenclature) belonged to different lineages. And like Robinson (1960) seven years earlier, Tobias saw that "Zinj" was indeed "dentally highly specialized" and had been subjected to "intensive selection pressures." But unlike Robinson, Tobias did not say what those pressures were, or what "Zinj" was dentally specialized for.

The strongest point — the "cardinal point" — of the dietary hypothesis, according to Robinson, is the disparity in sizes of canines and cheek teeth between robust and gracile australopithecines. Robust individuals tend to have smaller canines associated with larger cheek teeth than gracile individuals (Robinson 1956; Tobias 1967). Robinson claimed that this dental disparity was evidence that robust australopithecines were vegetarians. Not necessarily so, said Brace (1963, 1967), the disparity may merely reflect differences in australopithecine body size. Robinson (1963a, 1963b) agreed this might b etrue, but only in part. Large cheek teeth in robust hominids may be correlated with their presumed large body mass, but positive allometry cannot be invoked to explain why robust hominids have relatively small canines. But the question remains: why was a negative allometric growth rate selected in the canine segment of robust early hominids? Further, what is the causal relationship between small canines and a vegetarian diet?

A causal relationship between diet and the small canine-large postcanine complex, some might claim, was given by Jolly (1970) who, arguing by analogy from the diet and morphology of the gelada baboon, *Theropithecus*, suggested that the complex was an adaptation for chewing "small, hard, solid objects." "Many foods," Jolly says, "are small, hard, solid and of more or less spherical shape but only seeds of grasses and annual herbs are widespread enough in open country to be a likely staple."

In this article I test the hypothesis that robust and gracile australopithecines had substantially different diets, that their dental differences are caused by occupation of different niches, that they belonged to separate lineages, and that they were generically distinct. I suggest a modified dietary hypothesis for the evolution of the robust australopithecines and the emergence of *Homo*.

DIET AND TOOTH WEAR

Tooth wear can be defined as the loss of enamel, dentine, and cementum by erosion, abrasion, attrition, or any combination of these. Erosion is the loss of the calcified tissues of a tooth by nonbacterial acids. Abrasion is the loss of the dental hard tissues by contact with foreign objects introduced into the mouth or by contact with grit in the diet. Attrition is the loss of the calcified tissues by occlusal and approximal contact with other teeth.

Erosion is diagnosed by decalcified enamel, dentine, or cementum. No evidence was found for *in vivo* erosion of australopithecine teeth. Five types of abrasion are recognized: occupational, artificial, ritual, tooth cleaning, and dietary. Of these only the dietary type was found in early hominids. This is diagnosed by presence of scratches, microgouges, and chips. Attrition may occur during mastication and bruxism. Occlusal attrition is diagnosed by shiny, polished areas of enamel (sheared enamel). In early hominids, shiny, polished enamel was produced by tooth-to-tooth contact during chewing: no evidence was found for bruxism.

The micromorphology of worn tooth surfaces offers clues about the diet. The extent of tooth chipping gives a measure of the amount of grit in the diet, and the intensity of shine of sheared enamel as well as the depth of the facet reveals the force and frequency of tooth-to-tooth contacts, and this, as we shall now see, gives an indication of the physical consistency of the food.

Teeth frequently contact one another during chewing (Yurstas and Emerson 1954; Graf and Zander 1963; Adams and Zander 1964; Beyron 1964; Pameijer et al. 1969; Glickman et al. 1969). More tooth-to-tooth contacts occur when soft, mushy food is chewed; the teeth puncture the soft bolus, striking one another, whereas with hard, tough food occlusal contacts are either prevented or occur less often or with less force (Anderson and Picton 1957; Ahlgren 1966; Goodkind et al. 1970).

Because contacts that occur during chewing produce occlusal enamel attrition facets (Weinberg 1961), we would expect that individuals who habitually chewed soft food would have teeth more attrited than those who habitually chewed harder food. This was tested and found to be true for two populations known to have diets different in physical consistency, namely South African Caucasoids and Bushmen. Examination of teeth in the dried crania and mandibles of fifty South African Caucasoids and twenty-four Bushmen in the Department of Anatomy,

University of the Witwatersrand, revealed that the Caucasoids had deeper and more polished occlusal enamel facets than Bushmen. Assessment of the shine and depth of occlusal enamel facets thus seems to be a valid method for deciding whether two hominid populations ate food substantially different in physical consistency.

Ideally for valid comparison, both populations should be represented by a large number of teeth of each class and from all age groups. For the South African early hominids, this criterion is met only for the robust australopithecines at Swartkrans and, to a lesser extent, for the gracile australopithecines at Sterkfontein.

The extent of attrition was assessed subjectively under a low-power binocular microscope. On the average, the shine and depth of the facets were the same at Swartkrans and Sterkfontein. Comparison of Swartkrans and Sterkfontein homologues of the same age revealed no substantial difference in either the brightness or the depth of the sheared enamel. For this reason I conclude that probably the Swartkrans and Sterkfontein hominids ate food similar in physical consistency. From my observations on the facets, I think it improbable that robust australopithecines at Swartkrans ate more "small, hard, solid objects" (seeds) than gracile australopithecines from Sterkfontein.

This is not to deny that robust australopithecines ate seeds. Of course, we cannot exclude the possibility of seed eating; indeed it seems likely the australopithecines ate seeds — but only when seeds were in season. Dr. R. A. Lubke of the Department of Botany, University of the Witwatersrand, tells me that grass seeds of today are available for two, or at most three, months of the year. If conditions on the South African highveld today are similar to those of the past, seeds probably were not present year round. This is another reason that makes it unlikely that the small canine of the robust australopithecines is an evolutionary adaptation for chewing seeds.

The incidence of tooth chipping in australopithecines has been used both to support and to refute Robinson's vegetarian-omnivore hypothesis. Robinson (1954, 1956, 1962a, 1963a) claimed that the robust had more chipped teeth than the gracile australopithecines, and this was evidence that the robust forms ate more grit-laden roots, bulbs, and tubers. Tobias (1967) rejected this inference because the chips he examined were "similar in size, character, and number per jaw" in both robust and gracile specimens. The chips Tobias examined were all "rather large," and these he thought must have been produced during bouts of bone chewing.

I evaluated these conflicting claims by examining the teeth of the

South African australopithecines under a low-power binocular microscope. An enamel chip is defined as a flake scar equal to or greater
than 0.1 millimeters. The surface features of rounding and scratching
were used as criteria for sorting chips that were produced during an
individual's lifetime (ante-mortem chips) from those produced after
death (post-mortem chips). Unless otherwise qualified, the word "chip"
in the following discussion means an ante-mortem chip.

In a sample of 589 erupted deciduous and permanent teeth, fifty
chips were found spread among forty teeth representing an estimated
twenty-nine individuals. Of the six chipped teeth that comprised Tobias'
sample, only one (the M^3 of Sts 53) can be accepted as an ante-mortem
chip; the other five, by my criteria, are post-mortem chips.

The fifty chips were sorted into two groups according to size: forty-
seven were small (0.1 to 2.8 millimeters) and are called microchips,
three were large (approximately 4 millimeters) and are called macro-
chips. I calculated three ratios of microchipping for the permanent teeth
of Swartkrans, Sterkfontein, and Makapansgat:
1. Chipped teeth = Number of chipped teeth/Number of worn teeth
2. Chipped cheek teeth = Number of chipped cheek teeth/Number of
worn cheek teeth
3. Multiple chipped cheek teeth = Number of chipped cheek teeth
with multiple chips/Number of chipped cheek teeth.

In addition, multiple chipping was expressed as the average number
of chips per chipped cheek tooth. Excluded from these calculations
were the Kromdraai, Sterkfontein Extension, Cooper's B, and Taung
teeth because samples from these sites were too small. I also excluded
the teeth in SK 15 + SK 18a + SK 43 and the teeth in SK 45 + SK
80/847/846b because I believe, like Robinson (1953) and others (Clarke
et al. 1970), that these two individuals are not small robust australopithecines but early members of the genus *Homo* (see below). Thus the
comparison of tooth chipping was made between the robust australopithecines of Swartkrans and the gracile australopithecines of Sterkfontein (type locality) and Makapansgat.

The average number of chips on a cheek tooth was Swartkrans: 1.2,
Sterkfontein: 1.1, and Makapansgat: 1.0; and as Table 1 shows, the
indices of chipping differ to the order of 1, 2, and 3 percent among the
three sites. Swartkrans does not show the highest value for any of the
three indices. This demonstrates that there is no large difference in
tooth chipping between robust and gracile australopithecines. It seems
unlikely that robust australopithecines ate more "grit-laden roots, bulbs,
and tubers" than gracile australopithecines. My observations on the in-

cidence of tooth chipping suggest that the robust and gracile australopithecines did not differ substantially in the amount of grit in their food
and drinking water.

Table 1.   Chipped permanent teeth from Sterkfontein, Swartkrans, and Makapansgat (percent)

Indices	Sterkfontein	Swartkrans	Makapansgat
(1) Chipped teeth	5.9	6.8	7.1
(2) Chipped cheek teeth	5.5	7.7	8.8
(3) Multiple chipped cheek teeth	14.2	12.9	0

TOOTH FORM AND FUNCTION IN AUSTRALOPITHECINES

Here I attempt to identify the major trends in the australopithecine
dentition.

First, incisal wear planes vary on recently erupted australopithecine
upper central and lateral incisors. Robust hominids from Swartkrans
tend to have more or less horizontal wear planes. At Sterkfontein
and Makapansgat, in contrast, the gracile australopithecines tend to
have a much more beveled upward, inward wear surface on their recently erupted upper incisors. The type of incisor wear is abrasion,
not attrition. That is, australopithecine incisors are worn, not by
tooth-to-tooth contacts, but by contact with dietary grit.

The problem is why the bevels of the wear planes vary. A partial
solution is found in the observation that gracile australopithecines
tend to be more prognathous; the incisor segment of the arch is convex anteriorly. In contrast, robust australopithecines have a more
orthognathous maxilla; the incisor segment is flattened, and runs more
or less straight across from one canine alveolus to the other (Robinson
1956; Tobias 1967). In modern man, proclined upper incisors are
found in prognathous maxillae, whereas retruded or vertically implanted upper incisors more commonly occur in orthognathous upper
jaws (Hasund and Ulstein 1970). Among the australopithecines, "Zinj"
(OH. 5) has the flattest face and the most vertically set upper incisors
(Tobias 1967).

Thus far a correlation is seen between incisor wear planes, incisor
proclination, and prognathism. This brings us to the cause — the morphogenetic mechanism — underlying the variation in prognathism. Immediately we turn to the premaxilla because this is the bone that develops between the two maxillae anteriorly and the bone that carries

the upper incisors. The observation that completes our argument is Ashley Montagu's (1935) finding that prognathism in primates is correlated with growth at the premaxillary suture. In short-faced primates the suture fuses early, but in longer-faced forms sutural obliteration is late. Ashley Montagu noted that the premaxillary suture remained open longer in Negroes than in Caucasoids. No doubt, he reasoned, this accounts for the pronounced prognathism of Negroes.[2]

For the australopithecines we are left only to conclude that the variation we see in incisor wear planes, incisor proclination, and subnasal maxillary prognathism (perhaps even subnasal maxillary morphology) probably resulted from variation in the time the premaxillary suture took to become obliterated. In robust individuals the suture fused early. In gracile individuals the suture remained open longer.

We now turn to the question of why a short growth period at the suture was selected. What advantage was conferred to an australopithecine that had a short period of premaxillary suture growth, a flat maxilla, and vertically implanted upper incisors? Looking at the upper incisors we see that they wear flat as the individuals grow older. But in some, flat incisal wear developed earlier. These individuals were the ones that had flatter incisal wear planes to begin with: the robust australopithecines. Comparing "Zinj" (OH. 5) with Sts 52a + b from Sterkfontein corroborates that claim. To judge from eruption of third molars, the two hominids are dentally the same age. The upper incisors of orthognathous OH. 5 are worn flat; those of prognathous Sts 52a + b are worn with an upward, inward bevel. This means that the upper incisors of "Zinj" wore flat at an earlier age.

Flat incisal wear is evidence of an edge-to-edge occlusion (Weidenreich 1937; Hojo 1954; Begg 1965). Coupling that with the fact that incisors wore flat at an earlier age in robust than in gracile individuals brings us to the conclusion that an edge-to-edge incisor occlusion developed earlier in the former than the latter. That, I suggest, is an adaptation for crushing. In the flat faced fossil from Olduvai (OH. 5), the upper central and lateral incisors probably erupted directly into an edge-to-edge bite. From the time they erupted until the time of

---

[2] Priority on this point, as Ashley Montagu acknowledges, goes to Hamy, who in 1868 observed the correlation between loss of the premaxilla and facial profile in Negroes. Six years before Ashley Montagu's publication, Professor Wood Jones laid it down as an anatomical truth that "... by the sixth month, as a rule, the suture between it [the premaxilla] and the maxilla is closed, that in *prognathous skulls,* and in cases of rickets and hydrocephalus the closure may be delayed ..." (italics mine). "All this," proclaims Wood Jones is 1929, "is a universally recognized anatomical fact concerning the formation of the palate ...."

death, the incisors in "Zinj" almost certainly were used for crushing. Seemingly, incisor crushing was being selected in australopithecines, and this was achieved by early obliteration of the premaxillary suture.

Moving distally, we come to the canines and to the problem of the relatively small canine of robust australopithecines. Failure heretofore to find a selective advantage for canine reduction in robust australopithecines is due largely, I think, to previous workers having overlooked the fact that the functionally important parameter of a canine is neither length nor breadth, but height.

Robust australopithecines tend to have low canines that project little or not at all beyond the occlusal plane, whereas in gracile australopithecines the canine apex is sharper and projects beyond the occlusal plane. Speaking of unworn, permanent maxillary canines at Swartkrans, Robinson (1956) said: "In no case is the apex a sharp point." Besides confirming this, I can add that the WORN upper canine of Sts 52a + b from Sterkfontein bears a sharper apex than almost all the UNWORN homologues from Swartkrans. The permanent upper canines of SK 92, SK 85 + SK 93, and MLD 11 are unerupted and hence ideal for comparison of canine apices. In the Swartkrans canines the apices are rounded off. In contrast, the apex on the Makapansgat canine is high and pointed.

As Robinson's (1956) measurements testify, unworn mandibular canines from Swartkrans are lower incisocervically than homologues from Sterkfontein. Regrettably, a similar metrical comparison cannot be made between homologous upper canines, because all those from Sterkfontein are worn. However, my observations on occlusion of the upper canine suggest that upper canines of robust australopithecines are lower in height than upper canines of gracile australopithecines. The buccal d$\underline{c}$-facet on the Taung dm$_1$ runs the length of the mesiobuccal ridge of the mesiobuccal cusp, whereas in the Swartkrans dm$_1$'s of SK 64, SK 3978 and SK 63 the facet produced by the upper deciduous canine is confined to the buccal end of that ridge. This is evidence of a difference in overbite and hence canine incisocervical height.

In the permanent dentition, we find that Sts 52a + b and Sts 49 at Sterkfontein have buccal $\underline{C}$-facets on their P$_3$'s, whereas at Swartkrans buccal $\underline{C}$-facets are not seen on any P$_3$'s — not even on P$_3$'s of three individuals (SK 857, SK 831, and SK 6 + SK 100) that are dentally younger than Sts 52a + b, and not even on a recently erupted P$_3$ (SK 55a + b). This is evidence that the permanent upper canine of these four Swartkrans individuals was lower incisocervically than the upper canines of Sts 52a + b and Sts 49 from Sterkfontein.

Why were low cusped canines selected in robust australopithecines? Presumably they conferred some advantage during chewing. To judge from the wear on the permanent molars, SK 839 + SK 852 is dentally younger than Taung. Accordingly we would expect SK 839 + SK 852 to have a more projecting upper canine and thus more of a canine overbite. To the contrary, the canine is less projecting and there is no overbite. The dc of this Swartkrans child is worn flat and occluded edge-to-edge (better surface-to-surface) with dm₁. Thus relative to Taung, we can say that SK 839 + SK 852 developed an edge-to-edge canine occlusion at an earlier age. We can also say that had SK 64, SK 3978, and SK 63 lived longer they also would have acquired an edge-to-edge canine bite earlier than Taung. The magnitude of the overbite in Taung, which can be seen by manually articulating the upper and lower teeth in centric occlusion, suggests that had Taung lived, an edge-to-edge bite of the upper deciduous canine probably never would have developed; the canine would have been shed first.

In the permanent dentition, it is almost certain that had SK 857, SK 831, SK 6 + SK 100, and SK 55a + b lived longer, their upper canines would have worn flat into an edge-to-edge (surface-to-surface) occlusion with P₃ at an earlier age than in Sts 52a + b and Sts 49 from Sterkfontein. (With age, an edge-to-edge bite develops in both robust and gracile australopithecines.) As noted earlier, "Zinj" and Sts 52a + b are dentally the same age. Since the upper canines of "Zinj" are worn flat and those of Sts 52a + b are worn with a bevel, we can conclude that an edge-to-edge canine bite developed at an earlier age in "Zinj."

Our observations suggest that robust early hominids acquired an edge-to-edge occlusion of their deciduous and permanent upper canines at an earlier age than gracile early hominids. Most likely, the reason is that robust upper canines were genetically lower in height. Low cusped canines were selected presumably because they wore flat into an edge-to-edge occlusion at an early age. Thus for most, if not all, of their life, robust individuals had a canine occlusion that was well suited for crushing. From their apparent rapid rate of wear, I suspect that the upper canines of "Zinj" erupted almost directly into an edge-to-edge bite. Just as the incisors did little or no incising, the canines in robust australopithecines, especially in hyper-robust forms like "Zinj," did little or no slicing.

Canines may influence molar grinding. The angle at which the lower molars slide upward and inward into centric occlusion along the incline planes of the upper molars — the so-called "grind" angle

— depends, in part, upon the height of the upper canine and, in turn, the extent of the canine overbite. In persons with marked canine overbite and steep canine guidance, the closing stroke tends to be steep, while persons with small canine overbite and slight guidance have a larger lateral deviation of the mandible during the last part of the closing stroke (Shepherd 1960; Koivumaa 1961; Ingervall 1972).

Canine guidance of molar grinding was present in both robust and gracile australopithecine children with recently erupted deciduous canines. Probably robust australopithecine children with deciduous canines lost their canine overbite and canine guidance at an earlier age than gracile australopithecine children. In some gracile children (e.g. Taung) canine overbite and canine guidance was present at least until the first permanent molars erupted.

Guidance of molar grinding by the permanent canine was seemingly not present in robust australopithecines; no buccal C-facets were found on robust australopithecine P₃'s. In gracile australopithecines, canine guidance was present only in adolescents and young adults. Guidance was lost with age as abrasion leveled the canine cusp, unlocked the overbite, and established an edge-to-edge occlusion.

Low canines in robust australopithecines conferred a twofold advantage: (1) low canines permitted early acquisition of an edge-to-edge bite, thereby increasing the effectiveness of crushing, and (2) low canines permitted early loss or absence of canine guidance of molar grinding, thereby allowing for early development of an eccentric grinding component.

Examining Robinson's (1956) measurements of unworn canines, a correlation is seen between canine height, length, and breadth: low canines are short and narrow, and high canines are long and broad. Since canine length and breadth seemingly have little or no influence on the masticatory cycle, that is to say on how an individual chews, I incline to the view that reduction in canine length and breadth seen in robust australopithecines is a pleiotropic effect of reduction in canine cusp height. Reduction in canine cusp height, as discussed below, probably is a manifestation in the canine segment of a process of reduction in cusp height that extends along the tooth row from central incisor to third molar. Before examining that possibility we turn to the process of molarization of the deciduous molars and their permanent successors, the premolars.

As can be seen from the specimens, molarization of the australopithecine dm₁ involves an elevation or upgrowth of the lingual end of the mesial marginal ridge, resulting in a "squaring-off" of the mesiolingual corner of the tooth, a realignment of the anterior fovea and mesial marginal ridge at a right angle to the long axis of the occlusal surface, and an overgrowth of the mesiolingual occlusal groove with closure of the lingual end of the anterior fovea.

The degree of molarization of dm_1 varies among the specimens. The position of the mesiolingual occlusal groove and alignment of the anterior fovea in the SK 852 dm_1 from Swartkrans is intermediate between the less molarized Sts 24 dm_1 from Sterkfontein and the more molarized TM 1536 dm_1 from Kromdraai. Variation in degree of molarization is seen not only among dm_1's from Swartkrans, but also in dm_1's on opposite sides of the same Swartkrans mandible. The right dm_1 of SK 61 has a well-developed mesiolingual groove which escapes to the mesial surface. The left dm_1 of SK 61 lacks such a groove. Contrary to what Robinson (1956) seems to imply, my observations on twenty-one dm_1's belonging to thirteen early hominids suggest that the difference in molarization of the early hominid dm_1 is not one of kind, but one of degree.

Molarization of dm_1, that is elevation of the mesial marginal ridge, increases the surface area available for crushing. Developmentally this may be very simple. Enamel is produced by ameloblasts. Once the definitive thickness of enamel is reached, the ameloblasts die. Perhaps variation in thickness of mesial marginal ridges reflects variation in ameloblast life spans. In robust dm_1's the ameloblasts in the mesial marginal ridge lived longer to produce more enamel; in gracile dm_1's the mesial marginal ridge ameloblasts died earlier. The morphogenetic mechanism underlying molarization of early hominid dm_1's might have been a gene complex regulating death rates of ameloblasts.[3]

Molarization of dm_1 and molar cusp enlargement may be independent processes. In TM 1536 from Kromdraai, molarization of dm_1 has occurred without mesiodistal and buccolingual expansion of the M_1 cusps. The dm_1 of TM 1536 is much more molarized than any Swartkrans homologue, but the TM 1536 M_1 is much smaller in breadth and length than any Swartkrans M_1; it is similar in size to the M_1's of the gracile australopithecines of Sterkfontein (Robinson 1956).

Variation in mesial marginal ridge morphology occurs also in P_3's. Robinson (1956) reported that in Swartkrans P_3's the distal buccal groove is better developed than the mesial buccal groove, whereas in Sterkfontein P_3's the converse holds: the mesial is better developed

---

[3] It is hoped that my ongoing studies on the morphology of replicated enamel rod ends and fractured enamel prisms of early hominids will reveal some aspects of the life history of the ameloblast.

than the distal buccal groove. In MLD 2 from Makapansgat, I found that the left P₃ had a better-developed distal buccal groove, while the right P₃ had a better-developed mesial groove. In other words, this so-called gracile australopithecine has a mix of robust and gracile dental features. In premolar morphology, MLD 2 from Makapansgat is intermediate between a Sterkfontein gracile hominid and a Swartkrans robust hominid.

Turning to the cheek teeth cusps we find variation among the australopithecines in premolar and molar cusp height. I compared Swartkrans and Sterkfontein premolar and molar homologues that were unerupted, and premolar and molar homologues from these two sites that were almost identically worn. Although unmeasured, it was apparent from inspection that robust hominids from Swartkrans tended to have cheek teeth with lower cusps than gracile australopithecines from Sterkfontein. Referring to the buccal and lingual cusps on Swartkrans P₃'s, Robinson (1956) remarked: "Neither has sharp apices in any of the specimens to hand, the cusps being low and bluntly rounded. When only very slightly worn no traces remain of apices. . . ." Of the Swartkrans M¹, Robinson (1956) said: "The cusps are all relatively low and rounded. When entirely unworn there may be a moderate apex to each cusp but after the slightest wear the cusps are low, rounded tubercles." I found that in Swartkrans premolars and molars, dentine is seen first AFTER the cusps are leveled, whereas in Sterkfontein premolars and molars, the first dentine exposure appears BEFORE the cusps are worn flat. Since there seemed to be no appreciable difference in occlusal enamel thickness, as judged from inspection of worn enamel rims as well as from focusing up and down through the enamel, the most likely reason that dentine was reached relatively earlier in robust cheek teeth was that the cusps were lower and less projecting.

As noted earlier, low-cusped cheek teeth increase the horizontal grinding component of the closing stroke. Because of their low cusps and almost horizontal incline planes, robust australopithecines probably had a more horizontal contact glide path into centric occlusion than gracile australopithecines.

Reduction in cusp height, I believe, was the major trend in the evolution of the robust australopithecine dentition. Because of the functional integration of the canine and the cheek teeth (obviously there would be no selective advantage if cusp height reduced in cheek teeth but not in canines, or cusp height reduced in canines but not in cheek teeth), the question arises whether there might be some sort of unitary genetic control over cusp height. More evidence for a cusp height field in australopithecines is found in SK 27, a Swartkrans hominid which Robinson (1956) regarded as a dentally aberrant *Paranthropus*. Present are the completed but unerupted crowns of I², C̲ and P³. The M¹'s are recently erupted. Robinson (1956) noted that the lateral incisor and canine of SK 27 are incisocervically long — in fact they are longer incisocervically than any other australopithecine I² and C̲. In the P³ the mesial and distal lingual cusp ridges are the same length. Probably this symmetry of lingual ridges is a consequence of elevation of the lingual cusp. The cusps on M¹ are higher than any other equally worn Swartkrans M¹, and they are just as high as equally worn M¹'s from Sterkfontein. In SK 27 we see evidence in I², C̲, P³, and M¹ of a developmental process of cusp elongation. The elongation of the incisor, the canine, and the cusps on the premolar and first molar in SK 27 is evidence, I suggest, of the effect of a field for cusp height.

The cheek teeth cusps of robust australopithecines besides being low are broad and long. As the cusps became low, they seem to have flattened out and pushed the occlusal base mesiodistally and buccolingually. The mesiodistal and buccolingual expansion of robust hominid cheek teeth cusps perhaps resulted (1) from selection acting directly on cusp breadth and length, or (2) from selection for larger bodies, or (3) from a pleiotropic effect of selection for reduction in cusp height. Whatever the selection process, the result was the same: an increase in breadth and length of the occlusal table for crushing.

Morphologists agree that genes act mainly by influencing the rate and timing of developmental processes. This means that the variation we see among the australopithecines, or between two typical robust and gracile australopithecines, in incisor implantation; in canine, premolar, and molar cusp heights; in mesial marginal ridge morphology; and in molar cusp breadth and length may be very simple genetically. There is no need to invoke a multitude of mutations to account for the dental variation seen among the australopithecines. The appearance of a new pattern of alleles by genetic recombination may have accelerated or depressed (say) mitotic rates of osteoblasts in a suture or ameloblasts in a tooth germ.

The presumed small "genetic difference" among australopithecine dentitions; the existence of australopithecines such as MLD 2, SK 27, and TM 1536 evincing an admixture of "typical" robust and gracile dental characters; and, most important of all, the absence of evidence for an appreciable difference in diets point to two conclusions: (1) the "gracile" australopithecines at Taung, Sterkfontein, and Makapansgat are not generically distinct from the "robust" australopithecines at Swartkrans and Kromdraai, and (2) the australopithecines belong to one lineage with a trend toward increased robustness and increased efficiency for dental crushing and grinding.

The robust *Australopithecus* found at Swartkrans, and possibly Kromdraai, may have evolved from a gracile *Australopithecus* such as was found at Sterkfontein (the Sts and TM specimens) or at Makapansgat. The MLD 2 specimen with its curious amalgam of Sterkfontein–Swartkrans dental characteristics may represent a temporal *forme de passage* linking the early gracile *Australopithecus* of Sterkfontein with the later robust *Australopithecus* of Swartkrans. In this view the Makapansgat australopithecines are seen as morphological "intermediates" between the early gracile *Australopithecus* of Sterkfontein and the later robust form at Swartkrans. Before this interpretation can be accepted, more specimens are urgently needed as well as clarification of the dating of the South African sites, especially in the light of Wells' (1969) suggestion that, contrary to views of Cooke (1963, 1967), Makapansgat may be older than Sterkfontein, and thus may be the oldest of the South African cave deposits.

In the lineage leading from the earlier gracile to the more recent robust *Australopithecus,* the major trend in masticatory function was increased effectiveness of crushing and grinding. The selective factor, I suggest, was occupation of a collector niche in the absence of tools to prepare the food extraorally. The evolution of the robust from the gracile australopithecine probably reflects an increasing morphological adaptation to this niche.

THE STERKFONTEIN *HOMO*

At Sterkfontein the Sts and TM fossils were found in the eastern part of the cave, and because the type specimen of Broom's *Plesianthropus* was found here, the eastern part of the deposit came to be called the Sterkfontein Type site. Eighteen meters west of the Type excavation, miners had exposed a pocket of breccia which was called the West Pit. It was here, in 1955, that C. K. Brain found the first Sterkfontein stone tools, a discovery which prompted Robinson to excavate the West Pit breccia. To the enlarged West Pit, Robinson (1962b) gave the name Sterkfontein Extension site. In the Sterkfontein Extension (West Pit), Robinson found a dm² and M¹ (Se 255), an M² (Se 1508), a lingual half of a probable M² (Se 1579), a $\underline{C}^|_|$ (Se 1937), and a lingual half of a

P³ (Se 2396). Robinson (1962b) assigned these teeth to *Australopithecus*, save for Se 2396 which is catalogued as "*?Homo?erectus* (Telanthropus)." Tobias (1965) pointed out that the M¹ of Se 255 was smaller than those of *A. africanus* and approached the homologues of *H. habilis*. Because of the small size of the P³ and the M¹, the reduction of the metacone of the Se 1508 M², and the median position of the lingual ridge in the Se 1937 C̄ — characteristics not present in the TM and Sts specimens from the eastern part of the Sterkfontein cave — I tentatively assign the five Se specimens to *Homo* and not *Australopithecus*. The only tooth class shared at present by the Sterkfontein and Swartkrans *Homo* is the P3; both the SK 18a P₃ and the Se 2396 P³ are small and have thin enamel.

THE SWARTKRANS *HOMO*

In early 1949, Robinson found at Swartkrans a mandible bearing the left three molars and the right M₂ and M₃ (SK 15), an isolated P₃ (SK 18a) believed to belong to the mandible, and the proximal end of a radius (SK 18b) presumed to be from the same individual. The buccal half of an isolated P₄ (SK 43) was found at the same time and cataloged as belonging to the SK 15 mandible. Two months after these discoveries, an incomplete mandibular corpus with the right M₁ and M₂ (SK 45) and a palate with an I² stump and fragmented P³ (SK 80) were unearthed at Swartkrans. The SK 15 mandible was described as the remains of a human-like creature, *Telanthropus capensis* (Broom and Robinson 1952). In 1953, Robinson referred SK 18a, SK 18b, SK 45, and SK 80 to *T. capensis,* and in 1961, he eliminated *T. capensis* and transferred all the specimens to *Homo erectus.*

In 1970, R. J. Clarke observed that SK 847, a cranial fragment with a left M³, articulated perfectly along a break with the SK 80 maxilla. Moreover, a portion of a left temporal (SK 846b) could be brought into union with SK 847. The combined cranial complex of SK 80/847/846b was classified as *Homo* sp. indeterminate (Clarke et al. 1970). Clarke and Howell (1972) compared the cranial morphology of SK 80/847/846b with other Swartkrans hominids, adducing evidence that, contrary to Wolpoff (1971), this specimen is not a small, robust australopithecine but an early member of the genus *Homo.*

I now describe dental characteristics that suggest that SK 80/847/846b is *Homo* and not *Australopithecus.*

The wear pattern on the M³ of SK 80/847/846b is unique. This tooth has been worn more on the buccal than on the lingual half of the occlusal surface, and the first dentine exposure is on the mesio-buccal cusp. In all other early hominid M³'s, sufficiently worn for this characteristic to be discerned, the lingual half of the occlusal surface is more abraded than the buccal half, and the first dentine exposure is on the mesiolingual cusp. The pattern of abrasion on the SK 80/847/846b M³ is the most common pattern of wear on M³'s of modern man. Murphy (1959) found that in Australian aborigines, dentine is usually exposed first on the mesiolingual cusps of M¹ and M², but on the mesiobuccal cusp of M³. Of this Murphy said: "There can be little doubt that it is a significant difference."

The wear pattern seen on the M³ of SK 80/847/846b is part of a helicoidal occlusal wear plane (Campbell 1925; Moses 1946; Acker-mann 1963). In a helicoidal or "twisted" occlusal plane two zones can be distinguished, a mesial and a distal. The mesial zone includes the first molar and the mesial third of the second molar, while the distal zone embraces the distal two-thirds of the second molar and the whole of the occlusal surface of the third molar. The wear slopes of the two zones differ. In the mandible, the mesial zone is beveled down-ward and outward ("pitched buccally"), whereas the distal zone is beveled downward and inward ("pitched lingually"). In the maxilla the pitch of the two zones is reversed. Thus, in a helicoidal plane the buccal half of M³'s occlusal surface would be more worn than the lingual half. The helicoidal occlusal wear plane is a reflection of dif-ferences in width between upper and lower dental arches. In the mesial zone, the upper arch is wider than the lower (positive overjet); at the place of transition between the two zones, the *pas helicoid,* both arches are equally wide (zero overjet); and distally in the region of the third molar, the upper is narrower than the lower dental arch (negative overjet).

In the sample of early hominid mandibles in South Africa, the only specimen with a helicoidal occlusal plane is SK 45. Closer study under the binocular microscope reveals that the distinctive pockmarking or microgouging of the occlusal enamel of the SK 80/847/846b M³ is seen in the SK 45 M² as well. Moreover, the color and stain of the two bones is almost identical. Because of these three reasons — helicoidal occlusal planes, occlusal enamel microgouging, and stain-ing and color of the bones — I believe that SK 45 and SK 80/847/846b belonged to the same individual. The fact that a helicoidal wear plane and negative M³ overjet is present in SK 45 + SK 80/847/846 but absent in other South African early hominids is regarded as evidence that this individual is a member of the genus *Homo* and not *Australopithecus*.

A unique pattern of molar wear is seen in the SK 15 mandible. The three buccal cusps and the mesiolingual cusp of the M_1 have almost equally sized dentine exposures, a feature which is not seen in any other Swartkrans M_1's. In the M_2 of SK 15, dentine has appeared almost simultaneously on the hypoconid and hypoconulid. In all other Swartkrans M_2's, the exposure on the hypoconid appears before the exposure on the hypoconulid, as judged from the substantial size difference between these dentine exposures.

The teeth of SK 15 + SK 18a + SK 43 are small (Robinson 1953) and seemingly have thin enamel. To judge from the width of the enamel rims, the molar teeth of SK 15 had thinner occlusal enamel than any other Swartkrans molars that have equal-sized dentine exposures. The mesial surfaces of the left M_1 and right M_2 of SK 15 are carious. These are the only two South African early hominid teeth with approximal caries. Clement (1956), who described the lesions, said they were typical of those associated with "the breakdown of the contact point and the subsequent interproximal impaction of food debris." The presence in SK 15, but absence in other Swartkrans hominids, of approximal caries suggests that SK 15 had a relatively rapid rate of molar approximal attrition. Another comparison illustrates the high rate of approximal attrition in SK 15. The M_2's of SK 23, SK 34, and SK 15 are at a similar stage of occlusal wear, but relative to M_2, the M_1 of SK 15 is much more attrited approximally. The seemingly rapid loss of approximal enamel in SK 15 molars is consistent with the observation on occlusal enamel rims that molar enamel is thinner in SK 15 than in the other Swartkrans molars. My observations on the East Rudolf molars (KNM. ER 808) that have been assigned to *Homo* confirm the suspicion that small teeth have thin enamel. Dentally, early *Homo* is distinguished from *Australopithecus* by possession of small teeth with thin enamel.

Their smaller teeth, their apparently thinner enamel, and their lightly built mandibles suggest that early members of *Homo* chewed less vigorously. Unlike *Australopithecus*, who seemingly crushed and ground the food mainly with the teeth, early *Homo* did most of this crushing and grinding probably outside the mouth with tools. In *Australopithecus* the food was prepared intraorally by teeth. In early *Homo* the food was prepared extraorally by tools. Wherever in Africa we find the teeth of early *Homo* we find his tools: at Sterkfontein, at Swartkrans, at Olduvai, at East Rudolf and at Omo.

The first *Homo* was the individual that invented a new method of food preparation by using a tool instead of his teeth to crush and grind the food. To this early hominid we owe our existence.

REFERENCES

ACKERMANN, F.
1963   The helicoid principle in human dental occlusion and articulation. *International Dental Journal* 13:532–557.

ADAMS, S. H., H. A. ZANDER
1964   Functional tooth contacts in lateral and in centric occlusion. *Journal of the American Dental Association* 69:465–473.

AHLGREN, J.
1966   Mechanism of mastication: a quantitative cinematographic and electromyographic study of masticatory movements in children, with special reference to occlusion of the teeth. *Acta Odontologica Scandinavica* 24 (Supplement 44):1–109.

ANDERSON, D. J., D. C. A. PICTON
1957   Tooth contact during chewing. *Journal of Dental Research* 36: 21–26.

ASHLEY MONTAGU, F. M.
1935   The premaxilla in the primates. *Quarterly Review of Biology* 10: 32–59 and 181–200.

BEGG, P. R.
1965   *Begg orthodontic theory and technique.* Philadelphia: Saunders.

BEYRON, H.
1964   Occlusal relations and mastication in Australian aborigines. *Acta Odontologica Scandinavica* 22:597–678.

BRACE, C. L.
1963   Book review of *Evolution und Hominisation*, edited by G. Kurth. *American Journal of Physical Anthropology* 21:87–91.
1967 . Environment, tooth form, and size in the Pleistocene. *Journal of Dental Research* 46:809–816.

BROOM, R., J. T. ROBINSON
1952   *Swartkrans ape-man*, Paranthropus crassidens. Transvaal Museum Memoirs 6.

CAMPBELL, T. D.
1925   *Dentition and palate of the Australian Aboriginal.* Adelaide: Hassel.

CLARKE, R. J., F. C. HOWELL
1972   Affinities of the Swartkrans 847 hominid cranium. *American Journal of Physical Anthropology* 37:319–335.

CLARKE, R. J., F. C. HOWELL, C. K. BRAIN
1970   More evidence of an advanced hominid at Swartkrans. *Nature* 225:1219–1221.

CLEMENT, A. J.
1956 Caries in the South African ape-man: some examples of undoubted pathological authenticity believed to be 800,000 years old. *British Dental Journal* 101:4–7.

COOKE, H. B. S.
1963 "Pleistocene mammal faunas of Africa, with particular reference to Southern Africa," in *African ecology and human evolution.* Edited by F. C. Howell and F. Bourlière, 65–116. Chicago: Aldine.
1967 "The Pleistocene sequence in South Africa and problems in correlation," in *Background to evolution in Africa.* Edited by H. W. Bishop and J. D. Clark, 175–184. Chicago: University of Chicago Press.

GLICKMAN, I., J. H. N. PAMEIJER, F. W. ROEBER, M. A. M. BRION
1969 Functional occlusion as revealed by miniaturized radio transmitters. *Dental Clinics of North America* 13:667–679.

GOODKIND, R. J., J. H. BUTLER, R. C. SCHULTE
1970 Tooth contact relationships as revealed by intraoral telemetry (a preliminary report). *Northwest Dentistry* 49:362–366.

GRAF, H., H. A. ZANDER
1963 Tooth contact patterns in mastication. *Journal of Prosthetic Dentistry* 13:1055–1066.

HASUND, A., G. ULSTEIN
1970 The position of the incisors in relation to the lines NA and NB in different facial types. *American Journal of Orthodontics* 57:1–14.

HOJO, M.
1954 On the pattern of the dental abrasion. *Okajimas Folia anatomica Japonica* 26:11–30.

INGERVALL, B.
1972 Tooth contacts on the functional and non-functional side in children and young adults. *Archives of Oral Biology* 17:191–200.

JOLLY, C. J.
1970 The seed-eaters: a new model of hominid differentiation based on a baboon analogy. *Man* 5:1–26.

KOIVUMAA, K. K.
1961 Cinefluorographic analysis of the masticatory movement. *Suomen Hammaslääkärisveran Toimituksia* 57:306–336. (Quoted in Ingervall 1972.)

MOSES, C. H.
1946 Studies of wear, arrangement and occlusion of the dentition of humans and animals and their relationship to orthodontia, periodontia and prosthodontia. *Dental Items* 68:953–999.

MURPHY, T.
1959 The changing pattern of dentine exposure in human tooth attrition. *American Journal of Physical Anthropology* 17:167–178.

PAMEIJER, J. H. N., I. GLICKMAN, F. W. ROEBER
1969 Intraoral occlusal telemetry. III: Tooth contacts in chewing, swallowing and bruxism. *Journal of Periodontics* 40:253–258.

ROBINSON, J. T.
1953 *Telanthropus* and its phylogenetic significance. *American Journal of Physical Anthropology* 11:445–501.
1954 Prehominid dentition and hominid evolution. *Evolution* 8:324–334.
1956 *The Dentition of the Australopithecinae.* Transvaal Museum Memoirs 9.
1960 The affinities of the new Olduvai australopithecine. *Nature* 186:456–458.
1961 The australopithecines and their bearing on the origin of man and of stone tool-making. *South African Journal of Science* 57:3–13.
1962a "The origin and adaptive radiation of the australopithecines," in *Evolution und Hominisation.* Edited by G. Kurth, 120–140. Stuttgart: Gustav Fischer.
1962b Australopithecines and artefacts at Sterkfontein, I: Sterkfontein stratigraphy and the significance of the Extension site. *South African Archaeological Bulletin* 17:87–107.
1963a Australopithecines, culture and phylogeny. *American Journal of Physical Anthropology* 21:595–605.
1963b "Adaptive radiation of the australopithecines and the origin of man," in *African ecology and human evolution.* Edited by F. C. Howwwell and F. Bourlière, 385–416. Chicago: Aldine.
1967 "Variation and taxonomy of the early hominids," in *Evolutionary biology*, volume one. Edited by Th. Dobzhansky, M. K. Hecht, and W. C. Steere, 69–100. New York: Appleton-Century-Crofts.
1972a *Early hominid posture and locomotion.* Chicago: University of Chicago Press.
1972b The bearing of East Rudolf fossils on early hominid systematics. *Nature* 240:239–240.

SHEPHERD, R. W.
1960 A further report on mandibular movement. *Australian Dental Journal* 5:337–342.

TOBIAS, P. V.
1965 New discoveries in Tanganyika: their bearing on hominid evolution. *Current Anthropology* 6:391–411.
1967 *Olduvai Gorge,* volume two: *The cranium and maxillary dentition of* Australopithecus (Zinjanthropus) boisei. London: Cambridge University Press.

WEIDENREICH, F.
1937 The dentition of *Sinanthropus:* a comparative odontography of the hominids. *Paleontologia Sinica* 10:1–180.

WEINBERG, L. A.
1961 The prevalence of tooth contact in eccentric movements of the jaw: its clinical implications. *Journal of the American Dental Association* 62:402–406.

WELLS, L. H.
1969 Faunal subdivisions of the Quaternary in Southern Africa. *South African Archaeological Bulletin* 24:93–95.

WOLPOFF, M. H.
    1971   Is the new composite cranium from Swartkrans a small robust
            australopithecine? *Nature* 230:398–401.
WOOD JONES, F.
    1929   *Man's place amongst the mammals.* London: Edward Arnold.
YURSTAS, A. A., W. H. EMERSON
    1954   A study of tooth contact during mastication with artificial den-
            tures. *Journal of Prosthetic Dentistry* 4:164–174.

An Interpretation of the Bone Assemblage from the Kromdraai Australopithecine Site, South Africa

C. K. BRAIN

INTRODUCTION

The significance of Kromdraai lies in the fact that the first robust australopithecine, which was described by Broom (1938) as *Paranthropus robustus*, came from here in 1938. Further australopithecine remains were recovered from the site in 1941, but no associated faunal remains were forthcoming except for three cercopithecoid specimens. These were originally described as *Parapapio coronatus* (Broom and Robinson 1950) but are now assigned to *Papio angusticeps* and *Cercopithecoides williamsi* (Freedman and Brain 1972).

In 1941 Broom conducted an excavation in an adjacent cave breccia site close to the original exposure on the Kromdraai hilltop. This site, which produced abundant faunal remains but no hominids, came to be known as the Kromdraai Faunal Site or KA. The australopithecine site was later designated KB.

The Kromdraai deposits consist of the calcified fillings of two parallel cave galleries that trend approximately east-west and are exposed at almost exactly the same elevation (Brain 1958). In the past it has been customary to associate the fauna from KA with the hominids from KB and to assume contemporaneity. It now appears that such an assumption is unfounded.

In an attempt to obtain further information about the KB deposit,

Particular thanks are due to the Wenner-Gren Foundation for Anthropological Research in New York for support, without which, this and other studies on australopithecine bone accumulations could not have been made. I would also like to thank Dr. L. Freedman and Dr. Q. B. Hendey for their work on the Kromdraai fauna.

an excavation was undertaken by the writer during 1955 and 1956 in decalcified breccia along the northern wall of the exposure. The original roof of the KB cave has been removed by erosion and the dolomite wall of the cave is preserved in its original form only along the southern side of the deposit. On the northern side it has largely disappeared through solution, and the breccia, which was in contact with it, has been severely decalcified.

The remaining part of the cave may be reconstructed as an elongated solution gallery, which appears to have had its opening at the eastern end. Stratification in the breccia filling is inclined downwards toward the west. At the eastern end, the lower part of the deposit consists of a coarse mosaic of chert fragments set in calcium carbonate, while the upper levels there are of a finer grain and represent a calcified dolomite soil. Slightly further west, the whole thickness of the deposit seems to have been a fine-grained reddish brown breccia. Occasional stalactites embedded in the upper levels suggest that these were in close proximity to the original dolomite roof.

The 1955–1956 excavation extended to a depth of sixteen feet (4.88 meters) and exposed the solid breccia still clinging to the southern cave wall. Bedrock was not reached and the entire profile apparently consisted of breccia, which had been decalcified *in situ*. Abundant microfaunal remains derived from the breccia were present throughout; bone fragments from larger animals were also present. A total of almost 5,000 fragments (excluding microfaunal elements) came from the excavation and for purposes of the analysis have been kept in three groups:

Layer 1: surface–six feet (1.83 meters).
Layer 2: six–twelve feet (1.83–3.66 meters).
Layer 3: twelve–sixteen feet (3.66–4.88 meters).

When dealing with a decalcified breccia deposit, the possibility of later additions to the fossil assemblage cannot be excluded. However in this case, australopithecine remains were found in the upper levels, suggesting that the whole profile was probably of australopithecine age.

An overall analysis of the KB bone accumulation is presented in this paper. The identifiable cercopithecoid remains have recently been described (Freedman and Brain 1972) as have the carnivores (Hendey 1973). Bovid remains are being studied by E. S. Vrba, while the microfauna is receiving attention from D. H. S. Davis and T. N. Pocock.

When these results are published it will be possible to draw more complete conclusions about the ecological conditions at the time of the accumulation.

THE BONE ACCUMULATION

The present discussion excludes bones from animals classed as microfauna. These, which come largely from rodents, insectivores, and birds, represent the prey of owls which roosted in the cave. The sample under review consists of every other bone fragment recovered during the excavation. Layer 1 yielded 2,897 pieces; 972 came from Layer 2 and 1,116 from Layer 3, making a total of 4,985 specimens. Fragmentation was extreme; 70 percent of the total have a maximum length between one and three centimeters (see below).

The bone fragments were sieved from the decalcified breccia and then brushed in running water to clean them. The collection from each layer was then sorted into (1) fragments from animals that could be identified specifically or recognized with reasonable certainty; (2) miscellaneous fragments of bovid and nonbovid origin; or (3) bone flakes. These are defined elsewhere (Brain 1974) but consist of fragments from the shafts of long bones. They lack articular ends and, by definition, consist of less than half the cylindrical diameter of the shaft.

HOMINID REMAINS

The hominid remains from Kromdraai fall into two groups: those recovered between 1938 and 1941 by Broom and those from the excavation of 1955–1956. They all come from the upper part of the deposit and may be listed as follows:
1. 1938–1941 remains.

Paranthropus robustus

Type skull, TM 1517. Found June 8, 1938.
These remains consist of the left side of the braincase and face, the right mandibular corpus, eight isolated teeth or tooth fragments as well as the following postcranial bones closely associated in the breccia: distal end of right humerus, proximal end of right ulna, right astragalus, two metacarpal fragments, and seven phalanges (or fragments thereof).

TM 1602 Found 1938
Right maxillary fragment with roots of M^1–M^3 and part of the palate.
TM 1536 Found 1941
Mandibular fragment with erupting right I_1, right di_2–M_1; left dc and dm_1.
2.   1955–1956 remains.
TM 1600
Two mandibular fragments associated with the following isolated teeth: left P_3, M_2, and M_3
TM 1601
Isolated teeth: left dm_1, C, P_3, P_4, M^1
TM 1604
Isolated left dm_2
TM 1605
Iliac fragment with part of the acetabulum

On the basis of a detailed study, Mann (1975) concluded that the hominid remains come, in all probability, from six individuals. His estimated ages of the individuals are given in Table 1.

Summarizing the results, Mann concluded that two individuals fall into the one–five year age class, two into six–ten year class and two into the sixteen–twenty year class, the latter being regarded as mature.

CERCOPITHECOID REMAINS

Identifiable cercopithecoid remains have recently been studied by Freedman and Brain (1972). On the basis of cranial parts, three species were recognized (*Papio robinsoni*, *P. angusticeps*, and *Cercopithecoides williamsi*); the postcranial bones were not separated taxonomically.

Papio robinsoni

Material allocated to this species consists of four maxillary and mandibular pieces, together with eighty-five isolated teeth. The occurrence of these fragments in the three layers is listed in Table 2.

They come from a minimum of eighteen individuals, eleven of which were juveniles. The classification of individuals into age classes is given in Table 5.

A total of eleven individuals come from Layer 1, four from Layer 2, and three from Layer 3.

Papio angusticeps

Material allocated to this species consists of five mandibular fragments, one maxillary piece with two associated teeth, and eighteen isolated teeth. Included here are two mandibular specimens (previously numbered KA 196 and KA 197), which were discovered on the surface at the time of Broom's original investigations and were classified then as *Parapapio coronatus*. Occurrence of the specimens in each layer is listed in Table 3.

The specimens come from a minimum of fourteen individuals, three of which were juvenile. The classification of individuals into age classes is given in Table 6. They come from Layer 1 (one individual), Layer 2 (two individuals), and Layer 3 (four individuals).

Cercopithecoides williamsi

Referred material consists of a calvaria, mandibular fragment, and eleven isolated teeth, derived from a minimum of five individuals. The calvaria, previously numbered KA 195, was described as *Parapapio coronatus* by Broom and Robinson (1950). Table 4 lists the occurrence of the specimens in each layer.

A separation of the individuals into age classes is made in Table 7. They come from Layer 1 (two individuals) and Layer 3 (three individuals).

Cercopithecoid, sp. indet.

A total of 367 bone fragments from the three layers were clearly of cercopithecoid origin but could not be specifically identified. Largely of postcranial origin, the fragments are listed under skeletal parts in Table 8.

BOVID REMAINS

As yet, no specific identifications of bovid fossils from Kromdraai B have been published although the specimens are being studied by E. S. Vrba of the Transvaal Museum. The unidentified bovid remains are divided into four size classes according to a system published elsewhere (Brain 1974). The size classes are based on live weights of the antelope, as follows:

Table 1.   Estimated ages of the hominid remains

Specimen number	Age in years based on Mandibular teeth	Maxillary teeth
TM 1601	2 ± 1	2½ ± ½
TM 1536	2½ ± ½	
TM 1604	6 ± 1	
TM 1517	19 ± 1	20 ± 1
TM 1600	19 ± 1	

Table 2.   *Papio robinsoni*

	Layer 1	2	3	Total
Cranial and maxillary fragments	2	0	0	2
Mandibular fragments	2	0	0	2
Isolated deciduous teeth	47	2	4	53
Isolated permanent teeth	24	5	3	32
	75	7	7	89

Table 3.   *Papio angusticeps*

	Layer 1	2	3	Total
Cranial and maxillary fragments	0	0	1	1
Mandibular fragments	5	0	0	5
Isolated deciduous teeth	3	1	1	5
Isolated permanent teeth	9	1	5	15
	17	2	7	26

Table 4.   *Cercopithecoides williamsi*

	Layer 1	2	3	Total
Cranial and maxillary fragments	1	0	0	1
Mandibular fragments	0	0	1	1
Isolated deciduous teeth	0	0	0	0
Isolated permanent teeth	6	0	5	11
	7	0	6	13

Table 5.   *Papio robinsoni*

Age class	Layer 1	2	3	Total
Juvenile	7	2	2	11
Immature adult	0	0	0	0
Young adult	1	1	0	2
Adult	2	1	1	4
Old adult	1	0	0	1
	11	4	3	18

Table 6. *Papio angusticeps*

Age class	Layer	1	2	3	Total
Juvenile		1	1	1	3
Immature adult		1	0	0	1
Young adult		2	0	2	4
Adult		4	0	1	5
Old adult		1	0	0	1
		9	1	4	14

Table 7. *Cercopithecoides williamsi*

Age class	Layer	1	2	3	Total
Juvenile		1	0	1	2
Immature adult		0	0	0	0
Young adult		1	0	1	2
Adult		0	0	0	0
Old adult		0	0	1	1
		2	0	3	5

Table 8. *Cercopithecoid, sp. indet.*

Fragments of:	Layer	1	2	3	Total
Skull		41	0	14	55
Tooth		30	12	5	47
Vertebrae:					
Cervical		0	7	0	7
Thoracic		2	0	1	3
Lumbar		1	2	1	4
Sacral		0	0	0	0
Caudal		33	2	6	41
Rib		52	0	0	52
Scapula		1	0	1	2
Pelvis		2	3	1	6
Humerus		2	0	2	4
Radius		8	2	1	11
Ulna		4	0	2	6
Femur		9	3	3	15
Tibia		4	0	0	4
Metapodial		10	5	3	18
Calcaneum		5	2	2	9
Astragalus		2	0	1	3
Phalanx		50	11	6	67
Miscellaneous		0	0	4	4
Limb bone shaft		9	0	0	9
		265	49	53	367

Antelope   I: up to 50 pounds or 23 kilograms.
Antelope II: 50–300 pounds; 23–136 kilograms.
Antelope III: 300–600 pounds; 136–272 kilograms.
Antelope IV: more than 600 pounds or 272 kilograms.

In terms of living antelope, the size classes would be roughly delimited as follows:
Antelope   I: up to the size of a female grey duiker
Antelope II: grey duiker size to that of hartebeest
Antelope III: hartebeest size to that of sable
Antelope IV: larger than sable

A total of 222 bone fragments of bovid origin, which could be placed in size classes, are listed in Table 9. The fragments come from an estimated minimum of twenty-four individual antelope, although the extreme fragmentation of the bones suggests that a far greater number of individuals might well have been involved.

In addition, 556 bone fragments were found to be of probable bovid origin, although they could not be placed in antelope size classes. The distribution of these fragments in the layers was as follows: Layer 1 — 379; Layer 2 — 145; Layer 3: — 32.

CARNIVORE REMAINS

Canis sp. indet., Jackal
Layer 1: one individual, based on a premaxillary fragment.
Layer 2: one individual, based on two isolated teeth, a metapodial fragment, and phalanx.
Layer 3: two individuals, based on a maxillary fragment and three isolated teeth.
Viverra sp. indet., Civet
Layer 3: one individual, based on the distal end of a humerus.
Herpestes sp. indet., Mongoose
Layer 1: one individual, based on an isolated tooth.
Layer 2: one individual, based on a mandibular fragment.
Hyaena cf. brunnea, Brown Hyaena
Layer 1: one individual, based on an isolated tooth.
Layer 2: one individual, based on a metapodial fragment.
Layer 3: one individual, based on a phalanx.
Proteles sp. indet., Aardwolf
Layer 2: one individual, based on a mandibular fragment.

Table 9. Bovid remains according to size classes

Fragment of:	Layer 1			Layer 2			Layer 3				Totals
	Antelope I	Antelope II	Antelope III	Antelope I	Antelope II	Antelope III	Antelope I	Antelope II	Antelope III	Antelope IV	
Horn core	1	12	1	1				4	6		25
Cranium			1								1
Mandible		3	1								4
Tooth	6	12	2	2	4	14	1	1	3		45
Vertebrae:											
Cervical		2				1					3
Thoracic	1	6	1			2		1			11
Lumbar	1	1						1			3
Sacral											
Caudal									2		2
Rib		10	9			1		1	1		22
Scapula					1						1
Pelvis											
Humerus	1	2		1			1				5
Radius and ulna			2			2	2		3		9
Femur			1		1						2
Tibia					1	1	2	1			5
Carpal and tarsal		2	2		1		1			1	7
Calcaneus	1	4			1	1	1	1			9
Astragalus	1					2	1				4
Metapodial		2			1	2	3	2		1	11
Phalanx	2	11	4	1	9	4	7	7	4		49
Other		2	1					1			4
	14	69	25	5	19	30	23	22	13	2	222
Individual animals (estimated minimum numbers)	2	6	2	1	2	3	2	3	2	1	24

? *Megantereon sp. indet.*, Sabre-tooth Cat
Layer 2: one individual based on four metapodial fragments, three phalanges, an astragalus, and calcaneus.

? *Dinofelis sp. indet.*, False Sabre-tooth Cat
Layer 3: one individual based on a metapodial fragment.

Panthera pardus, Leopard
Layer 1: one individual based on a distal radius and proximal ulna fragment.
Layer 3: one individual based on an astragalus and two phalanges.

Unidentified remains

Forty-two fragments from Layers 1 and 2 were recovered. Although from carnivores, they could not be placed taxonomically.
Available particulars are listed in Table 10.

Table 10.   Carnivore indet. fragments

Fragment of	Layer 1	Layer 2	Layer 3	Total
Tooth	10	2	0	12
Skull	4	0	0	4
Pelvis	0	1	0	1
Limb bone	0	1	0	1
Metapodial	9	0	0	9
Phalanx	15	0	0	15
Total	38	4	0	42

OTHER MAMMALS

cf. *Lepus sp.*, Hare
Layer 1: one individual based on an isolated tooth, atlas vertebra, two humerus fragments, and a metapodial.
Layer 3: one individual based on a mandibular fragment.
Procavia sp., Hyrax
Layer 1: one individual based on distal end of humerus.
cf. *Potamochoerus sp.*, Bushpig
Layer 3: one individual based on an isolated tooth.
Mammalian coprolites
Layer 1: three of jackal size; one of mongoose size.
Indeterminate nonbovid bone fragments
Layer 1: 268 miscellaneous unidentified fragments, apparently not of bovid origin were recovered.
Layer 2: 58 such fragments were found.
Layer 3: 171 such fragments were found.

BIRD REMAINS

Most of the bird remains were included with the microfaunal elements being studied by Davis and Pocock. A report on the birds has appeared in print (Pocock 1970) with identifications based largely on postcranial bones. The following were identified:
Tyto (cf. Barn Owl) — one individual.

Francolinus (Francolin) — two individuals.
Coturnix (Quail) — eight individuals.
Turnix (Button quail) — eleven individuals.
Crex (Crake) — one individual.
Scolopacidae (Waders) — two species, one individual of each.
Agapornis (Lovebird) — fourteen individuals.
Agapornis (Lovebird) — larger species, one individual.
Sturnidae (Starlings) — twelve individuals.
Hirundinidae (Swallows) — large species, three individuals; medium
   species, four individuals; small species, two individuals.
cf. *Anthus* (Pipit) — fifteen individuals.
cf. *Estrilda* (Waxbill) — eight individuals.
cf. *Cisticola* (Warbler) — three individuals.
cf. ? *Passer* (Sparrow or Bishop) — two individuals.
cf. ? *Textor* (Masked Weaver) — one individual.
Indeterminate passerines — twenty individuals.

In Pocock's list the collection of avian remains was treated as a
unit without reference to the layers from which they came. In addition
to this material, a single piece of ostrich eggshell was recovered from
Layer 1, and two claws of a large raptor came from Layer 2.

REPTILE REMAINS

cf. *Testudo sp.*, Tortoise
Layer 1: two individuals, based on four limb bones, one carapace
         fragment, one plastron fragment.
Layer 3: one individual, based on a coracoid fragment.
cf. *Cordylus giganteus*, Giant girdled lizard
Layer 1: one individual, based on six-pointed dermal plates, probably
         from the tail base and two caudal vertebrae.
cf. *Crocodylus niloticus*, Crocodile
Layer 3: one isolated tooth.

FRAGMENTATION AND SIZE DISTRIBUTION OF THE BONES

Perhaps the most striking feature of the bone accumulation is the
extreme fragmentation of the individual pieces. The specimens are
generally evenly stained with manganese dioxide indicating that subsequent artificial breakage, such as during the excavation, has only

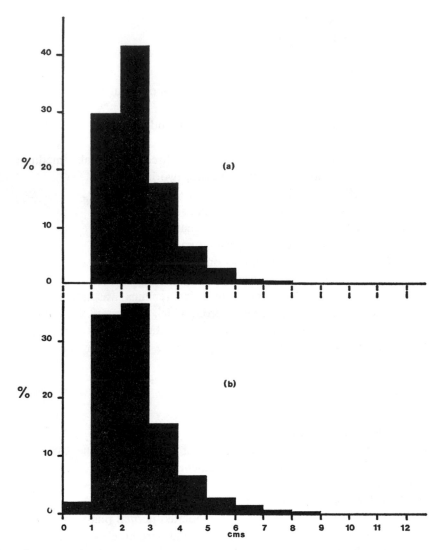

Figure 1. (a) Histogram showing the lengths of bone flakes from the Kromdraai australopithecine site; the analysis is based on 2,887 pieces. (b) A similar analysis for all 4,985 fragments of bone from the deposit

occurred in very few cases.

The maximum length of every fragment recovered was recorded, and these, for the bone flakes, are listed in Table 11. Lengths for all fragments are given in Table 12. Results are plotted in Figure 1 (a) and (b). It is immediately apparent that the majority of pieces have lengths of between one and three centimeters.

Table 11. Bone flakes

Bone flake length in cm	Layer 1 Number	Layer 1 Percent	Layer 2 Number	Layer 2 Percent	Layer 3 Number	Layer 3 Percent	Total Number	Total Percent
0–1	3	0.2	3	0.5	9	1.2	15	0.5
1–2	524	34.7	131	20.9	198	26.5	853	29.6
2–3	652	43.1	268	42.7	278	37.2	1,198	41.5
3–4	205	13.6	141	22.5	157	21.0	503	17.5
4–5	72	4.8	59	9.4	56	7.4	187	6.5
5–6	35	2.4	15	2.4	31	4.1	81	2.8
6–7	9	0.6	7	1.1	11	1.5	27	0.9
7–8	8	0.5	3	0.5	4	0.6	15	0.5
8–9	1	0	0	0	1	0.1	2	
9–10	0	0	0	0	2	0.3	2	
10–11	2	0.1	0	0	0	0	2	0.2
11–12	1	0	0	0	1	0.1	2	
	1,512	100.0	627	100.0	748	100.0	2,887	100.0

Table 12. All bone pieces

Bone frag. length in cm	Layer 1 Number	Layer 1 Percent	Layer 2 Number	Layer 2 Percent	Layer 3 Number	Layer 3 Percent	Total Number	Total Percent
0–1	66	2.3	11	1.1	11	1.0	88	1.8
1–2	1,212	41.8	215	22.1	287	25.7	1,714	34.4
2–3	1,000	34.5	401	41.3	408	36.6	1,809	36.3
3–4	351	12.1	197	20.3	213	19.1	761	15.3
4–5	132	4.6	96	9.9	93	8.3	321	6.4
5–6	69	2.4	27	2.8	51	4.5	147	2.9
6–7	30	1.1	16	1.6	23	2.1	69	1.4
7–8	18	0.7	4	0.4	13	1.2	35	0.7
8–9	6	0.2	3	0.3	5	0.4	14	0.3
9–10	3	0.1	0	0	5	0.4	8	0.1
10–11	4	0.1	2	0.2	3	0.3	9	0.2
11–12	3	0.1	0	0	2	0.2	5	
12–13	1	0	0	0	2	0.2	3	
13–14	0	0	0	0	0	0	0	
14–15	1	0	0	0	0	0	1	0.2
15–16	0	0	0	0	0	0	0	
16–17	0	0	0	0	0	0	0	
17–18	1	0	0	0	0	0	1	
	2,897	100.0	972	100.0	1,116	100.0	4,985	100.0

Table 13. Identified animals

Taxon	Common name	Number of individuals in each layer			Total individuals
		1	2	3	
Paranthropus robustus	Robust australopithecine	6 (4 juveniles, 2 adults)	0	0	6
Papio Robinsoni	Baboon	11 (7 juveniles, 4 adults)	4 (2 juveniles, 2 adults)	3 (2 juveniles, 1 adult)	18
Papio angusticeps	Baboon (smaller species)	9 (1 juvenile, 8 adults)	1 (juvenile)	4 (1 juvenile, 3 adults)	14
Cercopithecoides williamsi	Colobid monkey	2 (1 juvenile)	0	3 (1 juvenile)	5
	Antelope classI Small antelope	2	1	2	5
	Antelope class II Medium antelope	6	2	3	11
	Antelope class III Large antelope	2	3	2	7
	Antelope class IV Very large antelope	0	0	1	1
Canis sp. indet.	Jackal	1	1	2	4
Viverra sp. indet.	Civet	0	0	1	1
Herpestes sp. indet.	Mongoose	1	1	0	2
Hyaena cf. brunnea	Brown hyaena	1	1	1	3
Proteles sp. indet.	Aardwolf	0	1	0	1
?Megantereon sp. indet.	Sabre-tooth cat	0	1	0	1
?Dinofelis sp. indet.	False sabre-tooth cat	0	0	1	1
Panthera pardus	Leopard	1	0	1	2
cf. Lepus sp. indet.	Hare	1	0	1	2
Procavia sp. indet.	Hyrax	1	0	0	1
cf. Potamochoerus sp. indet.	Bushpig	0	0	1	1
cf. Testudo sp. indet.	Tortoise	2	0	1	3
cf. Cordylus giganteus	Giant girdled lizard	1	0	0	1
cf. Crocodylus niloticus	Crocodile	0	0	1	1
22	22	47	16	28	91

THE FAUNAL ASSEMBLAGE AS A WHOLE

Table 13 lists the animals which have been specifically or tentatively identified. Ninety-one individuals, belonging to twenty-two taxa are involved.

It is of interest that the six australopithecine individuals (four of which are juveniles) are restricted to the upper level of the deposit. During the accumulation period of the lower two-thirds of the cave deposit, australopithecines were either not present in the area, or, for some reason, their remains failed to find their way into the bone accumulation.

The baboon *Papio robinsoni* is represented by at least eighteen individuals, eleven of which were juvenile. This species is very similar in most respects to the extant *P. ursinus* and may well be a direct ancestor of it. Slightly smaller was *P. angusticeps*, which is represented by fourteen individuals, of which only three were juveniles. Why there should be fewer juveniles represented in this species than in *P. robinsoni* is not known. The colobid monkey *Cercopithecoides williamsi* is less frequent in its appearance (five individuals).

As reflected in Table 13, there is a consistent scattering of antelope remains throughout the deposit. The greatest number of individuals come from the medium size range (live-weight, 50–300 pounds) although in Layer 3 there is at least one individual of eland size.

There is an interesting variety of carnivores represented by the remains: jackal, civet, mongoose, brown hyaena, aardwolf (the first occurrence in a pre-Holocene context), sabre-tooth, false sabre-tooth, and leopard. It is not impossible that the cave was used as a carnivore lair from time to time; the presence of carnivore coprolites tends to support this.

Remains of other mammals are from hare, hyrax, and bushpig. Among reptiles, small species are included among the microfauna, while larger ones are represented by tortoise, girdled lizard, and crocodile.

THE CAVE AND ITS ENVIRONMENT

From what remains of the cave, it is clear that it took the form of an elongated solution gallery, at least 100 feet (thirty meters) long and perhaps twenty feet (six meters) wide, running downward and westward from the original entrance. Soil, rock, and debris formed a talus slope within the gallery with stratification sloping gently away from the entrance. Indications are that the gallery filled right to the roof and that subsequent erosion removed both the roof and the original entrance area. The filling was calcified into a solid breccia, but this suffered subsequent decalcification along the north wall. The decalcification of the breccia and solution of the cave wall in this area was probably brought about as a result of rainwater standing in a shallow depression on the hilltop.

The abundant presence of microfauna derived from owl pellets throughout the deposit indicates that the original cave form was such that it was favored by owls for purposes of day-roosting. At present, two species of owl contribute to microfaunal accumulations in caves in the Transvaal: the Barn Owl, *Tyto alba,* and the Spotted Eagle Owl, *Bubo africanus.* Both favor caves with fairly large entrances leading into a twilight zone where ledges along the walls serve as suitable perches for roosting during the day. The presence of occasional coprolites also suggests that the site cave was used by carnivores. Modern caves of this kind are frequently used by jackals, hyaenas, and leopards, particularly when they are rearing young.

The extreme fragmentation of the bones suggests that these might well represent food remains of primitive men. Bone food remains of Stone Age peoples from other cave sites in Southern Africa show a very similar pattern of fragmentation (e.g. Brain 1969). The pattern seems to be extremely consistent, both over a wide geographic area as well as through time (Brain 1974). The bones were presumably broken with hammerstones for the extraction of marrow and the fragments were then discarded.

Evidence of stone culture is meager at the Kromdraai australopithecine site. As previously reported (Brain 1958), the only indications of deliberate use of stone were one unquestionable artifact in chert, three less convincing flakes, and one broken quartzite pebble. It is not impossible that artifacts were concentrated closer to the entrance in a part of the deposit that has since been lost by erosion. It is also conceivable that the bones were broken with hammerstones which had not been artificially fashioned.

On the basis of the faunal remains, a picture has started to emerge of the kind of habitat in which the animals could have lived. The picture is likely to be further clarified when information becomes available on the microfaunal and antelope species.

On the subject of the birds which formed part of the KB microfauna, Pocock (1970: 6) has concluded:

Quail, button quail, pipits and perhaps also cisticolas were quite common, confirming the grassland character of the environment. Flocks of starlings occurred being preyed upon as they roosted in streamside or marsh vegetation. Swallows may have fallen victim in the same way especially if they were non-breeding migrants, or they may have built their mud nests, perhaps colonially, in the very cave frequented by the owl. Swifts doubtless also used the cave, nesting in the crevices, or perhaps commandeering some of the swallow nests. Non-breeding migrants probably did occur, crakes, sandpipers and ruffs from the steppes and tundra of a glaciated Europe. Thus far this is not at all different from the present, but there is an interesting difference in the occurrence of small members of the parrot family, one species evidently rather common .... A further difference, this time a negative rather than a positive inference, is the comparative rarity if not absence of seed-eating passerines such as sparrows, weavers, bishops, queleas, widows, canaries and waxbills ... Hence we may conclude that in the Pleistocene grassland environment of Kromdraai the seed-eating ecological niches were largely occupied by small psittacines, rather than the euplectine weavers of the present. This accords well with the idea that the weavers [Ploceidae] are a modern group originating perhaps in Asia which invaded Africa and underwent an extensive adaptive radiation there in comparatively recent times.

Most of the animals represented by the larger bone fragments are not clear indicators of the habitat in which they lived. Some, such as the leopard and brown hyaena, have in fact a very wide environmental tolerance. Nevertheless others are more helpful. The giant girdled lizard, for instance, is restricted today to certain open grassland areas of the highveld, while the bushpig definitely requires some dense cover. The colobid monkey *Cercopithecoides* presumably required trees, while the crocodile indicates the presence of perennial water.

The present evidence of the fauna indicates that the habitat during the accumulation of the KB deposit was an open grassland, which included dense vegetation and standing water along the course of what today is the Blaauwbank River.

Studies on the cercopithecoids (Freedman and Brain 1972) and carnivores (Hendey 1973) suggest that contemporaneity between the Kromdraai Faunal and Australopithecine Sites was unlikely. We are forced to conclude that although the KA and KB galleries were adjacent and at the same level, they opened to the surface at different times.

In conclusion, the question remains as to how the australopithecine bones found their way into the Kromdraai deposit. It appears that a good deal of the skeleton of the type specimen of *Paranthropus robustus*, TM 1517, may have been present on the cave floor at the time of fossilization. Some of the skull was lost by weathering of the enclosing breccia; this may have applied to other skeletal elements as well. When he described the endocranial cast of this specimen, Schepers (1946) concluded that the presence of a "large flint-like rock" in the calcified cast could be taken as evidence of deliberate interpersonal violence. He suggested that the australopithecine had died as a result of the rock penetrating its left parietal bone after being hurled by an adversary. In a subsequent review of the evidence for interpersonal violence among South African australopithecines, the present writer has questioned this evidence (Brain 1972). Because only the left side of the cranium has survived in the breccia, it is impossible to decide how complete it was at the time of fossilization. The stone, almost certainly a piece of chert, such as is common in the breccia, could easily have entered the brain-case in a manner less dramatic than that suggested by Schepers.

Although the evidence for deliberate violence on TM 1517 may not be convincing, the possibility remains that this individual was killed by hominid hunters. Other possibilities are that it died naturally in the vicinity of the cave or was dragged there by one of the many carnivores known to have existed at the time.

Remains of the other australopithecine individuals are far more fragmentary and are largely restricted to isolated teeth or skull fragments. The damage which they have suffered is indistinguishable from that shown by remains of other animals represented.

There are two cave sites in the Transvaal which have yielded remains of robust australopithecines: Kromdraai B and Swartkrans. It has been suggested (Brain 1970) that those at Swartkrans were largely food remains of leopards, which used the site as a lair and feeding place. The overall nature of the Swartkrans bone accumulation is very different from that of the KB collection, where fragmentation of the bones has been far more intense.

It is tentatively suggested that the KB bone fragments represent food remains of hominid hunters. Nevertheless the variety of carnivores represented in the collection suggests that the site may have been used by some of these animals.

REFERENCES

BRAIN, C. K.
  1958   *The Transvaal ape-man-bearing cave deposits.* Transvaal Museum Memoir 11.
  1969   Faunal remains from the Bushman rock shelter, Eastern Transvaal. *South African Archaeological Bulletin* 24:52–55.
  1970   New finds at the Swartkrans australopithecine site. *Nature* 225 (5238):1112–1119.

1972 An attempt to reconstruct the behaviour of australopithecines: the evidence for interpersonal violence. *Zoologica Africana* 7(1):379–401.

1974 Some suggested procedures in the analysis of bone accumulations from Southern African Quaternary sites. *Annals of the Transvaal Museum* 29(1):1–8.

BROOM, R.
1938 The Pleistocene anthropoid apes of South Africa. *Nature* (3591): 377–379.

BROOM, R., J. T. ROBINSON
1950 A new sub-fossil baboon from Kromdraai, Transvaal. *Annals of the Transvaal Museum* 22:242–245.

FREEDMAN, L., C. K. BRAIN
1972 Fossil cercopithecoid remains from the Kromdraai australopithecine site (Mammalia: Primates). *Annals of the Transvaal Museum* 28:1–16.

HENDEY, Q. B.
1973 Carnivore remains from the Kromdraai australopithecine site (Mammalia: Carnivora). *Annals of the Transvaal Museum* 28: 99–112.

MANN, A. E.
1975 Paleodemographic aspects of the South African australopithecines. *University of Pennsylvania Publications in Anthropology*, number one, Philadelphia.

POCOCK, T. N.
1970 Pleistocene bird fossils from Kromdraai and Sterkfontein. *Ostrich* (Supplement) 8:1–6.

SCHEPERS, G. W. H.
1946 "The endocranial casts of the South African ape-men," in *The South African fossil ape-men, the Australopithecinae*. Transvaal Museum Memoir 2(2):167–272.

Sexual Dimorphism in the Australopithecines

MILFORD H. WOLPOFF

INTRODUCTION

The question of sexual dimorphism is of considerable potential importance in any attempt to reconstruct the ecology, behavior, or phylogeny
of the Lower Pleistocene hominids. Three different approaches have been
used in discussions of possible sexual dimorphism within this sample.
First, sexes have been ascribed individually to many of the specimens in
initial descriptions (Broom and Robinson 1952; Broom, Robinson, and
Schepers 1950; Broom and Schepers 1946; Dart 1949a, 1949b, 1962;
Leakey 1972). Second, morphological variation in specific features has
been used to sex specimens and establish the extent of dimorphism. For
instance, von Koenigswald (1954) assumed that crania with sagittal crests
were male. Robinson considered the extent of sexual dimorphism in the
South African gracile and robust samples based on tooth size variation,
and suggested that dimorphism was slightly greater in the graciles (1956).
Third, there is a hypothesis that the South African gracile australopithecines are females and the robusts males. I mention this with some reluc-

I am deeply indebted to C. K. Brain and E. Voigt of the Transvaal Museum;
P. V. Tobias and A. Hughes of the Department of Anatomy, University of the
Witwatersrand; and M. D. M. Leakey, M. D. Leakey, and R. E. F. Leakey of the
National Museums of Kenya, Centre for Prehistory and Palaeontology, for permission to examine the fossil hominid material in their possession, and for the
help and encouragement given to me during my visit. I thank Dr. C. O. Lovejoy
and the laboratory personnel at Kent State University for their extensive preparation and help in sexing the Libben sample used. I am grateful to the Cleveland
Museum of Natural Science for use of the Hamann-Todd collection. Finally, I
thank T. White for his help in preparing this manuscript. This research was supported by NSF Grant GS-33035.

tance, for although the hypothesis is a part of the oral tradition of physical anthropology (see, for instance, the *Nature* editorial in volume 228: 315), it is without source or author. In "disproving" the hypothesis, Holloway (1970) quotes Brace (1969) as its source, as does Pilbeam (1972) in a paper expending considerable effort in its refutation. However, an examination of both Brace publications quoted (Brace 1969; Brace, Nelson, and Korn 1971) reveals only the statements that australopithecines might be expected to have more sexual dimorphism than *Homo*, and that as a result, the taxonomic designations of certain specimens may be based on variation due to sexual dimorphism rather than that due to genetic isolation and differing adaptive patterns. I intend to return to the original approach of sexing individual specimens and then on this basis to attempt to quantify the nature and extent of sexual dimorphism in this hominid sample.

All Lower Pleistocene hominids will be discussed in this work. They will be treated separately in four groups and together as a single temporal sample. The four groups are South African graciles, South African robusts, East African *"Homo,"* and East African robusts. These correspond to commonly recognized taxa. However, their treatment as separate sets is in no way meant to prejudice the taxonomic level of distinction (e.g. subspecific, specific, generic, etc.), nor is it meant to imply that distinctions between them are at the same level. Designations of particular specimens follow common literature usage. The combined temporal sample will be referred to as "australopithecine." The name is used as a convenient title for the sample and is not meant to imply the taxonomic unity of the sample at any particular level.

DETERMINING SEX

Once sex has been established, sexual dimorphism can be observed and quantified in many characteristics of both cranial and postcranial skeletons. Conversely, if sex is unknown, these characteristics may be useful in determining it. In *Homo,* the most accurate sexing criteria are in the pelvis (Krogman 1962). Of these, features of the os pubis are reported to yield unusual accuracy (Phenice 1969). My observations on material of known sex from the Hamann-Todd collection confirm this accuracy. Unfortunately, only one australopithecine skeleton may be sexed from the os pubis. In STS 14r, the ventral arc is very well defined, the neck of the pubic symphysis is narrow, the subpubic angle is broad, and the inferior surface of the ramus is concave. In all features STS 14r is female.

No cranial material is associated with the postcranial skeleton.

Because dental remains of the australopithecines outnumber all other remains combined, it is useful to attempt determination of sex from the dentition alone. In most modern human studies, the canine shows the greatest sexual dimorphism (Gonda 1959). This relation is generally true in the nonhuman primates, although in some taxa the lower first premolar is more dimorphic than the canine. Several studies indicate that the dimorphism is greater in the breadth dimension than it is in length (Mijsberg 1931; Garn, Lewis, and Kerewsky 1964, 1966a, 1966b). This may be the result of greater environmental influence on the population distribution of length because of interstitial wear (Wolpoff 1971b). Other evidence, based on brother-sister pairs, demonstrates genetic control for tooth size sexual dimorphism (Garn et al. 1967). Variation indicates that there is a canine field of sexual dimorphism and some level of relationship between dimorphism in tooth size and body size (Garn, Lewis, and Kerewsky 1966b; Garn et al. 1967). Taken together, these studies suggest that the greatest differences in the dentition due to sexual dimorphism can be expected in the labial-lingual diameter (breadth) of the canine, that these differences have a significant amount of genetic control (heritability), and that they bear some relation to sexual dimorphism in other characteristics of the body.

Not all studies of *Homo* population tooth breadth show the greatest sexual dimorphism in the canine. Indeed, one of Garn's studies of "Ohio whites" leaves the lower canine with the least dimorphism of any mandibular tooth. Table 1 indicates sexual dimorphism in tooth breadth for seven human and four nonhuman primate groups. Dimorphism is expressed by the index (100 times the ratio) of male mean to female mean minus 100. Data are included for the Aleuts (Moorrees 1957), Australian aborigines (Barrett et al. 1964), Japanese (Miyabara 1916), Javanese (Mijsberg 1931), Lapps (Selmer-Olsen 1949), "Ohio whites" (Garn, Lewis, and Kerewsky 1966a), Tristanites (Thomsen 1955), as well as the nonhuman taxa *Alouatta caraya* (Zingeser 1967), *Papio ursinus* (Freedman 1957), *Pan troglodytes* (Schuman and Brace 1954), and *Pan gorilla* (Pilbeam 1969). In the nonhuman primates, dimorphism is greatest in the canine, excepting *Alouatta,* where the canine dimorphism is exceeded by that of the lower first premolar. Because PM_1 is part of the canine growth field and is functionally integrated with C^1 in the nonhuman primates, the general observation of high canine dimorphism does not seem to be contradicted. Among the seven human populations, canine breadth sexual dimorphism is greatest in most, but not all, cases. An average dimorphism value was calculated for each tooth as an indi-

Table 1. Breadth sexual dimorphism for individual teeth in primates. Dimorphism is given in terms of ratios of male and female means $\dfrac{100 \times M}{F} - 100$. The *Homo* value is the average of population values for each tooth

	Aleuts	Australian aborigines	Japanese	Javanese	Lapps	Ohio whites	Tristanites	Average (*Homo*)	*Alouatta caraya*	*Papio ursinus*	*Pan troglodytes*	*Pan gorilla*
I^1		6.0	0.0	7.2	4.9	4.6		4.5	10.0	12.8	0.0	
I^2		5.8	3.1	6.3	2.8	7.4		5.1	13.3	14.3	4.3	
C^1	3.9	5.2	6.3	9.0	6.6	6.1	5.7	6.1	28.9	50.0	21.2	42.8
P^1	1.4	2.8	2.2	4.3	3.1	5.9	1.8	3.1	20.0	14.5	2.8	5.2
P^2	1.1	2.4	2.2	5.4	3.0	6.5	1.3	3.1	9.5	11.0	2.4	5.7
P^3									10.6			
M^1	1.2	3.4	3.6	5.4	4.7	5.8	3.1	3.9	11.6	7.3	1.7	5.6
M^2	0.7	3.3	6.4	7.3	6.8	6.5	3.0	4.9	9.1	10.4	2.8	6.5
M^3	0.6	1.3	8.0	4.7	5.5		5.5	4.3	12.3	10.3	2.2	6.2
I_1		6.7	3.5	7.3	4.4	3.6		5.1	3.2	10.8	0.0	
I_2		5.7	1.6	5.0	4.7	3.6		4.1	7.9	10.5	3.4	
C_1	4.6	4.5	5.5	9.7	8.6	2.3	6.2	5.9	27.4	64.7	23.6	36.1
P_1	3.2	1.6	1.3	6.5	3.6	6.0	1.4	3.4	40.0	35.4		16.3
P_2	3.2	2.3	3.7	3.7	3.2	5.8	0.5	3.2	16.3	13.6	2.6	6.8
P_3									14.0			
M_1	3.4	3.6	0.9	2.8	3.5	4.1	1.3	2.8	12.7	15.4	2.2	5.6
M_2	2.8	2.7	2.9	2.9	4.7	11.0	2.0	4.1	11.3	14.6	1.5	7.6
M_3	−2.6	2.2	4.2	2.0	3.5		4.3	2.3	10.9	10.4	3.5	8.0

cation of the SPECIES (rather than POPULATION) characteristic tooth breadth dimorphism distribution. These average values clearly show that the canine is the most dimorphic tooth for the species as a whole.

Indeed, a recent attempt to develop discriminant functions for sexing based on tooth dimensions (Ditch and Rose 1972) uses canine breadth in all six functions reported. Neither canine length, nor length or breadth of any other tooth, is used in all six functions. Apparently, canine breadth is the most important single measurement in discrimination.

In sum, it appears that canine breadth is the best single dental indicator of sex for a wide range of primates. Consequently, one would expect it to be the best dental indicator for australopithecines and the best vehicle for studying sexual dimorphism.

Canine breadth is measured as the maximum labial-lingual diameter perpendicular to the medial-distal axis of the tooth. The corresponding measurement for the nonhuman primates is entirely homologous and

analogous. There are several coincidental advantages in using this measurement. Maximum breadth is inevitably in the cervical region, in spite
of the wide range of morphological variation in human canines (Taylor
1969). Thus, the breadth measurement is unaffected by even the most
extreme occlusal wear. In addition, breadth of the root below the cervical
region closely corresponds to the crown breadth. Consequently, one
would expect a close relationship between canine breadth and canine
socket breadth. This expectation was tested for the australopithecine
sample by measuring canine sockets with canines whenever possible.
Calculation revealed that the correlation of socket to tooth breadth was
0.96, and the regression slope was not significantly different from 1.0.
Therefore, it is possible to use socket breadth to estimate tooth breadth
with a high degree of accuracy. This procedure was followed, greatly
expanding the available sample. All specific cases are indicated in the
appropriate tables.

SPECIMENS

All the Lower Pleistocene hominid specimens were observed and measured by the author. The individual canine or canine socket breadth dimensions are given in Tables 2 and 3. STS 3 is considered a maxillary
canine, as it was originally described (Broom, Robinson, and Schepers
1950). After examination of this worn tooth and comparison with known
mandibular and maxillary specimens, I find as many morphological reasons for calling it maxillary as mandibular. The decision to consider it
maxillary follows the original reasoning based on its distinctive size. The
tooth is significantly larger than any other canine of either jaw. If it were
a mandibular canine, and not anomalous, the corresponding maxillary
tooth would have dimensions almost, if not fully, within the gorilla
range of variation. STS 2 was not considered because the breadth measurement cannot be taken. The breadth measurement on the STS 5
socket was carefully checked by additional cleaning of the internal area.
The area of the STS 71 socket had been ground and polished. It was not
possible to clearly identify the original socket borders, so the published
socket measurement was used. TM 1528 is considered maxillary rather
than mandibular as reported by Robinson (1956) because of the clear
convexity and lingual tubercle development in the cervical portion of the
lingual face. SE 1937 was originally published as a mandibular canine
(Robinson 1962). I believe it is maxillary because of the well-developed
lingual tubercle. It closely matches the TM 1512 canine in both mor-

Table 2.   Australopithecine maxillary canine and canine socket breadths in millimeters

South African Gracile		Robust		East African "*Homo*"		Robust	
STS 3	12.1	TM 1517[1]	9.4	ER 803	9.0	ER 816	9.5
STS 5[1]	8.9	SK 4	10.6	OH 39	9.3	OH 5	10.0
STS 17[1]	10.2	SK 12[1]	12.0	OH 15	11.9	OH 30	9.1
STS 48	9.5	SK 13[1]	8.0			Chesowanja	8.5
STS 52	9.9	SK 27	10.4				
STS 53[1]	8.5	SK 38	10.0				
STS 71[1]	10.0	SK 46[1]	10.0				
TM 1511[1]	11.0	SK 47[1]	8.6				
TM 1512	9.2	SK 48	9.2				
TM 1514[1]	10.2	SK 52[1]	10.1				
TM 1527	8.8	SK 55	9.4				
TM 1528	9.0	SK 65	10.2				
SE 1937	9.0	SK 79[1]	8.9				
MLD 6[1]	8.3	SK 80[1]	9.4				
MLD 9[1]	9.0	SK 83	10.5				
MLD 11/30	10.1	SK 85/93	9.6				
		SK 86	8.9				
		SK 95	8.4				
		SK 845	11.4				
		SK 884	8.8				
		SK 1590	8.7				

[1] Breadth of the canine socket is used.

Table 3.   Australopithecine mandibular canine and canine socket breadths in millimeters

South African Gracile		Robust		East African "*Homo*"		Robust	
STS 7	11.0	TM 1517	8.8	ER 730[1]	8.2	ER 729	10.1
STS 36	10.5	SK 23	8.0	ER 992	9.2	ER 802	9.1
STS 50	9.8	SK 29	8.5	OH 7	9.8	ER 810[1]	10.0
STS 51	9.2	SK 34	8.8	OH 16	10.1	ER 818[1]	10.9
STS 52	10.2	SK 74[1]	9.2	OH 13	7.4	OH 30	7.7
MLD 18	8.9	SK 87	9.4	OH 37	9.6	Omo L7	10.0
MLD 27[1]	9.0	SK 94	8.5	ER 1483	11.4	Omo L74	9.1
MLD 40	9.1	SK 858	8.0	ER 1501	9.4	Omo L58[1]	10.5
		SK 876	10.8			Natron	8.4
		SK 1596	10.1				

[1] Breadth of the canine socket is used.

phology and wear. SK 92 is broken at the base, so that accurate labial-lingual measurements cannot be taken. The socket breadth measurement for MLD 9 is a minimum estimate. The socket may have been broader. I do not believe that the MLD 13 canine root is hominid. The preserved height is 32 millimeters and the dimensions at the distal break show little evidence of significant tapering. The partially erupted SK 63 canine was not used because I could not take accurate measurements at its base. SK 94 was originally described as a lower canine (Robinson 1956). Robinson later changed the entry to maxillary in the Transvaal Museum catalog. I believe the tooth is mandibular, as first suggested, because there is no lingual tubercle development, the distal buccal groove is only weakly developed, and the wear angulation better matches that of known mandibular specimens. SK 96, an unerupted tooth, is clearly not completely formed and the measurements cannot be used. There are two additional canines listed by Robinson in the 1956 monograph. One is misidentified, as SK 84 is a metacarpal. SK 84 is actually SK 845. The second, SK 820, does not appear in the catalog. It is unerupted and not completely formed.

Table 4 gives breadth measurements for all *Homo erectus* canines. I

Table 4. *Homo erectus* maxillary and mandibular canine and canine socket breadths in millimeters

Maxilla		Mandible	
OH 11[1]	10.6	OH 22	9.4
Java 4	11.9	Sangiran 8	8.3
Java 17	10.5	Java B[1]	**9.6**
Peking		Java C	8.5
C1	9.9	Sangiran 7	**11.0**
D2	9.8	Lantian	8.5
F4	10.4	Peking	
H4	8.2	AN 16	9.0
L1	10.6	B1	8.2
L2	9.8	B4	9.5
O1	9.5	C2	10.4
Ternifine	10.0	H1	8.7
Rabat	10.0	G1	10.1
Beriro	9.9	I1	8.7
		K1	9.3
		Ternifine 1[1]	10.0
		2[1]	11.0
		3	10.7
		Mauer	8.5
		Rabat	9.5
		Casablanca	9.0

[1] Breadth of the canine socket is used.

Table 5. Neanderthal maxillary and mandibular canine and canine socket breadths in millimeters

Maxilla		Mandible	
Krapina		Krapina	
46/47	10.6	E	9.8
E	9.6	H	9.1
86.1.1	10.0	I	11.5
86.1.2	9.9	D	8.7
86.1.3	9.6	86.2.2	8.4
86.2.1	10.3	86.2.3	9.9
91.1	11.4	91.11	9.8
91.2	10.6	91.12	9.4
91.3	9.6	91.16	10.1
91.4	9.4	Amud 1	8.5
91.5	11.2	Arcy-sur-Cure 2	9.5
91.6	10.3	Circeo 3	8.9
91.7	10.1	Ehringsdorf child	8.5
91.8	10.2	Ehringsdorf adult	8.8
91.9	10.8	Hortus 2	7.5
91.10	10.0	Hortus 6	7.5
91.13	9.9	Jersey	10.0
91.14	10.1	Lazaret	9.4
91.15	8.8	La Ferrassie	9.9
Africanthropus	9.0	La Quina 5	9.0
Amud 1	9.5	Le Moustier	9.5
Arcy-sur-Cure 3	9.9	Monsempron b	9.0
Broken Hill	10.9	Ochoz	9.8
Croz-del-dua	8.6	Petralona 4	9.0
Jebel Irhoud 2	10.0	Regordou	10.0
Kulna	9.6	Shanidar 2	9.6
La Ferrassie	11.2	Skhūl 2	8.4
La Quina 5	10.0	Skhūl 4	8.0
Le Moustier	10.0	Skhūl 5	8.5
Monsempron h	9.5	Skhūl 10	7.0
Omo 1	8.1	Spy 1	8.3
Petralona 1	9.1	Spy 2	8.8
Petralona 2	10.0	Subaluk	9.9
Petralona 3	10.0	Tabun 1	8.3
Qafzeh 6	10.0	Tabun 2	9.0
Qafzeh 7	10.0	Sipka	7.0
Qafzeh 8	10.2		
Saccopastore 2	9.2		
Shanidar 1	10.7		
Shanidar 2	8.5		
Shanidar 4	10.0		
Skhūl 1	8.0		
Skhūl 4	8.5		
Skhūl 5	9.5		
Skhūl 6	9.6		
Spy 1	9.0		
Spy 2	10.0		
Tabun 1	8.8		
Tabun B	9.0		
Tangier	10.7		

measured all the Olduvai specimens. The socket measurement for Java B mandible was taken from the Wenner-Gren cast. The accuracy appears great because measurements of the cheek teeth on this cast come within 1 percent of published measurements for the specimen. The Java 17 cranium was published by Sartono (1971), and the Ternifine canine and canine socket measurements by Arambourg (1963). Sources for the other specimens are given in a separate publication (Wolpoff 1971a).

Neanderthal canine breadths are given in Table 5. I measured the canines of Skhūl 5 and Skhūl 6, as well as Tabun B and the Tangier maxilla. All the Krapina canines were measured by Brace, and these measurements are used here with his kind permission. The Amud canines were published by Suzuki and Takai (1970), Hortus and Lazeret by de Lumey and Piveteau (1969), Omo by Day (Leakey, Butzer, and Day 1969), Kulna by Jelinek (1967), Petralona by Kannelis and Savas (1964), and Qafzeh by Vallois and Vandermeersch (1972). Sources for remaining specimens are in another publication (Wolpoff 1971a).

CANINE BREADTH FREQUENCY DISTRIBUTIONS

As a basis for interpreting fossil hominid distributions, it is important to determine the canine breadth frequency distributions for living primates of known sex. Data for *Pan gorilla* are given in Table 6 (see also Figure 1). The specimens were sampled from a data set measured by the author

Table 6. Frequency distribution of maxillary and mandibular canine breadths in absolute numbers of a *Pan gorilla* sample. Data are given by sex and for the pooled sample

Breadth in millimeters	Maxilla Female	Male	Both	Mandible Female	Male	Both
8.0– 8.9				1		1
9.0– 9.9	1		1	14		14
10.0–10.9	15		15	27		27
11.0–11.9	21		21	7		7
12.0–12.9	11		11	1	3	4
13.0–13.9	2	1	3		13	13
14.0–14.9		8	8		17	17
15.0–15.9		12	12		12	12
16.0–16.9		15	15		3	3
17.0–17.9		8	8		1	1
18.0–18.9		4	4		1	1
19.0–19.9		1	1			
20.0–20.9		1	1			

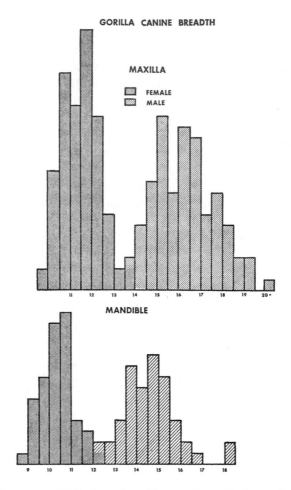

Figure 1.   Frequency distribution of maxillary and mandibular canine breadth in millimeters for *Pan gorilla*. One hundred upper and lower dentitions were used, and $N = 50$ for each sex

and by P. Mahler at the American Museum and the Cleveland Museum of Natural History. No mountain gorillas are included in the sample. Only specimens with known sex were utilized. In both mandible and maxilla there is virtually no overlap between male and female distributions. The combined distributions are very clearly bimodal, and the separate modes represent sex to a high degree of accuracy. To determine accuracy, the combined distributions were split at the class of minimum frequency between the modes (13.0–13.9 millimeters for the maxilla, 12.0–12.9 millimeters for the mandible), and the specimens within this class were split evenly between the larger and smaller mode. The means for each side of the divided distribution were then calculated and compared with the actual male and female means. In the male, mean was overestimated by this procedure by 0.2 millimeters, but the female estimate was exact. In the mandible, the male mean was overestimated by 0.2 millimeters, and the female mean by 0.1 millimeter.

Data for *Pan troglodytes* are presented in Table 7 (see also Figure 2). The specimens were sampled from a data set consisting of individuals

Table 7. Frequency distribution of maxillary and mandibular canine breadths in absolute numbers for a *Pan troglodytes* sample. Data are given by sex and for the pooled sample

Breadth in millimeters	Maxilla Female	Male	Both	Mandible Female	Male	Both
7.0– 7.9	1		1	2		2
8.0– 8.9	20		20	21		21
9.0– 9.9	20	4	24	19	3	22
10.0–10.9	8	11	19	6	11	17
11.0–11.9	1	16	17	2	21	23
12.0–12.9		9	9	0	6	6
13.0–13.9		9	9		4	4
14.0–14.9		1	1		3	3
15.0–15.9					1	1
16.0–16.9						
17.0–17.9					1	1

measured at the American Museum and the Cleveland Museum of Natural History by the author and P. Mahler, as well as Liberian chimpanzee specimens from the Museum of Comparative Zoology measured by C. L. Brace. Only specimens of known sex were used. No pygmy chimpanzees are included. The mandibular combined sample is bimodal in Table 7 and in Figure 2, which has twice as many classes. The maxillary sample is less strongly bimodal. Figure 2 shows the separate modes, but Table 7, with half the classes (i.e. the class ranges are twice as great as shown in the figure) shows no evidence of bimodality. In both maxilla and mandible the modes are separated by a gap of less, but not particularly low, frequency. If the mandibular distribution is split at the class of minimum frequency between the modes, following the procedure described in the analysis of the gorilla sample, the estimated female and male means are surprisingly accurate. The known male mean is overestimated by 0.4 millimeters, and the female mean estimate is exact. When this procedure is followed for the maxilla, both male and female means are overestimated by 0.1 millimeter. This accuracy is particularly interesting in light of the extensive overlap between male and female distributions in both

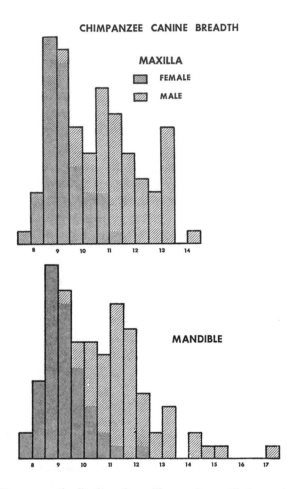

Figure 2. Frequency distribution of maxillary and mandibular canine breadth in millimeters for *Pan troglodytes*. One hundred upper and lower dentitions were used, and $N = 50$ for each sex

jaws. Analysis of both African pongid distributions suggests that when bimodality is present, division of the modes accurately estimates male and female MEANS, even though the distributions may overlap.

The Libben sample was chosen to exemplify *Homo* because it represents a preindustrial biological population with a large number of associated pelves and crania. In all cases, sex designation was based on the pelvis, and whenever possible characteristics of the os pubis (Phenice 1969) were used. Each individual was sexed independently by two observers, C. O. Lovejoy and myself, and the few specimens for which agreement could not be reached based on the pelvis were disregarded. In all cases these were individuals without a pubis. All canines were measured by the author, and no sockets were used. Table 8 shows the resulting distributions (see also Figure 3). Male and female distributions

Table 8. Frequency distribution of maxillary and mandibular canine breadths in absolute numbers for a *Homo sapiens* sample. This Amerind group from Libben probably represents an actual biological population. Data are given by sex and for the pooled sample

Breadth in millimeters	Maxilla Female	Male	Both	Mandible Female	Male	Both
6.0– 6.4						
6.5– 6.9				2		2
7.0– 7.4	1		1	8	2	10
7.5– 7.9	10	1	11	10	6	16
8.0– 8.4	13	6	19	3	12	15
8.5– 8.9	8	19	27		6	5
9.0– 9.4	1	12	13		5	5
9.5– 9.9		4	4		1	1
10.0–10.4		1	1			
10.5–10.9						

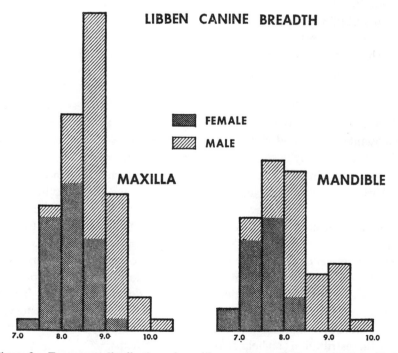

Figure 3. Frequency distribution of maxillary and mandibular canine breadth in millimeters for the Libben Amerind population. Forty-three male and 33 female maxillary canines and 32 male and 23 female mandibular canines were used

are clearly different. However, the modal frequencies for each are close enough together so that the combined distribution is unimodal. Individual sexes could not be ascertained on the basis of the combined distributions alone. Comparison with the few other studies that present male and female distributions separately (Miyabara 1916; Selmer-Olsen 1949) indicates that the unimodal combined distribution based on distinct male and female distributions is the usual condition for *Homo* populations. It is interesting that gibbons, with a sex ratio within the range of *Homo* population means (see Table 13), distribute exactly the same way. Distributions for the sexes are distinct, although they overlap. The modal values are close enough together so that the combined distribution is unimodal.

As samples of the three living taxa most closely related to the australopithecines, the hominoid distributions discussed are of particular relevance in interpreting the canine breadth frequency distribution of the Lower Pleistocene hominids. The three living species do not present three separate and distinct models of sexual dimorphism. Rather, they fall on a continuum with *Pan gorilla* at one end and *Homo sapiens* at the other. Neither extreme is unique among the higher primates, as baboons approximate and surpass the gorilla condition, while the sexual dimorphism distribution for gibbons closely resembles that of man.

This variation leaves us with no clear expectation for Lower Pleistocene hominid sexual dimorphism. Two factors make predictions difficult. First, no concrete information yet exists to show whether hominids derive from a primate form with extensive (gorilla- or baboonlike) sexual dimorphism or whether the ancestral hominid stock had less pronounced dimorphism. One could argue that if the earliest hominids occupied a baboonlike niche, and if very early cultural behavior was relatively ineffective, especially in supplanting canine functions under selection leading to sexual dimorphism, then one might expect early hominids to have had greater dimorphism, similar to that of baboons. On the other hand, if *Ramapithecus* is an ancestral hominid, and if all known specimens have been correctly identified, one might expect early hominids to have followed a more chimpanzeelike model of sexual dimorphism, because the *Ramapithecus* sample shows no indication of extensive dimorphism. Second, even if it were known that hominids descended from a primate form with extensive sexual dimorphism, we do not know how far removed in either time or morphological space the Lower Pleistocene hominids are from the ancestral condition. In sum, only the actual canine breadth distribution can help resolve these problems.

Tables 9 and 10 give the frequency distributions of maxillary and mandibular canine breadths for three fossil hominid groups and *Homo sapiens.* Data for the individual fossil specimens are given in Tables 2–5. The *Homo sapiens* sample represents a world-wide distribution re-

Table 9. Frequency distribution of hominid maxillary canine breadths in absolute numbers. The data are given by individual specimens in Tables 2, 4, and 5

Breadth in millimeters	Australo-pithecine n = 44	Pithecan-thropine n = 13	Neander-thal n = 50	*Homo sapiens* n = 288
6.0– 6.4				
6.5– 6.9				1
7.0– 7.4				3
7.5– 7.9				33
8.0– 8.4	3	1	2	84
8.5 8.9	9	0	5	81
9.0– 9.4	12	0	6	49
9.5– 9.9	3	5	11	27
10.0–10.4	10	3	17	5
10.5–10.9	2	3	6	5
11.0–11.4	2	0	3	
11.5–11.9	1	1		
12.0–12.4	2			
12.5–12.9				

Table 10. Frequency distribution of hominid mandibular canine breadths in absolute numbers. The data are given by individual specimens in Tables 3, 4, and 5

Breadth in millimeters	Australo-pithecine n = 35	Pithecan-thropine n = 20	Neander-thal n = 35	*Homo sapiens* n = 349
6.0– 6.4				2
6.5– 6.9				18
7.0– 7.4	1		1	66
7.5– 7.9	1	0	3	88
8.0– 8.4	4	2	6	87
8.5– 8.9	5	5	5	53
9.0– 9.4	9	5	8	24
9.5– 9.9	3	3	7	10
10.0–10.4	6	3	3	1
10.5–10.9	4	1	1	
11.0–11.4	2	1	0	
11.5–11.9			1	
12.0–12.4				
12.5–12.9				

ported by me in 1971 with the addition of the Libben canines. Figure 4 shows that in both jaws the fairly large Neanderthal sample is clearly unimodal and is different from *Homo sapiens* only in average breadth. The *Homo erectus* sample, although considerably smaller in number,

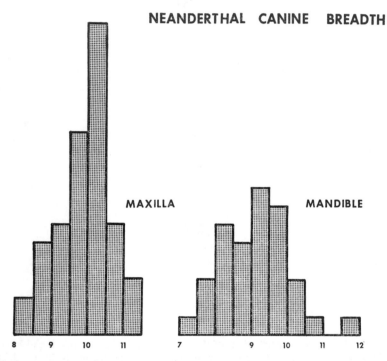

Figure 4. Frequency distribution of maxillary and mandibular canine breadth in millimeters for Neanderthals. The maxillary sample size is 50, and the mandibular 35

also appears unimodal (see Figure 5). However, it is of some interest that in both maxilla and mandible THE AUSTRALOPITHECINE SAMPLE IS BIMODAL (see Figure 6).

In both jaws the modes are distinct and separate, with only a few specimens between them. Tables 11 and 12 break down the Lower Pleistocene hominid distribution in terms of four subsamples. Table 11 shows that the South African gracile and robust samples are separately bimodal for the maxillary canine. The modes are in the same range, and the section point is the same. The East African sample is too small to show modality of any sort. Table 12 indicates mandibular canine breadth. The sample size is 28 percent smaller than the maxillary sample, and the individual distributions in the South African sample are not as well defined. The South African robusts are apparently bimodal, with the smaller mode

HOMO ERECTUS - CANINE BREADTH

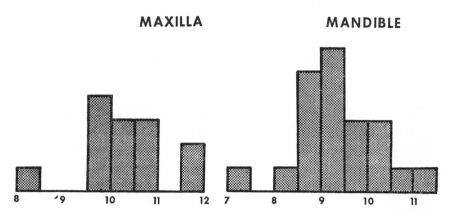

Figure 5. Frequency distribution of maxillary and mandibular canine breadth in millimeters for *Homo erectus*. The maxillary sample size is 13 and the mandibular 20

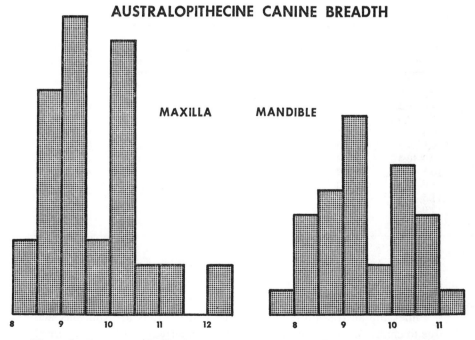

Figure 6. Frequency distribution of maxillary and mandibular canine breadth in millimeters for the combined Lower Pleistocene hominid sample. Sample size for the maxilla is 44 and for the mandible 35

Table 11.   Maxillary canine breadth distribution for four Lower Pleistocene hominid subsamples, based on data given in Table 2. Designations of particular specimens follow common literature practice

Breadth in millimeters	South African		East African		All Lower Pleistocene specimens
	Gracile	Robust	"Homo"	Robust	
7.0– 7.4					
7.5– 7.9					
8.0– 8.4	1	2			3
8.5– 8.9	3	5		1	9
9.0– 9.4	5	4	2	1	12
9.5– 9.9	1	1	0	1	3
10.0–10.4	4	5	0	1	10
10.5–10.9	0	2	0	0	2
11.0–11.4	1	1	0	0	2
11.5–11.9	0	0	1	0	1
12.0–12.4	1	1	0	0	2
12.5–12.9					

Table 12.   Mandibular canine breadth distribution for four Lower Pleistocene hominid subsamples, based on data in Table 3. Designations of particular specimens follow common literature practice

Breadth in millimeters	South African		East African		All Lower Pleistocene specimens
	Gracile	Robust	"Homo"	Robust	
7.0– 7.4			1		1
7.5– 7.9	0	0	0	1	1
8.0– 8.4	0	2	1	1	4
8.5– 8.9	1	4	0	0	5
9.0– 9.4	3	2	2	2	9
9.5– 9.9	1	0	2	0	3
10.0–10.4	1	1	1	3	6
10.5–10.9	1	1	0	2	4
11.0–11.4	1	0	1	0	2
11.5–11.9					
12.0–12.4					
12.5–12.9					

more frequent than the larger. The East African robusts are clearly bimodal, and the section point for both robust samples is the same.

Either the australopithecine bimodal distributions are spurious and due to chance or they are the result of an underlying biological cause. I believe it is unlikely that the bimodal distributions are due to chance for a number of reasons. First, whatever the odds are against sampling a bimodal distribution out of a unimodal underlying distribution, the odds are multiplicative against getting two independent bimodal distributions. The samples are virtually completely independent: only three specimens have both maxillary and mandibular canines. Thus, if the odds were one out of ten against a bimodal sample drawn from a unimodal distribution (and I suspect that one out of ten is much too high), the chances of picking two independent bimodal samples (mandible and maxilla) would be *one out of one hundred*. Second, if the bimodality in the combined sample were spurious, it would be unlikely that bimodality occurring in the smaller sample sets would be exactly the same. Third, sampling the Neanderthal distribution is an analogous case allowing an interesting comparison. The sample size is quite similar and the Neanderthal sample consists of individuals widespread in both time and space. Yet the Neanderthal sample is clearly unimodal. Fourth, if the separate modes are taken to indicate sex, and if mean values are calculated for each mode, the "male-female" ratios for maxilla and mandible are almost identical, as is true for other primate samples (see Table 13). Because the samples are independent, this would be very unlikely if the bimodal distributions in mandible and maxilla were attributable to chance. The resemblance to patterns known to be due to sexual dimorphism extends to small detail. For instance, Table 13 shows that for all primate samples but one the male-female ratio in the mandible is equal to or slightly greater than the maxillary ratio. The mandibular ratio in the australopithecines is slightly greater. Fifth, there is no evidence that the bimodality is site-specific. That is, one site is not contributing most of one mode while another contributes the majority of specimens in the other. The bimodality is not sample-specific for the four subsamples considered. Thus, the bimodality does not result from combined distribution of different but overlapping samples or taxa. The chances of all these factors occurring together are phenomenally low unless there is an underlying biological reason for the australopithecine distribution. CONSEQUENTLY, I BELIEVE THE AUSTRALOPITHECINE BIMODAL DISTRIBUTIONS ARE DUE TO SEXUAL DIMORPHISM.

I suggest this as the most likely explanation of the data and consider it a working hypothesis. It is of some interest to explore the implications and ramifications.

Table 13 indicates some statistics and indexes that can be used to quantify the nature and degree of sexual dimorphism in a number of primates. Gorilla, chimpanzee, australopithecine, and Libben data are as given in Tables 2, 3, 6, 7, and 8. The gibbon sample, *Hylobates moloch*, was measured by L. Greenfield at the American Museum. The

Table 13. Statistical data for quantification of sexual dimorphism in canine breadth for primate samples. Male, female, and combined means are given, as well as male, female, and combined standard deviations and male and female sample sizes. Statistics expressing sexual dimorphism are the index of male to female means, the ratio of the difference between male and female means to the standard deviation of the combined sample, the index of this difference to the mean of the combined sample, and the results of a Student's t calculation. The individual sexes of all specimens except the australopithecines are known.

| | Means | | | Standard deviation | | | Sample size | | $\dfrac{100\,M}{F}$ | $\dfrac{M\text{-}F}{SD_B}$ | $\dfrac{100\,(M\text{-}F)}{B}$ | t |
	Male (M)	Female (F)	Both (B)	M	F	B	M	F				
Maxilla												
Gorilla	16.31	11.40	13.85	1.4	0.9	2.7	100	100	143	1.81	35.4	29.44
Chimpanzee	11.61	9.19	10.40	1.2	0.8	1.6	50	50	126	1.50	23.1	11.77
Australopithecine	10.51	8.95	9.73	0.7	0.4	0.9	17	26	117	1.73	16.0	9.31
Libben	8.87	8.19	8.53	0.5	0.4	0.5	43	33	108	1.26	8.0	6.59
Australian aborigine	9.12	8.67	8.90	0.6	0.4		41	36	105		5.6	4.07
Aleut	8.47	8.15	8.31	0.4	0.4	0.5	65	44	104	0.62	3.9	4.15
Japanese	8.40	7.90	8.15	0.5	0.3	0.4	142	52	106	1.19	6.1	7.18
Javanese	8.50	7.80	8.15	0.6	0.7		136	43	109		8.6	6.61
Lapp	8.18	7.67	7.93	0.6	0.5	0.6	197	167	107	0.81	6.4	8.95
Tristanite	9.38	8.87	9.13	0.5	0.5	0.7	211	190	106	0.75	5.6	9.44
Gibbon	5.29	4.92	5.11	0.3	0.4	0.4	18	18	108	0.93	7.2	3.16
Mandible												
Gorilla	14.54	10.31	12.43	1.2	0.7	2.4	50	50	141	1.80	34.0	26.26
Chimpanzee	11.72	9.19	10.46	1.5	0.9	1.8	50	50	128	1.43	24.2	10.23
Australopithecine	10.29	8.72	9.51	0.4	0.5	0.9	13	18	118	1.74	16.5	9.35
Libben	8.34	7.52	7.93	0.6	0.4	0.6	32	23	111	1.28	10.3	5.96
Australian aborigine	8.39	8.03	8.21	0.5	0.4		41	36	105		4.4	3.61
Aleut	7.93	7.58	7.76	0.6	0.5	0.6	74	57	105	0.61	4.5	3.55
Japanese	7.70	7.30	7.50	0.4	0.3	0.4	146	48	106	0.95	5.33	7.07
Javanese	7.90	7.20	7.55	0.5	0.5		139	42	110		9.3	8.54
Lapp	7.55	6.95	7.25	0.4	0.4	0.7	211	190	107	0.91	8.3	14.24
Tristanite	8.97	8.45	8.71	0.7	0.7	0.7	54	43	106	0.75	6.0	3.88
Gibbon	5.12	4.65	4.89	0.5	0.3	0.5	19	19	110	0.96	9.6	3.34

data are used with his kind permission. Sources for the remaining human groups have already been given. The table presents male, female, and combined sample means, standard deviations, and sample sizes. Four statistics are used in quantifying the extent of sexual dimorphism. First, male and female means are compared in a simple index giving a percentage difference. Second, the difference between male and female means is divided by the standard deviation of the combined sample, thus weighting this difference by the variability in the sample. Third, an index is made of the difference between means divided by the average of the combined sample, weighting the difference by canine size. Fourth, the value of Student's *t* calculated between the means is given. The *t* values are all significantly different at the 0.1 percent level. Individual sexes in all cases except the australopithecines are known. In the australopithecines, the least frequent class between the modes was divided in half, with the larger individuals considered males and the smaller considered females. For the maxilla and mandible this section point is at 9.7 millimeters. I justify this procedure on the basis of analysis, already described, for gorillas, with more distinctive bimodality than australopithecines, and for chimpanzees, with less. In both cases it was found that when separate modes appear, the male and female mean estimates based on a division between the modes is surprisingly close to the actual male and female mean values, even though there may be extensive overlap of the distributions. This is apparently true because when overlap occurs, it is symmetric. Consequently, the procedure of dividing the modes seems an accurate estimator of the difference between the mean values, although it may be a less accurate estimator of individual sex.

In terms of the frequency distributions, bimodality in the autralopithecines seems more distinctive than it is in chimpanzees. The separate modes in the chimpanzee maxilla are close together, compared with the variation in the sample. In the mandible they are somewhat further apart, and the distribution is slightly more bimodal. However, even in this case, the least frequent class is not much smaller than the modes. For gorillas the least frequent class is much smaller than the modes, and the australopithecine distribution lies midway between the two in this feature. No other hominid groups are bimodal. The statistic that best shows this relation is the difference between male and female means weighted by the standard deviation of the combined sample. This ratio is higher for the australopithecines than it is for chimpanzees even though the male-female index of means is greater in the chimpanzee. In other words, while sexual dimorphism is greater in the chimpanzee, variation within each sex is also greater, obscuring bimodality in the combined sample. Variation is usually inversely related to selection, and one might infer that the australopithecines were under more intense selection for sexual dimorphism than are chimpanzees. The other measures show that the average degree of sexual dimorphism is greater in the chimpanzees, suggesting that the extent of sexual dimorphism under selection in the australopithecines is less. These two inferences are not contradictory, but rather suggest that the pattern of sexual dimorphism in the australopithecines is not the same as that of chimpanzees.

In these respects the australopithecines are more like gorillas or baboons. However, there are two important differences. First, both relative and absolute measures of variation are less in the australopithecines for either sex or for the combined sample. Second, the australopithecine canine breadths are reduced to Mid-Pleistocene hominid size. Maxillary average breadths in *Homo erectus* and the Neanderthals are 10.2 millimeters and 9.8 millimeters, and the corresponding mandibular breadths are 9.3 millimeters and 9.0 millimeters.

While in distinctness of the modes australopithecines lie somewhere between chimpanzees and gorillas, the extent of the difference between the modes falls about midway between chimpanzees and the human groups. In both male-female mean index and male-female mean difference weighted to the combined average, the australopithecines lie completely outside the ranges for human groups, or any reasonable extension of these ranges. It is unlikely that this difference is due to larger average canine size than *Homo* because the Mid-Pleistocene hominid canines are also large, and the distributions are clearly unimodal. Thus, the pattern of sexual dimorphism in the australopithecines is distinct from *Homo*. This distinction lies only in the average difference between means for the sexes. Combined sample means, as mentioned, are nearly the same for australopithecines and Mid-Pleistocene hominids, and combined sample standard deviations are also almost identical. Variation and size, in other words, follow the Mid-Pleistocene *Homo* pattern, while the male and female distributions do not.

In sum, the australopithecines have a more distinct pattern of mode separation than the chimpanzee, and one might expect less overlap in male and female distributions. The actual difference between the modes is less than that of chimpanzees but significantly greater than for *Homo*. The variations of the combined sample and the average breadth follow the Mid-Pleistocene *Homo* pattern.

SEXING INDIVIDUAL AUSTRALOPITHECINES SPECIMENS

The presence of clear bimodality in australopithecine canine breadths allows some estimation of individual specimen sexes. Discriminant function analysis has shown that this is possible in a unimodal distribution (Ditch and Rose 1972), and the accuracy should be much greater under bimodal conditions. However, it is unlikely that every individual in the "male" australopithecine mode is actually male, and every individual in the "female" mode actually female. Even the gorilla distribution shows some overlap.

Consequently, I have calculated estimated error functions for gorilla, chimpanzee, and a *Homo* population (Libben). The three step-functions are given in Table 14. In the three samples, there is almost no overlap of

Table 14. Calculated sexing error step-functions for three primate groups. Range between the male and female means was divided into four equal quartiles, and the percentage of males within each quartile was calculated. Percentage of males below the female mean can be taken as 0, and of females above the male mean as 100

	Percent males in quartiles from female to male mean			
	1 F–25 percent	2 26 percent– 50 percent	3 51 percent– 75 percent	4 76 percent–M
Maxilla				
Gorilla	0	1	99	100
Chimpanzee	33	38	71	92
Libben	17	33	75	77
Mandible				
Gorilla	0	0	100	100
Chimpanzee	15	50	79	93
Libben	32	43	67	83

males below the female mean and females above the male mean. The range between the two means was broken into four equal quartiles, and the percentage of males within the quartile sample calculated. These percentages form the basis of the error functions, expressing the probability that an individual designated male within that quartile is actually male. Designations of male above the male mean or female below the female mean are nearly, if not completely, certain. Generally speaking, the function is steepest in gorilla and shallowest in Libben, although more chimpanzee male maxillary canines extend into the female range than is the case in Libben, while for the mandibular canines the opposite is true.

Which error function is most applicable to the australopithecines? The

Table 15. Maxillary and mandibular section points for the quartiles between male and female means. An estimated error step-function is given as the probability that male designation within the quartile is correct. Probability of males below the female mean is 0 and of females above the male mean is 1.0

| | Australopithecine section points for quartiles from female to male mean | | | |
	1	2	3	4
Maxilla	8.9–9.3	9.3–9.7	9.7–10.1	10.1–10.5
Probability of male in quartile	.16	.23	.82	.90
Mandible	8.7–9.1	9.1–9.5	9.5–9.9	9.9–10.3
Probability of male in quartile	.15	.31	.82	.92

answer is probably none, as the australopithecine pattern of sexual dimorphism is not exactly like any of the samples. Mode separation is clearer than in the chimpanzee sample, while the degree of sexual dimorphism is less. As a conservative means of estimating the australopithecine expected error step-function, I have averaged the three functions. I believe this estimate is conservative because of the clear separation of australopithecine modes. If there were extensive overlap of males into the female range, and vice versa, the class between the modes would be far more frequent than it is, as in the chimpanzee situation. The estimated australopithecine error function and the ranges for the four quartiles between the means are given in Table 15. The probability of males below the female mean and females above the male mean can be taken as close to zero from the available evidence. Using Tables 2 and 3 with Table 15, sex of any australopithecine individual can be determined and the probability of error estimated.

It is of some interest to compare sexes determined here with previously published statements. Table 16 gives this information for thirty specimens. There is disagreement in nine instances. For every one of these the estimated probability of correct sexing was not 1.0. Some of the disagreements require explanation. Broom's sexing of TM 1517 as male (1939) was done with some hesitation because the Kromdraai skull was the only adult of its species. Between 1946 and 1950 there was a change in the sexing of some Sterkfontein crania. Before the large canine STS 3 was discovered, TM 1511 was considered male. With the discovery of STS 3, Broom changed his mind and in the end classified every Sterkfontein cranium as female. A comparison of Tables 2 and 11 shows that the South African gracile maxillary sample, much larger now than it was then, is clearly bimodal. Three of the crania he classified as female, TM 1511, STS 17, and STS 71, fall in the male mode. Because TM 1511 is

Table 16. Comparisons of individual australopithecine published sexes with sex determined in this article

Specimen	Sex determined in this work	Probability of correct sexing	Sex given in literature	Reference	Page
TM 1511	M	1.00	M	1	47
TM 1512	F	.84	F	1	47
TM 1514	M	.90	M	1	47
TM 1527	F	1.00	F	1	57
STS 3	M	1.00	M	2	39
STS 5	F	1.00	F	2	15
STS 7	M	1.00	M	2	34
STS 17	M	.90	F	2	24
STS 36	M	1.00	M	3	276
STS 50	M	.82	M	1	53
STS 51	F	.69	F	1	57
STS 52	M	.82	F	3	277
STS 71	M	.82	F	2	39
MLD 6	F	1.00	F	4	189
MLD 9	F	.84	F	5	335
MLD 18	F	.85	F	3	269
MLD 22	F	.85	M	3	269
MLD 40	F	.85	M	3	269
SK 12	M	1.00	M	6	6
SK 13	F	1.00	F	6	Plate 5
SK 23	F	1.00	F	6	18
SK 27	M	1.00	M	6	26
SK 34	F	.85	M	6	16
SK 46	M	.82	F	6	14
SK 47	F	1.00	F	6	29
SK 48	F	.77	F	6	10
SK 55	F	.77	M	6	35
SK 74	F	.69	F	6	23
SK 85/93	F	.77	F	6	35
TM 1517	F	.77	M	7	328

References:
1. Broom and Schepers (1946)
2. Broom, Robinson, and Schepers (1950)
3. Dart (1962)
4. Dart (1949a)
5. Dart (1949b)
6. Broom and Robinson (1952)
7. Broom (1939)

the second largest canine, if it is considered female, the gracile maxillary sample consists of one male and fifteen females. My feeling is that Broom's initial determination was correct, and his subsequent sexing of STS 17 and STS 71 should be considered with this in mind.

SK 46 and SK 48 come out as different sexes, although neither sexing is with absolute certainty. This seems unusual in view of the similarities between the crania. They were both sexed initially as female in view of comparisons with SK 12. I believe it possible that they are both the same sex, and I take this result to indicate the presence of some overlap between male and female distributions. Whatever the sex, there is clearly extensive variation within both male and female distributions. If SK 46 is male, the corresponding dimensions of specimens such as SK 12 and SK 845 are considerably larger. If, on the other hand, it is female, corresponding dental dimensions of SK 21 and SK 47 or cranial dimensions of SK 80/847 are considerably smaller.

STS 5 (Mrs. Pleis) was initially described as female, and this work suggests the same conclusion. There has been some recent discussion as to whether STS 5 may actually be male in view of the fact that its cranial capacity is the highest for any South African gracile adult. Unfortunately, cranial capacity estimates for the other specimens are based on reconstruction of at least one endocranial dimension determined by the average of the missing dimension in the specimens exhibiting it (Holloway 1970). This procedure tends to reduce observed variation in the sample and to make subsequent comparisons less certain. There are only two canine breadth dimensions smaller than the STS 5 value in the South African gracile sample, and on this basis I find it highly likely that the specimen was female.

STS 52, the complete Sterkfontein maxilla and associated mandible, comes out as male. The mandibular canine is more strongly male than the maxillary tooth. The other two specimens with maxillary and mandibular canines are TM 1517 and OH 30. Both are female, and in both cases the mandibular tooth is more strongly female (smaller error estimate) than the maxillary. Because the measures of dimorphism are slightly greater in the mandible than in the maxilla, these data support the inference that sexual dimorphism is more pronounced in the mandible.

OH 7 is classified as a male. However, it falls in the intermediate class and has the smallest male canine. The sexing of this specimen is probably the least certain for the sample. Excluding OH 7, only OH 15, OH 16 and ER 1473 of the East African "*Homo*" sample are male. All others, including the small Ileret mandibles ER 730 and ER 992, appear to be females. OH 5 is classified as male, while the Chesowanja cranium has one of the smallest female canines, which is well below the female mean. The large Rudolf mandibles, such as ER 729 and ER 818, come out as male.

SEXUAL DIMORPHISM IN OTHER FEATURES

The combined distribution for breadth in molars of both jaws shows no
definite evidence of bimodality. The second molar is the most dimorphic
tooth in *Homo*, after the canine. The combined australopithecine distributions for upper and lower second molars were clearly unimodal. Consequently, sexual dimorphism could not be established for other teeth independently.

Using the canine sexing criterion, there is some difference between the
postcanine dentitions of males and females in the South African samples
and in the East African robust sample. The East African *"Homo"* male
sample is too small for statistical treatment. Overlap between sexes is
extensive in the South African samples. For instance, the M^1 of the male
robust specimen SK 27 is smaller than five out of seven South African
robust females, and the M^1 of the male gracile specimen MLD 11/30
falls midway in the female range.

Table 17 shows maxillary molar breadth dimensions for the sexable
Lower Pleistocene hominid specimens. Of the subsample comparisons,
only the male-female robust South African samples are significantly different on the 0.05 level for M^1. Clearly, sample size limits the value of
these comparisons. Still, it is of interest that the male sample is uniformly
larger than the female for each subset. Differences are greatest in the
breadth of the maxillary first molar.

Tabe 17. Statistics for maxillary molar breadth in the four Lower Pleistocene
hominid subsamples. Breadths were used only for specimens that could be sexed
by the canine or canine socket. All measurements are in millimeters

	M^1 Breadth			M^2 Breadth			M^3 Breadth		
	X	Range	N	X	Range	N	X	Range	N
South African									
Gracile female	13.5	12.8–14.5	4	15.0	14.4–16.3	3	15.0	14.6–15.3	2
Gracile male	14.3	13.2–16.5	5	15.5	14.5–16.8	5	15.5	15.0–17.8	5
Robust female	14.2	12.8–14.9	7	15.3	14.3–16.3	4	16.1	15.3–17.1	4
Robust male	15.9	14.0–17.9	6	15.9	14.7–16.9	3	16.8	16.4–17.2	3
East African									
"Homo" female	11.0		1	12.5		1	13.5		1
"Homo" male	13.7		1	15.8		1	16.8		1
Robust female	15.2	14.9–15.5	2	17.0		1	17.1		1
Robust male	17.9		1	20.5		1	21.4		1

Table 18 shows mandibular molar breadth dimensions for the sexable
Lower Pleistocene specimens. None of the subsample differences in
sexual dimorphism have statistical significance. However, males again

Table 18. Statistics for mandibular molar breadths and mandibular corpus breadth and height in the four Lower Pleistocene hominid sub-samples. Measurements were used only for specimens that could be sexed by the canine or canine socket. Figures given for the corpus measurements are averages and are followed by sample size in parentheses. All measurements are in millimeters

| | M1 Breadth | | | M2 Breadth | | | M3 Breadth | | | Mandible | | | |
	X	Range	N	X	Range	N	X	Range	N	Height at P_4/M_1	Breadth at P_4	Height at M_1/M_2	Breadth at M_1/M_2
South African													
Gracile female	12.7	12.3–13.1	2	14.3	13.8–14.8	2	14.0	13.9–14.1	2	36.4 (1)	21.4 (2)	34.3 (2)	24.9 (2)
Gracile male	13.9	13.1–14.6	3	15.4	13.8–17.2	3	15.0	13.0–17.2	3	38.2 (2)	20.5 (2)	37.0 (2)	20.4 (1)
Robust female	14.0	13.2–15.0	6	14.9	14.3–16.4	6	14.3	13.2–16.0	4	39.3 (3)	22.5 (4)	36.4 (4)	24.4 (3)
Robust male	14.9	14.6–15.9	2	15.5	15.1–15.8	2	15.7	15.6–15.7	2	45.0 (1)	29.5 (1)	44 (1)	33.0 (1)
East African													
"*Homo*" female	11.5	10.9–12.0	4	12.4	11.8–13.5	4	12.1	11.6–12.5	3	31.4 (5)	18.7 (5)	30.8 (5)	19.5 (5)
"*Homo*" male	12.7	12.5–12.8	2	14.3	13.8–14.7	3	14.4		1	42.0 (1)	23.7 (2)	41.7 (1)	24.5 (1)
Robust female	15.0	14.5–15.4	2	16.1		1	16.0		1	42.7 (2)	24.9 (2)	40.4 (2)	29.6 (2)
Robust male	16.5	15.2–18.7	3	18.0	18.0–18.0	3	17.5	15.6–18.7	4	47.8 (5)	29.3 (5)	45.8 (5)	27.7 (5)

are uniformly larger than females. In the mandible, breadth differences in each subsample are about the same for all three molars. The mandibular East African sample is larger than the maxillary sample, and consequently the subsample sexual dimorphism indicated in Table 18 is of more significance.

Average molar size was calculated for males and females in the combined sample. In the maxilla dimorphism is greatest in M^1. The difference is significant on the 0.05 level. Dimorphism in the other maxillary molars is not significantly different. Almost exactly the opposite pattern occurs in the combined mandibular sample. Dimorphism is least in M_1 and greatest in M_3. The sex difference in M_2 and M_3 is significant at the 0.05 level. Dimorphism in these two molars is greater than in any of the maxillary teeth.

In sum, it appears that canine breadth dimorphism is not completely independent of breadth dimorphism in the molars, although the latter is less extensive and not bimodal. Because there is some amount of post-canine tooth size dimorphism, it is tempting to suggest that large gracile specimens such as MLD 2 and STS 1 are males and that small robust specimens such as SK 21, SK 81, SK 45, SK 1587, and SK 1588 are females. However likely, these designations cannot be established with the same degree of accuracy as can designations for specimens with canines or canine sockets.

Table 18 also indicates data for mandibular heights and breadths of sexable specimens. All observations were taken on the original specimens by the author. Sample size for East African *"Homo"* males is small, including ER 1483 and the juvenile OH 7 breadth value at P_4. The only East African robust female mandible is Natron, which is quite large when compared with possible females, albeit without canines, such as ER 727. Even so, mandibular height is uniformly greater in the males of each subsample. Mandibular breadth is quite another matter. In the South African gracile comparisons and in the East African robust comparison at M_1/M_2, the mandibles are actually broader in the female sample. While this reversal does not occur in the South African robust sample, it should be noted that there is only one male specimen with mandibular dimensions, SK 12. It is possible, if not likely, that in larger sexable samples male breadths would be uniformly greater than female breadths. However, these limited data indicate that sexual dimorphism is far more pronounced in mandibular height than in mandibular breadth. Table 19 shows the distribution of corpus heights at M_1/M_2 for the four subsamples. Canine sexes, where available, are indicated. For the South African sample, known males are uniformly larger than females in this measure.

The only unsexed specimen appearing is MLD 34. It falls within the female distribution. East African "*Homo*" specimens include males and females. The East African robust sample seems to show a natural gap between ER 819 (height = 39.1 millimeters) and ER 725 (height = 42.7 millimeters). Only three of the specimens are sexed by the canine, and of these, one possible male, ER 810, falls in what might be considered the female distribution. The ER 810 canine falls at the low end of the male range based on a canine socket measurement. Consequently, it is possible that the specimen is mis-sexed, although I would not like to base the case for dimorphism in the East African robust mandible height distribution on this possibility. A final determination must await more sexable specimens.

In sum, it appears that for a mandibular corpus without canines or

Table 19.   Distribution of mandibular corpus height in millimeters for the four Lower Pleistocene hominid subsamples. Specimens are given in size order, and a possible gap between male and female distributions is indicated. Canine sexes, when available, are given

South African Gracile	Robust	Mandible height at M_1/M_2 East African "Homo"	Robust
MLD 18 (F) 33.1	TM 1517 (F) 34.1	OH 13 (F) 24.7	ER 727 34.7
MLD 34 34.7	SK 23 (F) 36.2	ER1501 (F) 30.4	ER 728 36.0
MLD 40 (F) 35.5	SK 34 (F) 41.0	OH 37 (F) 32.2	ER 733 38.3
		ER 992 (F) 32.7	ER 810 (M) 38.3
		ER 730 (F) 34.0	Natron (F) 38.8
			ER 805 39.0
STS 7 (M) 37.0	SK 12 (M) 44.0	ER1483 (M) 41.7	ER 819 39.1
STS 36 (M) 37.0			ER 725 42.7
			ER 801 43.7
			ER 729 (M) 44.3
			ER 726 46.9
			ER 403 47.6
			ER 404 49.0
			ER 818 54.5

canine sockets, the corpus height and the breadth of the last two molars are probably the best sexing criteria.

Sexing individual specimens allows some conclusions to be made about variation in cranial features. However, the sample size of few features is large enough to allow adequate statistical treatment. Sagittal cresting occurs in all adult South African males for which observations of the appropriate area can be made (SK 46 and SK 52). SK 46 actually has a preserved crest. SK 52 is not preserved in the sagittal region. However, the temporal ridge closely parallels the superior orbital border to the approximate midpoint of the orbit where the specimen is broken. The direct medial extension of the temporal ridge behind the orbit is inevitably associated with anterior sagittal cresting for strictly mechanical reasons (Wolpoff 1974a).

Of the three reported female crania, cresting occurs in SK 48. There is no crest on SK 80/847 (Wolpoff 1974a). Finally, the morphology of the sagittal area and the position of the temporal ridge medial to the very lateral corner of the orbit on SK 79 could not be determined in spite of attempts to further clean the matrix in these areas. Consequently, the presence or absence of cresting could not be established.

In the South African gracile sample, the female cranium STS 5 is uncrested. In the male STS 71 the temporal lines meet at bregma, although no crest is formed. The male specimen STS 17 has a temporal ridge that extends to within 10 millimeters of the midline closely paralleling the superior orbital border. Although the regions medial and posterior to the ridge are missing, it is likely that the specimen had a sagittal crest (Wolpoff 1974a).

In the East African robust specimens that can be sexed, OH 5 is crested, while it is likely that the Chesowanja female is not (Walker 1971). Unfortunately, ER 406, which is crested, and ER 732 and ER 733, which are not, cannot be sexed by canine or canine socket size. The closest approach of the temporal lines in both ER 732 and ER 733 is 24 millimeters. These are much closer together than the closest approach of the lines in the South African gracile female STS 5, 40 millimeters, or the robust female SK 80/847, 48 millimeters.

The two East African "*Homo*" crania which can be sexed are both from Olduvai, OH 7 and OH 16. OH 16, a male, is uncrested. The closest approach of the temporal lines is 28.5 millimeters. In OH 7, probably a male, the closest approach of the temporal lines is 55 millimeters. The age of OH 7 is fourteen to fifteen years. In the East African samples, the question of eventual cresting in the adult is unclear because the ontogeny of cresting is largely unknown. SK 27, an eight- to ten-year-old male robust specimen from South Africa, has a minimum distance between the temporal lines of 74 millimeters. In three of the four uncrested East African specimens, OH 16, ER 733, and Chesowanja, the third molars are either completely unworn or show only the slightest wear on the tips of the mesial cusps. These are the only data bearing on the dental or chronological age of crest formation, and it is apparent that any or all of these specimens might have developed crests after occlusal eruption of M3. Consequently, cresting as a marker of sexual dimorphism in the East African samples can be neither established nor denied.

In the South African samples it appears that cresting is more likely in males than in females and that the incidence of cresting is slightly greater in the robust sample, in that some robust females may have crests and some gracile males may not. This difference is likely attributable to the average body size difference (Wolpoff 1974b).

Sample size for most other calvarial features is inadequate for statistically verifiable generalizations in either the South or East African samples. Cases from South Africa, where the sample size is greater than one, allow only hints of what the variation might be like. Cranial lengths measured from porion or mastoidale are greater in the robust male sample (n = 2) than the female sample (n = 3). The length difference also occurs in the only parietal sagittal comparison possible, SK 80 and SK 46. The sexable gracile sample is too small to allow length comparisons. Male gracile cranial breadth (n = 2) seems greater than female (n = 1). No robust male breadths are possible.

South African sample size for facial features is somewhat greater. In facial breadths the female samples are the same or even slightly larger than males, whereas in facial heights the males seem slightly larger, especially in measures of the zygomatic process of the maxilla. None of the facial differences, excepting the latter, are great enough to predict statistical significance with larger sample size.

From the limited information available, the South African samples appear to show more dimorphism in the cranium than in the face. The greatest facial dimorphism occurs in the region affected by the size of the masseter. With even these small samples, it is apparent that extensive overlap between males and females occurs.

The extent of sexual dimorphism in the postcranial skeleton can only be glimpsed because only three bones can be sexed. STS 14 can be directly sexed as female, TM 1517 is associated with a mandible and cranium both sexed as female, and STS 7 is associated with a mandible sexed as male. As Table 20 indicates, the reconstructed height based on the estimated length of STS 14 is considerably less than the reconstructed height based on the length of STS 7 (see Wolpoff 1973 for a detailed discussion of the height reconstructions). Broom equates the size of the TM 1517 humerus and talus fragments with a female Bushman (Broom and Schepers 1946). The comparable dimensions of these bones are only slightly larger than those reported for a female pygmy (Broek 1938) with a 262-millimeter-long humerus and a 362-millimeter-long femur. Estimated height for the pygmy is about midway between heights estimated for STS 14 and STS 7, and based on comparable dimensions, TM 1517 is no more than 10 percent larger than the pygmy female. In sum, the

Table 20. Some postcranial bone maximum comparisons for three Lower Pleisto-cene hominid subsamples. Comparisons were not possible for the East African *"Homo"* sample. Measurements are given in millimeters and are followed by the percentage difference. STS 14e is a second lumbar. STS 73 is an upper lumbar and is compared with STS 14e because it is the largest in the STS 14 lumbar column. The femur length for STS 14 and the estimated humerus length for STS 7 are given. The indirect comparison is between estimated body heights (see Wolpoff 1973). ER 738 and ER 736 are the largest and smallest published femurs from East Rudolf attributed to the robust sample. TM 1517 and SK 860 are distal humerus frag-ments. Finally, SK 853, a third lumbar, is compared with SK 3981b, a terminal lumbar. The direct percentage differences are given. However, the actual body size difference indicated is greater. This can be seen from the corresponding L_t/L_3 percentages given for STS 14. In almost all cases the Sterkfontein L_t is smaller than the L_3. In the Swartkrans comparison L_3 is the smaller vertebra, suggesting that the individuals concerned were even more different in vertebra size than the direct comparisons show

			Percentage	
South African gracile sample				
	STS 14e	STS 73		
Dorsal cranial-caudal centrum thickness	20.3	21.3	105	
Ventral cranial-caudal centrum thickness	19.5	19.8	102	
Dorsal-ventral cranial centrum length	20.5	24.3	119	
Transverse cranial centrum breadth	24.1	32.0	133	
	STS 14	STS 7		
Estimated limb length	285	310		
Estimated height	1220	1610	132	
South African robust sample				
	TM 1517	SK 860		
Medial-lateral breadth above olecranon fossa	33	39	118	
Anterior-posterior breadth	13	24	185	
Proximal fossa border to distal bone border	32	35	109	
Posterior breadth of trochlea	17.5	22.0	129	
	SK 853 (L_3)	SK 3981b (L_t)		STS 14 percent
Dorsal cranial-caudal centrum thickness	16.0	21.4	134	84
Ventral thickness	15.9	19.3	121	98
Dorsal-ventral cranial centrum length	19.2	24.0	125	97
Transverse cranial breadth	27.4	39.3	143	116
Dorsal-ventral caudal centrum length	18.5	20.7	112	79
Transverse caudal breadth	29.1	33.0	113	94
East African robust sample				
	ER 738	ER 736		
Circumference below lesser trochanter	80	118	148	
Anterior-posterior diameter	23.2	34.6	149	
Medial-lateral diameter	27.2	38.8	143	

male australopithecine is considerably larger than either female, and the two female specimens show extensive variation.

Unfortunately, sample size does not allow generalization beyond this, and it is surely no surprise that males are larger than females. The limited data hint at the possibility that the degree of body size sexual dimorphism may be greater than is usually the case within *Homo sapiens* populations, although it may not exceed the extremes within the whole species. Table 20 shows that the range of size variation within each Lower Pleistocene hominid subsample is great, even though there are only a few specimens available for comparison. How much of this variation is due to sexual dimorphism remains unknown. While the comparison of sexable postcranial bones suggests this contribution might be great, the extensive overlap between cranial, mandibular, and dental features of sexed specimens for a far larger sample must be taken into account. Given that no two specimens can be presumed in the same biological population, the confusion of interpopulation and intrapopulation variation is inevitable. However, the subsample molar breadths given in Tables 17 and 18, showing females of some samples larger than males of others in many cases, suggest that size variation between populations exceeds variation due to sexual dimorphism within them for the combined sample. In this pattern, the Lower Pleistocene hominids follow a pattern like modern man and unlike gorillas.

CONCLUSIONS

The Lower Pleistocene hominid specimens appear to show pronounced sexual dimorphism in canine breadth. Given individual sexing by this criterion, less pronounced dimorphism is shown in certain other features. Male and female modal ranges in canine breadth are the same for all four subsamples, while dimorphism in the other features discussed can only be established for each subsample independently. If these dimorphisms result from average male-female differences in body size and robustness, it appears that the total Lower Pleistocene sample has more body size and robustness variation between these subsamples than within them.

The canine dimorphism itself requires explanation. Australopithecine canines are totally hominid in function. The canines wear to the plane of the postcanine dentition, and all known P_3 specimens are nonsectorial, molarized teeth. On the other hand, unworn canines are pointed and the roots are large compared with later hominids. Because of the high rate of attrition and the low crown, these canines clearly do not function as do the canines of nonhuman primates. On the other hand, it is possible that the retention of sexual dimorphism, pointed crowns, and large roots are "holdovers" from a time in the not-distant (australopithecine) past when the canine-premolar complex had a different function.

While this explanation is possible, I personally do not like "holdover" explanations for morphological features. In addition, the demonstration of a delayed maturation rate coupled with shortened birth spacing, and the adaptations to bipedal locomotion and striding gait, all argue for some period of time prior to the Lower Pleistocene in which there was extensive selection resulting from cultural behavior. It seems to me that this period of selection would have also affected sexual dimorphism in the canines if dimorphic canines were truly functionless.

Brace (1973) suggests that early hominids, as terrestrial primates, might be expected to show a large degree of sexual dimorphism, possibly even exceeding the African pongids. He argues (1973: 240):

> While it has been noted that the development of culture has drastically altered the nature of the selective forces that have acted to shape the human physique ... it should also follow that the earlier the hominid the less effective was the cultural solution to environmentally imposed obstacles to survival.

How might this model apply to the Lower Pleistocene hominids? It is apparent that by the Lower Pleistocene, cultural selection had already led to considerable morphological changes in the cranial and postcranial skeleton, as well as changes in both structure and function of the canine itself. Sexual dimorphism in the canine does not exceed that of African pongids, and in fact is considerably less than that of gorillas. For the total sample, body size variation between populations seems to exceed sexual dimorphism within them, even though sexual dimorphism is more pronounced than in modern man. Reduction of canine size, pattern of attrition, and considerable alteration of P_3 morphology suggest that culture had, for some time, replaced the canine as an offensive and a defensive weapon. Consequently, the existing dimorphism probably does not result from possible differences in sexual roles concerned with offensive and defensive behavior directly affecting the canines.

Canines have other functions in the nonhuman primates which could be influenced by selection due to cultural behavior. Of these, probably the most important are food preparation and maintenance of dominance. If there was a significant difference in the diets of male and female australopithecines, the existing dimorphism might result from the ineffectiveness of early hominid culture in supplanting the anterior dentition in food preparation. However, there is no evidence suggesting such a dietary difference, and in any event, it seems to me that even the simplest stone tools would effectively replace the cutting function of the anterior dentition in a creature that shows flat canine and incisal wear soon after eruption.

Dimorphism due to the differential use of canines in dominance displays is a second possibility. Here again, the problem with this explanation arises when considering the importance of cultural behavior. If tools and weapons were important enough to allow canine size reduction, selection for bipedal locomotion for carrying, and delayed maturation for effective transmission of cultural behavior, it is probable that they had also replaced the canines in dominance displays. Either of these explanations may in actuality be correct, but on the basis of the present evidence they do not seem likely.

As an alternative, I propose the hypothesis that canine size dimorphism in the Lower Pleistocene hominids is a secondary sexual characteristic, as is the case in modern man. I suggest that the larger male canines are linked to larger and more robust body size in the males of each australopithecine population. Dimorphism in body size could result from the lesser effectiveness of culture and technology, which selected for significantly larger males in these early terrestrial hominids. For instance, if there were sexual differentiation in hunting and scavenging, the use of weapons only effective at close quarters would surely select for size and strength in males. This hypothesis cannot be easily tested because we cannot identify actual australopithecine populations. Other evidence suggests extensive size variation between populations, so that a mixture of specimens, even in a temporally and geographically restricted sample, probably gives little indication of what population variation was like. However, one can infer that if canine dimorphism was great within actual australopithecine populations, quite possibly body size dimorphism was also extensive. I present these suggestions, then, as the best of a series of possible explanations.

One other inference can be gained from the demonstration of significant canine dimorphism in the Lower Pleistocene. One would expect that earlier hominids, or protohominids, should similarly have pronounced canine sexual dimorphism, and if terrestrial, body size dimorphism as well. This prediction should specifically apply to *Ramapithecus*. Given that the known canines and canine sockets are uniformly small, it is possible that male canines for this taxon have yet to be correctly identified.

SUMMARY

A clearly bimodal distribution in canine breadth occurs in the Lower Pleistocene hominid sample. Sexing individual specimens on this basis suggests the presence of both males and females in the four subsamples discussed. The average difference between sexes for australopithecines is not as great as for chimpanzees, but the variation within each sex seems less, so that the distributions of australopithecine males and females are less overlapping. The difference between the modal means for australopithecines is significantly greater than for *Homo*, although the variability of the combined australopithecine sample and the average canine breadth dimension follow the Mid-Pleistocene *Homo* pattern.

Other characteristics show some evidence of sexual dimorphism. Three specimens with sexable postcranial remains show an extensive male-female difference. Mandibular corpus height appears to be a good indicator of sex within each subsample. However, the cranial, mandibular, and dental features that show evidence of dimorphism also show extensive variation between the four subsamples considered. Dimorphism is greater in the mandibular teeth than in the maxillary ones.

As the best of a number of possible explanations, I suggest that the presence of canine dimorphism is a secondary sexual characteristic, linked to sexual dimorphism in body size. Extensive body size variation occurs between the known samples, so that within-population sexual dimorphism in body size can only be inferred. This inference fits the general model of greater dimorphism in body size resulting from lesser cultural effectiveness in Lower Pleistocene hominid adaptation.

REFERENCES

ARAMBOURG, C.
1963 Le gisement de Ternifine I. *Archives de l'Institut de Paléontologie Humaine, Mémoire* 32:37–190.
BARRETT, M. J., T. BROWN, G. ARATO, I. V. OZOLS
1964 Dental observations on Australian Aborigines: buccolingual crown diameters of deciduous and permanent teeth. *Australian Dental Journal* 9:280–285.
BRACE, C. L.
1969 The australopithecine range of variation (abstract). *American Journal of Physical Anthropology* 31:255.
1973 "Sexual dimorphism in human evolution," in *Man in evolutionary perspective*. Edited by C. L. Brace and J. Metress, 238–254. New York: Wiley.

BRACE, C. L., H. NELSON, N. KORN
1971   *Atlas of fossil man.* New York: Holt, Rinehart and Winston.
BROEK, A. J. P.
1938   Das Skelett einer weiblichen Efe-Pygmäe. *Zeitschrift für Morphologie und Anthropologie* 40:121–169.
BROOM, R.
1939   A restoration of the Kromdraai skull. *Annals of the Transvaal Museum* 19:327–329.
BROOM, R., J. T. ROBINSON
1952   *Swartkrans ape-man,* Paranthropus crassidens. Transvaal Museum Memoir 6. Pretoria: Transvaal Museum.
BROOM, R., J. T. ROBINSON, G. W. H. SCHEPERS
1950   *Sterkfontein ape-man,* Plesianthropus. Transvaal Museum Memoir 4. Pretoria: Transvaal Museum.
BROOM, R., G. W. H. SCHEPERS
1946   *The South African fossil ape-men, the Australopithecinae.* Transvaal Museum Memoir 2. Pretoria: Transvaal Museum.
DART, R. A.
1949a The cranio-facial fragment of *Australopithecus prometheus.* *American Journal of Physical Anthropology* 7:187–214.
1949b A second adult palate of *Australopithecus prometheus.* *American Journal of Physical Anthropology* 7:335–338.
1962   A cleft mandible and nine other lower jaw fragments from Makapansgat. *American Journal of Physical Anthropology* 20:267–286.
DE LUMLEY, M., J. PIVETEAU
1969   Les restes humains de la grotte du Lazaret. *Mémoires de la Société Préhistorique Française* 7:223–232.
DITCH, L. E., J. C. ROSE
1972   A multivariate dental sexing technique. *American Journal of Physical Anthropology* 37:61-64.
FREEDMAN, L.
1957   The fossil Cercopithecoidea of South Africa. *Annals of the Transvaal Museum* 23(2):121–262.
GARN, S. M., A. B. LEWIS, R. S. KEREWSKY
1964   Sex difference in tooth size. *Journal of Dental Research* 43:306.
1966a Sexual dimorphism in the buccolingual tooth diameter. *Journal of Dental Research* 45:1819.
1966b Relationship between sexual dimorphism in tooth-size and body-size studies within families. *Archives of Oral Biology* 12:299–301.
GARN, S. M., A. B. LEWIS, D. R. SWINDLER, R. KEREWSKY
1967   Genetic control of sexual dimorphism in tooth size. *Journal of Dental Research* 46:963–972.
GONDA, K.
1959   On the sexual difference in the dimensions of human teeth. *Journal of the Anthropological Society of Nippon* 67:151–163.
HOLLOWAY, R. L.
1970   Australopithecine endocast (Taung specimen, 1924): a new volume determination. *Science* 168:966–968.

JELINEK, J.
1967 Der Fund eines Neandertaler Kiefers (Kulna) aus der Kulnahöhle in Mähren. *Anthropologie* 5(1):3–19.

KANNELIS, A., R. SAVAS
1964 Kraniometriki Meleti ton *Homo neanderthalensis* ton Petralonen. *Epistimeniki Epetiris tis Physikomathematikis Sholos* 9:65–92.

KROGMAN, W. M.
1962 *The human skeleton in forensic medicine.* Springfield: Thomas.

LEAKEY, R. E. F.
1972 Further evidence of Lower Pleistocene hominids from East Rudolf, North Kenya, 1971. *Nature* 237:264–269.

LEAKEY, R. E. F., K. W. BUTZER, M. H. DAY
1969 Early *Homo sapiens* remains from the Omo River region of southwest Ethiopia. *Nature* 222:1132—1138.

MIJSBERG, W. A.
1931 On sexual differences in the teeth of the Javanese. *Koninklijke Akademie van Wetenschappen te Amsterdam*, Series B 34:1111–1115.

MIYABARA, T.
1916 An anthropological study of the masticatory system in the Japanese (1): the teeth. *Dental Cosmos* 16:739–749.

MOORREES, C. F. A.
1957 *The Aleut dentition.* Cambridge: Harvard University Press.

PHENICE, T. W.
1969 A newly developed visual method of sexing the *os pubis*. *American Journal of Physical Anthropology* 30:297–302.

PILBEAM, D. R.
1969 *Tertiary Pongidae of East Africa: evolutionary relationships and taxonomy.* Peabody Museum Bulletin 31:1–185.
1972 Adaptive response of hominids to their environment as ascertained by fossil evidence. *Social Biology* 19:115–127.

ROBINSON, J. T.
1956 *The dentition of the Australopithecinae.* Transvaal Museum Memoir 9. Pretoria: Transvaal Mureum.
1962 Australopithecines and artifacts at Sterkfontein. Part 1: Sterkfontein stratigraphy and the significance of the Extension site. *South African Archaeological Bulletin* 17:87–107.
1970 Two new early hominid vertebrae from Swartkrans. *Nature* 225:1217–1219.
1972 *Early hominid posture and locomotion.* Chicago: University of Chicago.

SARTONO, S.
1971 Observations on a new skull of *Pithecanthropus erectus* (*Pithecanthropus VIII*) from Sangiran, Central Java. *Proceedings of the Koninklijke Akademie van Wetenschappen, Amsterdam*, Series B 74:185–194.

SCHUMAN, E. L., C. L. BRACE
1954 Metric and morphologic variations in the dentition of the Liberian chimpanzee. *Human Biology* 26:239–268.

SELMER-OLSEN, R.
  1949   An odontometrical study of the Norwegian Lapps. *Skifter det Norske Videnskaps-Akademi I Oslo, Mathematisk-Natur-videnskapelig Klasse* 65(3):1–168.

SUZUKI, H., F. TAKAI
  1970   *The Amud man and his cave site.* Tokyo: University of Tokyo.

TAYLOR, R. M. S.
  1969   Variation in the form of human teeth II: an anthropological and forensic study of maxillary canines. *Journal of Dental Research* 48:173–182.

THOMSEN, S.
  1955   *Dental morphology and occlusion in the people of Tristan da Cunha.* Det Norske Videnskaps–Akademi, Oslo 25.

VALLOIS, H. V., R. VANDERMEERSCH
  1972   Le crâne mousterien de Qafzeh (*Homo VI*). *L'Anthropologie* 76: 71–96.

VON KOENIGSWALD, G. H. R.
  1954   *Pithecanthropus, Meganthropus*, and the Australopithecinae. *Nature* 173:795–797.

WALKER, A.
  1971   Late australopithecine from Baringo district, Kenya: partial australopithecine cranium. *Nature* 230:513–514.

WOLPOFF, M. H.
  1971a *Metric trends in hominid dental evolution.* Case Western Reserve University Studies in Anthropology 2. Cleveland: Case Western Reserve University Press.
  1971b Interstitial wear. *American Journal of Physical Anthropology* 34:205–228.
  1973   Posterior tooth size, body size, and diet in South African gracile australopithecines. *American Journal of Physical Anthropology* 39:375–394.
  1974a Sagittal cresting in the South African australopithecines. *American Journal of Physical Anthropology* 40:397–408.
  1974b The evidence for two australopithecine lineages in South Africa. *Yearbook of Physical Anthropology* 17:113–139.

ZINGESER, M. R.
  1967   Odontometric characteristics of the Howler monkey (*Alouatta caraya*). *Journal of Dental Research* 46:975–978.

Discussion

[Susan Cachel presented a summary of her paper].

SACHER: Miss Cachel, what place does the factor of speed in the prey have in your theory on gracile and robust australopithecines? And how do you relate your theory to the problem of Pleistocene extinctions? The larger, and presumably slower, animals preferentially went to total extinction, which would have left the robust australopithecines without any prey to pursue, if they did not adapt to pursue smaller and speedier animals.

CACHEL: I did not consider the matter of Pleistocene extinctions. Nor did I consider the speed of the animals being pursued. Pleistocene extinctions of large prey may have contributed to the demise of robust australopiths, although I do not believe that megaherbivores were exploited by these forms.

WOLPOFF: Your reconstruction is very interesting. We need more hypotheses like this one as a basis from which to interpret that vast mosaic of variation in the australopithecines. How does the massive size of the postcanine dentition in the australopithecines relate to your concept that they were hunters?

CACHEL: The massive size of the posterior dentition in *A. robustus* can best be explained by allometry. In mammalian groups that differ in size it appears that the posterior part of the dentition is being emphasized relative to the anterior part of the dentition. That which Robinson considered the major criterion of the dietary hypothesis can best be explained by allometry.

WOLPOFF: Do you appreciate the fact that in gracile australopithecines with an estimated body weight of perhaps fifty to sixty pounds, the postcanine dentition is fully within the range of modern gorilla? In fact it is only about 10 percent smaller than the gorilla average. The problem is not just to explain the robust australopithecines. It is to explain the massive dentition of *A. africanus*.

CACHEL: It is not simply a question of absolute size, it is the comparison of anterior dentition to posterior dentition which is telling. Accordingly *A. africanus* clearly does not have its posterior dentition developed to the extent that the robust form does.

TOBIAS: I too found Sue Cachel's hypothesis very interesting. We have suffered in the past from thinking too much in terms of unifactorial analyses. There is no reason why the divergences of lineages should have been accompanied or caused by a single set of factors. This hypothesis is an additional point in the total pool of ideas about divergence. In your paper (see Cachel, this volume) you refer to the decreasing size of the robust australopithecines in time. I am not quite sure what you base that on. In fact it would seem that there was a trend to increasing size. For instance at Omo, where we have a very well dated series, the earliest teeth of the robust form are not extremely robust, but the later ones become more and more robust. Bob Eckhardt's paper (see Eckhardt, this volume) is also factually wrong in that the earliest hominids at Omo (about 3.1 million years B.P.) are not the extremely robust mandibles. There are only a few isolated teeth. The very robust specimens come later in the Omo sequence and are dated nearer to two million than to 3.1 million years.

ECKHARDT: We are not at variance, Phil, my statement was that the earliest mandibles from Omo are extremely robust.

TOBIAS: Your statement put them at about 3.1 million years and they are not nearly that old. There are only a few isolated teeth at 3.1 million years. The mandibles are more recent in time.

ECKHARDT: What date? My statement did not put the Omo mandibles at 3.1 million years ago. It put the Omo remains in general, jaws and teeth, in this time range. The Omo deposits are generally known to cover a substantial period of time. It should also be realized that all dates under discussion here have an error factor associated with them.

TOBIAS: About two million years B.P.

ECKHARDT: My dating was Clark Howell's dating.

TOBIAS: I am quoting dating from Clark Howell's laboratory last week.

CACHEL: Dr. Tobias, I was using a statement in one of your papers concerning decreasing robusticity with time. I assume that my ideas would be able to explain that statement. It is not an integral part of the thesis.

TOBIAS: I may have said that earlier. At that stage I did not believe what Professor von Koenigswald had claimed. But the newer datings have shown him to be right and myself wrong. I do not think it is essential to your hypothesis either. I am glad you pointed that out.

[Dr. John Wallace presented a summary of his paper.]

AUDIENCE: To what extent is it possible to recognize sexual dimorphism in these forms?

WOLPOFF: I attempted to determine how much sexual dimorphism occurs in the australopithecines. There is only one specimen that can be sexed by its pubic bone, viz. STS 14. It is a female. But there are no associated jaws. In man and great apes, the canine tooth is probably the best dental vehicle for sexing. It shows the most dimorphism. And in the canine, breadth shows the most dimorphism. I plotted canine breadth measurements of the australopithecines. At Sterkfontein and Makapan there are bimodal distributions roughly equivalent with that in the chimpanzee. At Swartkrans there is a bimodal distribution roughly equivalent to the chimpanzee. This is true for the mandibular and the maxillary canines in samples separately as well as combined. I can think of no way of explaining this other than as a result of sexual dimorphism. The bimodal distribution is in fact a distribution of males (the larger mode) and females (the smaller mode) with very little overlap between them. Thus I infer that the amount of sexual dimorphism in the australopithecines is greater than that in any other hominid, and is something like what we find in chimpanzees. Looking at the crania which contain canines, or at least canine sockets, there is no necessary relationship between body size and sexual dimorphism. That is, there seem to be both large and small males, and large and small females. The most likely explanation for this in a population context is that each of these sites are samples of a number of polytypic populations which differ significantly in body size from each other. It is likely that there is more variation in australopithecine populations due to sexual dimorphism than would normally be the case in modern man. This must be kept in mind when we employ models of human variation in order to infer how much variation we should expect in the australopithecines.

TOBIAS: We should be very grateful to Milford Wolpoff and Loring Brace for having forcibly, if not always quite acceptably, drawn our attention to the need to take more care in considering sexual dimorphism in future studies. I think that the point is very well taken and I go along with everything that Milford said in his last remarks.

ECKHARDT: Among the available candidates for hominid ancestry only *Gigantopithecus* is represented by large enough samples to make statements about sexual dimorphism. It very clearly was a sexually dimorphic primate.

Plates

Plate 1. River Sutlej and the Siwalik Hills at Bilaspur, Himachal Pradesh, India

Plate 2. A panoramic view of the Siwalik Hills around Haritalyangar, Bilaspur, Himachal Pradesh

Plate 3.   The Cuesta Scarp, known locally as *Hari-Ka-Tibba,* at Haritalyangar; it is from this scarp that most of the hominoid fossils have been recovered at Haritalyangar

Plate 4.   The deep brown or red clay of Nagri beds, yielding primate fossils at Haritalyangar; Cuesta Scarp (*Hari-Ka-Tibba*), Haritalyangar

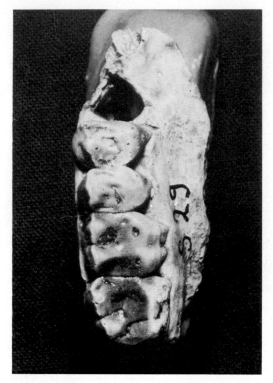

Plate 1.   Cast of the maxillary fragment **YPM** 13799 perpendicular to the level of occlusion

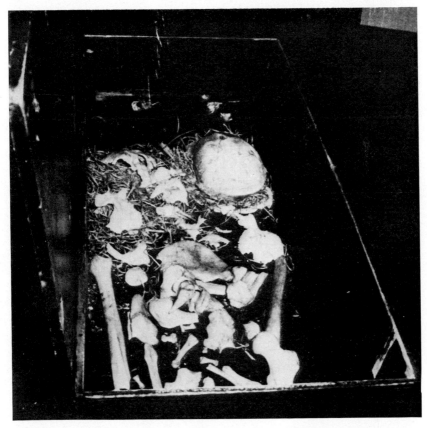

Plate 1.   Footlocker possibly containing some fossils from Choukoutien

Plate 1.   Lateral view

Key to Plates 1 through 6:

a.   *Homo erectus ngandongensis XI* (cast). Syn.: *Homo (Javanthropus) soloensis XI.*

b.   *Homo erectus erectus VIII* (original). Syn.: *Pithecanthropus (erectus) VIII.*

c.   *Homo erectus pekinensis* (cast). Syn.: *Sinanthropus pekinensis.*

d.   *Homo neanderthalensis* (cast).

Specimens in Plates 1–6 are of the same scale.

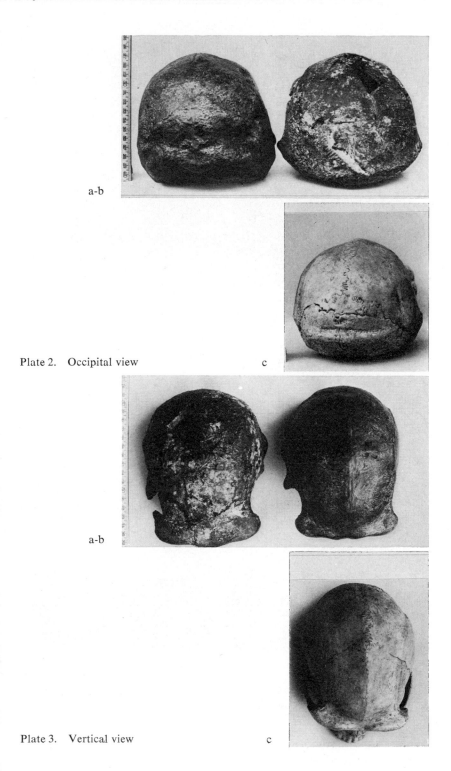

Plate 2.   Occipital view

a-b

c

Plate 3.   Vertical view

a-b

c

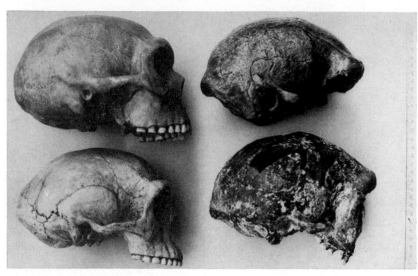

d-a

c-b

Plate 4. Lateral view

b-c

Plate 5. Occipital view

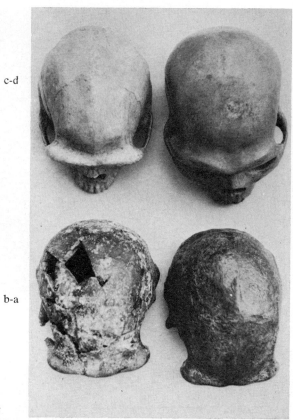

c-d

b-a

Plate 6.   Vertical view

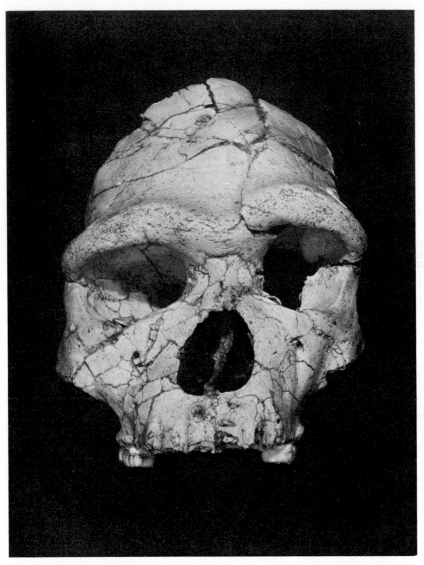

Plate 1. Skull of Tautavel man, found at the Caune de l'Arago (Pyrénées Orientales), 22 July 1971

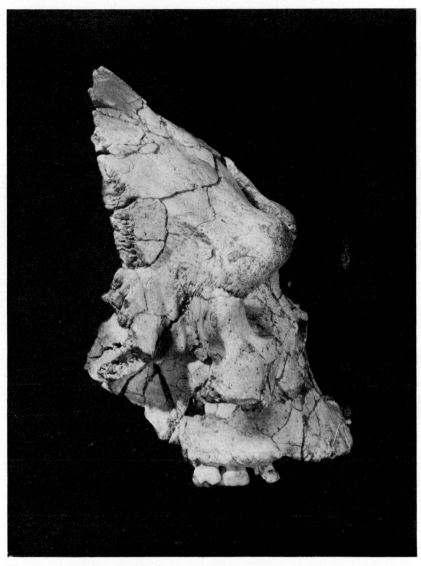

Plate 2.   Tautavel man; side view

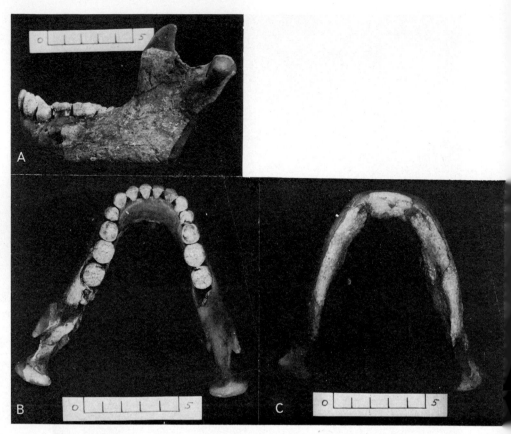

Plate 1.   Left lateral (A), occlusal (B), and inferior (C) aspects of the mandible from Zaskalnaya. Restored parts are darker than the fossil bits

SECTION FOUR

The Fate of the Chinese Homo erectus
Specimens That Were Lost in 1941

The Peking Man Fossils:
Progress of the Search

CHRISTOPHER G. JANUS

Anthropologists are normally quiet men, hardly suited to intrigue and mysterious plots meant to be executed in bad lighting and isolated corners. But the missing Peking Man fossils have crossed over the lines and turned placid scientists into sleuths and laboratory specimens into secret booty.

More than a year has passed since I became involved in the search. It has been a year of strange twists and bizarre coincidences, a time of intense investigations by amateurs and professionals. But certain events give me reason to believe that we may be close to recovering the long-lost Chinese Man from Peking, or at least to proving that the thirty-year mystery can never be solved.

The Peking Man fossils comprise the remains of some forty individuals, *Homo erectus,* the creatures who preceded modern man by as much as 500,000 years. They were found in digs which began in 1921 and continued through 1937. Until they were unearthed from the rocky soil of Choukoutien, only the two specimens of Java Man, found in 1891, pointed to *Homo erectus* as an ancestor of modern man. Peking Man (originally called *Sinanthropus pekinensis*) left no doubt in the minds of researchers that it was a true man, a man who knew how to use tools and fire.

In those terms, the dust settles over the drama and the Peking Man fossils take on major scientific importance, as the largest collection of *Homo erectus* remains (more than 150 specimens) ever found and proof that early man roamed widely throughout Asia.

This would be of interest only to an anthropologist except for a series of events that occurred in North China in the days just before

For plates, see p. v, between pp. 288–289

Pearl Harbor. Because of the Japanese threat to the mainland in November, 1941, the Chinese government made arrangements with the United States Marines, who were evacuating North China to ship the fossils to the American Museum of Natural History in New York, for safekeeping. The fossils were packed and sent to a United States Marines camp near the port city of Chinwangtao, where they remained until the war broke out and all the marines were taken prisoners. The fossils, packed in marine footlockers, were supposedly left in the camp and have not been seen since. Nobody really knows whether they were lost in the confusion, stolen by someone who understood their value, or destroyed by ignorant invaders.

When I went to China in May, 1972, I knew little about Peking Man. The whole story was told to me during my visit to the digs at Choukoutien, a small village southwest of Peking. My Chinese hosts felt sure that the fossils still existed. They had a "contract" with the Americans, they said, a "contract" with the United States Marines to recover them. They were adamant. The fossils were more than anthropological wonders — they were of great importance to the Chinese people. The Maoists had incorporated the discovery of the fossils into their political dialectic. Peking Man was proof that pure proletariat labor and the use of tools had developed man.

But now the Peking Man Museum, standing only yards from Dragon Bone Hill, where the fossils were unearthed, is missing its most valuable possessions. It is a castle without its crown jewels, a Louvre without its Mona Lisa. And it will remain that way until Peking Man is found.

The Chinese had asked me to help them locate their lost Peking Man. I was fascinated by the challenge. As soon as our group arrived back in Hong Kong from China, reporters besieged us with questions, not about our trip, but about Peking Man. Could I find the fossils? Did I have a plan? Where would I begin the search?

I decided to offer a $5,000 reward for information leading to the recovery of the fossils. The story of the reward received worldwide attention, and by the time I returned to America, hundreds of responses had poured in.

A year has passed. The search has become a complex and sometimes bizarre adventure. A woman who described herself as a friend of the late Edgar Snow telephoned me in June, 1972. She said that she was the widow of an ex-Marine and that she had the fossils. Her husband had told her just before he died that he had obtained them through violence and that he was leaving them to her as his legacy.

I met this woman on the observatory deck of the Empire State Building (this location was her idea, not mine), where she showed me a snapshot of an open footlocker containing what appeared to be a collection of bones (Plate 1). Before I could convince her to let an expert authenticate a specimen, she panicked at the sight of a tourist who had pointed a camera in our direction and she fled. I have not seen this woman again.

But she did telephone me once more and agreed to send me a copy of the photograph. It is not a good picture, but it shows a fossil skull that has piqued the interest of several prominent anthropologists, who think it may be Peking Man. The woman would not tell me her name. My only contact with her now is through a man who claims to be her attorney. He has called me several times.

He claims that his client is in great danger because of the collection of fossils, "which after all, is stolen property," and demands that we get written assurance from the United States State Department that she will not be prosecuted for having them. Mr. Francis B. Tenny, director of the Office of East Asian and Pacific Programs for the State Department, has written us a letter saying that the return of the fossils to the Chinese is in the national interest and that whoever possesses them will not be prosecuted. But the letter was not sufficient for the woman's lawyer. Now he wants me to secure a letter from the People's Republic of China guaranteeing that they will not harm his client.

The attorney also suggests that the fossils are worth at least $500,000 dollars. I am not averse to raising this money if the fossils are indeed Peking Man, but I am somewhat surprised by the lawyer's pushiness. At times he sounds more like a promoter than a member of the bar.

Another lead has come from a Chinese-American man in New York who has told me that a friend of his in Taiwan has the fossils. This man is not interested in reward money, but he is adamant about conducting the search in total secrecy. He is afraid of all the publicity that surrounds my involvement and he assures me that I am naive and do not understand the great danger we are in. I have met this man several times and I know his name. He is a complex individual who constantly complains that I do not understand the ramifications of the search, that I do not understand the Chinese mind. He has called me a dreamer or a madman. But he says that when all the excitement dies down, he will tell me the name of his friend, and the search can proceed according to his wishes.

Just a few weeks ago, I received a telephone call from a Russian gentleman who claims to have been a teacher in Shanghai during and after the war. He had seen a news story which stated that $100,000 was offered for the return of the Peking Man fossils and he wanted to know if the reward had been claimed. I explained that the reward was firm. Then he told me that after the war, in 1945, he had heard rumors that the fossils had been loaded aboard a Russian ship and sent to Yalta. He is in Yalta now, looking for the fossils, and promises to contact me when he returns. If he finds Peking Man, the story takes on a new twist. Would the Soviets, themselves cool toward Peking, turn the fossils over to the People's Republic?

Our search has also uncovered important information concerning the transfer of the fossils from the Peking Man Museum to the North China Marines. I have talked with Mrs. Claire Taschdjian, a biology teacher now living in New York, and the only person I know who has actually handled the fossils. She worked as a secretary at the Peking Union Medical College in 1941, and it was she who packed the fossils for shipment to the United States. She has supplied me with a complete inventory of the specimens. She has also told me the story of the search for the fossils in 1942-1943 by the Kompetai, the Japanese secret police. The Kompetai questioned her as often as twice a week and they also interrogated and even tortured other officials of the Peking Union Medical College. Their tactics stopped abruptly in 1943, and Mrs. Taschdjian thinks the Japanese might have discovered the whereabouts of the fossils.

Another important figure in the search is Dr. William T. Foley, a prominent Manhattan physician who with his assistant, Herman Davis, was attached to the North China Marines in 1941. The footlockers containing the fossils were turned over to Dr. Foley and were sent with his own baggage by train to Chinwangtao. Davis, stationed at Camp Holcomb, took custody of the footlockers when they arrived. Both men deny actually seeing the contents of the footlockers which supposedly contained Peking Man. Dr. Foley entrusted his own foot-lockers to several Chinese friends when he was taken captive, but he tells me that to reveal their identities could be dangerous for them.

Other developments have turned the search into a complicated mixture of plots and counterplots. The State Department has revealed that it is very interested in finding the fossils, if they are in the United States, and returning them to the Chinese. However, this introduces the political implications of the search, because it is possible that the Nationalist Chinese government has the fossils and it is unlikely that they would want them returned to the People's Republic.

What lies in the future is more investigation, negotiations, and discussions with the Empire State Building woman, the Chinese gentleman in New York, the Russian gentleman in Yalta, and others. I plan to go to Taiwan and follow up leads there. And, of course, an important step in the search will involve a return to the Chinese mainland and a visit to the World War II sites where the fossils were presumably left. Many people close to the search, especially a number of the North China Marines, have told me that they believe the Peking Man fossils are still in China if, indeed, they are anywhere.

If we find the fossils, not only will we clear up the thirty-year-old mystery surrounding their disappearance but we will also initiate important new scientific study. The fossils have not been dated by means of the sophisticated techniques developed during the last thirty years. We do not know how old they really are.

From what I have learned this past year, from intuitions, from leads and scattered bits of information, from numerous interviews, I am convinced that the Peking Man fossils still exist and I think that we can locate them and return to the Chinese the gemstone of their anthropological beginnings. In the process, we can rid science of the cloak-and-dagger intrigue that has surrounded Peking Man. It is fascinating, the stuff of which good novels are made, but certainly maddening to the scientist who simply wants to focus his microscope on a piece of prehistoric man and get on with his work.

Discussion

[Mr. Christopher Janus presented a summary of his paper].

VON KOENIGSWALD: May I relate my part of the story. I was a prisoner under the Japanese. It is absolutely impossible to keep things like foot-lockers in the prison camp. After the war there was a rumor that the Peking skulls were still in China. The Chinese did receive a number of "fossils" from Shanghai, but these turned out to be very well made casts. The original specimens were lost in China. My wife and I were able to save the Javanese fossils and they were brought from Java to the United States after the war. At the American Museum of Natural History, New York, we divided the material. Weidenreich took the Solo skulls and I kept *Pithecanthropus*. Professor Watson, a very well known paleontologist from London, visited us. While talking with Weidenreich he saw the skulls on Weidenreich's desk. They clearly were original skulls to a paleontologist. But he did not ask any question about them. Because everybody linked Weidenreich to *Sinanthropus*, Watson must have thought that they were the original *Sinanthropus* skulls. He went back to London and told students that he had seen the *Sinanthropus* skulls in New York. We know exactly how this news reached the Chinese. One week later Radio Peking announced that it was not true that the Peking material was lost. It was in the Osborn Tower of the American Museum of Natural History. Professor Watson had seen it. I received a letter from my friend Kenneth Oakley inquiring what I thought about the story. I told him what had happened. Oakley gave my story to a friend and the Chinese suddenly stopped the propoganda. They now said that all the material was lost except one skull. And this skull was in the American

Museum of Natural History. That is what I know about the original specimens of Peking man. I have seen a picture of a box full of human bones (see Plate 1 of Janus, this volume). Now this is clearly one skeleton of a modern man. In the box are parts which are not known from Peking Man, e.g. a complete pelvis, nearly complete long bones, and foot bones.

JANUS: What about the skull? Harry Shapiro, Glenn Cole, and a few other people told me that the skull has the dimension of Peking Man.

VON KOENIGSWALD: Yes, but the skull is too complete to be Peking Man. The Peking skulls are broken. They would not have put an original Peking skull in a box and then parts of a modern skeleton around it. I wish you the best!

TUTTLE: Would anyone other than Professor von Koenigswald like to step forth and collect the reward?

HOWELLS: I agree with Ralph von Koenigswald that this is not the Peking stuff. Not the skull either. I do not see that it can be matched to any of the known specimens. Another possibility is that the Upper Cave material, which was sent out at the same time, might be in the box. But the inventory of Upper Cave material consists of three good skulls, one skull top of an adult, and skeletal parts of three juveniles; altogether skeletal and cranial parts of about seven individuals. I looked at Weidenreich's dublications on the skulls and this skull cannot be matched to any of them. I do not even know whether there was an inventory of the postcranial material from the Upper Cave anywhere. But I do not think so. On the whole, I have looked very carefully at this picture (see Plate 1 of Janus, ¡his volume. It looks like the skeleton of almost anybody that had been forgotten about and dug up again. Dr. Janus did not tell us what Dr. Foley said about the shipment of the Peking and Upper Cave material from Peking to Chinwangtao, which is a seaport. Now there have been stories, of unknown origin, about its having been dumped in the water and lost that way. What actually happened was that it was in a couple of boxes with a lot of Marine gear. It was sent in three railway cars to Chinwang-tao, not to the docks but to a little Marine camp there, Camp Holcomb. The three cars arrived on the morning of December 8, 1941. (Dr. Foley was a Marine medical officer then, and had frequently visited Camp Holcomb). The eighteen Marines who had come down with the cars learned that they were at war. They took baggage out of the cars, set up a small perimeter and placed a machine gun on one box that had fossils in it. That is what one of the Marines, Herman Davis, says. The Japanese sent four men to ask the Marines to surrender. The Marines arrested the four Japanese instead. Then they got in touch by hand radio with the Marine commander in Tientsin, who said do not be silly, do what the

Plate 1. Left to right: Professor William W. Howells, Dr. Phillip V. Tobias, Mr. Christopher Janus, and Professor G. H. R. von Koenigswald examining and discussing a photograph (see Plate 1 page v of the Plates, between pages 288–289) of a footlocker purportedly containing remains of Peking Man (Photograph by George Sacher)

Japanese say and surrender. They did. They were parted from their baggage and sent to Tientsin. The baggage was to follow them. Well, there is a lot of confusion as to what followed after that. But it is the last time anybody was in contact with the baggage in any authoritative way. The important thing is that Camp Holcomb is better than a mile away from the waterside. So there is no reason to think that the bones went into the water at that point.

ADDENDUM: *January 3, 1974, by Prof. W. W. Howells*

Howells conferred with Janus and Tobias following the session, and the latter insisted that the skull, taken by itself looked important. Consequently, on returning to Harvard, Howells compared the photo directly with Weidenreich's casts of the Locus L skulls, which he had not done before. He found complete correspondence in all visible details between the photo and the cast of Skull II, Locus L (Skull XI of the total series), and is now satisfied that the photo contains the original or a good cast of that skull, together with various modern cranial and post-cranial bones.

SECTION FIVE

Revised Concepts of Early Man in Java

Early Man in Java: Catalogue and Problems

G. H. R. VON KOENIGSWALD

I previously published a summary of pre-Trinil human remains in Java (von Koenigswald 1969). I will now review the present state of affairs in Java, where altogether five different human types are known and three different faunal units can be distinguished.

NGANDONG FAUNA

Homo soloensis, Solo man, is a Javanese representative of Neanderthal man. New excavations at the type site of Ngandong have yielded no additional remains, but Professor T. Jacob has discovered (but not yet published) a new find at a new site in the Solo valley (personal communication).

The avian remains from Ngandong point to a slightly colder climate than that of today. Water buffaloes with enormous horn spreads of more than two meters indicate a more open country, not the typical rain forest conditions. We have thus correlated the Ngandong stage with the Würm glaciation in Europe and Asia. In addition, the astonishingly advanced bone culture and the completely rounded stone balls (often called "bolas") would hardly fit in an older period. Therefore, in spite of the primitive character of the Solo skulls, we see no reason to change our original correlation.

The rock fissures of Punung and Patjitan, in our opinion, are post-Trinil. A few isolated teeth, not yet published, indicate the presence of man here.

TRINIL FAUNA

The famous hominid of the Trinil fauna is the classic *Pithecanthropus* or *Homo erectus*. Recently, Sartono (1972) has discovered at Sangiran *Pithecanthropus* VII, a nearly complete skull with part of the face preserved. The skull has not yet been fully prepared and described.

The two large upper molars discovered by Dubois at Trinil in 1891–1892, which he regarded as belonging to *Pithecanthropus*, do not belong to an orang, as other authors have suggested, but to *Meganthropus*. The completely worn upper molar is not a third but a second molar; the unworn tooth is a third molar of a different individual.

DJETIS FAUNA

The *Pithecanthropus* from these layers is *Pithecanthropus* or *Homo modjokertensis*. In spite of stratigraphical and morphological considerations, Weidenreich formerly regarded this as just a male *erectus*; later he noted the differences and called the male skull from Sangiran (*Pithecanthropus* IV) *Pithecanthropus robustus*. From this skull we have a fine palate. A small fragment of a second palate was recently found by Sartono (1974).

The lower jaw of *Pithecanthropus* B, which I originally referred to as *erectus*, belongs instead to *modjokertensis*. Elsewhere, I have stressed the great primitiveness of the dentition. Now that absolute dates are available, the differences with *erectus* can no longer be dismissed as simple variability; rather, they show the typical characteristics of this early hominid.

No *Meganthropus palaeojavanicus* skull is known. Robinson (1953) was the first to compare this form with *Paranthropus*. For morphological and stratigraphical reasons (the faunas of South Africa and Java are too different and have no species in common), we cannot fully accept his view, but we now agree that *Meganthropus* is certainly "australopithecoid." There are some morphological considerations for this, but the main reason is that *Meganthropus* occurs in the same layer as *Homo modjokertensis*, and it seems very unlikely that two different representatives of the genus *Homo*, s.str. would occur side by side.

Pithecanthropus dubius still is insufficiently known. The body of the mandible is not inflated as in *Meganthropus* (and in most Australopithecinae). Both lower premolars are double-rooted, which is normal in anthropoids but which has not yet been observed in *Homo*.

Perhaps the most significant result since the last report was published is the first absolute date for the Djetis fauna. The fauna was first recognized in eastern Java near the town of Modjokerto, where it is intercalated in marine layers. Because the mollusk fauna contains 32 percent extinct species, Martin (1933) thought that it probably dated from the upper Pliocene. But the mammalian fauna, first collected by Cosijn (1932), includes specialized *Stegodon*, *Leptobos*, and *Machairodus*. After much discussion with the geologists and paleontologists of the Geological Survey in Bandung, we finally placed the whole faunal complex in the Lower Pleistocene and regarded it as the "Javanese Villafranchian." Shortly afterward the same fauna was observed at Sangiran; there the Djetis beds are much better developed and contain a number of species that are absent from Modjokerto, where apparently only the upper level is represented. At Sangiran the marine basal layers (*Turritella*-Clay) contain 55 percent extinct mollusks, indicating a lower marine level than at Modjokerto; this certainly dates from the Pliocene.

We have gone into so much detail because it is Modjokerto that yielded the first human fossil from the Djetis Beds, and from the locality where the skull was found we now have the first absolute date for this stage. The skull is that of an infant, very thin and only fourteen centimeters long. It was found in a shallow excavation by Andojo, one of the Indonesian assistants working for Ir. Duifjes, who mapped the area. By accident, this excavation was the only one in that region. Andojo had observed the skull of a *Leptobos* partly exposed by erosion and he excavated the fossil; just underneath it, at a depth of less than one meter, he discovered the human skull. Although it is not directly comparable to the Trinil skull cap, because of the differences in individual age and fauna, we felt that we could give a separate name to this apparently new *Pithecanthropus*. We had been asked to publish the first description in Holland. In my original manuscript the name *Pithecanthropus modjokertensis* had to be changed to *Homo modjokertensis* because at that time (1936) Professor Dubois regarded "his *Pithecanthropus*" as an anthropoid and thus no apparently human skull could be called *Pithecanthropus*.

But there were other difficulties, too. Several scientists could not believe that such a small, thin, human skull could be fossilized at all. I was quite astonished to discover that Weidenreich, in a joint article with me, had added in a separate footnote: "On the basis of my study of the original I have now come to the conclusion that this infantile skull reallly represents a *Pithecanthropus* child" (von Koenigswald and Weidenreich 1939: 927).

At Sangiran we were not able to find suitable material for a potassium/argon date of the Djetis. But Jacob and Curtis (1971) relocated the original site of the Modjokerto skull and were able to take datable samples. Because of impurities of the tuff sample, the possible errors are quite large. The date is 1,900,000 ± 400,000 years. But Curtis (1970, personal communication) assured me: "My feeling about the date is that it is more likely to turn out to be quite a bit older [than 1,900,000 years] than younger."

This date without any doubt places the Djetis in the Villafranchian. It must, however, be remembered that this determination is good for the upper Djetis only; the lower part might be considerably older. The section at Sangiran (for the Djetis alone) is about 100 meters thick. (At Olduvai one hundred meters of sediment cover a time span of nearly 2,000,000 years, but the rate of sedimentation in these two localities is not directly comparable.)

The new date also clarifies the correlation of our Javanese stratigraphy. For many years we have been contradicted by Hooijer (1968a, 1968b), who, because of the remains of primitive elephants, had put the Pliocene/Pleistocene boundary much lower than had the Geological Survey. In Europe the first true elephants arrive with the beginning of the Pleistocene, but in Africa — and apparently in Asia too — *Elephas* occurs in layers 4,000,000 years old, which are certainly Pliocene. Thus Hooijer's arguments are no longer valid.

Although *Homo modjokertensis* is still insufficiently known, in some ways it is not simply another *H. erectus*. Measured in time, the distance between *H. modjokertensis* and *erectus* is of about the same magnitude as that between *H. erectus* and *H. sapiens*. Thus the differences between the former two hominids cannot be dismissed on grounds of variability. If the canine in the palate of *H. modjokertensis* were just a little stronger, the dentition alone would not distinguish this *Homo* from an anthropoid.

The Lower Pleistocene age also explains why the dentition of *H. modjokertensis* has so much in common with the jaws of Hominid 13 from Olduvai (whatever "*Homo habilis*" might be), as was demonstrated by Tobias and myself.

There can be no doubt that *Meganthropus* was contemporaneous in the Djetis with *Homo modjokertensis* and in the Trinil with *Homo erectus*. Thus, at Sangiran as at Olduvai, Omo, and East Rudolf (and most probably in southern China, too), two branches of the human family tree are represented. In *Homo* we find the steady increase in brain capacity that leads to *Homo sapiens*; in the Australopithecinae the capacity remains on the anthropoid level. The unilineal theory of the descent of man, of orthogenesis without deviation, can no longer be defended. There is no reason why the family tree of man should be so much simpler than that of a horse or an elephant.

REFERENCES

ARAMBOURG, C., J. CHAVAILLON, Y. COPPENS
 1969 Résultats de la nouvelle mission de l'Omo (2e campagne 1968). *Centre de Recherche, Académie des Sciences, Paris* 268:759–762.
BOUMAN, K. H.
 1938 The brain-convolutions of the *Pithecanthropus erectus* of von Koenigswald. *Acta Neerlandica Morphologiae, Normalis et Pathologicae* 2:1-3.
COSIJN, J.
 1932 Voorlopige mededeling over het voorkomen van fossiele beenderen in het heuvelland ten noorden van Djetis en Perning (Midden Java). *Verhandelingen van het Geologisch – Mijnbouwkundig Genootschap voor Nederland en Koloniën (Geology Series)* 9:135–148.
HOOIJER, D. A.
 1952 Fossil mammals and the Plio-Pleistocene boundary in Java. *Proceedings of the Koninklijke Nederlandse Akademie van Wetenschappen, Amsterdam* 55B:436–443.
 1968a "The Middle Pleistocene of the Near East," in *Evolution und Hominisation* (second edition). Edited by G. Kurth, 82–85. Stuttgart: G. Fischer Verlag.
 1968b "The Middle Pleistocene of Java," in *Evolution und Hominisation* (second edition). Edited by G. Kurth, 86–90. Stuttgart: G. Fischer Verlag.
HOWELLS, W. W.
 1966 *Homo erectus. Scientific American* 215:46–53.
JACOB, T.
 1964 A new hominid skull cap from Pleistocene Sangiran. *Anthropologica*, n.s. 6:97–104.
 1966 The sixth skull cap of *Pithecanthropus erectus. American Journal of Physical Anthropology* 25:243–260.
 1972a The absolute date of the Djetis beds at Modjokerto. *Antiquity* 47:148.
 1972b New hominid finds in Indonesia and their affinities. *Mankind* 8:176–181.
JACOB, T., G. H. CURTIS
 1971 Preliminary potassium-argon dating of early man in Java. *Contributions of the University of California Archaeological Research Facility* 12:50.

KAPPERS, C. U. A., K. H. BOUMAN
1939   Comparison of the endocranial casts of the *Pithecanthropus erectus* skull found by Dubois and von Koenigswald's *Pithecanthropus* skull. *Proceedings of the Koninklijke Nederlandse Akademie van Wetenschappen, Amsterdam* 42:30–40.

MARKS, P.
1953   Preliminary note on the discovery of a new jaw of *Meganthropus* von Koenigswald in the lower Middle Pleistocene of Sangiran, Central Java. *Indonesian Journal of Natural Science* 1, 2, 3:26–33.

MARTIN, K.
1933   Eine neue tertiäre Molluskenfauna aus dem Indischen Archipel. *Leidsche Geologische Mededelingen* 6(1):7–32.

MC GREGOR, J. H.
1925   Recent studies on the skull and brain of *Pithecanthropus*. *Natural History* 25:544–559.

ROBINSON, J. T.
1953   *Meganthropus*, australopithecines and hominids. *American Journal of Physical Anthropology* 11:1.
1968   "The origin and adaptive radiation of the Australopithecines," in *Evolution und Hominisation* (second edition). Edited by G. Kurth, 150–175. Stuttgart: G. Fischer Verlag.

SARTONO, S.
1961   Notes on a new find of a *Pithecanthropus* mandible. *Publikasi Teknik Seri Paleontologi* 2:1–51.
1964   On a new find of another *Pithecanthropus* skull. *Bulletin of the Geological Survey of Indonesia* 1:2–5.
1967   An additional skull cap of a *Pithecanthropus*. *Journal of the Anthropological Society of Nippon* 75:83–93.
1968   Early man in Java: *Pithecanthropus* skull VII, a male specimen of *Pithecanthropus erectus* (I). *Proceedings of the Koninklijke Nederlandse Akademie van Wetenschappen, Amsterdam* series B, 71, (5).
1971   On the stratigraphic position of *Pithecanthropus* mandible C. *Proceedings of the Institut Teknologi Bandung* 4:91–102.
1972   Discovery of another hominid skull at Sangiran, Central Java. *Current Anthropology* 13(1):124–126.

TOBIAS, P. V.
1966   A re-examination of the Kedung Brubus mandible. *Zoölogische Mededelingen* 41:307-319. Leiden: Rijksmuseum van Natuurlijke Historie.

VON KOENIGSWALD, G. H. R.
1935   Die fossilen Säugetierfaunen Javas. *Proceedings of the Koninklijke Nederlandse Akademie van Wetenschappen, Amsterdam* 38: 188–198.
1936   Erste Mitteilung über einen fossilen Hominiden aus dem Altpleistocän Ostjavas. *Proceedings of the Koninklijke Nederlandse Akademie van Wetenschappen, Amsterdam* 39:1000–1009.

1956   Remarks on the correlation of mammalian faunas of Java and the Plio-Pleistocene boundary. *Proceedings of the Koninklijke Nederlandse Akademie van Wetenschappen, Amsterdam* 59:204–210.

1968a "Das absolute Alter des *Pithecanthropus erectus* Dubois," in *Evolution und Hominisation* (Second edition). Edited by G. Kurth, 195–203. Stuttgart: G. Fischer Verlag.

1968b Observations upon *Pithecanthropus* mandibles from Sangiran, Central Java. *Proceedings of the Koninklijke Nederlandse Akademie van Wetenschappen, Amsterdam* 71:1–9.

1969   Java: Prae-Trinil Man. *Proceedings of Eighth International Congress of Anthropological and Ethnological Sciences, Tokyo* 1:104–105. Tokyo: Science Council of Japan.

VON KOENIGSWALD, G. H. R., A. K. GHOSH

1973   Stone implements from the Trinil beds of Sangiran, Central Java, volume one. *Proceedings of the Koninklijke Nederlandse Akademie van Wetenschappen, Amsterdam* 76:1–34.

VON KOENIGSWALD, G. H. R., F. WEIDENREICH

1939   The relationship between *Pithecanthropus* and *Sinanthropus*. *Nature* 144:926–929.

Morphology and Paleoecology of Early Man in Java

TEUKU JACOB

Between 1889 and 1941 remains of at least thirty-one individual fossil men were discovered in Indonesia, or more precisely in East and Central Java (Jacob 1973). Most of these finds are pithecanthropines. They consist of skulls, skull caps, skull bones, or skull-bone fragments of at least 19 individuals; mandibles or mandibular fragments of 5 individuals; limb bones or fragments thereof of 7 individuals; and a number of isolated teeth.

Since 1952, additional fossils have been discovered belonging to at least 17 individuals, and almost all of them are pithecanthropines. The finds comprise skulls, skull caps, or skull fragments of at least 11 individuals; jaw fragments of 4 individuals; and a number of isolated teeth.

This paper reviews the morphology of pithecanthropines, based on the finds particularly of the last twenty-odd years (Tables 1 and 2), paying special attention to the morphology of the skull, the mandible, and the teeth; and attempts to correlate them to their environment and antiquity, as far as these are known at present.

The author expresses his gratitude to the Wenner-Gren Foundation for Anthropological Research, New York; the Department of Education and Culture, Jakarta; and Gadjah Mada University and its College of Medicine, Jogyakarta, for supporting the research reported in this article. Mr. Johannas, Director; Mr. T. Soeradi, Museum and Documentation Section; and Mr. Darwin Kadar, Paleontology Section, of the Directorate of Geology, Bandung, gave permission to study human fossils in their collection; and the Indonesian Paleoanthropological Research Project made available research facilities.

Mr. Ngadimin, Department of Pathology, Gadjah Mada University College of Medicine, helped in the preparation of some photographs. And the Ford Foundation, Jakarta, has enabled the author to present this report at the 9th International Congress of Anthropological and Ethnological Sciences, Chicago, September 1973.

Table 1.   Hominine skulls discovered in Indonesia

Site	Number[1]	Fossil	Year of discovery
			1889–1939
Wajak	1	Skull	1889
	2	Skull fragments	1890
Trinil	2	Calotte	1891
Ngandong	1	Calotte	1931
	2	Frontal bone	1931
	3	Calotte	1931
	4	Parietal fragment	1931
	5	Calotte	1932
	6	Calotte	1932
	7	Calvaria	1932
	8	Parietal fragment	1932
	11	Parietal bones	1933
	12	Calotte	1933
	13	Calotte	1933
	14	Calvaria	1933
Perning	1	Calvaria	1936
Sangiran	2	Calotte	1937
	3	Calotte	1938
	4	Calvaria	1938–39
			1963–1973
Sangiran	10	Calotte, zygomatic bone	1963
	12	Calotte	1965
	13	Skull fragments	1965
	14	Skull base fragments	1966
	17	Calvaria	1969
	18	Skull fragments	1970
	19	Occipital fragment	1970
	20	Skull fragments	1971
Sambungmachan	1	Calotte	1973

[1] Numbers are given in chronological order of discovery at individual sites.

Table 2.   Hominine upper and lower jaws discovered in Indonesia

Site	Number	Fossil	Year of discovery
			1889–1941
Wajak	1	Mandible and maxilla	1889
	2	Mandible and maxilla	1890
Kedung Brubus	1	Mandibular fragment	1890
Sangiran	1	Mandibular fragment	1936
	4	Maxilla	1939
	5	Mandibular fragment	1939
	6	Mandibular fragments	1941
			1952–1973
Sangiran	8	Mandible	1952
	9	Mandibular fragment	1960
	15	Maxillary fragments	1968–69
	17	Maxilla	1969

I assign the skull of 1969 (Sangiran 17, from Sangiran, north of Surakarta) and the skull cap of 1973 (Sambungmachan 1, from Sambungmachan, east of Sragen) to Solo man, because their metric (Table 3) and non-metric traits correspond very closely to those of the Ngandong remains, although they were both found in the Kabuh formation, of Middle Pleistocene age. Stratigraphically, they are closer to *Pithecanthropus modjokertensis* of the Puchangan formation of the Lower Pleistocene; in qualitative traits, however, they resemble *P. soloensis*, while in quantitative traits, as apparent in Table 3, they are intermediate between the two. The close relationship between *P. soloensis* and *P. modjokertensis* will be described later in this discussion; the close similarities between Solo or Ngandong man and the pithecanthropines have been described earlier (Jacob 1967; Weidenreich 1951).

THE SKULL

The most important feature of a pithecanthropine skull is the position of the maximum breadth at or near the base (Jacob 1971). While the general size of the brain has increased since the australopithecines, the cortex is still relatively and proportionately less developed than in *Homo sapiens*. This fact is reflected in the low parietobasal index (the ratio between the distance between the parietal bosses and the maximum cranial breadth) in the pithecanthropines (about 75; in *Homo* it is around 100). Besides this, we notice the parasagittal depression or flatness. Because of this, the skull has a gable-shaped appearance in occipital view: the sides of the pentagon are formed by the two parasagittal flatnesses, the inferiorly-diverging parietal walls, and the occipital torus as a wide base, and its angles are formed by the sagittal torus as apex, the parietal eminences, and the euryon at the base.

The position of the euryon at the base of the skull is due not only to the pronounced supramastoid crests; even if these structures are excluded in the measurement, the point of maximum breadth is still to be found at the base.

At the front of the skull, the underdevelopment of the cerebral cortex is revealed by the receding forehead (or the high frontal sagittal curvature index), the marked postorbital constriction (or the low frontoparietal index), and the prominent supraorbital torus. It is also evident from the low skull vault (low auricular or basion-bregma height, or low supraorbital height index; LeGros Clark 1955).

At the back of the skull, the small cortex is reflected in the low height of the occipital plane (or lambda-inion cord) and the occipital angulation at the torus. Endocranially, the low internal inion (entinion) is due not to the expansion of the cortex, but to the small size of the cerebellum. The vertical distance between the entinion and ectinion (external inion) varies between 21 and 38 millimeters in the pithecanthropines, while in modern man they almost always coincide (Weidenreich 1951). In other words, in the pithecantropines the ectinion-opisthion distance is twice or more the entinion-opisthion distance.

The small, flat, and almost equilateral parietal bones constitute additional evidence. Furthermore, the temporal squama is small, low, and triangular in shape. The sides of the triangle are formed by the supramastoid crest as base, the sphenotemporal suture as the vertical anterior border, and the squamous suture as the straight posterior border.

In the face or viscerocranium, the dominance of the heavy masticatory apparatus is clearly noticeable, but this is not an exclusively pithecanthropine characteristic. The large teeth, especially the molars, are related to the robusticity of the alveolar portion and the absence of the canine fossa. Well-developed masticatory muscles necessitate the development of buttresses on the facial skeleton, such as the broad nasal root, the thick supraorbital torus, the thick frontal process of the zygomatic bone, and the well-marked temporal lines. In Solo man, as exhibited by Sangiran 17, the cheekbone is large and its base is also thick, with a strong zygomaxillary tuberosity.

The thickness of the middle portion (between the nasal and temporal portions) of the supraorbital torus varies between 11 and 19 millimeters; the temporal portion wings backwards and downwards. In Solo man the torus shows signs of disintegration in the supraglabellar region. The ratio between the minimum frontal breadth and the length of the supraorbital torus is between 81.7 and 85.5. No trace of a lacrimal fossa is observable.

Pithecanthropus has a broad nose, probably as an adaptation to the climate. The face, at least of Solo man, is also broad, owing to the protruding cheekbone.

To compensate for the massive viscerocranium, we have in the back of the head strong nuchal muscles, which in turn bring about a wide nuchal area, a prominent occipital torus, and a high ectinion (or a low ratio between the lambda-inion cord and the inion-opisthion cord). In Solo man the upper border of the torus is rounded as in other pithecanthropines, but the lower border is sharp, and forms a triangular prominence at the inion; this structure continues downwards as

Table 3. Cranial measurements in Asiatic pithecanthropines (in millimeters)[1]

Measurement	P. erectus	P. lantianensis	P. pekinensis	P. modjokertensis	Sangiran 17	Sambungmachan 1	P. soloensis
Cranial breadth	130 –147	± 149	137 – 143	156	160	151	144 – 155
Cranial length	176.5–184	± 189	188 – 199	199	208	199	192.5– 220.3
Cranial index	68.8– 76.5	± 73.0	71.4– 72.6	62.8	76.9	75.9	65.2– 75.6
Cranial capacity (in cc)	775 –975	780	915 –1225	900	1125	1035	1140 –1300
Auricular height	89 –102	± 87	93.5– 105	90	113	119	105 – 111
Basion-bregma height	105?		115?	102			124 – 131
Breadth-height index[2]	67.9– 73.4	± 58.4		72	70.6	72.2	86.1– 89.1
Length-height index[2]	50.3– 55.4	± 46.0		45.2	54.3	54.8	59.5– 64.4
Cranial circumference (maximum)	525?		556 – 582?		606	574	
Supraorbital height index	63 – 67				64.6		
Minimum frontal breadth	79 – 85		81.5– 91	78	103	106	102 – 112.5
Transverse frontoparietal index	60.3– 67.4		59.7– 64.1	62.4	64.4	70.2	70.9– 73.6
Biparietal breadth	116 –131		131 – 140	125	120	121	98 – 116
Parietobasal index[3]					75	80.1	66.5– 78.5
Interporion distance	115 –135		141 – 151	156	133	119	120 – 132
Transverse arc	258 –270		277 – 310		290	300	293 – 315
Transverse curvature index	42.6– 52.3		47.4– 54.8		45.9	39.7	40.1– 41.9
Nasion-opisthion cord	134?–142		145 – 147	144	150?		143 – 151
Nasion-opisthion arc			263 – 293		359		342 – 360
Total sagittal curvature index	44.4		43.6– 44.8		41.8		39.4– 44.2
Lambda-inion cord	43 – 50		45 – 56		69	59	56 – 67
Lambda-opisthion cord	75 – 84?		85 – 86	78	93		81 – 89
Lambda-opisthion arc	101 –113		114 – 155	117	142		108 – 124
Occipital sagittal curvature index	74.2– 75.7		72.9– 77.8	72.3	65.5		67.3– 74.6
Occipital angle[4]	103°–115°		98° – 106°	91°		112°	91° – 102°
Parietal angle[5]	115°–120°					136°	
Height of temporal squama	37		29 – 39		44	39	46.9[6]

Table 3.   (Continued)

Measurement	P. erectus	P. lantianensis	P. pekinensis	P. modjokertensis	Sangiran 17	Sambungmachan 1	P. soloensis
Facial breadth			148		158?		
Biorbital breadth			111		107		
Nasal breadth	33		30	36	32		29 [7]
Height of zygomatic bone	33		31.5		41		
Thickness of zygomaxillary margin	9				16		
Palatal depth	12		12	14	12?		
Length of supraorbital torus					126	124	110 – 124
Thickness of supraorbital torus	9 – 19	14–17	11.2–19.6		15–19	14–17	11 – 22
Vault bone thickness	6 – 24	7–24	4.6–23		8–22?	6–19	7 – 22
Ectinion-entinion distance	25 – 32		27.5–38		30	27	21 – 38
Length of foramen magnum				39	37?		41 – 45
Breadth of foramen magnum	35			29	29		29 – 31.5
Breadth of occipital condyle	11 – 12			13.4	12		9 – 11
Basion-hormion distance	25				28		34.5– 35.2
Breadth of basilar portion	22				23		23.2– 24.5
Basilar portion index	88				82.1		65.9– 71

[1] Compiled from LeGros Clark (1955), Jacob (1966, 1967, 1972, 1973), Weidenreich (1943, 1945, 1951), and Woo (1966). Juveniles are excluded.
[2] As height, either the auricular height or the basion-bregma height is used.
[3] Ratio between the distance between parietal bosses and maximum cranial breadth.
[4] Angle made by the occipital and nuchal planes.
[5] Angle at the parietal boss in transverse plane.
[6] Mean value.
[7] Breadth of choanae.

an incomplete external occipital crest. Crests and fossae for the neck muscles are well developed, but these are not exclusively pithecanthropine characteristics.

The base of the skull possesses several traits peculiar to *Pithecanthropus*. In the posterior portion of the external cranial base we notice the foramen magnum angulated into two planes: the posterior plane corresponds to the nuchal plane and the anterior one to the plane of the basisphenoid (Jacob 1967, 1972). This is due to the posterior position of the foramen magnum and the extensive nuchal area. Muscular crests are furthermore present in the surroundings of the foramen magnum, such as the basioccipital crests and the retromastoid tuberosities.

In the subcerebral portion of the cranial base we observe the absence of the foramen lacerum and of the petrooccipital fissure. Consequently, the pterygoid nerve and emissary veins might pass respectively through the sphenopetrosal fissure and the oval foramen. The petrotympanic axis is angulated; the tympanic axis runs transversely, while the petrous one turns obliquely forwards and medianwards. Above the external acoustic porus a tegmen is present (the tegmen pori acustici, or suprameatal tegmen), accentuated by the well-developed supramastoid crest.

In Solo man the condition of the oval foramen is interesting because it is situated in a fossa, together with an accessory foramen on its medial side and sometimes also with the spinous foramen. The accessory oval foramen probably serves as passage for the accessory meningeal vessels (Jacob 1967).

The mandibular fossa of *Pithecanthropus* is also peculiar. It is deep, and the articular tubercle is large; the squamotympanic suture runs transversely along the convexity of the fossa, and not on its posterior wall. This wall is formed by the large and thick tympanic plate, and lies in an oblique (not vertical) plane. The vaginal crest is absent. All these peculiar features on the cranial base might be classified among the group of skeletal variants described by Berry (1968) as polygenic discontinuous traits. They may seem to be trivial details to those who look at human evolution as a broad process, but they could be used as genetic markers to identify and differentiate populations. To be sure, some of the features described above have never been reported in any other hominine skulls.

The occipital condyles in Solo man exhibit a posterior extension of the articular surface which forms a concavity. This must be related to the relative imbalance of the skull on the vertebral column; the concavity, being covered by cartilage during life, accommodates the articular fovea of the atlas in hyperextension and anteflexion of the head, allowing some anteroposterior movement to increase the range of up and down facial movement (Jacob 1967).

In all pithecanthropine specimens the bones of the skull vault are thick, with maximum thickness obviously found at the bosses and superstructures.

The middle meningeal groove pattern demonstrates constantly the strong posterior branch and its low division from the main stem. At the base of the arborization, this stem or the anterior branch is protected in a bony canal (the Sylvian crest) of the parietal bone for some distance (Jacob 1966, 1967).

In many features Sambungmachan 1 resembles Ngandong 1, 7, and 14 (skulls I, IV, and XI); the resemblance is not only in gross morphology and continuous traits, but also in discontinuous morphological details. The similarity is also very close between Sambungmachan 1 and Sangiran 17; the latter is more robust, and although its occipital torus is the same as in *P. erectus,* it has an incomplete external occipital crest. In a few features *P. modjokertensis* resembles *P. soloensis* more than it does *P. erectus,* for example, in the large mastoid process, the occipital torus, and the external occipital crest.

THE MANDIBLE AND TEETH

The size and shape of the lower jaws in *Pithecanthropus* are influenced by the large teeth and the strong masticatory musculature. Since the mandibles show great variation and were never found associated with the skull, they cause some problems in taxonomic assignment.

Meganthropus mandibles are thick both in the alveolar portion (20 millimeters) and at the base (14 millimeters). The teeth are larger than in pithecanthropines. Simian shelves are absent, and likewise the chin eminence.

In *Pithecanthropus* the base of the mandible is as narrow as in modern man (11 millimeters), although its alveolar portion is thick (18 millimeters). This condition is not reflected by the robusticity index (47–59) which is based on the maximum thickness of the corpus (Jacob 1964a).

Powerful masticatory stresses are reflected in the strong lateral torus on the corpus and the transverse tori on the lingual aspect of the symphysis. Mandibles of Solo man should be more robust than in *P.*

erectus. The dimensions of the mandibular fossa in Sambungmachan 1 match those of Solo man (length 17–32 millimeters, breadth 17–25 millimeters, depth 13–17 millimeters; Jacob 1967).

The teeth are relatively large, especially the lower cheek teeth. Reduction of the posterior molars is less evident in the lower dentition. Five cusps are present in the lower molars, and also protostylids.

Upper premolars usually have two roots, whereas in *P. modjokertensis* the upper first premolar has three roots (von Koenigswald 1964a). In the mandible, two-rooted premolars are also present (von Koenigswald 1968). Dental attrition is heavy, and the canine, while possessing a long root, is not projecting.

MORPHOLOGICAL VARIATIONS

Whereas in *Pithecanthropus* the total morphological pattern is consistent, variations are evident in the available skeletons of the Javanese pithecanthropines. Supraorbital tori, for example, vary in thickness, continuity, and shape. In Solo man, while the neck musculature seems to be stronger than in *P. erectus,* as indicated by the sharp, well-developed inferior border of the occipital torus and the well-marked subtoral fossae, the supraorbital torus displays signs of breakdown in the supraglabellar region.

The sagittal torus also shows variation, but it never forms a sagittal crest and it does not serve as attachment for the temporal muscles. In lateral view, the torus exhibits an undulating contour, in some specimens more than in others. The undulations are brought about by the glabellar eminence, supraglabellar fossa, bregmatic eminence, postbregmatic depression, obelionic depression, lambdoid protuberance, supratoral groove, inion (or triangular prominence), and subtoral groove. These alternating convexities and concavities are not evident on the cerebral aspect of the skull.

Cranial capacities vary between 800 and 1,300 cubic centimeters, the smaller end of the range being occupied by *P. erectus* and the larger end by *P. soloensis*. But even in the larger skulls, the base is always the broadest.

The occipital torus sometimes extends laterally to the asteriac process; in other cases, it stops before reaching the lateral angle of the occipital plane. Occasionally, there is a triangular prominence in-the-making in *P. erectus,* accompanied by a sharp lower border of the occipital torus; this condition is found in Sangiran 12. As mentioned earlier, Sangiran 17 has no triangular prominence, but the external occipital crest is present.

Supramastoid crests vary from slightly marked to 6 millimeters thick. The suprameatal spine is present in *P. modjokertensis* and *P. soloensis*, but absent in *P. erectus*. In *P. soloensis* (including Sambungmachan 1) the external acoustic porus is large and usually round, and its walls are thicker. The sphenoid bone also joins in forming the entoglenoid process of the mandibular fossa.

The mastoid process is small in *P. erectus*, but large in *P. modjokertensis* and *P. soloensis*. Air cells are usually abundant in the mastoid process, and extend into the supramastoid crest and the jugular process of the occipital bone (Jacob 1966, 1967). The sphenoid sinus is large and sometimes multilocular; the air cells are also found in the pterygoid process (Jacob 1967, 1973). Furthermore, ethmoidal sinuses and sphenoethmoidal recesses are present. The maxillary sinus is large, too, and the frontal sinus is simply compartmented, not of cauliflower type, and never extends beyond the supratoral groove and the middle portion of the supraorbital torus (Jacob 1972, 1973).

Zygomatic bones are small in *P. erectus* (Sangiran 10), whereas in *P. soloensis* (Sangiran 17) they are large and robust; in the latter, the zygomaxillary tuberosity is well-developed and, therefore, the zygomaxillary border is thick. The inferior border of the piriform aperture is not bounded by crests (Jacob 1966, 1972, 1973).

In Solo man, the margin of the foramen magnum is thickened so as to form lips (labium foraminis magni). A basionic process for the apical ligament of the axis is sometimes formed at the anterior end of the foramen (Jacob 1972). Muscular crests for the deep neck muscles are present in different degrees on the basilar portion of the occipital bone.

The middle meningeal groove pattern shows variations in the relative size of the posterior branch, the level of division of the main stem, and the site of ramification of the middle branch. In Solo man, the oval foramen is situated in a common fossa with an accessory foramen; sometimes the two foramina are confluent, and the spinous foramen may join in the fossa lateral to both (Jacob 1967).

THE DATE

P. modjokertensis lived between 2.3 and 1.5 million years ago, as dated by the K/Ar (potassium-argon) method on pumice from the

Djetis beds at Kepuhklagen (Perning, Modjokerto), where a child skull was discovered in 1936 (Jacob and Curtis 1971); and on andesite from the Djetis beds at Kebonduren near Kedung Brubus, below the level of the juvenile mandible found in 1890 (Curtis, personal communication, 1972). *P. erectus* lived from about one million to half a million years ago. Dates obtained from pumice from the sites of Sangiran 10 and 12 give an average of 830,000 years (Curtis, personal communication, 1972). Dates obtained from tektites from Sangiran give an average of 710,000 years, while a date from basalt from the level above the Kabuh beds at Patiayam gives a result of 0.50 ± 0.06 million years (von Koenigswald 1964b, 1964c).

Still a problem is the antiquity of *P. soloensis*. In 1962 we found stone balls in Sangiran similar to those reported from Ngandong, which made us speculate that remains of Solo man must also be present in Sangiran (Jacob 1964b; von Koenigswald 1951). In 1967, after studying the Ngandong fossils, the author came to the conclusion that Solo man resembles *Pithecanthropus* very closely (Jacob 1967), as was also reported by Weidenreich and others. In 1969 a skull (Sangiran 17) was found in the Middle Pleistocene Kabuh formation of Sangiran showing many characteristics of Solo man. The skull was recovered from the lower layers of Kabuh at East Puchung (Sartono 1972). In 1973 a skull cap was found at Sambungmachan, Sragen, between Sangiran and Trinil, on the bank of the Solo River. As mentioned previously, the skull cap, recovered from the boundary beds, the lowest layer of the Kabuh formation, has characteristics of Solo man. Table 3 shows its resemblance to Sangiran 17, *P. modjokertensis,* and the Ngandong skulls.

Consequently, we have to allow a greater antiquity to Solo man. The author thinks that *P. soloensis* evolved from *P. modjokertensis* at the beginning of the Middle Pleistocene, and survived into the Upper Pleistocene.

The fauna associated with pithecanthropine finds in Sangiran, Sambungmachan, Trinil, and Ngandong are the following (Hooijer 1957; von Koenigswald 1940, 1951): *Stegodon, Elephas, Bibos, Bubalus, Axis, Cervus, Muntiacus, Tragulus, Duboisia, Antilope, Hippopotamus, Sus, Rhinoceros, Tapirus, Pongo, Symphalangus, Hylobates, Macaca, Presbytis, Felis, Cuon, Megacyon, Mececyon, Epimachairodus, Nestoritherium, Ursus, Hyaena, Viverriculus, Viverra, Paradoxurus, Arctitis, Lepus, Rattus, Rhizomys, Manis, Crocodilus, Gavialis, Batagur, Trionyx, Chitra,* etc.

The presence of long-horned *Bubalus palaeokerabau* and hugeantlered *Cervus palaeomendjangan* indicates that the habitat was not a dense tropical rain forest (Schuster 1911; von Koenigswald 1951). It might have been woodlands, with grassland and swamps. Schuster concluded that the climate was about 6° Centigrade cooler than at present; most of the fossil plants from Trinil are members of subtropical vegetation. The distribution of tropical forest and open grassland in Indonesia might have been different during the Pleistocene from what it is at present. The above inferences and speculations should be verified by pollen analyses, and we await the reports of studies carried out by Dr. W. van Zeist, University of Groningen, on samples from the black clay of Sangiran and Perning for information on the paleoclimate and flora of the Pleistocene pithecanthropine habitat.

CONCLUSIONS

From the above discussion it is evident that the skulls of *Pithecanthropus* show a good number of definite characteristics which are exclusively pithecanthropine, while some others it shares with other early hominines or isolated groups of modern men. The first-mentioned traits are more influenced by genetic factors, while the latter are more subject to environmental influence. The total morphological pattern, a result of interaction between genes and environment, is consistent throughout the various pithecanthropine populations, and easily distinguishes them from any other hominines.

The relative underdevelopment of the cerebral cortex, especially the frontal and parietal lobes, results in the low position of the euryon, marked parietal angulation, parasagittal flatness, small quadrangular parietal bones, low triangular temporal squama, low occipital plane, occipital angulation, low receding forehead, and marked postorbital constriction.

The masticatory apparatus is well developed, as evidenced by the large teeth, thick alveolar processes of the jaws, strong lateral tori of the mandibles, symphyseal transverse tori, robust mandibles, absence of the canine fossa, retention of supernumerary dental roots, broad nasal root, horizontal supraorbital torus ending in a lateral wing, and marked temporal lines. As compensation for the protruding viscerocranium there develop in the back of the head strong neck muscles, resulting in a large nuchal plane, strong occipital torus, and well-marked muscular crests for superficial and deep nuchal muscles. These features are not exclusively pithecanthropine characteristics.

Typically pithecanthropine among the hominines are some cranial features, such as the tegmen pori acustici, the absence of the foramen lacerum and petrooccipital fissure (probably due to the robust petrous and tympanic portions of the temporal bone and the relatively small size of the brain), the absence of the vaginal crest, the angulated petrotympanic axis, and the construction of the mandibular fossa. The distance between the internal and external inion is considerable. The posterior branch of the middle meningeal artery is larger than or equal to the anterior; both branches ramify at a lower level from the main stem. Cranial capacities vary between 800 and 1,300 cubic centimeters. And lastly, vault bones are thicker than in earlier or later hominids, although this trait may be found in some isolated groups among these as well.

Pithecanthropus lived from around two million years to around 200,000 years ago. *P. erectus* lived between more or less 900,000 and 600,000 years ago. It seems that *P. modjokertensis*, who lived in the Lower Pleistocene, evolved into *P. soloensis* at the beginning of the Middle Pleistocene. Thus, Solo man was contemporary with *P. erectus* for a certain period of his history, but survived into the Upper Pleistocene.

Pithecanthropus lived in or near the edge of woodlands, and near rivers, lakes, or inland seas; the remains of ruminants with considerable horn spread and huge antlers suggest that the habitat was not a dense jungle. While all the finds were secondarily deposited by stream or volcanic action, several fossils of both hominines and animals are surprisingly intact. It seems that fluctuation in temperature was not too drastic in Pleistocene Indonesia, but the distribution of forest and grassland may have differed from the present condition. The difference in animal genera during the stages of the Pleistocene might be not too remarkable, but this might be due to slight changes in paleoclimate and physical environment. Paleobotanic and paleoclimatic studies need to be intensified in future paleoanthropological research in Indonesia.

REFERENCES

BERRY, R. J.
    1968   "The biology of non-metrical variation in mice and men," in *The skeletal biology of earlier human populations*. Edited by D. R. Brothwell, 103–133. Oxford: Pergamon Press.

HOOIJER, D. A.
1957 The correlation of fossil mammalian faunas and the Plio-Pleistocene boundary in Java. *Proceedings of the Koninklijke Nederlandse Akademie van Wetenschappen, Amsterdam*, series B, 60:
1–10.

JACOB, T.
1964a A human mandible from Anjar urn field, Indonesia. *Journal of
the National Medical Association* 56:421–426. Djakarta.
1964b *Fosil-fosil manusia dari Indonesia*. Jogjakarta: Universitas Gadjah
Mada.
1966 The sixth skull cap of *Pithecanthropus erectus*. *American Journal
of Physical Anthropology* 25:243–269.
1967 *Some problems pertaining to the racial history of the Indonesian
region. Utrecht:* The Netherlands.
1971 Diagnosis *Pithecanthropus*. *Gadjah Mada Journal of the Medical
Sciences* 3:191–200.
1972 New hominid finds in Indonesia and their affinities. *Mankind*
8:176–181.
1973 Palaeoanthropological discoveries in Indonesia with special reference to the finds of the last two decades. *Journal of Human
Evolution* 2:473–485.

JACOB, T., GARNISS H. CURTIS
1971 Preliminary potassium-argon dating of early man in Java. *Contributions of the University of California Archaeological Research
Facility* 12:50.

LE GROS CLARK, W. E.
1955 *The fossil evidence for human evolution*. Chicago: University of
Chicago Press.

SARTONO, S.
1972 Discovery of another hominid skull at Sangiran, Central Java.
Current Anthropology 13:124–126.

SCHUSTER, JULIUS
1911 "Die Flora der Trinil-Schichten," in *Die Pithecanthropus-Schich-
ten auf Java*. Edited by M. Lenore Selenka and Max Blancken-
horn, 235–257. Leipzig: Verlag von Wilhelm Engelmann.

VON KOENIGSWALD, G. H. R.
1940 Neue *Pithecanthropus*-Funde 1936–1938. *Wetenschappelijke Me-
dedeelingen, Dienst van den Mijnbouw in Nederlandsch-Indië* 28.
1951 "Introduction," in Morphology of Solo man, by Franz Weidenreich. *Anthropological Papers of the American Museum of Natural History 43*, (3)'211–221.
1964a The importance of teeth in the study of early man. *International
Dental Journal* 14:343–358.
1964b Potassium-argon dates and early man: Trinil. *Report of the Sixth
International Congress of Quaternary 1961* 4:325–327.
1964c The problem of tektites. *Space Science Reviews* 3:433–446.
1968 Observations upon two *Pithecanthropus* mandibles from Sangiran,
Central Java. *Proceedings of the Koninklijke Nederlandse Akademie van Wetenschappen, Amsterdam*, series B, 71:99–107.

WEIDENREICH, FRANZ
  1943   The skull of *Sinanthropus pekinensis:* a comparative study on a
         primitive hominid skull. *Palaeontologia Sinica*, n.s. D (10) 127.
  1945   *Giant early man from Java and South China.* Anthropological
         Papers of the American Museum of Natural History 40(1):1–134.
  1951   Morphology of Solo man. *Anthropological Papers of the Amer-
         ican Museum of Natural History* 43(3):205–290.
WOO JU-KANG
  1966   The skull of Lantian man. *Current Anthropology* 7:83–86.

Implications Arising from
Pithecanthropus VIII

S. SARTONO

THE SUBDIVISION OF *PITHECANTHROPUS*

In most discussions of *Pithecanthropus* populations considerable emphasis is placed on contrasts in certain features of their cranial vaults and dentition, as well as stratigraphic differences of their sites.

One theory, most lucidly championed by von Koenigswald (1968c), is that *Pithecanthropus* can be subdivided into three types on the basis of morphological and stratigraphical differences. Accordingly, *Meganthropus* is regarded as a taxon distinct from *Pithecanthropus* and most probably an independent Asiatic offshoot from the main hominid line. According to von Koenigswald, this subdivision is summarized in Table 1.

In connection with the subdivision indicated in Table 1, the synonyms of available specimens of *Pithecanthropus* are summarized in Table 2. LeGros Clark (1964) proposed the specific nomen *Homo erectus* to replace the generic nomen *Pithecanthropus*. This proposed nomen is included in the genus *Homo* but specifically distinct from *Homo neanderthalensis* and *Homo sapiens*. Consequently, he used the nomen

I have profited greatly from repeated critical discussions and suggestions from Professor von Koenigswald of the Senckenberg Museum (Germany), who has an untiring devotion to and is an unparalleled authority on *Pithecanthropus*. Sincere appreciation is also due to the Geological Survey of Indonesia in Bandung (Java, Indonesia) which not only facilitated my visits to the Javanese Pleistocene hominid sites, but also allowed me to study those specimens in its Paleontological Laboratory. The necessary plates and figures in this paper have been made by Mr. Subardiman of the Geological Survey of Indonesia and Cik Haidar Ludin from the Department of Geology of the Universiti Kebangsaan Malaysia; to both of them I am very grateful.

For Plates, see pp. vi–ix, between pp. 288–289

Table 1.   Types of *Pithecanthropus*

Pithecanthropus erectus:
     seems to be confined to Middle Pleistocene Trinil beds and is comparable
     to *Sinanthropus pekinensis* from China and to the *Pithecanthropus* skull
     from the upper part of Bed II of Olduvai.
Pithecanthropus modjokertensis:
     confined to Early Pleistocene Djetis beds and can be distinguished from
     erectus by a heavier and more primitive dentition as well as lesser brain
     capacity. It seems unlikely that he is the direct ancestor of this type. *Modjo-*
     kertensis is comparable to *Pithecanthropus lantianensis* from China, and
     according to dentition is comparable to *Homo habilis* from the lower part
     of Bed II of Olduvai.
Pithecanthropus dubius:
     has the most primitive root system in the lower premolars known in early
     man. Probably confined to the lowest levels of the Pleistocene of Sangiran.

Table 2.   Synonyms of *Pithecanthropus*

Pithecanthropus erectus	
(Dubois)	*Pithecanthropus I* (von Koenigswald)
	Pithecanthropus II (von Koenigswald)
	Pithecanthropus III (von Koenigswald)
	Pithecanthropus VI (Jacob)
	Pithecanthropus VII (Sartono)
	Pithecanthropus VIII (Sartono)
Pithecanthropus modjokertensis	*Homo modjokertensis* (von Koenigswald)
(von Koenigswald)	*Homo soloensis* p.p. (Dubois)
	Pithecanthropus B (von Koenigswald)
	Pithecanthropus robustus (Weidenreich)
	Pithecanthropus IV
	Pithecanthropus V
Pithecanthropus dubius	*Pithecanthropus C* (Sartono)
(von Koenigswald)	

Homo erectus Chinese variety for *Sinanthropus pekinensis* and *Homo erectus* Javanese variety for *Pithecanthropus erectus*. In renaming *Pithecanthropus* he intended that *Homo erectus* should include all fossil men which morphologically have much in common with *Pithe-canthropus erectus* (Dubois). In recent years, there has developed a tendency to rename *Homo erectus* (Javanese variety) *Homo erectus erectus*, while *Homo erectus* (Chinese variety) should be *Homo erectus pekinensis*. Some students of fossil man elaborate further, saying that the nomen *Pithecanthropus erectus* should be retained, because it has priority over *Homo erectus*. Consequently *Homo erectus erectus* should be designated *Pithecanthropus erectus erectus*, while *Homo erectus pekinensis* should be designated *Pithecanthropus erectus pekin-ensis* (for nomenclature see Table 6, p. 352).

On September 13, 1969, an almost complete cranium was unearthed from Middle Pleistocene deposits at Sangiran (Central Java, Indonesia). Based on stratigraphic and morphological considerations, it was assigned the specific designation *Pithecanthropus (erectus) VIII*. I reported this discovery in previous works (Sartono 1971, 1972, 1973a, b). Here I will discuss the cranial capacity and craniograms of *Pithecanthropus VIII* and will compare it with other *Pithecantropus* skulls, viz. *Pithecanthropus, I, II, IV*, and *VII. Pithecanthropus III and VI* are not well enough preserved and are not sufficiently informative for detailed purposes of this study though they will be mentioned occasionally. *Pithecanthropus V* is considered to be a juvenile. Thus it will not be included in comparisons among adult specimens.

Meganthropus palaeojavanicus (von Koenigswald) is only represented by mandibular fragments. In this article comparisons will not be made between *Meganthropus* and *Pithecanthropus* because I believe them to represent different genera.

I will, however, compare the cranial capacities and craniograms of *Pithecanthropus* and *Homo (Javanthropus) soloensis* (Oppenoorth). The taxonomic status of the latter group of fossils is still equivocal.

BACKGROUND AND OBJECTIVES

Examination of *Pithecanthropus VIII* indicates that it does not mirror the "common" *Pithecanthropus* morphology represented by previous specimens. Its dentition is smaller than the *modjokertensis* type but larger than the *erectus* type. Its supraorbital ridges are strongly developed and far more heavily built than those of *Pithecanthropus I, II*, of reconstructed *III* and *IV*, and of all known *Homo soloensis* and *Sinanthropus*.

I do not aim to contradict the *Pithecanthropus* phylogenies of von Koenigswald and Clark. Instead I hope to show that stratigraphic and morphologic evidence obtained from *Pithecanthropus* is still increasing. Further work and re-evaluation of already obtained data are necessary to solve the *Pithecanthropus* problem. In order to pursue this the geology of the various *Pithecanthropus* sites and laboratory samples need to be studied further. Consequently, I will discuss the problem and urge further field and laboratory studies. I will not present conclusive results.

THE NATURE OF *PITHECANTHROPUS* CRANIOGRAMS

I assigned the latest skull to *Pithecanthropus (erectus) VIII* (Sartono 1971, 1972) on the basis of stratigraphic and morphological evidence. However, a closer study of this specimen reveals certain features which are different from those of other *Pithecanthropus* skulls. These differences are not just variations or sexual differences. The most conspicuous difference is the size of the skull of *Pithecanthropus VIII* versus those of *Pithecanthropus I, II, III, IV*, and *VII*. Raw measurements of the skulls (Table 3) do not demonstrate the extent of these differences very well. But differences are excellently exhibited by craniograms (Figures 1, 2, and 3). Figure 6 shows craniograms of *Pithecanthropus* and *Homo soloensis*. Those of *Pithecanthropus I, II,* and *VII* are almost coincident with each other in morphology and size. Only the occipital torus is more protuberant posteriorly in *Pithecanthropus VII* than *Pithecanthropus I* and *II*. Based on this feature and other characteristics I proposed that *Pithecanthropus VII* is a male specimen and that *Pithecanthropus I* and *II* are females (Sartono 1968). The similarity of craniograms of *Pithecanthropus, I, II, III,* and *VII* is even more surprising if we consider that all of them were found in beds of the same age, i.e. the Trinil beds for *Pithecanthropus I* and the Kabuh beds for *Pithecanthropus II, III* and *VII*. Both of these beds are of Middle Pleistocene age.

The craniogram of *Pithecanthropus IV* evidences that its skull vault is longer frontally, in part because of well-developed supraorbital ridges. I should mention that the frontal region is reconstructed, but the fact does not escape us that the skull vault of *Pithecanthropus IV* is flatter, lower, and has a more inclined frontal than *Pithecanthropus I, II, III,* and *VII*. It came from the Lower Pleistocene Putjangan beds.

The most recent specimen obtained from Middle Pleistocene beds is *Pithecanthropus VIII*. Figure 1 shows that the craniogram of this specimen is distinctly different from those of all other available *Pithecanthropus*. It is not only much larger, but also longer especially in its frontal region because of very heavy supraorbital ridges. Although the differences of craniograms of *Pithecanthropus VIII*, on one hand, and *Pithecanthropus I, II, III,* and *VII*, on the other, are so remarkably distinct, the former specimen still retains the characteristic features of *Pithecanthropus*, that is the low, flattened almond-shaped skull vault with strongly protruding eye-ridges. However, its occipital torus is not as well developed as those of *Pithecanthropus IV* and *VII*. Instead it is quite similar to *Pithecanthropus I, II,* and *III*

Table 3. Comparative measurements

Number of centi- meters	Measurement	Pithecanthropus skulls					Sinan- thropus (average)	Homo soloensis (average)
		erectus				*robustus* IV		
		I	II	VII	VIII			
1	Maximum: **g — op**	183	176.5	191.8	204	199	193.6	209
4	Nasion — opisthocranion: n — op	179	—	182.3	190	192.5	189	198.7
8	Nasion — basion line: n — ba	108	—	—	118	113	105.5	113.5
9	Nasion — opisthion line: n — o	142	134?	137.4	140	144	145.3	153.4
10	Horizontal occipital: o — op, projected to **FH**	41	42	—	54	53	48.3	50.7
11	Bregma position, projected to g — op	77.5	64?	—	51	85	77.3	77.7
12	Lambda position, projected to g — op	162	153	—	177	172	172	176.6
13	Bregma position, projected to n — o	55	44	—	30	64	56.7	61.4
14	Lambda position, projected to n — o	143	134	—	148	152	148.2	162
15	Inion position, projected to n — o	172	164.5	—	188	185?	180.3	195.4
20	Breadth (maximum)	134?	135	—	162	158?	141	146
26	Interporial: po — po	135	114	129.9	145	156	145.5	148
33	Distance between temporal lines: lp — lp	—	67	80.8	105	78	93.5	112.8
34	Basi — bregmatic: ba — b	105	105?	—	132	102	115?	122.5
56	Frontal chord: n — b	100	90?	—	118	99	109.8	116.7
58	Parietal arch: b ⌒ l	91	94	105	145	89	102.5	107.4
59	Parietal chord: b — l	87.5	90.1	150.3	149	90	96.2	102
60	Occipital arch: l ⌒ o	103	101	114	140	117	114	116.8
61	Occipital chord: l — o	78	75	83.1	88	78	84	88.2
74	Cranial capacity in cubic centimeters	900	775	900	1,029	900	1,043	1,100

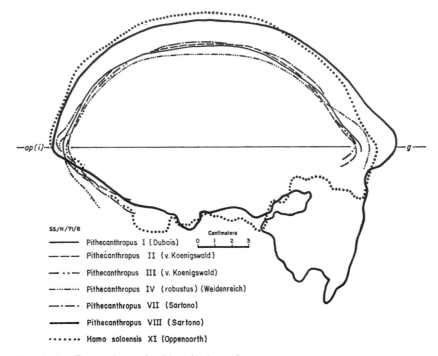

SS/H/71/8

——— Pithecanthropus I (Dubois)

— — — Pithecanthropus II (v. Koenigswald)

— ·· — Pithecanthropus III (v. Koenigswald)

—···—··· Pithecanthropus IV (robustus) (Weidenreich)

—·—·—· Pithecanthropus VII (Sartono)

——— Pithecanthropus VIII (Sartono)

······· Homo soloensis XI (Oppenoorth)

Centimeters
0 1 2 3

Figure 1.   Comparison of mid-sagittal craniograms

in this feature.

We may thus consider the craniograms of *Pithecanthropus* in two groups; those of *Pithecanthropus I, II, III, IV,* and *VII* clustering and almost overlapping each other, and that of *Pithecanthropus VIII* distinctly separated from the earlier specimens (Figure 1). The first group belongs to the small-brained and the latter to the large-brained *Pithecanthropus.* Within the small-brained group we may distinguish the craniograms of *Pithecanthropus I, II, III* and *VII* which are especially similar to one another and that of *Pithecanthropus IV* which is slightly smaller. Recall that *Pithecanthropus IV* is of Early Pleistocene age while the others are of the Middle Pleistocene.

The difference in size between the large-brained and small-brained *Pithecanthropus* is demonstrated also in Figures 2 and 3. Here we see that the horizontal and coronal craniograms of *Pithecanthropus VIII* are distinctly larger than those of *Pithecanthropus II* and *VII.* From these figures we may also conclude that the skull vault of *Pithecanthropus VII* is broader, and possibly also longer than *Pithecanthropus II.*

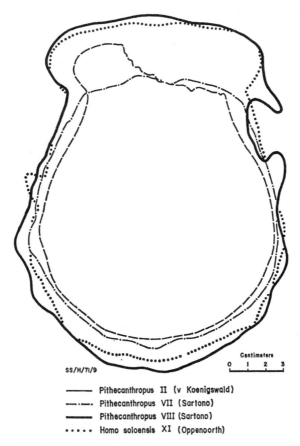

SS/H/71/9

Centimeters
0   1   2   3

——— Pithecanthropus II (v Koenigswald)
—·—· Pithecanthropus VII (Sartono)
——— Pithecanthropus VIII (Sartono)
· · · · Homo soloensis XI (Oppenoorth)

Figure 2.   Comparison of horizontal craniograms

In Plate 1 the lateral views of *Pithecanthropus VIII* (original), *Sinanthropus* (cast), and *Homo soloensis XI* (cast) are compared. The similarity in the shape of the skull vaults between *Pithecanthropus VIII* and *Sinanthropus* is clear. The typical *Pithecanthropus* skull profile is exhibited by *Sinanthropus* with its low, flat and almond-shaped cranium. We also observe that the occipital of *Pithecanthropus VIII* is somewhat pointed as a result of its well-developed torus occipitalis, which is slightly similar to that of *Homo soloensis*. The supraorbital ridges of *Pithecanthropus VIII* and *Homo soloensis XI* are heavy and otherwise remarkably similar.

An interesting feature is demonstrated by the supraorbital torus of *Pithecanthropus VIII*. Its anterior contour is a straight line with a forward swelling in its median part. In *Pithecanthropus I* it is almost

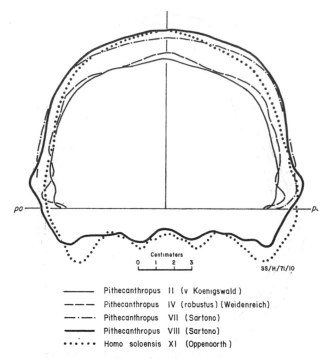

Figure 3.   Comparison of coronal craniograms

straight. In *Pithecanthropus II* it probably also is nearly straight as evidenced by the left fragment. That of *Sinanthropus XII* is straight with a median swelling which shows a distinct convexity superiorly. This feature is also demonstrated by *Homo soloensis XI*, which unlike *Sinanthropus XII*, has a distinct retroversion toward the lateral ends of the supraorbital torus thereby forming a slightly curved margin. This lateral retroversion is stronger in Neanderthal specimens. The anterior contour terminates as a more pronounced rounding in recent man (see Figure 9).

According to Weidenreich (1945) the ontogenetic development of the supraorbital torus, which can be seen in the gradual reduction of the supraorbitals, is closely connected with the evolution of mankind. The supraorbitals tend to retrogress and to become part of the face and orbit thereby conforming to the circular contour of the cranium. The supraorbitals not only protect the eyes but also relate closely to the gradual increase of the braincase in the course of man's evolution (see also Plates 3 and 6).

If we compare the lateral views of *Pithecanthropus VIII, Sinan-*

thropus, and *Homo soloensis XI* on one hand with that of *Homo neanderthalensis* on the other (see Plate 4) the difference between them is very pronounced. The skull of *Homo neanderthalensis* is rounded posteriorly, and thus distinct from those of *Pithecanthropus VIII, Sinanthropus,* and *Homo soloensis XI.* But anteriorly it is somewhat similar to *Sinanthropus.* The torus occipitalis of *Pithecanthropus VIII* is relatively lower than that of *Sinanthropus* and *Homo soloensis XI.* Toward its median part the profile of *Pithecanthropus VIII* is more similar to *Homo soloensis XI* than to *Sinanthropus* which is lower and consequently also relatively flatter.

Although the transverse contour of the cranium of *Pithecanthropus VIII* is similar to those of other *Pithecanthropus,* the shape of its forehead is different. This is higher than other *Pithecanthropus* and if compared to that of *Homo soloensis XI* it is more inclined. But the midsagittal contour of *Homo soloensis XI* is higher in the crest and lambda area and shorter toward the supraorbitals. The incline of the frontal bone with regard to the g-op(i) line as shown in the midsagittal craniograms can be seen in Figure 10. Those of the small-brained *Pithecanthropus* are more inclined than the large-brained *Pithecanthropus, Sinanthropus,* and *Homo soloensis.* The latter are more inclined than those of *Homo sapiens.* Furthermore, the frontal of *Pithecanthropus IV* is slightly more inclined than other small-brained *Pithecanthropus.*

If we compare the occipital views of *Pithecanthropus VIII, Sinanthropus, and Homo soloensis XI* with that of *Homo neanderthalensis* the difference is clear. The occiput of *Homo neanderthalensis* is narrow at the base and well-rounded and higher in its median part. Its general configuration approaches that of *Homo sapiens* more than those of *Homo soloensis, Pithecanthropus VIII,* or *Sinanthropus* (see Plate 5).

Based on the overall similarity of the skull vaults and craniograms of *Pithecanthropus VIII, Sinanthropus,* and *Homo soloensis XI,* I believe that *Pithecanthropus VIII* is nearer to *Homo soloensis* and *Sinanthropus* than to small-brained *Pithecanthropus.* I submit that just as *Sinanthropus* is a variety of *Pithecanthropus, Pithecanthropus VIII,* is more closely related to *Homo soloensis.*

STRATIGRAPHIC POSITIONS OF *PITHECANTHROPUS*

So far, in Java, there are four important areas in which Pleistocene hominids have been discovered (Table 4; Figure 4).

Table 4.   Distribution of Javanese Pleistocene hominid skulls in time and space

Area	Age	Hominid	Number of skull
Ngandong (Madiun, East Java)	Upper Pleistocene	*Homo soloensis*	*I–XI*
Trinil (Madiun, East Java)	Middle Pleistocene	*Pithecanthropus erectus*	*I*
Sangiran (Solo, Central Java)	Middle Pleistocene	*Pithecanthropus erectus*	*II, III, VI, VII, VIII*
Sangiran (Solo, Central Java)	Lower Pleistocene	*Pithecanthropus modjokertensis*	*IV*
Perning (Modjokerto, East Java)	Lower Pleistocene	*Pithecanthropus modjokertensis*	*V*

Of the areas shown in Table 4, the Sangiran site offers the best opportunity to study the evolutionary development of the Javanese hominids (Figure 4). In this area I investigated the relationship between the relative increase of cranial capacities of *Pithecanthropus* and the stratigraphic positions of specimens within the Pleistocene deposits. In this way the evolutionary trends of these hominids may be demonstrated within the framework of their distribution in time and space during the Pleistocene.

Up to now, five *Pithecanthropus* skulls in the Middle Pleistocene Kabuh beds of Sangiran have been found. These are: *Pithecanthropus II, III, VI, VII* and *VIII*. All of them have been assumed to belong to the *erectus* type. Within the beds they occupy different stratigraphic positions (von Koenigswald 1940; Sartono 1964, 1967, 1972).

The Sangiran area is a dome in which the oldest rock formation consisting of Pliocene deposits, crops out in its central part encircled by Early and Middle Pleistocene beds. In this way, going from the central part of the dome outward we gradually encounter younger rocks. Consequently, at Sangiran the further a hominid site is located from the core of the dome, the higher it is stratigraphically and the younger will be the specimens contained therein. With this in mind, cross sections were made through the various *Pithecanthropus* sites and the average thickness of the stratigraphic columns of those sections was recorded. I found that there is a relationship between the stratigraphic

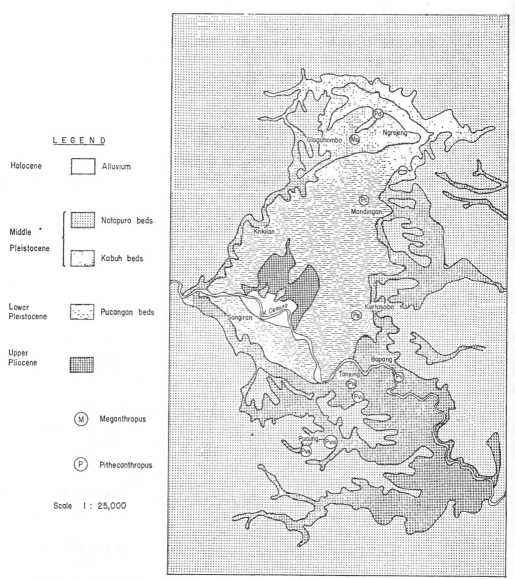

Figure 4. Sketch map of Sangiran site

positions of the various *Pithecanthropus* specimens and their respective cranial capacities, i.e. the higher their positions are within the
stratigraphic column the larger their skull volumes are (Figure 5).
Thus there is a tendency for increase in skull size, with the decrease
in age of *Pithecanthropus* specimens in the Sangiran sites. Note that
Pithecanthropus II, III, VI and *VII* are stratigraphically lower than

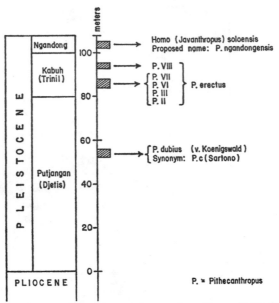

Figure 5.   Schematic illustration of the stratigraphic positions of *Pithecanthropus*

Pithecanthropus VIII (Figure 5). We may deduce from this that the small-brained *Pithecanthropus*, comprising *Pithecanthropus II, III, VI* and *VII*, are stratigraphically lower than the large-brained form represented by *Pithecanthropus VIII*.

Pithecanthropus I was found in Trinil (East Java) about sixty kilometers from the Sangiran area (Central Java). It is hard to place this specimen accurately in the stratigraphic sequence of the Sangiran site. But geological evidence indicates that *Pithecanthropus I* is from Trinil beds of Middle Pleistocene age. Based on the small cranial capacity which approaches the small-brained *Pithecanthropus* of Sangiran, there is a probability that stratigraphically it may be located lower than *Pithecanthropus VIII*.

The site of *Pithecanthropus IV* is, according to von Koenigswald (in Weidenreich 1945), from the Putjangan beds of Lower Pleistocene age. The skull vault of *Pithecanthropus IV* is distinctly smaller than other small-brained *Pithecanthropus*. Thus we obtain the sequence shown in Table 5.

In the Lower Pleistocene and in the lower and higher levels of the Middle Pleistocene of Sangiran two groups of *Pithecanthropus* have been documented. The small-brained *Pithecanthropus IV* was found in Lower Pleistocene deposits. The small-brained group also occurs in the lower levels up to the higher levels of Middle Pleistocene beds.

Table 5. Stratigraphic distribution of large- and small-brained *Pithecanthropus* in the Sangiran site

Pleistocene	Middle	higher levels	*Pithecanthropus VIII* (large-brained) *Pithecanthropus VII* (small-brained)
		lower levels	*Pithecanthropus III* (small-brained) *Pithecanthropus II* (small-brained)
	Lower		*Pithecanthropus IV* (small-brained)

By contrast the large-brained *Pithecanthropus* seems to be confined to the highest levels of Middle Pleistocene.

Pithecanthropus IV is smaller than other members of the small-brained group. So far, based on their cranial volumes alone, it is not possible to separate *Pithecanthropus IV* from *Pithecanthropus II, III* and *VII*. But the former specimen has more primitive traits and is geologically older than the other specimens. Further *Pithecanthropus IV* is of another type, i.e. *modjokertensis,* while the other members of the small-brained *Pithecanthropus* group belong to the *erectus* type.

THE *HOMO SOLOENSIS*

Specimens of *Homo soloensis* were excavated from an Upper Pleistocene river terrace in the village of Ngandong (residency of Madiun, East Java). This village is situated about sixty-two kilometers from Sangiran and about seventy-one kilometers from the residential town of Solo (or Surakarta) from which its specific name is derived.

General agreement has not been achieved concerning the taxonomic status of *Homo soloensis*. Oppenoorth (1932) designated the specimens *Javanthropus soloensis*. Later he renamed them *Homo soloensis* (Oppenoorth 1937) because he was convinced that they represented a Neanderthal type of man though one different from the European type. Dubois' view in 1932 that Ngandong man, like *Homo wadjakensis,* was a fossil form of *Homo sapiens,* contributed considerably to Oppenoorth's (1937) change of the nomen. Von Koenigswald (1933) and Vallois (1935) mentioned the similarities between Rhodesian and Ngandong men. Weidenreich (1951) concluded that the Ngandong skulls resembled those of *Pithecanthropus*. He suggested the nomen *Pithecanthropus soloensis* for those skulls. However, in order to avoid further taxonomic confusion, he eventually decided to replace this nomen with the vernacular "Solo man." I believe that this confuses the taxonomic status of this specimen. Weidenreich's diagnosis is shared by Coon (1963), Mayr (1963), Kurth (1965), and Jacob (1967), who provides a detailed description of the Ngandong skulls.

The craniograms of *Homo soloensis* are different from the small-brained *Pithecanthropus* and are more closely similar to those of *Pithecanthropus VIII* (Figures 1–3). It seems that the cranial length of *Homo soloensis* is reduced anteriorly (Figures 1 and 2) and concomitantly the skull is higher and narrower posteriorly (Figure 3). This evolutionary change may also have occurred between the skull of the Early Pleistocene *Pithecanthropus IV* and the Middle Pleistocene small-brained *Pithecanthropus*, possibly from *modjokertensis* toward the *erectus* type. The former has a more inclined frontal bone and a lower skull vault craniogram than the latter (Figure 1). The frontal inclination increases towards the large-brained *Pithecanthropus*, *Sinanthropus* and *Homo soloensis*, the largest inclination being possessed by *Homo sapiens* (Figure 10).

Figure 6 shows the minimum and maximum size of midsagittal craniograms of *Sinanthropus* and *Homo soloensis* (after Weidenreich 1951). The midsagittal craniogram of *Pithecanthropus VIII* falls entirely within the range of these specimens.

It is well known that cranial volumes of fossil hominids vary between certain maximum and minimum limits. Like cranial measurements, figures obtained from cranial volumes do not fully represent the morphology of the crania. But limits of cranial morphology can be obtained from their craniograms. Weidenreich (1951) illustrated the maximum and minimum cranial limits of *Sinanthropus* and *Homo soloensis*. In Figures 6 and 7 the maximum and minimum cranial limits of *Pithecanthropus* are combined with those of *Sinanthropus* and *Homo soloensis* as presented by Weidenreich. These figures show that the maximum and the minimum limits of *Sinanthropus* and *Homo soloensis* crania overlap each other, and that *Pithecanthropus VIII* is grouped with them. This may indicate that variations of cranial morphology of these specimens do not differ much from each other. If *Sinanthropus* is the Chinese counterpart of the Javanese *Pithecanthropus*, then — apart from Weidenreich's recognition (1951: 226) that there are fifty-six characters of *Pithecanthropus* out of fifty-eight similar to *Homo soloensis* (Jacob 1964) — *Pithecanthropus* and *Homo*

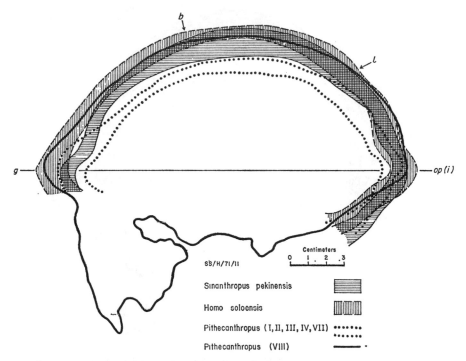

Figure 6.   Mid-sagittal craniograms of maximum and minimum limits of skulls

soloensis are indeed very close to each other. On the other hand, Figure 6 also shows that the limit of cranial extension of the small-brained *Pithecanthropus I, II, III, IV,* and *VII* falls outside those of *Homo soloensis, Sinanthropus,* and the large-brained *Pithecanthropus VIII.* Comparison of horizontal craniograms also demonstrates that the cranial limits of *Sinanthropus* and *Homo soloensis* are closely related to each other, and that of *Pithecanthropus VIII* is encompassed by them (Figure 7). On the other hand, those of the small-brained *Pithecanthropus* fall outside the limits of these hominids as well as being morphologically distinct from them.

LeGros Clark (1964) stated that *Homo soloensis* is a neanderthaloid. Their cranial capacities range between 1,140 and 1,300 cubic centimeters based on skulls *I, V,* and *VI* (Oppenoorth 1937) with an average of 1,100 cubic centimeters (Weidenreich 1945), those of *Homo neanderthalensis* are between 1,300 and 1,600 cubic centimeters (LeGros Clark 1964) with an average of 1,400 (Weidenreich 1945), those of *Sinanthropus* range from 850 to 1,300 cubic centimeters (LeGros Clark 1964) and those of *Pithecanthropus* are between 775 and

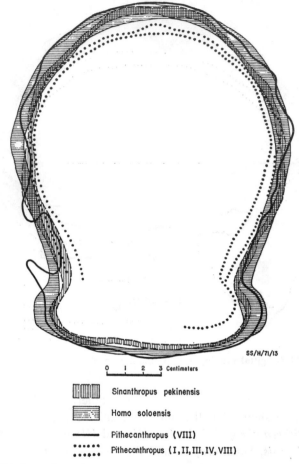

SS/H/71/13

0 1 2 3 Centimeters	
▦	Sinanthropus pekinensis
▤	Homo soloensis
——	Pithecanthropus (VIII)
••••••	Pithecanthropus (I, II, III, IV, VIII)

Figure 7.   Horizontal craniograms of maximum and minimum limits of skulls

1,029 cubic centimeters (Table 3 and Sartono 1968, 1971) with a mean of 902 cubic centimeters. Morphological characters of *Pithecanthropus*, *Sinanthropus*, *Homo soloensis*, and *Homo neanderthalensis* have been compared extensively by von Koenigswald (1940), Weidenreich (1945, 1951), Jacob (1967), and LeGros Clark (1964). Their observations provide an augmentary basis for the diagnosis of *Pithecanthropus* in relation to *Sinanthropus* and *Homo soloensis*, as follows:

1.   As in the case of *Pithecanthropus VIII*, from the size of its craniograms *Homo soloensis* can be distinctly separated from the group of small-brained *Pithecanthropus* which includes *Pithecanthropus I, II, III, IV* and *VII* (Figures 1 and 2).

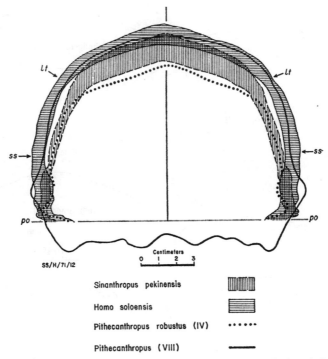

Figure 8.   Coronal craniograms of maximum and minimum limits of skulls

2.   Based on the size of its craniograms, *Homo soloensis* could be grouped into the large-brained *Pithecanthropus* which so far is represented only by *Pithecanthropus VIII* (Figure 6).

3.   The craniograms of *Pithecanthropus VIII* fall entirely within the maximum and minimum limits of those of *Homo soloensis* and *Sinanthropus* (Figures 6, 7, and 8).

4.   The cranial capacity of *Pithecanthropus VIII* (1,029 cubic centimeters) is still smaller than those of the average of *Sinanthropus* (1,043 cubic centimeters) and *Homo soloensis* (1,100 cubic centimeters (Table 3).

5.   The general contour of the supraorbital tori of *Homo soloensis* is almost the same as those of *Pithecanthropus* and *Sinanthropus*. Only their sizes are different. Those of *Homo soloensis, Sinanthropus,* and *Pithecanthropus VIII* are distinctly larger than *Pithecanthropus I* and *II* (Figure 9). Based on this, *Homo soloensis, Sinanthropus,* and *Pithecanthropus VIII* may be grouped as large-brained *Pithecanthropus* whereas *Pithecanthropus I* and *II* are in the small-brained group.

6.   The inclination of the frontal bones of *Homo soloensis* is almost

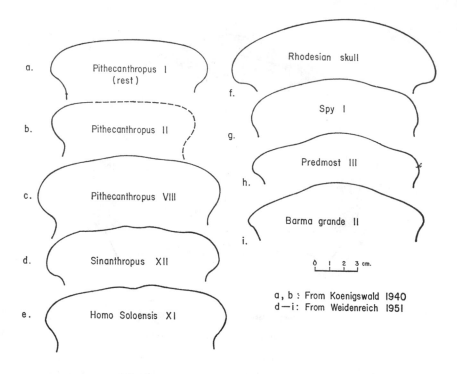

Figure 9.   Ontogenetic development of supraorbital tori

as steep as those of *Sinanthropus* and *Pithecanthropus VIII*, while those of *Pithecanthropus I, II, III, IV*, and *VII* are distinctly flatter. Based on this we may group *Homo soloensis, Sinanthropus*, and *Pithecanthropus VIII* within the large-brained *Pithecanthropus*, whereas the above remaining *Pithecanthropus* comprise the small-brained group (Figure 10). The inclination of the frontal bone of *Pithecanthropus IV* is distinctly smaller than in the other members of the small-brained *Pithecanthropus*. As mentioned earlier, this specimen is more primitive and geologically older than the other members of the small-brained *Pithecanthropus*.

Based on the foregoing discussions and extensive studies on *Homo soloensis* by earlier workers, I conclude that *Homo soloensis* is more closely related to *Pithecanthropus*, especially the large-brained group, than to *Homo neanderthalensis*. There are indeed certain features of *Homo soloensis* resembling *Homo neanderthalensis*, and this is why LeGros Clark (1964) did not group *Homo soloensis* with *Homo erectus* or *Homo neanderthalensis*, but instead designated them a special group of neanderthaloids. *Homo soloensis* may be another

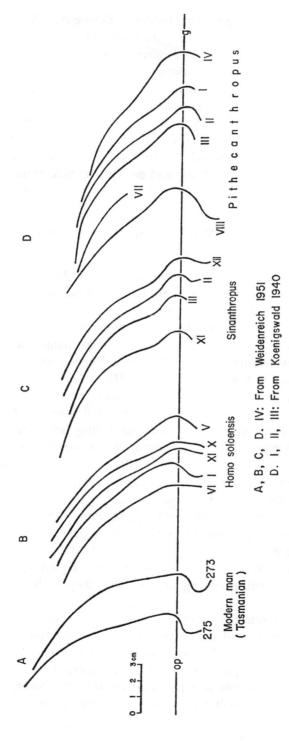

Figure 10. Ontogenetic development of the inclination of frontal bones

type of *Pithecanthropus*. But unlike Weidenreich (1945), I do not accept the nomen *Pithecanthropus soloensis*. Instead I propose the nomen *Pithecanthropus ngandongensis*, because the specimens were found in the village of Ngandong and not in the town of Solo which is seventy-one kilometers away.

This may prevent future workers from being confused as to the location of the only available site of Upper Pleistocene hominids in Java. I do not recommend the use of the term "Solo Man" for this Upper Pleistocene hominid, because we should make a distinction between the Upper Pleistocene and present-day Solo man.

THE EVOLUTIONARY DEVELOPMENT OF *HOMO ERECTUS*

The Pleistocene fossil men from Java, especially the large-brained *Homo erectus*, and from China are not very different from each other. But the nature of their craniograms, supraorbital tori, inclination of their frontal bones, and other morphological features described by earlier workers suggest that there were gradual changes in morphology indicating evolutionary changes during the Pleistocene.

In this section I will use the nomen *Homo erectus* instead of *Pithecanthropus*, *Sinanthropus*, or *Homo soloensis* because use of the latter implies that they were reproductively isolated from one another. The ability to interbreed is the key factor explaining how small differences could arise among those Pleistocene fossil men. Accordingly they should be considered as one species. By this view they are generally placed in the genus *Homo* but according to paleontological taxonomic procedures should retain the species name of *erectus*. No doubt more and more evidence of early man will be found. Therefore, for practical reasons, in previous sections of this article I used the nomina *Pithecanthropus*, *Sinanthropus*, and *Homo soloensis* to separate various fossil men scattered over an extensive region and of different geologic ages, while keeping in mind that they all belong to *Homo erectus*.

The above reasoning should not be taken to imply that I would place all known fossil men and "near-men" from the Pleistocene in *Homo*. *Meganthropus*, for instance, is different from *Pithecanthropus* and does not belong to *Homo erectus*. Per contra, all known *Pithecanthropus* specimens have much in common with each other.

In this section I will retain the designation of the types suggested by von Koenigswald (1968c). For instance, the mandible discovered in 1939 which he named *Pithecanthropus dubius* (von Koenigswald 1950) is so similar to the one I obtained in 1960 and designated *Pithecanthropus C* (Sartono 1961) that together they probably represent a separate type of *Pithecanthropus*. This is also the case with the mandible of 1939 which had been named *Pithecanthropus modjokertensis* which I believe represents a separate type of *Homo erectus*. I obtained another specimen of this type in 1969 (Sartono 1974).

Now what kind of conclusions can be drawn from the existence of the small- and large-brained *Homo erectus*? Are they different subspecies? In other words, do *erectus I, II, III,* and *VII* belong to a small-brained subspecies while *erectus VIII, pekinensis* and *ngandongensis* belong to a large-brained subspecies? These possibilities are worth exploring more thouroughly rather than brushing them aside for the sake of simplicity or because a multiplicity of taxonomic terms is confusing to us. Detailed knowledge of small morphological differences is required for a deeper understanding of the evolutionary progress of mankind. I agree with Leakey (1960: 30) that: "Since there can be no doubt that, as we find more and more evidence of early fossil man, the picture will become more complex rather than simplified . . ."

I tentatively proffer the following evolutionary scheme for *Homo erectus* during the Pleistocene. *Homo erectus* lived in Java and China and probably beyond these regions because *Pithecanthropus*-like hominids have been discovered in Africa and in Europe. Particularly in Java, two subspecies existed, the small-brained and the large-brained *Homo erectus* represented by *erectus I, II, III, IV, VII* and *erectus VIII, pekinensis, ngandongensis*, respectively. The small-brained subspecies lived from the Early Pleistocene until the middle part of the Middle Pleistocene, while the large-brained subspecies existed from the late part of the Middle Pleistocene almost until the end of the Upper Pleistocene. During the Early Pleistocene the primitive small-brained subspecies of *Homo erectus* in Java is represented by *modjokertensis* (cf. *Pithecanthropus robustus, Pithecanthropus IV*). Collaterally the form designated *dubius* (Syn.: *Pithecanthropus C*) existed. However, it is not known which of the two forms is oldest because the stratigraphic position of *modjokertensis* within the Early Pleistocene Putjangan beds is not known. On the other hand, the stratigraphic position of *dubius* has been located (Sartono 1970). Von Koenigswald (1968a: 102) stated that: "This must be according to our knowledge, the oldest mandible from Sangiran . . ." Their geographic distributions are unknown. If *Pithecanthropus modjokertensis* is conspecific with *Sinanthropus lantianensis* (von Koenigswald 1968c), the more primitive small-brained *Homo erectus* would have occupied an extensive area possibly extending from Southeast to East Asia.

The remains of the Javanese Early Pleistocene *Homo erectus* provide only a few indications of their evolutionary progress and origin. Morphologically speaking, *dubius* with its smaller teeth — especially the canine — looks more progressive than *modjokertensis* with its larger teeth and diastema. Von Koenigswald (1968c: 102) remarked that he could not agree with Weidenreich's arguments and so called that mandible *Pithecanthropus dubius* in 1950. To him the high position of the foramen mentale and the small canine were typically human.

I obtained a second specimen of *modjokertensis* in 1969 (Sartono 1974). Its exact stratigraphic position cannot be located, but it may have come from the upper levels of the Early Pleistocene Putjangan beds. I surmise that it is higher stratigraphically than *dubius* (cf. *Pithecanthropus C*).

So far, no *dubius* or *modjokertensis* specimens have been obtained from the overlying Middle Pleistocene Kabuh beds, and we do not know whether they became extinct at the end of the Early Pleistocene. It is more likely that the small-brained *erectus* of the Middle Pleistocene evolved from *dubius* than from *modjokertensis* because morphologically *erectus* is nearer to *dubius* than to *modjokertensis*.

We know more about the Javanese small-brained *Homo erectus* of the Middle than of the Early Pleistocene, which are supposed to be of another type, i.e. the *erectus*. The lowest specimen from Sangiran came from about five meters above the base of the Middle Pleistocene Kabuh beds. This is *erectus II*, a form morphologically more advanced than the Early Pleistocene *dubius* and *modjokertensis*. Higher in the stratigraphic profile we encounter *erectus III* of almost identical morphology to *erectus II*. *Pithecanthropus VI* is almost at the same stratigraphic level as *erectus III*. Its craniograms have not been published yet.

The *erectus VII* specimen was stratigraphically higher than *erectus II*, *III*, and *VI*. Its skull height is almost the same as these specimens but its skull is distinctly broader. Its cranial capacity is about 900 cubic centimeters compared to 775 cubic centimeters of *erectus II*. Based on the shape and size of its craniogram I regard it as a small-brained *erectus*.

The crucial change from the small-brained to large-brained *erectus* probably occurred within the time span between *erectus VII* and *VIII*. Stratigraphically this period is represented by a thickness of not more than ten meters. We do not know what processes took place within this short time. But the morphology of *erectus VIII* is distinctly different from all other *Homo erectus* specimens although it retains the basic morphologic pattern of the species. The skull became longer, broader, and higher, with very thick eyebrow ridges. The position of the occipital torus is relatively lower and the foramen magnum is more to the front than in other *Homo erectus*. Its upper teeth are smaller than those of *modjokertensis*, which is the only *Homo erectus* having upper teeth approximating those of *erectus VIII*. The curvature of its alveolar arch is amazingly like that of *Homo sapiens*. The increase of skull size probably gocs hand in hand with the formation of its relatively high forehead as judged by the increase in the degree of inclination of its frontal bone. The frontal inclination is the smallest in *modjokertensis*, increases in *erectus I, II, III, VII* and culminates in *erectus VIII, pekinensis* (cf. *Sinanthropus pekinensis*), and *ngandongensis* (cf. *Homo soloensis*) (Figure 10).

Frontal inclination increases even more to culminate with *Homo sapiens* (Figure 10). This ontogenetic development of the frontal bones may be the result of the increase in brain size from Early Pleistocene to recent time.

Compared to the increase in degree of inclination of the frontal bones, there is a decrease in size of the supraorbital tori in Pleistocene fossil men which may be related to the increase of brain size (Figure 9). In Figure 9 is shown the ontogenetic development of supraorbital tori in Javanese Middle and Upper Pleistocene *Homo erectus* (a, b, c, d, e) and other fossil men (f, g, h, i). In Javanese *Homo erectus* we note the difference in skull size of the small- and the large-brained forms. Although the shapes of their supraorbital tori remain almost the same, the size decreases between Middle and Upper Pleistocene. Comparing Figures 9 and 10 we observe that the increase in brain size from Early to Upper Pleistocene may be related to the increase of inclination of the frontal bones and decrease of the supraorbital tori. Very likely the change of shapes of supraorbital tori between small- and large-brained *erectus* (Figure 9) may be associated with the change in inclination of frontal bones (Figure 10). The conclusion which could be drawn from this is that whereas there is an increase in the inclination of frontal bones, there is a decrease in the size of the supraorbital tori. Change in these features may occur simultaneously with the increase in brain capacity during the Pleistocene period.

The fossil materials show that dramatic evolutionary changes occurred among *erectus* during the Middle Pleistocene. From the early part of this period we discovered only small-brained *erectus*; no large-brained specimens have been obtained. As discussed previously, small-brained *erectus* may have evolved from the Lower Pleistocene *dubius* and presumably not from the small-brained *modjokertensis* which possessed smaller skull size than the small-brained *erectus*. The small-brained *erectus* experienced physical changes during their evolutionary development as evidenced by *erectus VII* which is broader but only slightly higher than other small-brained *erectus* specimens of the early part of Middle Pleistocene (Sartono 1968) and possesses certain other distinctive morphological characteristics.

Since *erectus VIII* was discovered not much higher than *erectus VII*, we may assume that the small- and large-brained *erectus* lived contemporaneously in the same area during the late Middle Pleistocene. It seems that the small-brained *erectus* did not survive after the end of Middle Pleistocene and they may have been extinct before the end of that period. This may be deduced from the fact that they have never been discovered in the higher levels of the Middle Pleistocene or in Upper Pleistocene deposits of Java, in contrast with the large-brained *erectus* which are confined to the Upper Pleistocene and to the higher levels of the Middle Pleistocene and which have not been discovered in the lower levels of this period (Figure 11).

I will not detail the different views regarding the taxonomic status of *Homo soloensis* presented by earlier workers on this problem. *Homo soloensis* has been regarded as *Pithecanthropus*, Neanderthaloid, *Homo neanderthalensis*, and as a subspecies of *Homo sapiens*. Per contra, I believe that *Homo soloensis* is a type of *Homo erectus* and propose the designation *ngandongensis (vide supra)*. None of the eleven skulls has a brain volume smaller than those of the large-brained *erectus*. Their average size is larger than that of the *erectus VIII*. However, the brain volume of *erectus VIII* falls entirely within the limits of *ngandongensis*. Based on this and features of their craniograms and also considering the opinions of earlier workers on *Homo soloensis*, I believe that there is a very close evolutionary relationship between the large-brained *erectus* and *ngandongensis*, and of course also between both of these and the large-brained *pekinensis*, because we regard the latter as the Chinese counterpart of the Javanese *erectus*.

It is not unusual in paleontology for bio-stratigraphic units to cross time-stratigraphic units. This may be illustrated by the Middle Pleistocene deposits of Sangiran in connection with the vertical distribution

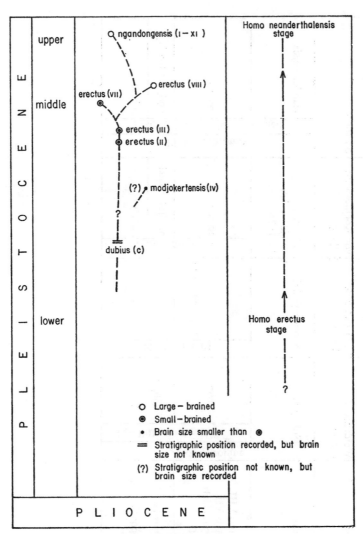

Figure 11.   Evolutionary progress of *Homo erectus* in time and space

of the large-brained *Homo erectus*. In fact one representative of this group is confined to the upper levels of Middle Pleistocene, but in Upper Pleistocene eleven large-brained *ngandongensis* have been discovered. In other words, large-brained *Homo erectus* as a bio-stratigraphic unit crosses the angular unconformity between the Middle Pleistocene Kabuh beds and the Upper Pleistocene Ngandong terraces which are the time-stratigraphic units. This is also the case for the small-brained *Homo erectus* which crosses the disconformity between the Early Pleistocene Putjangan beds and the Middle Pleistocene Kabuh

Table 6. Nomenclature of Javanese Pleistocene hominids

Age	Fauna	Hominid fossil	Weidenreich (1951)	Le Gros Clark (1964)	von Koenigswald (1968)	Sartono
Upper Pleistocene	Ngandong	Homo soloensis (I–XI)	Solo man	"Neanderthaloid"	Solo man (Weidenreich 1951: 216)	ngandongensis
Middle Pleistocene	Trinil	Pithecanthropus VIII, Pithecanthropus VII, Pithecanthropus II, III, Pithecanthropus I	erectus	Pithecanthropus	erectus	erectus
Lower Pleistocene	Djetis	Pithecanthropus IV, Pithecanthropus C	robustus ?	Homo erectus	modjokertensis / dubius	modjokertensis / dubius

Weidenreich (1951): Archanthropine; Pithecanthropus (erectus, robustus).
von Koenigswald (1968): Pithecanthropus (erectus, modjokertensis, dubius).
Sartono: Pithecanthropus; ? small-brained large-brained.

beds. The picture we obtain from this situation is that the small-brained *Homo erectus* is contained between the Early Pleistocene and about the middle part of Middle Pleistocene while the large-brained *Homo erectus* occurs between the upper part of Middle Pleistocene and the Upper Pleistocene. This is in contrast to earlier assumptions which suggest a rigid and strict age classification as follows: *dubius* and *modjokertensis* in Early Pleistocene, *erectus* and *pekinensis* in Middle Pleistocene, and *soloensis* (cf. *ngandongensis*) in Upper Pleistocene. My theory is based on an "open" subdivision of *Homo erectus* with regard to their respective ages. This agrees with the observations that evolutionary progress is continuous and that it need not be restricted by arbitrary geological divisions. Alternative interpretations of the evidence are illustrated in Table 7. They are premised on two different sets of assumptions.

First we may assume the existence of five subspecies of *Homo erectus* during the Pleistocene epoch: *dubius, modjokertensis, erectus, pekinensis,* and *soloensis.* Or we may assume that only two subspecies, which for the time being are provisionally called the small-brained and the large-brained subspecies, existed. Both of these schemes include *dubius, modjokertensis, erectus, pekinensis,* and *ngandongensis.* It should be recalled that a skull of *dubius* has not been found but its stratigraphic position (like *modjokertensis*) suggests that it belongs to the small-brained subspecies.

On the basis of present knowledge of Javanese *Homo erectus,* it is still difficult to conclude certainly whether the small-brained subspecies evolved into the large-brained subspecies. However, *erectus VII,* which is different in many ways from other small-brained *erectus,* lived almost contemporaneously with *erectus VIII.* This suggests that in Java the small-brained *Homo erectus* could have evolved into the large-brained *Homo erectus* during the late part of the Middle Pleistocene. Another possibility is that after evolving in an area outside Java (very likely Asia) the large-brained subspecies migrated to Java during the late part of the Middle Pleistocene period. Through long-term contact between small-brained and large-brained *Homo erectus* admixture between them could have resulted ultimately in the absorption and replacement of the indigenous by the migrant population.

We do not know whether *Pithecanthropus lantianensis* of China and *Homo habilis* of Africa also belong to small-brained *Homo erectus* although they have been compared to *modjokertensis* by von Koenigswald (1968c). In any case *Homo erectus* had a wide geographical

Table 7.   Subspecies and types of *Homo erectus*

Age	Specimen	Homo erectus I	II	
		Subspecies	Subspecies	Type
Upper Pleistocene	*Homo soloensis*	*soloensis*		*ngandongensis*
Middle Pleistocene	*Sinanthropus pekinensis*	*pekinensis*	Large-brained	*pekinensis*
	Pithecanthropus VIII	*erectus*		
	Pithecanthropus I, II, III, VII	*erectus*		*erectus*
Early Pleistocene	*Pithecanthropus IV*	*modjokertensis*	Small-brained	*modjokertensis*
	Pithecanthropus C	*dubius*		*dubius*

distribution, over Java, China, Africa, Europe, and possibly also to Australia. Of all those localities, at the present time Java offers most of the information on *Homo erectus* especially concerning the chronology and stratigraphic position of specimens.

It is generally accepted that *Homo erectus* arrived in Java from the Asian continent along with the southward migratory movements of the Pleistocene vertebrate fauna to Southeast Asia (von Koenigswald 1940; De Terra 1943; Weidenreich 1945). This migration eventually reached Timor, an island opposite the Australian mainland (Sartono 1973a), as suggested by Paleolithic artifacts found in *Stegodon*-bearing deposits in Flores (Maringer and Verhoeven 1970) and in Timor (Sartono 1969). Possibly this migration continued further to the south into the Australian mainland as has been suggested by the discovery of the Kow Swamp skulls in Victoria (Thorne 1971).

The following dates have been obtained in relation to *Homo erectus*:

1.   The Lower Pleistocene Djetis beds of East Java which contain the infant skull of Homo *modjokertensis* (cf. *Pithecanthropus modjokertensis, Pithecanthropus V, Homo erectus modjokertensis*) and which can be correlated with the Lower Pleistocene Putjangan beds of Sangiran in Central Java containing the small-brained *dubius, modjokertensis*, and also *Meganthropus* have been estimated to have an age of about 1.9 ± 0.4 million years. This preliminary figure was obtained by

potassium-argon dating of pumice tuff found in the Djetis beds. It is also assumed to be the age of the Putjangan beds containing the small-brained *Homo erectus* and *Meganthropus* (Jacob and Curtis 1971).

2.   Available potassium-argon dates on Indo-Australian tektites from the Middle Pleistocene Kabuh beds of Sangiran in Central Java are believed to be 700,000 years B.P. (von Koenigswald 1968b).

3.   The age of basalt from the Patiajam dome in the Gunung Muria area, Central Java, overlying leucite-bearing breccious beds containing a Middle Pleistocene Trinil fauna, is estimated at about 500,000 years (Evernden and Curtis 1965).

4.   The age of the Middle Pleistocene *Homo erectus pekinensis*, which belongs to the large-brained *Homo erectus* subspecies, is estimated at about 350,000 years (LeGros Clark 1964: 110).

5.   The age of *Homo soloensis*, with its Mousterian culture found in the Upper Pleistocene river terraces in the Ngandong area of East Java, has been estimated at between 100,000 to 60,000 years ago (Jacob 1967: 39).

6.   The age of the Kow Swamp skulls from Victoria, Australia, is believed to be 10,000 years (Thorne and Macumber 1972).

From the above dates it is inferred that the oldest *Homo erectus* may consist of the small-brained subspecies. In Java this small-brained *Homo erectus* lived contemporaneously with *Meganthropus* about 1.9 ± 0.4 million years ago. They include the small-brained sub-species of the type of *modjokertensis* and possibly also of *dubius*. This small-brained *Homo erectus* evolved into the small-brained *erectus* between 700,000 and 500,000 years ago. Eventually this small-brained *erectus* evolved into the large-brained *Homo erectus* of China and Java, respectively the type of *pekinensis* about 350,000 years ago and *ngandongensis* about 100,000 years ago. This evolutionary progression occurred via the Javanese large-brained *erectus*, i.e. *Pithecanthropus VIII*. Ultimately the large-brained *Homo erectus* may have evolved into a certain type or types on the Australian mainland, and produced the Kow Swamp skulls, at least 10,000 years ago.

The above evolutionary process of *Homo erectus* does not indicate that, because its oldest type has been found in Java, it had its origin on this island too. This reasoning is in contradiction to the Pliocene paleogeography of Southeast Asia which shows that the largest portion of this region was still occupied by sea during that time and that the Pliocene beds of Java are marked by a mixed facies of mostly marine and less continental facies. This indicates that very likely *Homo erectus* could not have originated in Java but that it had come from neighboring regions, probably from the Asian mainland. The deduction which can be drawn from this is that a primitive small-brained *Homo erectus* migrated from somewhere in the Asian main-land into Java and China, and in both of these regions they developed into a large-brained *Homo erectus*. Javanese large-brained *Homo erectus*, (so far it is not yet known which type) may have migrated toward Australia along the Lesser Sunda Islands chain. This is sug-gested by the preservation of many features of the large-brained *Homo erectus* in the Kow Swamp skulls which can only be explained by the existence of gene flow from Java to Australia. This contact may go as far back as 100,000 years ago when the last type of the large-brained Javanese *Homo erectus*, i.e. *ngandongensis*, became extinct and lasted up to about 10,000 years ago when the Kow Swamp people died.

In China unequivocal representatives of the small-brained *Homo erectus* have not been discovered. As assumed by von Koenigswald (1968b) *Pithecanthropus lantianensis* might represent this form and might have evolved into the large-brained *pekinensis*.

Then, what was the ancestral stock of the small-brained subspecies of *Homo erectus*? We do not know now. Future discoveries of *Homo erectus* may shed more light on its evolutionary development and may also provide more information on their migratory movements during the Pleistocene.

CONCLUSIONS

The foregoing discussion supports the following conclusions about *Homo erectus*:

1.   Based on overall morphology and size of craniograms there are two subspecies of *Homo erectus* which provisionally are called the large-brained and the small-brained subspecies.

2.   Each of the subspecies is represented by its own types:

a.   The large-brained subspecies is represented by *erectus VIII*, *pekinensis*, and *ngandongensis*.

b.   The small-brained subspecies is represented by *erectus I, II, III*, and very likely *VI, VII*, and *modjokertensis* also.

3.   I recommend the nomen *Homo erectus ngandongensis* instead of *Homo soloensis* (cf. *Javanthropus soloensis*, Solo man).

4.   Based on stratigraphic considerations, *Pithecanthropus dubius* and the infant skull of *Homo modjokertensis* may also be placed in the small-brained subspecies of *Homo erectus*.

5.   *Homo erectus modjokertensis* has a slightly smaller brain capacity

than the small-brained *Homo erectus erectus* and it is stratigraphically and chronologically older than this subspecies.

6.   The following ages have been obtained:

Holocene: ± 10,000 years.

Kow Swamp skulls with many features of the large-brained *Homo erectus*, especially the striking similarity between *erectus VIII* and Kow Swamp I.

Upper Pleistocene: ± 60,000 – 100,000.

Large-brained *Homo erectus ngandongensis*.

Middle Pleistocene: ± 350,000 years.

Large-brained *Homo erectus pekinensis*.

Middle Pleistocene: ± 500,000 – 700,000 years. At upper levels the large-brained *Homo erectus erectus VIII*. At lower levels the small-brained *Homo erectus erectus I, II, III, VII*, and very likely also *VI*.

Early Pleistocene: 1.9 ± 0.4 million years. (Possibly including Villafranchian).

Small-brained *Homo erectus modjokertensis* and *Homo erectus dubius*; possibly also *Pithecanthropus lantianensis*.

7.   In the absence of more data, I assume that *Meganthropus* is different from *Homo erectus*. *Meganthropus* occurs between the upper levels of Early Pleistocene and the lower levels of Middle Pleistocene

8.   An ancestral stock of *Homo erectus* may have arrived in Java from the Asian mainland and evolved respectively into *Homo erectus dubius* and *Homo erectus modjokertensis* during the Early Pleistocene about 1.9 ± 0.4 million years ago. The ancestral stock also may have arrived in China and evolved into *Pithecanthropus lantianensis*.

9.   It is possible that the small-brained *Homo erectus dubius* evolved into the small-brained *Homo erectus erectus* about 700,000 years ago and into the large-brained *Homo erectus erectus* around 500,000 years ago. Eventually the large-brained *Homo erectus erectus* evolved into the large-brained *Homo erectus ngandongensis* about 100,000 years ago.

10.   The morphology of small-brained *Homo erectus modjokertensis* suggests that it is not the direct ancestor of small-brained *Homo erectus*. Neither is *Meganthropus*.

11.   In China *Pithecanthropus lantianensis* may have evolved into *Homo erectus pekinensis* around 350,000 years ago.

12.   Although the large-brained *Homo erectus* was probably extinct at the end of the Pleistocene epoch, many of its characteristics were inherited by certain populations of *Homo sapiens* as demonstrated by the Kow Swamp skulls which possess many characteristics of *Homo*

erectus. In this case the similarity of the large-brained *Homo erectus erectus VIII* and Kow Swamp skull I is very striking indeed.

13.   The migration route of *Homo erectus* during the Pleistocene epoch from Asia to Java extended eastward along the Lesser Sunda Islands chain into Flores and then to Timor. This migration might have arrived eventually on the Australian mainland as indicated by the Kow Swamp skulls. These fossils suggest the existence of gene flow during the Pleistocene epoch between the *Homo erectus* and the Kow Swamp populations.

REFERENCES

CAMPBELL, B.
  1964   "Quantitative taxonomy and human evolution," in *Classification and human evolution*. Edited by S. L. Washburn, 50–74. London: Methuen.
  1968   The use of nomenclature in the study of recent and fossil man. *Symposia of the Society for the Study of Human Biology*, volume eight: *The skeletal biology of earlier human populations*. Edited by D. R. Brothwell, 19–29. Oxford and New York: Pergamon Press.
COON, C. S.
  1963   *The origin of races*. London: Jonathan Cape.
DE TERRA, H.
  1943   Pleistocene geology and early man in Java. *Transactions of the American Philosophical Society* 32(3):437–464.
EVERNDEN, J. P., C. H. CURTIS
  1965   The potassium-argon dating of Late Cenozoic rocks in East Africa and Italy. *Current Anthropology* 6:343–385.
HOWELL, W. W.
  1966   *Homo erectus. Scientific American* 215(5):46–53.
JACOB, T.
  1964   A new hominid skull cap from Pleistocene Sangiran. *Anthropologica* 6(1):97–104.
  1967   "Some problems pertaining to the racial history of the Indonesian region." Unpublished doctoral dissertation, Rijksuniversiteit Utrecht, The Netherlands.
JACOB, T., G. G. CURTIS
  1971   Preliminary potassium-argon dating of early man in Java. *Contributions of the University of California Archaeological Research Facility* 12:50.
KURTH, G.
  1965   "Die (Eu)Homininen," in *Menschliche Abstammungslehre*. Edited by G. Heberer, 357–425. Stuttgart: Gustav Fischer Verlag.

LEAKEY, L. S. B.
1960   "The origin of the genus *Homo*," in *Evolution after Darwin*, volume two: *The evolution of man*. Edited by Sol Tax, 17–32. Chicago: University of Chicago Press.

LE GROS CLARK, W. E.
1964   *The fossil evidence for human evolution*. Chicago: University of Chicago Press.

MARINGER, J., T. VERHOEVEN
1970   Die Steinartefakte aus der *Stegodon*-Fossilschicht von Mengeruda auf Flores, Indonesien. *Anthropos* 65:229–247.

MAYR, E.
1963   "The taxonomic evaluation of fossil hominids," in *Classification and human evolution*. Edited by S. L. Washburn, 332–346. New York: Wenner-Gren Foundation for Anthropological Research.

OPPENOORTH, W. F. F.
1932   *Homo (Javanthropus) soloensis*, een pleistoceene mensch van Java. *Wetenschappelijke Mededelingen Dienst van de Mijnbouw in Nederlandsch-Indie* 20.
1937   The place of *Homo soloensis* among fossil men. *Early Man* (Philadelphia 1937), 349–360.

SARTONO, S.
1961   *Notes on a new find of a* Pithecanthropus *mandible*. Publikasi Teknik Seri Paleontologi 2. Geological Survey of Indonesia.
1964   On a new find of another *Pithecanthropus* skull: an announcement. *Bulletin of the Geological Survey of Indonesia* 1(1):2–5.
1967   An additional skull cap of a *Pithecanthropus*. *Journal of the Anthropological Society of Nippon* 75, (754).
1968   Early man in Java: *Pithecanthrropus VII*, a male specimen of *Pithecanthropus erectus (I)*. *Proceedings of the Koninklijke Nederlandse Akademie van Wetenschappen, Amsterdam*, Series B, 71, (5).
1969   *Stegodon timorensis*: a pygmy specimen from Timor (Indonesia). *Proceedings of the Koninklijke Nederlandsche Akademie van Wetenschappen, Amsterdam* 72, 192–202.
1970   On the stratigraphic position of *Pithecanthropus* mandible *C*. *Proceedings of the Institut Teknologi Bandung* 4(4):91–102.
1971   Observations on a new skull of *Pithecanthropus erectus (Pithecanthropus VIII)* from Sangiran, Central Java. *Proceedings of the Koninklijke Nederlandsche Akademie van Wetenschappen, Amsterdam*, series B, 74(2).
1972   Discovery of another Hominid skull at Sangiran, Central Java. *Current Anthropology* 13(1):124–126.
1973a On Pleistocene migration routes of vertebrate fauna in Southeast Asia. *Geological Society of Malaysia Bulletin* 6:273–286.
1973b On cranial measurements of *Pithecanthropus erectus (Pithecanthropus VIII)*. Publikasi Teknik Seri Paleontologi 4. Geological Survey of Indonesia.

1974   Observations on a newly discovered jaw of *Pithecanthropus modjokertensis* from the Lower Pleistocene of Sangiran, Central Java. *Proceedings of the Koninklijke Nederlandsche Akademie van Wetenschappen, Amsterdam,* series B, 77(1).

THORNE, A. G.
1971   Mungo and Kow Swamp: morphologic variation in Pleistocene Australians. *Mankind* 8(2):85–90.
1972   *Pithecanthropus* and early man in Indonesia. *Geosurvey Newsletter,* IV, 46, 4. Geological Survey of Indonesia.

THORNE, T., P. G. MACUMBER
1972   Discoveries of Late Pleistocene man at Kow Swamp, Australia. *Nature* 238:316–319.
        8(2).

VALLOIS, H. V.
1935   Le *Javanthropus. L'Anthropologie* 45:71–84.

VON KOENIGSWALD, G. H. R.
1933   Ein neuer Urmensch aus dem Diluvium Javas. *Cbl. Mineral., Geol., Palaeont.* Abt. B, 1:29–42.
1940   Neue *Pithecanthropus*-Funde 1936–1938. *Wetenschappelijke Mededelingen Dienst van de Mijnbouw in Nederlandsch-Indie* 28.
1950   Fossil hominids from the Lower Pleistocene of Java. *Proceedings of the Ninth International Geological Congress, London, 1948* 9:59–61.
1968a   Observations upon two *Pithecanthropus* mandibles from Sangiran, Central Java. *Proceedings of the Koninklijke Nederlandsche Akademie van Wetenschappen, Amsterdam,* series B, 71:1–9.
1968b   "Das absolute Alter des *Pithecanthropus erectus* Dubois," in *Evolution und Hominisation.* (Second edition). Edited by Gottfried Kurth. Stuttgart: Gustav Fischer Verlag.
1968c   Java: Prae-Trinil Man. *Proceedings of the VIIIth International Congress of Anthropological and Ethnological Sciences, Tokyo,* volume one, 104–105. Tokyo: Science Council of Japan.

WEIDENREICH, F.
1945   Giant early man from Java and South China. *Anthropological Papers of the American Museum of Natural History.* 40(1):1–134.
1951   Morphology of Solo Man. *Anthropological Papers of the American Museum of Natural History* 43(3):205–290.

WOLPOFF, H. H.
1971   Vertesszöllös and the Presapiens theory. *American Journal of Physical Anthropology* 35(2).

An Explanation for the Diastema of Javan Erectus *Skull IV*

GROVER S. KRANTZ

In 1939 G. H. R. von Koenigswald discovered a pithecanthropine skull in what is now called the Djetis horizon of eastern Java. This specimen, known as skull IV, consists of the posterior two-thirds of the braincase and a palate with ten teeth. In all important characteristics the braincase is of the *Homo erectus* type. The palate and its dentition, however, are very unlike anything associated with *H. erectus* from Java or anywhere else.

Franz Weidenreich exhaustively described this and several other discoveries made just prior to World War II (Weidenreich 1945). He decided that skull IV represented a different, and more primitive, species than the first three skulls, which are now referred to the more recent Trinil horizon. The skull showed such peculiarities as an unusually large temporal pyramid on the endocranial floor and anteriorly converging temporal squama. As Weidenreich assumed the Trinil skulls would have had facial parts similar to those of "Sinanthropus," it was mainly the characteristics of the palate of skull IV that led him to designate it as a separate species, *Pithecanthropus robustus*. This genus designation is no longer in use today, and skull IV might now more properly be distinguished, following his reasoning, as a temporal subspecies of the Javan geographical variety of *Homo erectus*.

What is most peculiar about the palate of skull IV is that the canines are somewhat projecting, and there is a precanine diastema on both sides. These are pongid traits not found in *Australopithecus*, which almost certainly includes the ancestor of *Homo*. It is something of a mystery just how an *erectus* skull could show characteristics already lost by its distant ancestors. Hulse (1971: 214) complains that ". . . no one has advanced a satisfactory hypothesis to explain this fact." Several possible explanations will be mentioned here, including an original one that will be described at length (see Figures 1 and 2).

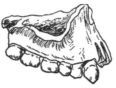

Figure 1.   Palate of Java skull IV. Right side is shown and illustrates the projecting canine, wear surfaces, and prognathism. (Redrawn from Weidenreich 1945.)

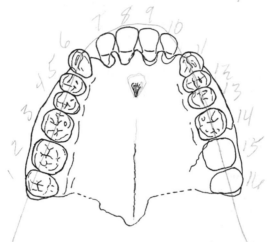

Figure 2.   Occlusal view of skull IV palate. The palate is drawn with tooth rows spread to original shape and the missing teeth filled in. The incisors are very conservatively restored. (Drawn from the cast.)

One explanation is that skull IV shows a reappearance of characteristics from a distant ancestor of perhaps several million years earlier. The number of such characteristics, which will be reviewed below, seems inordinately great to be accounted for this way.

Another suggestion depends on the idea that *Homo* is not a descendant of *Australopithecus*; thus the hominid type of dentition was evolved in two separate lines. This would mean that *Australopithecus* developed hominid dentition at an early date without significant increase in brain size, while the reverse was happening in the line leading to *Homo*. This would also mean that *Homo* has no Villafranchian ancestors, as even *H. habilis* has hominid dentition. Von Koenigswald's (1966) picture of the australopithecines as a separate line could perhaps be stretched to include this concept, but only with difficulty.

Still another explanation would be to take some of the ideas of Weidenreich and Carleton Coon on racial origins to a ridiculous extreme that neither proposed. It would postulate that racial separations already existed in a preaustralopithecine ancestor of *Homo,* and that racial mixing has been minimal since then. A characteristic of the Australoid line would then be a retardation in the evolution of hominid dentition so great as to exhibit in the Middle Pleistocene pongid traits that had already been lost in other lines two million years or more earlier. Aside from its obvious theoretical difficulties, this idea fails simply because other fossil material from Java at that time shows fully hominid dental traits (*Meganthropus* and *H. erectus* mandible B).

A fourth explanation is offered here which is based on the assumption that the braincase and palate are from two different individuals. It would follow that the source of the palate was not a hominid. This idea will now be explored in some detail.

The two skull parts do not contact each other, though they are reported to have been found in close proximity in the same deposit. Because there was also no overlap of parts, and their state of preservation was the same, the presumption of a single individual appeared obvious at the time. If one assumes that two individuals are involved, the real nature of the palate may then be considered strictly on its own merits.

The palate cannot have come from the same individual as skull IV because it is much too broad. The external palatal breadth, as found, but with two left molars added, is about 84 millimeters. It was somewhat crushed inward on the left side, and its reconstructed breadth is 94 millimeters (Weidenreich 1945: 32). I have checked this on the Wenner-Gren cast, which clearly shows each break, and find this breadth figure cannot be off by more than a millimeter without introducing some asymmetry. This may be compared with the distance between the centers of the mandibular (or glenoid) fossae of the temporals, which is no more than 91 millimeters.

In all hominid and anthropoid skulls the glenoid fossae are considerably farther apart than are the external alveolar borders on the palate. Yet here it is the palate which is broader.

In order to obtain some statistical meaning for this I measured the external palatine breadths and the distances between centers of glenoid fossae in a sample of seventeen *Homo sapiens* skulls. These were seven New Guinea natives, seven American Indians, one Caucasian, and the casts of Predmost and Skhūl V. The center of the glenoid fossa is not a precisely defined point, but when repeated measurements were within two millimeters I decided my procedure was satisfactory for present purposes.

Palatine breadths were expressed as a percentage of the interfossa breadths. These ranged from 58.9 percent to 74.2 percent, with a mean of 65.7 percent, and with a standard deviation of 4.16. For Java skull IV it is 103.3 percent, which is over nine standard deviations away from the *H. sapiens* mean.

The same measurements were made on casts of other hominids and various apes with results as shown in Table 1.

Table 1.   Palatine breadth in a selection of pongids and fossil hominids, expressed as a percentage of interfossa breadth

Hominids	Percentages	Pongids	Percentages
Broken Hill	71.2	Orangutan	67.8
Sinanthropus (recon.)	66.3	Chimpanzee (1)	69.2
La Chapelle	66.7	Chimpanzee (2)	73.7
Zinjanthropus	71.8	Gorilla (1)	64.8
Sterkfontein V	74.2	Gorilla (2)	70.8
		Gorilla (3)	60.7

These are all within the range found in the *H. sapiens* sample. None of these is a statistically useful sample, thus each high figure might be used as though it were a mean with the same rather great standard deviation as found for the *H. sapiens* sample. By this procedure, skull IV surpasses Broken Hill by 7.7 standard deviations; Sterkfontein V by seven standard deviations; and the chimpanzee by more than seven standard deviations.

Putting these figures another way, if skull IV had the same shape as Broken Hill, then its biglenoid diameter should have been 132 millimeters instead of its actual 91 millimeters. Similarly with *Australopithecus* proportions, it should have been 127 millimeters and with chimpanzee proportions 128 millimeters. There is no way these percentages or biglenoid breadths can be reconciled with the actual braincase supposedly associated with the palate.

From the palate there is another method by which one can approximate the positions of its corresponding glenoid fossae. In the major act of chewing, one condyle moves forward out of its socket and onto the preglenoid eminence, thereby moving the lower teeth toward the opposite side of the mouth and apart from the uppers. As the teeth come together on the working side, the opposite condyle slips back into its socket. On the working side of the jaw, dental occlusion is thus a side-to-side movement of the lower teeth against the uppers, with the condyle of that side acting as a center of rotation. The same is true for the other side of the jaws as they are used to chew.

The palate of skull IV shows significant wear on its teeth, which interlocked considerably with the mandibular dentition. The direction of movement of the lower teeth can clearly be seen from this wear to have been exactly perpendicular to the mesiodistal line of the cheek teeth. The condyle position, in order to accomplish this movement must also have been in line with these teeth. As the tooth rows diverge posteriorly, the condyles must have been considerably farther apart than the last molars. A drawing illustrates the condyle, and mandibular socket, positions as deduced from the palate (Figure 3).

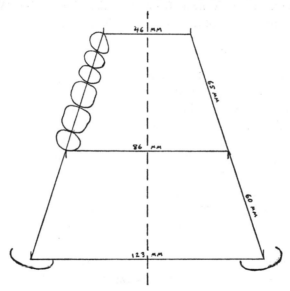

Figure 3. Diagram of reconstructed palate showing midlines of tooth rows ex‧ tended to locate centers of glenoid fossae. This gives only a minimum biglenoid breadth as it does not allow for spread of ascending rami

The result of this calculation is that the mandibular socket centers must have been about 123 millimeters apart rather than 91 millimeters as in the associated braincase. The distance from the palate to the fossae in the drawing is based on *Sinanthropus* proportions, and could have been greater. Also, because the occlusal plane slopes somewhat, the condyles will have been still farther apart in proportion to the height of the ascending ramus. The figure of 123 millimeters is thus a minimum value, while the actual biglenoid breadth was probably more on the order of 140 millimeters.

Two estimates of the distance between centers of the mandibular fossae agree with each other, and exceed that measured on the skull by some 45 or 50 millimeters. This should be sufficient to show that the palate was from some different being than was the braincase.

Weidenreich made a restoration of the entire skull IV, which is illustrated in his 1945 work, including a basal view. Careful measurement and comparison of contours show he had artificially spread the mandibular fossae some distance apart without any explanation. Still, they were much too close together to accommodate the palate breadth.

Treating the palate as though it were found alone, its affinities may now be assessed as pongid versus hominid. The following summary of its characteristics is drawn from the description by Weidenreich (1945) except where otherwise noted. The following traits are the pongid ones:

(1)   The cheek teeth form a straight row from canine to last molar with no curve as found in man. This makes the greatest breadth occur at the third molar rather than at the second. That the canine is part of this straight row is especially nonhominid. In *Australopithecus robustus* with a similarly straight row of cheek teeth, the anterior premolar forms the "corner" while the small canine is part of the more transverse anterior row.

(2)   Both canines project three millimeters beyond the occlusal levels of the adjacent teeth. They show considerable wear, exposing the dentine, and thus they originally projected even more. (Measured from the cast.)

(3)   The canine sockets and those of the missing lateral incisors are well separated — by 6.2 millimeters on the left and 5 millimeters on the right. This means there was a considerable diastema, which in the apes accommodates the projecting tip of the lower canine.

(4)   The upper canines are not worn flat, but have steeply sloped wear facets on their anterior surfaces caused by contact with the lower canines (LeGros Clark 1964: 101). These facets show the canines overlapped one another by at least four millimeters, and possibly much more. A loose incisor, identified by Weidenreich as a lateral one, has a distal wear facet which was likely caused by the lower canine, which thus filled the diastema well when the mouth was closed.

(5) The posterior surfaces of the upper canines also have sloped wear facets which correlate with reverse-sloped facets on the anterior premolars. These facets were worn by contact with the missing lower anterior premolar, which projected considerably. The mesiodistal length of this lower premolar was about eleven millimeters judging from the distance between the tips of the occluding upper teeth. The wear facets resulting from the lower second premolar indicate it had a length of only eight millimeters. Hominid lower premolars are of nearly equal length, while in apes the anterior one is longer because of its unicuspid, sectorial design. The missing lower dentition here had an elongated, projecting anterior premolar of apelike, not human, proportions. (Observed by the author on the cast.)

(6) While the upper incisors are lacking, their sockets call for very large, sloping teeth. An unprejudiced restoration of these teeth would make them very apelike and projecting.

(7) The molar crown enamel is somewhat wrinkled. While this is comparable to that found in *Sinanthropus*, it is more than in the Javan mandible B (an undoubted *H. erectus*), and is also very much like that in fossil orang molars from the same locality.

(8) LeGros Clark (1964: 101) reports that the anterior premolars had three roots as is normal in apes, but this is not evident in the cast.

(9) The palate is relatively smooth as in apes rather than ridged as in man.

(10) The palate surface rises rather gradually from front to back as in apes rather than rising abruptly, then continuing level as in man.

(11) Nasal breadth can be approximated at thirty-six millimeters, which is extreme by human standards and exceeds all other fossil hominids. Such a breath would be more common for an ape.

(12) Maxillary sinuses are exceptionally large with more apelike than human dimensions.

In contrast with the above traits, the palate shows the following more hominid characteristics:

(1) The canine shape is more spatulate than conical, and the degree of projection is much less than is usual in pongids.

(2) The molar rows diverge posteriorly rather than being parallel as in the large apes.

(3) Crown details of the premolars and molars are very human-looking according to most authorities, though orangutan teeth are often similar enough to make identification difficult.

(4)   There is a moderate development of a nasal spine looking more hominid than pongid.

(5)   The palate is quite "deep," as is usuall in man.

(6)   The root of the zygomatic arch arises above the first molar as in man rather than farther back as in most pongids, though not in female orangutans.

(7)   Two other fragmentary specimens of palates found by von Koenigswald reportedly show similar traits, but without the precanine diastema in one case.

This listing of traits, with twelve to seven in favor of an apelike morphology should not necessarily be taken as a relative weighting of the palate's affinities. Not all of these traits are necessarily of equal significance. Also, many of the traits could have been subdivided into several aspects, while others could have been combined under the same number. While its pongid features seem to predominate, they are not clearly overwhelming in this enumeration.

Of the apelike traits I would consider the most important to be the overlapping of projecting canines, the inferred type of lower anterior premolar, the diastema with inclined incisors, and the smooth palate. Of the human traits the most impressive are the spatulate canine form and the high palate. The breadth of the palate seems at first glance to be a more hominid trait, but is so great as to make it unique.

If it is assumed that this palate is indeed pongid, and not hominid, it now becomes the manlike traits which must be explained. Most of these traits are accounted for by making two assumptions: it is from a pongid with very little muzzle projection, and it is a female. These assumptions could explain the relatively small anterior dentition (small for an ape), the incipient nasal spine, and the anterior location of the zygomatic root. The size and morphology of the postcanine teeth are not greatly outside the range of living and fossil orangutans.

The height of the palate is exaggerated by its breakage but is still considerable and remains unexplained, as does the spatulate form of the canine. Still, these traits are relatively minor when compared with the far greater number of pongid characteristics.

The reported association of the palate with the *H. erectus* braincase can only be classed as pure coincidence. The lack of diastema in one of the two other reported specimens is based on a contact facet on the canine, but this could result from the lower canine as well as an upper incisor. A full description of these additional palatal fragments would be of value.

It is proposed here that the palate previously related to the Javan *Homo erectus* skull IV should be removed from this association and classed in the Pongidae on the basis of the traits enumerated above. More particularly it can be assigned to the genus *Pongo*, large Asiatic apes, because of its location and for reasons that have to do with a probable second specimen of the type.

The specimen is distinguished from that of *Pongo pygmaeus* by its spatulate upper canines, high palate, and great breadth. Because of its relatively small anterior teeth and incipient nasal spine, a very short muzzle is indicated. Accordingly a new species is proposed, *Pongo brevirostris*, with this palate being the type specimen.

There is another fossil from the Djetis horizon in Java which appears to be a second specimen of *Pongo brevirostris*. This is the mandible previously called Sangiran 1939, or *Pithecanthropus dubius*. The only available description of the detailed morphology of this specimen is again from Weidenreich (1945).

In size and gross morphology the Sangiran 1939 mandible fragment is, at first glance, between that of *Homo erectus* mandible B and the so-called *Meganthropus* mandibles. It is not, however, clearly distinguishable from the jaw of a female orangutan in most characteristics (see Figure 4).

Figure 4. Sangiran 1939 mandibular fragment: (A) outside or labial view, and (B) inside or lingual view (Redrawn from Weidenreich 1945)

The specimen consists of most of the right horizontal ramus with the first two molars, a stump of the second premolar, and sockets of the first premolar and canine. It is broken near enough to the symphysis to indicate clearly its shape, which is quite narrow near the inferior border. The shape of this symphysis is basically pongid and is extended into a true simian shelf. Here the torus transversus superior is much thicker (19 millimeters) than the torus transversus inferior (13.5 millimeters) as in all apes, whereas all hominids have just the reverse proportions.

The anterior premolar, if present, would be distinctive — in hominids it is bicuspid and mesiodistally short; in pongids it has a single sectorial cusp and is mesiodistally elongated. The tooth type can be determined by the disposition of its root sockets. In hominids the root is buccolingually wide and may be divided into two parts. In pongids there are two major roots, one distal and one mesiolabial in location.

The Sangiran 1939 mandible shows three openings in the region of the anterior premolar (see Figure 5). One opening is clearly a root socket (distolingual); another opening is labial to the first, and the third opening is mesial to the first. The labial opening appears to be a break in the bone, but if it is a socket, the premolar was of the hominid design. The mesial opening looks more like a root socket and would indicate a pongid sectorial premolar. Weidenreich clearly preferred to find the jaw to be hominid, but concluded the pongid premolar design was far more likely.

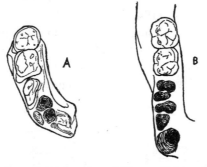

Figure 5. Occlusal views of (A) Sangiran 1939 mandible, and (B) orangutan mandible with premolars and canines removed (Redrawn from Weidenreich 1945)

Another significant trait is the vertical position of the mental foramen. It is located about half way down the side of the bone as in hominids rather than two-thirds of the way down as in pongids. What Weidenreich did not realize is that the level of this foramen is related to the root length of the canine. As this specimen had a relatively small canine for an ape, the foramen is understandably high-placed. The direction in which the foramen is oriented is forward as in apes.

Weidenreich's description includes a number of other traits and measurements of lesser importance most of which are matched or most closely approached only in orangutan jaws.

The Sangiran 1939 mandible is not simply that of a female orangutan, though it is clearly from an oranglike pongid. It differs from a typical ape in the same general way as does the palate of skull IV. It matches that palate for size and general build, and even the reconstructed lengths of the lower premolars are essentially the same. It would appear that these upper and lower jaws are from the same species. To assume otherwise would mean postulating two species of oranglike pongids in the Pleistocene of Java, both of which have short muzzles, small canines, and posteriorly diverging cheek-tooth rows.

A comparative inventory of Southeast Asian Pleistocene hominoids should now be reviewed. There now appear to have been at least six species if one includes the gibbon, which is not under consideration here. Of the other five species two are pongids, two hominids, and the last is of presently uncertain affinities.

1. *Pongo pygmaeus* is the most probable designation of numerous fossil teeth found from Java to South China and merits no further discussion here.

2. *Pongo brevirostris* is proposed, which would include the palate found with skull IV and the Sangiran 1939 mandible. An unknown number of fossil "orang-utan" teeth may also belong to this species.

3. *Homo erectus* is now well known from at least seven incomplete crania, three mandible pieces, and the Modjokerto child's skull. The more recent Solo skulls are morphologically of this type in all essential particulars, and differ only in the larger size of several specimens.

4. *Meganthropus paleojavanicus* is known from two mandibles, the first called Sangiran 1941, and a second, more damaged specimen, found after the war. These are entirely outside the possible size range of *H. erectus* and are now usually classed with the australopithecines. The size matches the well-known *A. robustus* mandibles, but the premolar morphology of the 1941 specimen is clearly more like *A. africanus*. This can be confirmed by the reader by comparing the premolars of the available Wenner-Gren casts of *A. robustus* and *africanus* with those of *Meganthropus*. The size contrast between these two types may be only a local phenomenon in parts of Africa, at best.

5. *Gigantopithecus blacki* is known from three mandibles and hundreds of isolated teeth from the Pleistocene of South China, and an older mandible from India called *G. bilaspurensis*. No specimens are presently known from Java. *Gigantopithecus* shows mixed hominid and pongid traits — small incisors but large canines, apparently bicuspid lower anterior premolars but a rather pongid-shaped mandibular symphysis. Its posteriorly diverging molar rows have suggested affinities with the palate of Java skull IV and the Sangiran 1939 mandible, but all the anterior dentition is quite differently proportioned. *Gigantopithecus* is the largest known primate and probably has no close relation to any of the other forms discussed here.

The proposed new species of *Pongo brevirostris* cannot safely be reconstructed beyond the jaws and glenoid fossae. It is the great distance between these fossae that is its most peculiar feature as this exceeds anything known among hominoids, excepting *Gigantopithecus* of course. I have drawn several sketches (not reproduced here) attempting to illustrate an oranglike skull with the modififed muzzle and broad base as indicated by the present analysis. Such a skull bears no particular resemblance to any other mammal, though the masticatory function appears to parallel that of hominids in some respects.

The widely spaced mandibular sockets allow a large space between them in which the foramen magnum could easily be shifted forward. If this were the case, a better balance of the head would also be facilitated by the known reduction of the muzzle. An equally likely interpretation would be that the skull base and intergonial space are expanded to accommodate an unusual development of the vocal appartus. The raised palate could be part of this design. Until more discoveries are made, these last ideas must remain as no more than speculations.

REFERENCES

HULSE, FREDERICK S.
   1971   *The human species* (second edition). New York: Random House.
LE GROS CLARK, W. E.
   1964   *The fossil evidence for human evolution* (second edition). Chicago: University of Chicago Press.
VON KOENIGSWALD, G. H. R.
   1966   *The evolution of man*. Ann Arbor: University of Michigan Press.
WEIDENREICH, FRANZ
   1945   Giant early man from Java and South China. *Anthropological Papers of the American Museum of Natural History* 40(1):1–134.

A Study on the Modjokerto Infant Calvarium

CANTEMIR RIŞCUŢIA

This article constitutes a brief preliminary report on the cranial capacity, age, and sex of the hominid child from Modjokerto, Java, based on graphic and plastic reconstructions of the skull and head that I performed in 1968 in Professor G. H. R. von Koenigswald's laboratory in the Geological Institute of the Rijksuniversiteit, Utrecht.

In order to determine the endocranial volume I conducted (1) a comparative morphological investigation of the fossil emphasizing topographic analysis; (2) a determination of the optimal orientation of the slightly asymmetrical calvarium; (3) a graphic reconstruction of the skull; (4) a plastic reconstruction of the skull; (5) a reconstruction of the endocranial cavity; and (6) the measurement of the cranial capacity.

I preferred to measure the endocranial volume directly instead of using computational formulae, because the extent of preservation of the calvarium permitted a quite reliable reconstruction of the endocranial cavity. The capacity measured directly with a liquid is 673 cubic centimeters. This value falls between the values given by Dubois (650 cubic centimeters) and Boule and Vallois (700 cubic centimeters).

The thickness of the skull walls varies between one-and-a-half and five millimeters according to topography. It might be that the actual thickness of the cranial walls was a little bit more than that measured on the fossil because of past influences of mineralization and the

I am grateful to Professor G. H. R. von Koenigswald, the discoverer of the Modjokerto infant calvarium, for the suggestion that I conduct this study and for providing access to the original fossil and other data and casts. I also thank Professor Dr. Ion Moraru, the Director of the Victor Babes Institute, Bucharest, for permitting me to undertake this project.

cleavage by mineral substitutes in the bone. If this is so, then for the same exocranial dimensions we should expect to encounter somewhat smaller endocranial capacities.

By simulating the endocranial capacity of the calvarium with a sphere of the same volume and by reducing by one, two, and three the radius of this sphere, we obtain the following values for its volume: 636.5, 601.4, and 567.6 cubic centimeters (reductions of the sphere radius correspond to hypothetical thickening of the bony walls of the calvarium). Thus, assuming that values for the thickness of the bone wall of the fossil might have been decreased from the original thickness of the bone by values ranging between zero, and two millimeters, the endocranial capacity of the Modjokerto child could have been between 601.4 and 673 cubic centimeters.

My age diagnosis is premised basically on the value of the cranial capacity. It has wider biological implications, regarding: (1) the evolutionary level of the brain and the skull capacity of the Djetis hominids; (2) the pattern of ossification of these hominids' skulls; (3) the approximate limits of their sexual dimorphism; and (4) the ontogenetical development of the skull and of the thickness of the skull bones.

Some authors (e.g. LeGros Clark 1964; Piveteau 1957) have mentioned "contradictions" in the morphology of this child's skull between characters which evidence a degree of maturity, like the frontal bone inclination, the supraorbital prominences, the narrowing of the postorbital regions, the ossification of the tympanic region, and the appearance of a torus occipitalis, and the apparent absence of the fontanella and features that indicate immaturity such as the small cranial capacity. But this apparent "contradiction" is placed in perspective by acknowledgement of the fact that the child from Modjokerto belonged to a hominid population with an average cranial capacity of 800 cubic centimeters instead of 900 cubic centimeters as was formerly believed. Wandel obtained an endocranial value of about 750 cubic centimeters from a reconstruction of the adult cranium from Modjokerto and Woo obtained a value of 780 cubic centimeters from the Lantian skull (von Koenigswald, personal communication). If the adult hominids from Modjokerto indeed had an average endocranial capacity of 800 cubic centimeters (or perhaps only 750 cubic centimeters) then interpolation of the Modjokerto child (with an endocranial capacity between 601.4 and 673 cubic centimeters) on a hypothetical diagram of the ontogenetic development of the skull capacity in these hominids gives it an age of 2.5 to 3.5 years. (I constructed the hypothetical diagram of the ontogenetical development of endocranial capacity in Modjokerto hominids on the basis of a diagram of development of endocranial capacity in recent man from data of Böning and Welcker (Martin and Saller 1959: 1219).

My diagnosis of sex took into account the presence of the trends toward skeletal maturation in relation to presumed age. I conclude that the Modjokerto child is probably male.

Recent results of radiometric dating techniques reported by Koenigswald (personal communication) demonstrate considerable antiquity of the Modjokerto deposits. This in large measure agrees with my inferences based on morphological reconstructions of the Modjokerto infant calvarium.

REFERENCES

LE GROS CLARK, W. E.
1964 *The fossil evidence for human evolution* (revised edition). Chicago: University of Chicago Press.

MARTIN, RUDOLF, KARL SALLER
1959 *Lehrbuch der Anthropologie.* Stuttgart: G. Fischer.

PIVETEAU, JEAN
1957 *Traité de paléonologie,* volume seven: *Vers la forme humaine. Le problème biologique de l'homme. Les époques de l'intelligence.* Paris: Masson.

VON KOENIGSWALD, G. H. R.
1936a Erste Mitteilung über einen fossilen Hominiden aus dem Altpleistocän Ostjavas. *Proceedings of the Koninklijke Nedelandsche Akademie van Wetenschappen, Amsterdam,* 39:1000–1009.
1936b Ein fossiler Hominide aus dem Altpleistocän Ostjavas. *De Ingenieur in Nederlandsch Indië* 3:149–157.

Discussion

[Dr. Jacob and Dr. von Koenigswald summarized their papers and illustrated them with slides].

TOBIAS: Dr. Jacob, has the date of 1.9 million years for the lower layers in Indonesia, which you and Dr. Curtis published, now been confirmed?

JACOB: We have two additional dated samples. One is from the Djetis Beds of Kebonduren near Kedung Brubus where the Kedung Brubus mandible was found. It is dated at 1.91 million years. The second additional date which is 1.89 million years was obtained from the same sample which gave the first date but with a smaller error. Altogether the three samples have an error of less than 15 percent.

VON KOENIGSWALD: Mr. Krantz (see Krantz, this volume) claims that a *Pithecanthropus modjokertensis* palate belongs to an orangutan. We measured it by his method. He seems to have erred. The width between the third molars is sixty-eight millimeters, not eighty-six millimeters. With the former dimension the palate fits the rest of the skull perfectly.

ADDENDUM: *September 13, 1973, by Prof. Grover Krantz*

My measurements of the breadth of the palate of Java skull IV are correct as given, and are the same as those determined by Franz Weidenreich. Our difference evidently follows from the nature of the fossil which is conspicuously broken through the socket of the first left incisor. The greater part of the left maxilla is shifted toward the midline and fossilized in that position. Both Weidenreich and I moved this part back to its

natural position and measured what was the original palate. Von Koenigswald's measurements are apparently taken from the fossil in its distorted
condition and thus have only minimal value.

*Revised Concepts of Early Man in
Europe and the U.S.S.R.*

Ante-Neanderthals of Western Europe

MARIE-ANTOINETTE DE LUMLEY

RISSIAN HOMINIDS

Human remains dated to the penultimate glaciation and discovered in the southern Mediterranean (Midi) are still fairly rare:

Grotte du Prince (Vintimille) — a pelvis associated with Acheulean industry;

Grotte du Lazaret (Nice) — a right parietal of a child and two teeth associated with Acheulean industry;

Orgnac III — two teeth associated with Acheulean industry;

Caune de l'Arago — eighteen teeth found isolated, phalanges, fragments of parietal bones, one mandible with six teeth in place (Arago II), a second portion of a mandible with five teeth (Arago XIII) and the anterior part of an adult skull (Arago XXI) associated with Tayacian industry;

La Chaise (cave-shelter Bourgeois Delaunay) — a skull cap, frontal and parietal bones, occipital, temporal, mandible and fragment of maxilla with three molars;

La Chaise (cave Suard) — fragment of skull cap (frontal and parietal), temporal and child's frontal with its mandible, three teeth;

Grotte de Fontéchevade — skull cap, fragment of mandible and radius, associated with Evenosian industry.

The recent discoveries, particularly those of the Caune de l'Arago at Tautavel have permitted us, only very recently, to gain some knowledge of these men.

The only complete skull that we know of Rissian man in France is that found at Tautavel. It may be compared with that of Steinheim

For Plates, see pp. x–xi, between pp. 288–289

man. Measurements of the curvature of the frontal bone give evidence of the flatness of the skull (platicranie) comparable with or greater than the majority of Neanderthals. The forehead however is not as flat as that found in some classic Archanthropus such as the *Pithecanthropus* and *Sinanthropus*, for example. There is no sagittal crest (Plates 1 and 2).

In examining the relative proportions of the frontal bone of Tautavel man, a longitudinal development is to be observed, greater than in most of the Neanderthals; however, it seems smaller transversally. A pronounced postorbital narrowing can be noticed. From above, the postorbital narrowing is easily distinguishable. It is distinctly more pronounced than that of the Neanderthal skulls and comparable with that of Steinheim. It is less pronounced than that of *Sinanthropus* and *Pithecanthropus*. Contrary to modern man, frontal bossing in the Neanderthalian adult is weakly developed; it is completely absent from the frontal of Tautavel man, as in Steinheim man.

The lateral crests of the frontal bone are prominent and very high The temporal fossae of the frontal bone are vast and deeper than those on the Steinheim and Neanderthal skulls.

The orbital torus (*sus-orbitaire*) is very pronounced. A superciliary arcade and a supraorbital arcade can be distinguished. They are partially separated by an oblique sulcus, running superiorly and laterally: the *sulcus supraorbitalis*. The supraorbital trigone is not separated off from the supraorbital arcade. The strongest region of the torus is approximately thirty millimeters from the sagittal region as in Steinheim man.

The glabella is depressed in comparison with the torus as in Steinheim man. The torus therefore does not constitute a continuous ridge as in Neanderthals but it is comparable to that present in Steinheim man. The depression over the supraorbital torus is shallow. It is less pronounced than on the frontal bone of Steinheim man. The supraglabellar depression is well delimited. The frontal sinuses are visible on X-ray. They are very small. Their size is not connected with the strong development of the torus. Sockets are large, low, and rectangular, much lower than those of the classic Neanderthals; their margins resemble those of Steinheim.

The interorbital distance is very large, it is comparable or slightly superior to the largest measurements found in Neanderthalians. Prognathism is very pronounced, with marked anterior positioning of the facial portion. This aspect is further emphasized by a pronounced alveolar prognathism. The upper maxilla is massive and robust. The lateral aspect is nearly flat, and as in Neanderthals has no canine fossa. It must be mentioned however that a slight depression is noticable in the La Ferrassie specimen. In Steinheim man, the canine fossa is deep and marked. In the classic Archanthropes, it exists apparently in *Sinanthropus*, but is absent in *Pithecanthropus* IV.

The palate is deep. The alveolar arcade is somewhat ipsiloid, the premolar and molar sockets are aligned. The individual had lost his two second premolars and their sockets are partially resorbed. M2 is the largest tooth and M3 is relatively small — M1 < M2 > M3. The occlusal aspect of the molars is relatively simple and there is no cingulum.

There is a very pronounced external mandibular ridge. It merges with the exterior alveolar line, and it is well developed at the level of M1 and M3. The same kind of ridge may be observed in Steinheim man, but it also exists in certain Neanderthals as for example La Ferrassie. On the internal aspect of the cranium, the frontal crest is relatively pronounced. The frontal depressions are not discernible. Vascular traces are few. The superior longitudinal sinus can be distinguished. The bulging of the encephalon must have been particularly developed, to conform with the great distance between the orbits. A first examination of the endocranium shows that the third frontal circonvolution was well developed and the "cap de Broca" must have been very pronounced.

The endocranial volume was relatively small, certainly smaller than that found in the average classic Neanderthals. But it was somewhat greater than that of Steinheim. Furthermore, the discovery of a number of parietals of ante-Neanderthals from Western Europe permits some very useful comparisons. The examination of these bones gives evidence of two types of ante-Neanderthal individuals among the Rissian population, in which the stage of hominization of the skull differs: (1) Lazaret man, with whom the man from La Chaise and Steinheim may be associated, and (2) Cova Negra man, with whom the fossils of Fontéchevade and Swanscombe may be associated.

Lazaret man like La Chaise and Steinheim is characterized by a long parietal bone in which the asterion is posteriorly situated, which indicates a poorly developed occipital rotation. Man from Cova Negra, like the Fontéchevade and Swanscombe specimens on the other hand, is characterized by a short subsquare parietal bone on which the asterion is located in a lower more anterior position, which would indicate a greater rotation of the occipital.

As a direct consequence of this difference in rotation, the temporal margin is, on the parietal bone from Lazaret, as in some pithecan-thropines, longer than the sagittal margin, whereas on the Cova Negra parietal, as on certain ante-Neanderthals from Western Europe (Fon-téchevade, Swanscombe) the temporal margin is distinctly shorter than the sagittal margin. This characteristic is to be found in most Neander-thals and in modern man.

The diagram comparing the height ratio of the sagittal and bregma-lambda chords shows that the child from Lazaret compares with the adult from La Chaise as a modern nine-year-old child would to a modern adult. It also shows that the Cova Negra parietal bone resembles modern man more closely than La Chaise.

The maximum height of the Lazaret parietal bone is comparable to or slightly less than that of Neanderthals; that of Cova Negra on the other hand is greater than that of the Neanderthals: it falls within the range of variation of present-day man and approximates that of Swanscombe.

Further, when examined from the anterior aspect, the Lazaret parietal bone like that from La Chaise has a weakly rounded cur-vature in the transverse plane. Cova Negra parietal on the other hand is markedly rounded in the transverse plane. The two parietals from Lazaret and La Chaise therefore seem less evolved than those of the Neanderthals. The Cova Negra parietal seems to possess certain char-acteristics more evolved than those of the Neanderthals.

These observations are confirmed by the study of the peri-biparietal spheres, which include parietals from the following points: bregma, lambda, and fronto-parietal. Delattre and Fenart (1960) have shown that the phenomena of ontogenetical "spherisation" of the human bi-parietal arch has been responsible for the creation on this same sphere of two other points: the asterion and the internal incisural point. In Pongidae, these two points are always situated outside the sphere be-cause of the negative rotation of the back of their skull during growth.

Some descriptive geometric constructions allow us to locate these points in comparison with the peri-biparietal sphere. In the Neander-thalian (Krapina Ba 1), the asterion and the internal incisural bridge are situated either on the sphere or inside it, as in modern man. The same disposition can be found in Cova Negra man, whose skull spherisation had thus reached the evolutionary stage of the Neander-thalians and of modern man. The asterion on the other hand is situated outside the sphere on the Lazaret parietal, which allows us to con-clude that skull spherisation is less evolved and that less positive rota-tion took place during ontogenesis.

The disposition of the meningeal sector shows once more the feeble occipital rotation of the parietal bone of Lazaret: the bregmatic and lambdatic branches are parallel and run superiorly, whereas on the Cova Negra parietal these two branches are more horizontally directed and present a fan-like aspect diverging posteriorly, as in modern man. In the same way, the difference in skull rotation of these two Rissian hominids explains why the general direction of the "Sylvian fissure" is very oblique in the Lazaret brain and almost horizontal on that of Cova Negra. The rare ante-Neanderthal mandibles however give evidence of a certain homogeneity between the Rissian hominids (Table 1).

The very different size of mandibles suggests an important sexual dimorphism: Arago XIII and Mauer belonging to male subjects and Arago II, Montmaurin and Asych to female individuals. Their dimensions are large: the mandible (external bicondyle diameter) in particular for Arago XIII, is of great width. Their alveolar arcades built above the basilar arcade are convex anteriorly; their symphyses are receding, the chin triangles are absent, digastric traces are entirely situated on the lower part of the bone, their genio-glossal fossae are deep, their *torus transversus inferior* and the marginal swellings are very thick, and their lateral proeminences are pronounced. But what is most remarkable, in particular in Arago XIII and Mauer, is the development of the alveolar planum and of the internal oblique line, the very low position of the geni-superior cavity and the chin cavities.

Their rami are high and very wide; their condyles are of large

Table 1. Data on mandibles

	Mauer	Montmaurin	Arago II	Arago XIII	Bañolas
Total length	122 mm	111 mm	108 mm	124.5 mm	107 mm
Total width	132 mm	133.5 mm	128 mm	158 mm	110 mm
Mandibular index	92.4	83.1	84.4	78.8	97.3
Thickness of lateral protuberance	21 mm	16 mm	17.3 mm	25 mm	16 mm
Robusticity index[1]	55.9	54.2	48.5	68.5	55.4
Basilar component					
Alveolar component	31.6	45.2	31.5	22.5	50.8
Symphysial angle	93°	98°	103°	106°	89°

[1] At chin cavity level.

dimensions, their coronoid apophyses are very short, low and wide; the sigmoid notches are lightly marked and their lowest points are posteriorly situated. The pharyngeal lines are well marked and the internal oblique lines pronounced. Their retro-molar triangles are vast; their retro-molar grooves are wide and deep. In Arago II and Mauer the rami are vertical in relation to the body of the mandible which is remarkably wide. In Arago XIII and Montmaurin the rami are slightly inclined.

The position of the alveolar component of the mandible of Arago II is like that of the fossil of Montmaurin and the Arago XIII one like that of Mauer. A mandibular depression giving evidence of a slight bony chin may be observed on Arago II; it is absent on Arago XIII and on Mauer and Montmaurin.

The dimensions of the teeth vary greatly. Some are of medium size and belong to female mandibles (Arago II, Montmaurin, Asych, Mauer), others of very large size belong to male type mandibles (Arago XIII for example). The molar cusp pattern is not very archaic.

In their overall dimensions and morphology the European ante-Neanderthal mandibles present a certain homogeneity, in a number of characteristics; however, they seem to differ from the mandibles of the pithecanthropines who lived at the same time on the other side of the Mediterranean in Africa and southeast Asia, *Atlanthropus*, *Pithecanthropus*, and *Sinanthropus*.

In the light of all these observations, the ante-Neanderthals of Western Europe show:

1. Archaic characteristics which allow us to consider that they are at an evolutionary stage near to that of the Archanthropes (*Homo erectus*): marked prognathism, very developed supraorbital tori, marked postorbital narrowing, frontal flattening, and in the mandible a strongly developed alveolar planum and the internal oblique line with a very low positioning of the superior genial foramina.

2. Characteristics which distinguish them from African and Asian Archanthropes; such as less pronounced supratoral sulcus, less pronounced postorbital narrowing, and absence of a sagittal crest.

3. Characteristics which sometimes resemble the West European classical Neanderthals such as absence of canine fossae in the man of Tautavel.

Much polymorphism must have existed in Rissian populations. Thus, the skull of Tautavel man may be compared with that of Steinheim in the marked postorbital narrowing, in the disposition of the torus and the supratoral sulcus, in the configuration of the sockets and in the small skull capacity. Other characteristics differ such as morphology of the maxilla and absence of a canine fossa.

In the study of the parietal bones, we have been able to show several individuals whose skull capacity differed. To the Lazaret specimen whose skull spherisation was apparently incomplete it is possible to add the Rissian men from La Chaise, Tautavel, and Steinheim. To the man of Cova Negra, whose skull spherisation was complete, it is possible to add those of Fontéchevade and of Swanscombe.

To conclude, from many morphological characteristics the West European ante-Neanderthals seem to belong to the same evolutionary phase as the archanthropines of Africa and Asia. They could however be situated on a parallel evolutionary branch (subphylum), which strengthens the hypothesis according to which several human groups evolved independently on different continents ("subgroups of independent evolution"). In the same way as one admits the polycentric origin of modern man, one can also imagine a polycentric origin of the paleanthropines (Neanderthalians).

REFERENCES

DELATTRE, A., R. FENART
    1960   *L'hominisation du crâne étudiée par la méthode vestibulaire*. Paris: Éditions du Centre National de la Recherche Scientifique.

Neanderthal Man: Facts and Figures

W. W. HOWELLS

Everyone agrees that Neanderthal man did in fact exist as a population in Europe during the Würm glacial before the Upper Paleolithic, that his cranial morphology was visibly different from modern man's, and that populations akin to this one were present in the Near East. Agreement stops there. How and when the population arose, what became of it, and how to relate it to other contemporary and later populations of the Old World are matters of dispute. They are not subjects of this article. Quite the reverse: I wish to say here that we could benefit from a period of quiet analysis. As a foreword I shall say that by "Neanderthal" I mean specimens of the European Würm, usually called "classic," plus certain Near Eastern ones: Tabun, Shanidar, Amud. I do not include Skhūl, Qafza, Ighoud, nor Petralona, and certainly not Broken Hill or Solo.

WHAT NEANDERTHAL MAN HAS DONE TO US

Primary among his offenses is his unrelenting stimulus to anthropological conjecture and strong personal feeling. All of us know about the quaint ideas attending his first recognition: idiot, pathological specimen, Cossack victim of rickets, etc., as well as half-erect antediluvian caricature of man (Gruber 1948; Eiseley 1954). And a century later? We have hypotheses suggesting he was a victim of rickets (Ivanhoe 1970), or eventually succumbed to respiratory

Research cited herein was supported by grants GS-664 and GS-2645 from the National Science Foundation.

diseases (Emiliani 1968), or as anatomically limited in linguistics articulation (Lieberman and Crelin 1971). Of course, ideas about required evidence are clearer now. Nevertheless, the element of conjecture is strong and permeates all attempts at understanding him, as we shall see.

He has also insidiously reflected the social and intellectual spirit of different times. In the ordered society before World War I it was natural that Boule should place him between a chimpanzee and a Frenchman. In the liberated air of today, when we relate first and ask questions afterwards, it is apparently more congenial to see him as a close, direct ancestor, who falls within the range of modern man physically; in fact, to doubt it seems to be consenting to a sort of evolutionary racism. This is not made explicit by authors reflecting this feeling but I doubt I am wrong. A writer in the American Anthropological Association *Bulletin* even holds that all anthropology, physical and other, is divisive, racist, and antihumanist "whenever we classify, differentiate or objectify." Before we accept the stupefying proposition he offers, that we abandon the study of human variation and rush back into a pre-Linnaean innocence, trampling poor Mendel and Darwin on the way, let us ask just how we are going to approach problems of evolution at all, both for ourselves and for the Neanderthals. By humanist revelation? Or how? This last is really the question before us.

Neanderthal man has served to launch, to enhance, and to mar anthropological careers. Perhaps he is like the Tar Baby — each time Brer Rabbit hit him another lick, he got stuck faster. Among Neanderthal's minor crimes is letting himself be found in the Neander Gorge in the first place, rather than in some spot with a shorter, more pronounceable name. [1] But more important is his primacy in the whole discovery of fossil hominids, which has caused him to be unduly focused and refocused upon. He has very much set a model for pre-

---

[1]   The spelling of "Neanderthal" appears to be a question of convention, nationality, and taste. In 1952 Vallois noted that, although German spelling had long dropped the "h" in a number of common words (nouns like "Thal," "Thier," verbs like "thun," adjectives like "roth" — these are my examples, not Vallois'), Anglo-Saxon writers continued to use the "h" in Neanderthal, and that French writers had also done so up to that point. Saying that no reason existed to retain a traditional form, he recommended that the spelling should henceforth be "Neandertal," as well as "*neandertalensis*" in formal taxonomic usage. French writers have almost unanimously adopted his advice, at least as to the first.

This is not quite the whole story. By the International Code of Zoological Nomenclature the original spelling of a scientific name must be preserved, in this case "*neanderthalensis*." On the German side, spelling depends on official dispensations. Confusion in spelling following the unification of Germany in the last century led to governmental creation of a "Rechtschreibungskonferenz" to deal with the prob-

modern man, while drawing everyone's gaze to events in one particular region, Europe. We should resist this hypnotic effect; nevertheless the wealth of his remains makes his central position inevitable.

WHAT WE HAVE DONE TO NEANDERTHAL MAN

This is known history also: the various overdone views concerning his bodily posture, or his taxonomic position (removed to separate genera, etc.), or assumptions about the uniqueness of his connection with Mousterian cultures. We have continuously projected onto him our own interpretations of history, anatomy, evolution, and genetics. We have accepted or rejected him as a direct ancestor, in Europe or elsewhere, although we are fully aware that the critical stratigraphical relations and the dates are not yet known, to say nothing of knowledge about actual transition.

Not much has been said about his obviously necessary derivation

---

lem, which in 1901 promulgated "Regeln für die deutsche Rechtschreibung nebst Wortverzeichnis," these rules being made obligatory for officials and for teaching in school, with the press and general public following along later. The rules for usage, grammar and spelling are incorporated in Duden's officially sanctioned dictionary of long standing: in volume one, "Rechtschreibung," the official spelling is given as "Neandertal." German writers have used this quite generally but not unanimously, probably more regularly now than a decade or so ago. Various other proper names, however, for towns or families, retain the "h," e.g. Thalgau, Winterthur, Rothschild.

As to writers in English, the British have preserved a fidelity to the original spelling, first breached, I believe, by Campbell in 1965. A vanguard of Americans has lately dropped the "h," probably in deference to Vallois' suggestion, or else simply from an awareness of common German spelling. (In two recent books on human evolution by Pilbeam, the English publication, 1970, keeps the "h" while the American, 1972, drops it.) Howell in 1952 noted Vallois' lead and followed it briefly, abandoning it subsequently. I cannot suggest any recognized rules or conventions. English has conventions of its own, of course (e.g. capitalizing national adjectives like "American," which the French do not), and it is also conservative in spelling ordinary words as well as names (e.g. Taylor). Possibly American users of "Neandertal" simply prefer rational spelling, as advocated by G. B. Shaw and the *Chicago Tribune* and as exemplified by "tonite" and "thru"; I do not know. Reasons are not stated as far as I am aware.

It seems to come down to a matter of observing a convention of consistency in English versus rational spelling OR following a German lead. I personally prefer "Neanderthal." The 1901 German ruling on "Neandertal" seems anomalous; and Ernst Mayr remarks to me that, since "*neanderthalensis*" is unchangeable, changing the original place name to "Neandertal," however correct, invites doubt and confusion. I thank Richard Metz and Dr. Hans Freiensehner for information on the history of German spelling.

from *Homo erectus* or how he achieved morphological individuality; more has been said on whether he had any individuality worth noting. The main fray relates to what became of him. The school which thinks he was replaced in Europe by invaders of modern physique has been called antievolutionary by Brace (1964). Livingstone (1969), using a computer simulation of genetic change (assuming different numbers of loci of additive genes and certain values of relative fitness), has argued that mean cranial length and cranial height could have shifted from Neanderthal to large modern values (a Mesolithic example) in the course of as little as 3,500 years. Brace contends that specialized stone tools of the Upper Paleolithic replaced the use of the front teeth for many purposes, relaxing selection in favor of large tooth size and allowing diminution of teeth and face; thus a rapid and direct evolution took place from Neanderthal to Upper Paleolithic men. Now these are just the kind of hypotheses I am objecting to. They pose what might have been without a second body of evidence as to what actually happened. In this case they require a sort of quantum evolution over perhaps ten millennia, followed and preceded by periods of about thirty millennia during which Europeans showed little change in basic cranial form, whether as Neanderthals or as moderns. [2]

Brace's 1964 article was a vigorous attack on the whole paleo-anthropological establishment, which he alleged to be ignorant of evolution and to be blindly opposed to direct descent in Europe. Powered by a style of insouciant effrontery, it has been influential (not inevitably among his targets, although some of them were startled into genuflections of varying depth); it appeared as a new orthodoxy to many spectators, which Brace may not have intended. He was certainly right about weaknesses in the views of many writers, if too free with insinuations as to their motives. At the same time, his cannonading was so wide-ranging that it concealed his own failure to provide evidence for an opposite view, legitimate as it may be. Except for his hypothesis about the dentition, his contribution was limited to a modification of Hrdlička's definition of Neanderthal man, which was given as "the man of the Mousterian culture prior to the reduction in form and dimension of the Middle Pleistocene face." This

---

[2]   It is true that dates defining such periods are not available for Western European materials, largely because of early excavation and loss of evidence. This merely emphasizes the necessity for having such dates eventually, before accepting simplistic answers or, for example, taking the Mt Carmel Tabun and Skhūl specimens as a single population.

epitomizes a view which ignores any real examination of the structure of the Neanderthal face (except to refer to it as the supporting architecture for the teeth), and also ignores, except for a reference or so to the *Homo erectus* or pithecanthropine features, the entire world outside of Europe and its fringes. Broken Hill and Solo are not mentioned. [3]

Colleagues of Brace (Brose and Wolpoff 1971) have attempted to fill this out by being more specific and inclusive, by broadening "Neanderthal" to include all fossils anywhere of post-Riss, premodern date. The result is a monster, whose morphological character is merely large cranial size and large brows and whose range of variation is simply illegitimate. I considered this in another place (Howells 1974). 1974).

TAKE TWO DEEP BREATHS

There are two principles we might follow in order to escape from the polemic atmosphere (provided we want to). They involve taking a real evolutionary view of man in the Upper Pleistocene, on the one hand, and making a real attempt to examine the physical features of the Upper Pleistocene specimens, on the other. I am not saying such efforts have not been made; they have, but they are little noticed in the smoke from the more flamboyant writing.

Suppose we could rearrange history a little, and have Chinese anthropologists make the first fossil discoveries known to science in Java and Choukoutien. As the Neanderthals then began to be found in Europe, they might first be recognized as a late, western form of Peking man, or they might simply be called western Solo man. It can hardly be supposed that this population would have given its name to Upper Pleistocene man generally or that, being essentially localized in the subcontinent of Asia known as Europe, it would have been proclaimed the source of all later men. I am saying only that we should turn our view around and recognize that, meager though the fossils are, the populations in the vast areas of tropical Africa and Asia are equally as important as the Neanderthals and are equally likely, or more so, to have been ancestral to modern man. This is obvious, and Weidenreich (1946) and Coon (1962) made it the basis for whole interpretations. But the idea is absolutely nonexistent in Brace's article, which mentions Weidenreich but talks of ancestors

---

[3] Except in his summary reply, following the article, to those who raised the point.

only as Neanderthals. The idea is also not contained in much of the other published thinking about Neanderthals. How evolutionary is that?

This leads, secondly, into differences between Neanderthals and these other neglected Upper Pleistocene populations. In anatomical comparison the accent has been on the grossest aspect or morphology, whether determined by inspection or by measurement. (I am not referring to the conscientious monographic studies of particular specimens or groups.) Because, for example, the Broken Hill skull is low and has large brows, and a big face and teeth, and because the Solo skulls have similar vault features, the grossness of comparison has led some thinkers to merge them with Neanderthals, not to discriminate. There has been surprisingly little attempt to specify the distinctions of the Broken Hill and Solo crania, as well as of many others like Skhūl. Note that Petralona has been readily accepted as a "classic" Neanderthal in spite of its plain differences. [4]

Such attempts at distinction have certainly been made. Morant in a series of "Studies of Paleolithic man" (1926–1930) made metrical comparisons among specific specimens or groups. He and Weidenreich (1943) found clear differences between Broken Hill and Neanderthals of Europe, and Weidenreich also saw similar clear distinctions between Neanderthal and Solo; unfortunately he never reached the comparative part of his monograph on the Solo material itself (1951). Howell's article in 1951 was significant because it was just the sort of thing I am pointing to: an attempt to discriminate defined populations by measurement of features of meaningful differentiation. (His conclusions are vitiated now by later datings affecting his groupings.) Sergi (1953) and Stewart (1970) are other examples, which have given attention, with careful measurement or record, to important specifics of form.

What I am getting at is not a catalogue of error but a matter of attitude. It is easy to generalize behind an appealing hypothesis. But we need to make a much more precise and systematic examination of the fossils in order to discover the features that really distinguish and characterize fossil populations; in this way it is possible to work toward understanding their evolution instead of hypothesizing on slender or nonexistent evidence. Such work is going forward in the case of early hominid evolution and the australopithecines; why not in the case of the Neanderthals? Should Livingstone really have used the measure-

[4] For a spelling out of some differences, as well as references to recent evidence of an earlier date for Petralona, see Hemmer 1972.

ments of skull length and height as important genetic characters in his model?

UNIVARIATE COMPARISONS

As I said, comparisons have often been made in the gross measurements of vault and face, and there is no doubt that Neanderthals are decidedly long, broad, and low in the vault, and long in the face; differences from modern man or Upper Paleolithic skulls (which are also large-sized) are significant, statistically speaking, whether or not there is overlap. Such comparisons have probably obscured more than they revealed because: (1) they are assumed to present a morphological pattern, (2) they often include as "Neanderthal" an unsorted rabble of Pleistocene skulls, and (3) estimates of variation are based on these uncritical groupings so that "overlap" has no meaning because the analysis is circular.

Ignoring all but morphological pattern, what *would* we like to learn from such comparisons? A glance tells us that Neanderthal skulls are long and low-headed and projecting in the face. Which element is primary? The retreating zygomatic arch has always been particularly striking visually. There is something about the positioning of teeth, masseter muscle origin, and temporo-mandibular joint that is unusual in Neanderthal. Before we accept facile assumptions about tooth size and "Middle Pleistocene face," we should try to get further into all this.

To begin with, take the general profile of the middle of the face. We may measure this from the axis through the ear openings to several points: nasion ["nasion radius" = NAR], subspinale [SSR], prosthion [PRR] and the forward edge of the first molar alveolus [AVR]. These measurements are defined and discussed in Howells (1973) with comparative material on seventeen populations of living man with a worldwide distribution. [5] The figures are shown in Table 1 (within the limitations of accuracy of reconstructions, casts, etc.). Measurements are on original specimens except as footnoted.

The figures indicate that the nasion region of Neanderthals is uniformly extended forward compared with modern man; large Upper Paleolithic or Mesolithic skulls fall between them. The difference be-

---

[5] Keith, for example in his study with McCown of the Mt. Carmel material, used a similar kind of profile measuring by drawing diagrams.

Table 1.   Figures concerning skulls of Neanderthals and modern man

	NAR	SSR	PRR	AVR
La Ferrassie[1]	117	120?	128	108
La Chapelle	110	120	131?	108?
Shanidar[1]	110	114	120?	101
Monte Circeo[2]	107?	113?	119?	—
Petralona[3]	103	112	120?	96
Broken Hill	104?	107?	121?	93?
Ighoud I[1]	103	106	118	99
Skhūl V	93	(102)[4]	113?	89
Qafza VI	101?	97	105	83
Lautsch I[1]	96	102	109	85
Predmost III[1]	108	114	118	95
Chandelade[1]	105	103	105?	82?
Afalou 5	102	101	111?	93
Afalou 9	96	97	102?	81
Teviec 11	101	104	108	87
Upper Cave 101[1]	109	107	113	95
Modern male skulls				
Mean, 17 populations	94.4	96.2	102.6	82.0
Standard deviation[5]	3.50	4.01	4.40	4.02
Highest population mean	99.8	102.8	110.4	88.3
	(Eskimo)	(Tolai)	(Tolai)	(Eskimo)

[1]   From a cast.
[2]   Estimated from measurement of profile photograph. Attempts to do the same from contour drawings published by Morant gave unsatisfactory results because of lack of the same landmarks used.
[3]   Measurements courtesy of Christopher Stringer.
[4]   Subnasal region missing in original and restored.
[5]   This is a generalized figure for single populations, not a figure for pooled skulls of modern man. It can be used to estimate a range for the population means on the last line, which approach the specimens tabulated more closely.

comes more pronounced in projection immediately below the nose. Of post-Neanderthals Predmost III approaches their figures. Broken Hill does so with respect to prognathism at prosthion.

A special distinction is the position of the first molar's leading edge [AVR]. Here Ighoud I is nearest Neanderthal figures. All these relations (for a reduced number of the skulls in Table 1) may be compared to modern man more easily by putting the figures in standard (z-score) form, based on the modern grand means with unit standard deviation (Table 2).

Horizontal profiles give further information. In Table 3 are (1)

Table 2. Figures concerning Neanderthal and other skulls

	NAR	SSR	PRR	AVR
La Ferrassie	6.45	5.94	5.77	6.48
La Chapelle	4.45	5.94	6.45	6.48
Shanidar	4.45	4.44	3.95	4.74
Broken Hill	2.73	2.70	4.18	2.75
Ighoud I	2.45	2.45	3.50	4.24
Skhūl V	−0.98	(1.45)	1.91	1.75
Qafza VI	1.88	0.20	0.54	0.26
Predmost III	3.88	4.44	3.50	3.25
Afalou 5	2.16	1.20	1.91	2.75
Lautsch	0.45	1.45	1.45	0.76
Upper Cave 101	4.16	2.70	2.36	4.22

measures of forward protrusion of nasion from the lateral edges of the frontal bone, and the angle formed at nasion [FMB = bifrontal breadth, NAS = nasion subtense to FMB, NFA = nasio-frontal angle]; and (2) forward projection, measured in the same fashion, of subspinale [SSS] from the zygomaxillary breadth [ZMB, between the zygomaxillary sutures at the masseter origin], and the angle at subspinale [SSA].

Table 3. Figures concerning Neanderthal and other skulls

	NAS	FMB	NFA	SSS	ZMB	SSA
La Ferrassie[1]	32	113	121°	41	117	110°
La Chapelle	24	114	134°	42	110	105°
Le Moustier[2]	20	107	139°	—	—	—
Shanidar[1]	21	111?	139°	36	109	113°
Broken Hill	27	124	133°	33	108	117°
Solo XI	17?	113?	146°?	—	—	—
Ighoud I[1]	19?	116?	141°?	30	109	122°
Skhūl V	15	114	151°	(29)	109	(124)°
Qafza VI	18?	114	145°	23	108	134°
Lautsch[1]	14	102	149°	23	102	131°
Predmost III[1]	19	109	142°	30	103	120°
Chancelade[1]	19	104?	140°?	25	96	125°
Afalou 5	20	108	139°	25	100	127°
Upper Cave 101[1]	21	110	137°	24	105	131°

[1] From casts.
[2] Cast of latest reconstruction, kindness of M. Wolpoff.

In absolute terms the frontal tends to be angled forward in the midline somewhat more in Neanderthals (La Ferrassie and La Chapelle being extreme); the same is true of Broken Hill but not of the only Solo specimen measurable in this respect. Forward angling of the subnasal region relative to the zygomaxillary junction (or forward edge of the masseter muscle) is much more marked; in this respect Broken Hill falls behind the Neanderthals and no other skull, of any period, approaches the values of the three Neanderthal specimens available. We seem to be closing in on an anatomical location relative to the forward edge of the masseter origin on the zygomatic arch, which has an extreme position in Neanderthals.

For further specification of this and further examination of profiling of the lateral part of the face, Table 4 provides additional information (for some measurements involved, see Figure 1):

NAR-EKR (nasion radius minus ectoconchion radius) measures the retraction of the lateral border of the orbit relative to nasion.

NAR-ZMR (nasion radius minus zygomaxillare radius) indicates the retraction of the zygomaxillare point, or junction of the zygomaxillary suture and the masseter origin, relative to nasion.

ZOR-ZMR (zygo-orbitale radius minus zygomaxillare radius) gives essentially the retraction of the lower end of the facial zygomaxillary suture from its upper end.

AVR-ZMR (M1 alveolar radius minus ZMR, above), essentially

Table 4. Figures concerning skulls of Neanderthals and modern man

	NAR-EKR	NAR-ZMR	ZOR-ZMR ·	AVR-ZMR
La Ferrassie	36	37	15	38
La Chapelle	30	35	16	33
Shanidar	31	34	15	25
Broken Hill	33	30	9	19
Ighoud I	25	26	9?	22
Skhūl V	21?	20?	9?	16?
Qafza VI	25?	24?	5	6
Lautsch I	19	18	5	7
Predmost III	24	21	10	8
Chancelade	25	25	13	2
Afalou 5	27	24	8	15
Teviec 11	22	25	11?	11?
Upper Cave 101	24	24	9	10
Modern males Mean,				
17 populations	22.0	20.8	7.6	8.3
Range of means	18.7–23.9	17.2–23.8	5.5–8.9	4.6–11.6
Standard deviation	2.92	3.43	2.19	3.26

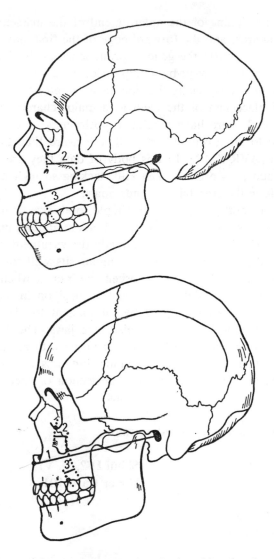

Figure 1. Some of the measurements given in the tables placed on a Neanderthal (an adaptation of Boule's restoration of La Chapelle) and a modern skull.

1 = **SSR**, subspinale radius from auditory meatus,

2 = **ZOR-ZMR**, difference between radius to **ZOR** (upper end of zygomaxillary suture) and to **ZMR** (lower end of suture).

3 = **AVR-ZMR**, difference between forward edge of alveolus of M^1 and **ZMR**, lower end of zygomaxillary suture (approximating forward limit of masseter muscle origin).

Note also the relative position of M_3 and the forward edge of the ascending ramus of the mandible. (The La Chapelle original mandible of course lacks the molar teeth, but these figures are diagrammatic and the mandible represents a typical Neanderthal specimen fairly) the relative positioning of the anterior end of the masseter origin on the zygomatic arch, and the forward edge of the first maxillary molar.

These figures confirm the general prominence of the facial midline [NAR] producing the swept-back impression of the sides in Neanderthals. They confirm especially the simultaneous retraction of the malar and forward placement of the teeth as a major character; the Neanderthals available here have a relative positioning of the first molar which is two to three centimeters further forward than the mean for modern man [AVR-ZMR]. In this body of data they are approached only by Ighoud I — even Broken Hill, lacking so high a value here and for AVR in the first table, stands apart.

Now this has nothing to do with simple tooth size or a large face; it is a real matter of positioning of teeth. Look at another manifestation of this, to which Coon (1962) has already drawn attention. Typically in Neanderthals, the mandibular third molar sits well forward of the anterior edge of the base of the ascending ramus when viewed in profile (see Figure 1). It may have such a position in modern jaws, but normally it is partly eclipsed by, or tangent to, the ramus; the same is true of non-Neanderthal Pleistocene jaws. The following list of mandibles is not meant to be comprehensive with respect either to adult Neanderthals or to other hominids, but it is broad enough to be indicative. It is based on my own inspection of specimens, casts, photographs, and published illustrations.

M₃ distinctly forward of ascending ramus:

La Ferrassie	Skhūl IV?, V, VI
La Quina 5	Upper Cave 101
Regourdou	Predmost III? IV?
Krapina G, J, plus one unnamed	
Monte Circeo III	
Tabun I, II	
Amud	
Shanidar I	
Subalyuk	

M₃ tangent to or partially behind ramus:

Montmaurin	Skhūl VII
Arago XIII	
Mauer	Upper Paleolithic: all others noted,

Haua Fteah I

Ternifine I, II, III

Sinanthropus GI, HI (as restored)

Pithecanthropus B

including Obercassel (female)

Barma Grande II, Grotte des

Enfants (male), Chancelade,

Predmost IX, X, Brünn III,

Combe Capelle, Teviec 11

The consistency of the designated Neanderthals, including the Near Easterners, is marked. Tobias (1967) noted that the feature distinguishes Haua Fteah, a supposed Neanderthal, from the others; most of the Skhūl jaws, on the other hand, come down on the Neanderthal side (as does the Old Man of Choukoutien, no Neanderthal). Two Predmost jaws are hard to judge from the existing material, but Predmost III would be conforming in this way to its definite facial extension seen in other measurements.

More important is the distinction between Neanderthals and accepted *Homo erectus* jaws, as well as those of Rissian or apparently Rissian date in Europe: Montmaurin and Arago XIII. Montmaurin may well be earlier. In any case, the consistency of the Neanderthal mandibles suggests that their associated skulls, where not known, corresponded in facial features to those of the particular specimens, which can be evaluated metrically.

MULTIVARIATE COMPARISONS

In 1968 I presented the results of a multiple discriminant analysis of seventeen worldwide modern series of crania, as a background for attempting to place the same three Neanderthal skulls whose casts were complete enough for testing (Howells 1970). These all fell at the limit, or beyond it, for scores of 834 modern male skulls in four of ten functions separately inspected, with Skhūl V also lying at the limit on one function. Predmost III, in spite of figures cited above and commonly expressed opinions that it has Neanderthaloid characters, showed no abnormal position on these functions; in fact, it varied (slightly) as often in a direction opposite to the Neanderthals as toward them. The same was true of other Upper Paleolithic (e.g. Chancelade) and Mesolithic skulls tested at the same time.

The main result was a finding that set Neanderthals outside the modern range. Interpretation of Neanderthal form, except for bringing out obvious facts relating to transverse facial profiles, was difficult, and raised a question about interpreting fairly deviant specimens introduced for classification into a discriminant analysis when they do not partake in the original computation of discriminants (Oxnard 1972). Bilsborough (1972) has given a brief report of a similar analysis, but based on the problem specimens themselves: European Neanderthals, Middle Eastern Neanderthals (Tabun I, II; Skhūl IV, V), and European Upper Paleolithic. His analysis uses Q-technique, leading also to D^2 distances; and his complete results should be interesting. He concluded that distance was less between the European Neanderthal and Upper Paleolithic groups than between either and the Near Eastern Neanderthal group (I would quarrel with the composition of the latter). His distance figures, however, do not clearly support his conclusion because there are more significant and larger overall distances between the Upper Paleolithic and the two Neanderthal groups than between the last two.

COMPARISONS BY FACTOR ANALYSIS SCORING

In the same study (Howells 1973) of seventeen cranial populations from all world regions I did a factor analysis based on the pooled within-group covariance (to exclude the effect of population differences and to produce generalized factors of individual variation). Eighteen such factors were scored for all individuals and for various further specimens. Here the nature of the variation is more explicit than with discriminant functions, and factors are supposedly more expressive of morphology than are raw measurements. The scores here are approximately in standard form (the modern population mean is zero and the standard deviation is 1.00 or slightly less *within* any population). That is to say, scores cited are in standard deviation units and related to a world mean of crania of the present.

Factor 1 (the order is arbitrary) "facial forwardness" (see Howells 1973: 129) is the most important factor of individual variation and is also important in population distinction because the whole orbital ring, with nasion, is the site of forward extension relative to the skull. The highest modern mean is Inugsuk Eskimos (+2.24). Neanderthal scores, all positive, are: La Ferrassie, 4.03; La Chapelle, 3.68; Shanidar, 4.18. Being between one and two standard deviations above the Eskimo mean, they are decidedly high in this character; the Eskimo mean itself is extraordinarily high, over two standard deviations above the world mean and nearly a full unit higher than the next population, Hawaiian.

Predmost III, with his very prominent face, has a score of 3.84 on this factor, but his "Neanderthal" character factorially seems to be embodied in this alone. He has no other noteworthy deviation on other factors. Broken Hill scores 0.53; Skhūl V, –0.02; Ighoud I, 1.73; Qafza VI, 1.16. Post-Neanderthals have the following scores: Chancelade, 2.36; Afalou 5, 1.26; Afalou 9, –0.70; Teviec 11, 1.68; Teviec 16, 1.21. It hardly needs saying that Factor 1 does not indicate a special relationship between Eskimos and Neanderthals. In other aspects of flatness in the orbital region they are of course very different. In *Factor 7*, "orbit horizontal profile," the Eskimo mean is –1.12, signifying marked horizontal flatness, while the Neanderthal figures are: La Ferrassie, +4.15; La Chapelle, +2.00; Shanidar, +0.41; Broken Hill is +3.53.

Factor 2, "subnasal flatness" or the reverse, reflects features already seen. The least flat, or most projecting relative to the malars, are Tasmanian skulls, with a mean score of –1.87. The Neanderthals are extreme, with La Chapelle at –5.21, La Ferrassie at –4.16, and Shanidar at –3.01. Broken Hill comes close with a score of –2.39. Others are Ighoud I, –2.13; Skhūl V, –1.98; Qafza VI, + 1.28. Later people may also be somewhat projecting: Teviec 11, –2.25; Teviec 16, –2.00; Predmost III, –1.76. But the Neanderthals are special. Once more the forward placement of the dentition relative to the malar region (and the masseter and temporal muscles) is brought to our attention.

A factor of upper facial height strangely produces no remarkable scores for Neanderthals, although they are indeed on the positive side. *Factor 5*, "upper facial breadth," also puts them somewhat on the positive side: La Chapelle, 3.05; La Ferrassie, 1.81; Shanidar, 2.35. But the visible fact, that the *relative* breadth of their upper facial skeleton is not a pronounced development, is also shown on this factor; with respect to it they are surpassed by Broken Hill (5.37), Qafza VI (4.89), Ighoud I (4.42), and Skhūl V (5.37). Here we see numerical evidence, which further separates Broken Hill on the one hand, and Qafza and Skhūl on the other, from Neanderthals. (The last two specimens have no other notable scores.)

SUMMARY

All these data should show that the Neanderthals were different from modern man (here nobody really disagrees, regardless of the pleas for "overlap") and from Skhūl V and Qafza VI and probably from

Ighoud I. The real question is *how* they were different, and whether they should be regarded as specialized.

From the above and other measurements we know that the Neanderthals had great face length, although in upper breadth they seem weak compared to Broken Hill and Solo. It seemed to Weidenreich (1943) that the supraorbital torus structure of *Homo erectus* had begun to disintegrate in them.

But one item of clear importance is the forward positioning of the teeth. This is unquestionably extreme: if the number of crania I have used here to show the fact is small, the conclusion may be backed up by the placing of the tooth row in numerous mandibles. The general feature may be evidence for Brace's idea of industrial tooth use by the Neanderthals. What are the implications?

Recall for the moment Brace's definition of Neanderthal man as having an unreduced "Middle Pleistocene face." (Neanderthal faces, of course, are all Upper Pleistocene.) What do we know about Middle Pleistocene faces? *Pithecanthropus* VIII, Arago, and Petralona were all found too late for Brace to consider. Otherwise we have Steinheim, Lantian, perhaps Broken Hill, and portions only of *Homo erectus* of Java and Choukoutien. These have not been sufficiently analyzed overall to answer the questions; but the indications are that, in the matter of details of facial projection, the Neanderthals differ from them as they do from modern man. Apparently in the "Middle Pleistocene face" the upper part is broader, but the upper nose is less forwardly placed (e.g. Petralona, Arago, Steinheim, *Pithecanthropus* VIII — little can be said about Peking or Solo, although they may have had a relatively forward nasion).

It is the jaws which must be called upon for general evidence on the forwardness of the teeth, although the cranium shows that Broken Hill evidently did not share this Neanderthal feature. The pre-Neanderthal jaws do not, on the basis of third molar-ascending ramus relations, show the same movement forward of the dention, regardless of size. The Arago face, however, on the basis of photographs (kindness of the de Lumleys) does seem to combine strong brows, and a somewhat recessed nose, with a more forwardly projecting palate. (This is a preliminary impression and must await the de Lumleys' own studies for validation.) So we may argue that the Neanderthal form is in fact a specialization, probably already in existence by the time of Saccopastore in the third interglacial, and is not a generalized, all-purpose leftover from the Middle Pleistocene. In other words, although there obviously were steps in many places between *Homo erectus* and modern man, steps which had "Middle Pleistocene faces," the Neanderthals do not represent one of them, but were a special line, perhaps flowing out of such antecedents as the Arago and La Chaise (Piveteau 1970) men of the Riss, and from older or provisonally older forms: Steinheim, Swanscombe, Petralona, Montmaurin, Vértesszöllös, and Mauer. Why they eventually specialized in this anterior development of the face is another matter. Did *only* Neanderthals hold things in their front teeth? We have a lot to learn about all other hominids before such conjectures are really worthwhile.

I agree with the essential idea Brace was expressing in 1964. Past views of Neanderthal man have often been blinkered by extraneous preconceptions. But this is true of present views as well. We need to see what we are looking at, not to fit it to a preferred scheme. I do not know whether or not the European or Near Eastern Neanderthals gave rise directly to any modern men, though I doubt it. Nor do I care. What I do care is that we go in for much more organized analysis of the evidence.

REFERENCES

BILSBOROUGH, A.
   1972   Cranial morphology of Neanderthal man. *Nature* 237:351–352.
BRACE, C. L.
   1964   The fate of the "classic" Neanderthals: a consideration of hominid catastrophism. *Current Anthropology* 5:3–43.
BROSE, D. S., M. H. WOLPOFF
   1971   Early Upper Paleolithic man and late Middle Paleolithic tools. *American Anthropologist* 73:1156–1194.
COON, C. S.
   1962   *The origin of races.* New York: Knopf.
DE LUMLEY, H., M.-A. DE LUMLEY
   1971   Découverte de restes humains anténéandertaliens datés du début du Riss à la Caune de l'Arago (Tautavel, Pyrénées-Orientales). *Comptes Rendus de l'Académie des Sciences de Paris* 272:1739–1742.
EISELEY, L. C.
   1954   The reception of the first missing links. *Proceedings of the American Philosophical Society* 98:453–465.
EMILIANI, C.
   1968   The Pleistocene epoch and the evolution of man. *Current Anthropology* 9:27–47.

GRUBER, J. W.
   1948   The Neanderthal controversy: nineteenth century version. *Scientific Monthly* 67:436–439.

HEMMER, H.
   1972   Notes sur la position phylétique de l'homme de Petralona. *L'Anthropologie* 76:155–162.

HOWELL, F. C.
   1951   The place of Neanderthal man in human evolution. *American Journal of Physical Anthropology* 9:379–416.
   1952   Pleistocene glacial ecology and the evolution of "Classic Neandertal" man. *Southwestern Journal of Anthropology* 8:377–410.

HOWELLS, W. W.
   1970   Mount Carmel man: morphological relationships. *Proceedings of the Eighth International Congress of Anthropological and Ethnological Sciences, Tokyo and Kyoto* 1:269–272.
   1973   *Cranial variation in man: a study by multivariate analysis of patterns of difference among recent human populations.* Peabody Museum Papers 67.
   1974   Neanderthals: names, hypotheses and scientific method. *American Anthropologist* 76:24–38.

IVANHOE, F.
   1970   Was Virchow right about Neandertal? *Nature* 237:577–579.

LIEBERMAN, P., E. S. CRELIN
   1971   On the speech of Neanderthal man. *Linguistic Inquiry* 2:203–222.

LIVINGSTONE, F. B.
   1969   Evolution of quantitative characteristics which are determined by several additive loci. *American Journal of Physical Anthropology* 31:343–361.

MORANT, G. M.
   1926–1930   Studies of Paleolithic man. *Annals of Eugenics* 1:257–276; 2:318–381; 3:337–360; 4:109–214.

OXNARD, C. E.
   1972   South African fossil foot bones: a note on the interpolation of fossils into a matrix of extant species. *American Journal of Physical Anthropology* 37:3–12.

PILBEAM, D.
   1970   *The evolution of man.* London: Thames and Hudson.
   1972   *The ascent of man: an introduction to human evolution.* New York: Macmillan.

PIVETEAU, J.
   1970   Les Grottes de La Chaise (Charente). Paléontologie humaine, I: L'homme de l'Abri Suard. *Annales de Paléontologie (Vertébrés)* 56:174–225.

SERGI, S.
   1953   I Profanerantropi di Swanscombe e di Fontéchevade. *Atti dell'Accademia dei Lincei* 14:601–608.

STEWART, T. D.
  1970   "The evolution of man in Asia as seen in the lower jaw," in *Proceedings of the Eighth International Congress of Anthropological and Ethnological Sciences, Tokyo and Kyoto* 1:263–266.

TOBIAS, P. V.
  1967   "The hominid skeletal remains of Haua Fteah (Appendix B)," in *Haua Fteah (Cyrenaica) and the Stone Age of the south-east Mediterranean.* Edited by C. B. M. McBurney, 337–352. Cambridge: Cambridge University Press.

WEIDENREICH, F.
  1943   The skull of *Sinanthropus pekinensis* ... *Palaeontologia Sinica,* n.s. D, 127(10). Peking.
  1946   *Apes, giants and man.* Chicago: University of Chicago Press.
  1951   Morphology of Solo man. *Anthropological Papers, American Museum of Natural History* 43(3):205–290.

Morphology of a Neanderthal Child from Kiik-Koba in the Crimea

EMANUEL VLČEK

HISTORY OF THE FIND AND THE DATING

In the course of archaeological excavations of the Mousterian settlement in the Kiik-Koba cave in the Crimea, the outstanding Soviet scholar Bonč-Osmolovski uncovered two inhumations of the Mousterian man. The excavations of the cave were started in 1925 and lasted for several seasons. The research workers uncovered a sequence of layers in the cave with two cultural horizons that may be ascribed archaeologically to the orbit of the Mousterian culture.

In the middle of the settlement area of the lower, that is, the earlier, Mousterian horizon in squares number twenty-five and twenty-one the inhumation of an adult individual was found. The grave-pit was cut in the rocky floor of the cave. During the Upper (later) Mousterian settlement of the cave, two-thirds of the contents of the grave were removed, together with the skeletal remains. Of the original skeleton, which was placed on its left side and slightly contracted, only the bones of the lower limbs and the skeleton of the hands remained *in situ*. The discovery of phalanges of the fingers and toes and one tooth scattered in the upper (later) horizon shows that a substantial part of the skeleton was removed from the grave-pit. During the later Mousterian settlement of the site, the bones of the skeleton were still connected with ligament. The removal of the skeleton may be explained by cult or other reasons.

Close to this adult burial and some thirty centimeters north of the original position of the head of the adult individual, the burial of a young child was found in a small grave-pit cut in the floor of the grave, in square number thirteen. This individual was placed on its left side, in a slightly contracted position, and the burial belonged to the Lower (earlier) Mousterian cultural horizon.

The lithic industry associated with the latter find belongs to the typical Mousterian. In absolute terms, both finds of Neanderthal man may be dated, in view of the stratigraphy of the sequence of horizons in the cave and of the paleontological and paleobotanical contents of the cultural horizons, to the start of the last glacial period, the early Würm.

Geological, stratigraphical, paleontological, and archaeological conclusions and evidence were published by Bonč-Osmolovski in the first part of his monograph "Paleolit Krima" [The Paleolithic of the Crimea] as early as 1940. In the second part, which appeared in 1941, the author elaborated the morphology of the hand skeleton of the adult individual from Kiik-Koba. In the third part, published in 1948 after the death of the author and edited by V. V. Bunak, the morphology of the skeleton of the foot and shin of the adult individual is elaborated. Recent works include studies by Gromov (1948), Ivanova (1965), and Klein (1965, 1969).

The remains from the second burial containing a young Neanderthal child, kept in the collections of the Institute of Ethnography of the Academy of Sciences in Leningrad, are described below.

THE STATE OF PRESERVATION OF THE CHILD SKELETAL REMAINS FROM KIIK-KOBA

The skeleton of the child was found in an undisturbed anatomical position, but in a very poor state of preservation. Of the skull only unrecoverable impressions in the clay are preserved; these were covered by bone dust. For this reason we find today at the Institute of Ethnography of the Academy of Sciences in Leningrad, under the inventory number 5496, only tiny fragments of the crushed calvarium. The skull was broken to fragments by the pressure of the stony earth, which later formed the cultural horizon.

Of the postcranial skeleton only some long bones, parts of long bones, the left ilium and the right scapula have been reconstructed. Bones of the right forearm and parts of the hand without fingers were found *in situ,* all embedded in a clump of clay from the cultural horizon. Of the tiny fragments it has been possible to separate isolated phalanges of fingers and toes, relatively well preserved bodies of vertebrae, and a number of fragmentary arches of vertebrae, as well as fragments of ribs.

ANTHROPOLOGICAL DESCRIPTION OF THE CHILD FROM KIIK-KOBA

The skeletal remains of the child from Kiik-Koba make it possible to study some problems of the development of the post-cranial skeleton of Neanderthal people at the age of five to seven months. The author would like to point to some differences in the proportions of upper and lower limbs, as well as to some important diagnostic features present on the skeleton of both limbs and thorax of the young Neanderthal child.

This study has been made possible by a reliable reconstruction of three long bones in their total length and by the relatively complete reconstruction of other bones. The femur measures ninety-eight millimeters, the fibula seventy-two millimeters, and the ulna seventy-two millimeters.

These long bones of the child from Kiik-Koba were then compared with the skeleton of a recent child, whose femur also measured ninety-eight millimeters. Such exact analogy enables scholars to study differences in the proportions of the individual parts of the lower and upper limbs and to guess at the height of the body and the age of the child from Kiik-Koba. In addition to these findings, the comparison of the structure of some long bones supplies marked, phylogenetically important features for the establishment of differential diagnostics between the Neanderthal and modern forms.

The results of this study are summed up in the following passages.

Body Height of the Neanderthal Child from Kiik-Koba

For the calculation of the body height we used the method introduced by Stewart (1948). The body height calculated on the basis of the length of the femur diaphysis for the Neanderthal individual from Kiik-Koba is sixty-four centimeters. For comparison we also calculated the body height according to the formulas of Smith (1945), Olivier and Pineau (1960), and, for the sake of completeness, also according to the method of Balthazard and Devieux (1921). According to the method of Smith the body height was 65.8 centimeters and according to that of Olivier-Pineau it was 66.06 ± 1.82 centimeters. A rather different result was achieved when we applied the method of Balthazard and Devieux — 62.9 centimeters.

Thus, on the basis of methods used for the calculation of body height of recent children according to the length of femur, the body height of the child from Kiik-Koba should be sixty-four to sixty-five centimeters. But after establishing that the Neanderthal child had a shorter shin, it was necessary to reduce its calculated body height by 7 percent of the total length of the shin, by six millimeters. Therefore, it will be necessary to adhere to the lower value of the calculated body height — sixty-four centimeters.

What effects upon the body height should be ascribed to the skeleton of the neck, to the skull, or to the position of big joints such as the knee or hip-joint, cannot be ascertained on the basis of the material we have today. It is possible to expect some corrections here also.

Age and Sex of the Kiik-Koba Individual

The calculated body height of the child from Kiik-Koba, when compared with that of recent children, corresponds to an age of about five to seven months.

The preserved fragments of the right ilium even point to the sex of the individual. The incisura ischiadica major is very narrow when compared with that of a recent European female child of the same age, and therefore the Neanderthal child from the Kiik-Koba cave was very probably a male.

Proportions of the Individual Parts of the Limb of the Neanderthal Suckling

In the metric and graphic comparison of the bones of the Kiik-Koba child with a recent individual, whose femur also measured ninety-three millimeters, striking differences in the proportions of the individual parts of the skeleton of both limbs have been found (see Table 1).

The differences in the length ratio of the individual parts of the upper and lower limb are expressed in two ways:

1. Proportionality indices (see Table 2).
2. Value in percent of the difference in the individual parts of both limbs.

As the femurs are of equal length, the shin of the Neanderthal child from Kiik-Koba is shorter than that of the modern child by seven percent. This means that the length of the shin of the Neanderthal individual represents only 93 percent of the length of the shin of the recent individual.

An inverse ratio is found in the comparison of the length of the forearms. The forearm of the Kiik-Koba child is longer by 10 percent than that of the recent individual. This means that it represents 110 percent of the length of the forearm of the recent child.

Thus, we find in the Neanderthal child the same proportions of limbs as in adult Neanderthal individuals. From this follows that the total body height of Neanderthal children is lower than that of modern children, the explanation being the shorter shin.

Table 1. Length in millimeters of long bones of the Neanderthal child from Kiik-Koba and of the recent child aged five months

Length of:	Kiik-Koba	Recent
humerus	(78) R	78
ulna	72	68
radius	—	60
femur	(98)	98
fibula	72	78
tibia	(78) R	80

Table 2. Comparison of proportionality indices of the Neanderthal child from Kiik-Koba and the recent child aged five months

Index	Neanderthal	Recent
femur-tibia	(79.6)	81.6
femur-fibula	73.4	79.5
humerus-ulna	(92.3)	87.2

Robusticity of Limb Bones of the Kiik-Koba Child

Generally, the bones of the child from Kiik-Koba display a relatively pronounced robusticity, particularly the diaphyses of the bones. This conclusion is based on the robusticity index of the femur (16.8 for the Neanderthal child and 13.8 for the recent child aged five months)

Table 3.   Robusticity of long bones of the Kiik-Koba child as compared with a recent child aged five months

Index of the cross-section of the diaphysis	Neanderthal	Recent
humerus	87.5	92.8
radius	72.7	88.9
ulna	100.0	77.8
fibula	88.9	100.0
Index of the robusticity of the femur	16.8	13.8

and on the indices of the cross-section of the central diaphysis of other long bones, as shown in Table 3.

The thickness of long bones in the child from Kiik-Koba is directly proportional to the thickening of diaphyses of the long bones. Their relation may best be studied on X-ray pictures.

Morphology of the Postcranial Skeleton

TRUNCAL SKELETON   Of the skeleton of the thorax there are only eleven vertebrae in various stages of preservation and nineteen fragments of arches of vertebrae. In comparing this material with vertebrae of a recent European child of the same age we do not find any pronounced differences.

In addition to the vertebrae fragments, several small fragments of ribs have also been preserved. These rib fragments show a markedly greater thickness and roundness of the lateral segments than do ribs of a recent child.

Table 4.   Width and thickness of ribs in millimeters

	Kiik-Koba	Recent
Costa I		
width of lateral segment	7.5	7.5
thickness of lateral segment	4.0	3.0
index	53.3	40.0
Costa III–IV		
width of lateral segment	7.0	8.0
thickness of lateral segment	4.0	2.5
index	57.1	41.2

As far as the shape and measurements are concerned, we find a pronounced difference between the ribs of the Kiik-Koba child and those of a recent European. The child from Kiik-Koba displays similar ratios, as do adult individuals (Boule 1911-1913; Gorjanovič-Kramberger 1906; Endo 1970).

SHOULDER GIRDLE

Clavicle   Of both clavicles there have been preserved only tiny fragments, which do not offer any reliable basis for examination.

Scapula   In the grave of the Kiik-Koba child a crushed right scapula was found. A part with the cavitas glenoidalis, the lateral part of the spina scapulae, the medial part of the acromion and also a part of the axillar border were recovered and reconstructed. Missing are the lower angle and the medial part of the scapula.

On the reconstructed fragment we may find some important features that set apart the Kiik-Koba child from a recent European individual.

The cavitas glenoidalis is of a symmetrical oval shape; the fossa articularis is mildly bulging. In the recent child the cavitas glenoidalis is rather kidney-shaped and has a straighter ventral border.

With respect to a cross axis of the scapula drawn below the spina scapulae, the cavitas glenoidalis displays a more dorsal turn than in the recent child. For this reason the cavitas glenoidalis in the Kiik-Koba individual is well visible from dorsal view.

On the fragment of the scapula it is possible to measure the axillo-glenoid and the spino-axillary angles (see Table 5).

Table 5.   Angles of the scapula

	Kiik-Koba	Recent
Axillo-glenoid	150°	134°
Spino-axillary	63°	45°

A very important feature of differential diagnostics, the sulcus marginalis on the axillary border, is not yet fully developed in such a young child. The axillary border in the Kiik-Koba individual is about one quarter thicker than in the recent child.

The whole length of the axillary border is rounded and without edge. Five millimeters below the lower border of the cavitas glenoidalis there is the suggestion of a ridge which turns in the caudal direction to the dorsal side of the scapula. On the axillary border in the recent child is a sharp edge.

If we study the features found on the scapula of the Kiik-Koba child, we find that the existing differences between the Kiik-Koba individual and the recent European child are practically of the same nature as those found in the study of adult individuals. On the whole, the scapula of the Kiik-Koba child is more robust. The shape of the cavitas glenoidalis is that of a broad oval; the fossa articularis is situated rather towards the dorsal side with respect to the transverse axis of the bone; the axillo-glenoid and spino-axillary angles are greater than those found in the recent child; and, finally, the axillary border is thicker and there is the suggestion of the development of sulcus marginalis (Boule 1911-1913).

All these findings point to the fact that typical Neanderthal features on the scapula are already fixed in the early postnatal period of the ontogenesis of the Neanderthal man.

CURVING OF THE DIAPHYSES OF FOREARM BONES IN THE KIIK-KOBA CHILD
One of the most striking features is the medio-lateral curving of the diaphysis of the radius and a considerable dorsovolar curving of the ulna. These curvings result in the spatium interosseum in the Kiik-Koba child being twice as wide as that in the recent individual aged five months.

The width of the spatium interossum in the Kiik-Koba individual is nine millimeters and in the recent child aged five months only four millimeters. This difference is also clearly reflected in the width-index of the spatium interossum, which in the Kiik-Koba child is 12.5 millimeters and in the recent child only 5.9 millimeters.

Thus, we may see that this feature, which is typical of the adult Neanderthal population, is clearly developed as early as five to seven months.

CURVING OF THE FEMORAL DIAPHYSIS IN THE KIIK-KOBA INDIVIDUAL   The back-to-front curving of the femoral diaphysis, which is also typical of adult Neanderthal individuals, is developed to a conspicuous degree in the young child from Kiik-Koba.

RETROVERSION OF THE UPPER EPIPHYSIS OF THE TIBIA IN THE KIIK-KOBA CHILD   In the child from Kiik-Koba striking retroversion of the upper epiphysis of the tibia at an angle of twenty-four degrees has been found; this is again a constant feature of adult Neanderthal individuals. In recent man this is characteristic of fetuses and new-born children and disappears in the course of later development. This feature is usually found in populations that spend a large part of their life in a squatting position; consequently, it is a functional feature.

REFERENCES

BALTHAZARD T., DEVIEUX
1921 Études anthropologiques sur le foetus humain. *Annales de Médicine Légale* 50:37–42.

BONČ-OSMOLOWSKI, G. A.
1940 *Paleolit Kryma.* Vypusk 1. Moscow-Leningrad: Akademja Nauk SSSR.
1941 *Paleolit Kryma.* Vypusk 2. Moscow-Leningrad: Akademja Nauk SSSR.
1948 *Paleolit Kryma.* Vypusk 3. Moscow-Leningrad: Akademja Nauk SSSR.

BOULE, M.
1911–1913 L'Homme fossile de la Chapelle-aux-Saints. *Annales de Paléontologie* 6:109–172; 7:105–192; 8:1–62.

ENDO, B.
1970 "Postcranial skeleton of the Amud man," in *The Amud Man and his cave site.* Edited by H. Suzuki and F. Takai, 231–245. Tokyo: Academic Press of Japan.

GORJANOVIČ-KRAMBERGER, D.
1906 *Der diluviale Mensch von Krapina in Kroatien.* Wiesbaden: C. W. Kreidel.

GROMOV, V. I.
1948 The palaeontological and archaeological basis of the stratigraphy of the continental deposits of the Quaternary period on the territory of the U.S.S.R. (in Russian). *Trudy Inst. geol. Nauk* 64(17): 1–45.

HEIM, M. J.-L.
1968 Les restes néandertaliens de La Ferrasie. Nouvelles données sur la stratigraphie et inventaire des squélettes. *Comptes rendus hebdomadaires des séances de l'Academie des sciences* 266:576–578.

IVANOVA, I. K.
1965 The geological age of fossil man (in Russian). *Nauka* 73–76.

KLEIN, R. G.
1965 The Middle Palaeolithic of the Crimea. *Arctic Anthropology* 3: 34–68.
1969 Mousterian cultures in European Russia. *Science* 165:257–265.

OAKLEY, K. P., B. G. CAMPBELL, T. I. MOLLESON
1971 *Catalogue of fossil hominids. Part II: Europe,* 318–319. London: British Museum of Natural History.

OLIVIER, G., H. PINEAU
1960 Nouvelle détermination de la taille foetale d'après les longueurs diaphysaires des os longs. *Annales de Médicine Légale* 40:141–144.

SMITK, S.
1945 *Forensic Medicine.* London: J. and A. Churchill.

STEWART, T. D.
1948 Medico-legal aspects of the skeleton. *American Journal of Physical Anthropology,* n.s. 6(3):315–321.

1960   "Détermination de la taille d'un enfant," in *Pratique Anthropologique*. Edited by G. Olivier, 259. Paris.

VALLOIS, H.
1932   L'omoplate humaine. Etude anatomique et anthropologique. *Bulletin de la Société d'Anthropologie* 3:3–153.

Palaeoanthropic Specimens from the Site Zaskalnaya VI in the Crimea

YU. G. KOLOSSOV, V. M. KHARITONOV, and V. P. YAKIMOV

In the eastern foothills of the Crimea, near the town of Belogorsk a new area of Mousterian sites was recently found. The massif of Ak-Kaya (White Rock), composed of nummulitic formations and sandy marls, rises here. In its northern part the massif is divided by the deep ravine of Krasnaya, several hundred meters long. All along the ravine its right slope is bordered by a steep rocky barrier about fifteen meters high, composed of nummulitic limestones of the Middle Eocene age. Caves, rock-shelters, and niches of different size are situated in it.

From 1964 to 1969 Ukranian archaeologists collected more than one thousand flint implements from the bottom and slopes of the Krasnaya ravine. These finds gave rise to the systematic excavations begun in the area. Pilot studies revealed fourteen palaeolithic sites. Between 1970 and 1972 some of them were excavated by the Crimean Palaeolithic Expedition under the direction of Kolossov. As a result four Mousterian sites have been found: Ak-Kaya III, and Zaskalnaya III, V, and VI. The latter two are multilayer sites.

At Zaskalnaya V deposits were 4.5 meters thick and showed four cultural layers of Mousterian age (Kolossov 1971a, b), while at Zaskalnaya VI deposits were three meters thick and contained five Mousterian layers (Kolossov 1973).

In 1970, at the site of Zaskalnaya V a fragment of occipital bone of a palaeoanthropic adult was discovered in a trench somewhat down the slope, among animal bones and Mousterian flint tools. It is being investigated now by Gokhman, a Leningrad anthropologist.

The second discovery of ancient human bones occurred in 1972 while excavating Zaskalnaya VI, situated seventy meters farther up the

For Plates, see p. xii, between pp. 288–289

Krasnaya ravine. This site is an ancient ruined grotto. Its collapsed roof is covered with the Mousterian layers. The uppermost layer lies directly below the soil in the horizon of rocky collapse. Layers II-IV are exposed below the collapse in the nummulitic sands. Layer V overlies the rocky floor of the cave. As a rule cultural layers are forty-five centimeters thick and are distinguished by the darkish color of the ashy-hearth strata. Layers III and IV and layers IV and V are separated from each other by sterile sediments. Cultural layers contain large amounts of fossil animal bones, flint flakes, and bone coal.

Faunal remains include bones of mammoth, horse, wild ass, reindeer, red deer, aurochs, and wolf. Sometimes groups of bones were found with their anatomical order preserved.

The flint industry is represented by a large number of tools of the Mousterian type: knives with straight or convex blades, side-scrapers, points that often are asymmetrical, and drawknives. The flint was lightly covered with a bluish or light grey patina. The numbers of tools were distributed as follows: layer I, 138; layer II, 1,200; layer III, 250; layer IV, more than 400. Excavations of layer V had just begun, so only few implements were available. All five cultural layers are characterized by a protoprismatic technique of flint-working. The flint industry represents the Mousterian tradition of bifacial manufacturing. Tools bifacially or partly bifacially worked are especially numerous in three upper layers, making up 41 percent of the total number of implements in layer I, 30 percent in layer II, and 17 percent in layer III. In layer IV such tools make up only 4 percent.

Oddly formed tools were also found. Among them were knives bifacially or partly bifacially worked with a platform for supporting the fingers, and scraper-knives of wedge or triangular shape. Tools of the first type are numerous in layers I, II and III. Layer II contains 8 percent of such tools; layer III, 4.5 percent; and layer IV, 0.7 percent.

Layer IV differs from the upper layers in that it contains numerous tools of comparatively small size, the average length being not more than five centimeters. Thus we detect a certain microlithic tradition in the flint industry of layer IV.

Preliminary analyses of the flint assemblage from four cultural layers of the Mousterian site of Zaskalnaya VI leads to some conclusions about continuity in the development of the stone industry of these layers with simultaneous indications of change in the tradition of flint working. While in layer IV the tradition of unifacial tool-working on the basis of protoprismatic technique is widely represented, in the three upper layers the tradition of bifacial tool-working is prevalent, although the former technique is still preserved. Of course thorough and detailed investigations of the whole flint assemblage with application of typological and statistical analysis must be made before we draw final conclusions.

When parts of rocky collapse were removed at the Zaskalnaya VI site human bones were found in cultural layer III. Cultural layer II was preserved *in situ* and twenty-five to thirty centimeters below it, layer III, with a marked ashy horizon, appeared. The human remains were found in this layer some 183 to 184 centimeters from our marked zero point, or seventy centimeters from the present surface. They lay in the southern part of the excavated area at a radius of forty centimeters. The layer yielded a fragment of the left side of the mandible with three teeth, fourteen isolated teeth, several small mandibular fragments, and eight fragments of metacarpal and manual phalangeal bones. Animal bones and flint tools were discovered nearby. One artifact merits special mention here: a spear-point 11.7 centimeters long, five centimeters wide and two centimeters thick, made of flat flint slab. The upper and middle parts of the tool are covered with bifacial facets while the lower part preserves some of the core. The point base is wide and the upper end is very sharp. We emphasize that the manufacture of different tools from pieces of flint slab-stone was characteristic of Mousterian peoples in this region.

As noted above, human skeletal remains were represented by several metacarpal and phalangeal bones in poor condition, plus some mandibular fragments. Thus, only a preliminary report on these fragments can be presented here. The mandibular specimen comprised part of the left half of the jaw broken at the alveolus of the first premolar. The ramus with the lower part of the left coronoid process and condyle were also preserved, the top of the latter being partly damaged. The posterior margin of the ramus, from the top of the condyle to the mandibular angle, was broken. The alveolar margin of the body was also damaged. From the right side of the jaw only a fragment of the basal surface of the body was preserved. A small piece of the basal part of the symphyseal region (twenty-one millimeters long) was preserved. It exhibits traces of the digastric fossae.

Luckily, all the teeth corresponding to this jaw were found. They were represented by two categories: milk teeth (right and left second molars) and permanent ones (the whole set of teeth from both sides of the jaw in different stages of development). The jaw therefore belonged to a child with changing dentition.

On the basis of these fragments and teeth, Elistratova, an experienced restorer from the D. N. Anuchin Institute and Museum of Anthropology, Moscow State University made an accurate full plastic reconstruction of the lower jaw (Plate 1). We are greatly indebted to Elistratova for this work.

According to the general appearance of the reconstruction we consider the jaw to be from a Neanderthal, not modern, type of man. This is evidenced by the structure of the frontal part of the mandible. The preserved piece of the lower border of the symphysial region, in spite of its small size, clearly exhibits Neanderthal characteristics. The line of the frontal surface of the mandibular body runs obliquely from the incisors thereby forming an oblique angle with the horizontal plane. The mandibular body in the part related to the incisors and canines is flattened and runs almost frontally, then turns and passes bilaterally at marked angles. This particularity in the structure of the frontal part of the lower jaw is present in the skulls of the Teshik-Tashian boy and many other representatives of Neanderthal man, as well as in the jaws of Archanthropes. In describing an infant skull from the Mousterian site of Staroselye, Roguinsky (1954) noted the flattening and frontal position of the incisor-canine mandibular part, among other typical Neanderthaloid features.

Another peculiarity distinguishing the mandible of the Zaskalnaya site from the jaw of modern man is the structure of coronoid and condyloid processes. The former probably was quite high, essentially higher than the latter. Its posterior border passes into the upper margin of the mandibular notch and approaches almost exactly the middle axis of the top of the condyle. This was noted in the child's jaw from the Teshik-Tash cave (Gremyatsky 1949). In modern man the posterior border of the coronoid process approaches the lateral part of the condyle, either covering it a little or running tangentially towards its top.

Due to the heights of the coronoid and condyloid processess, the notch itself is deep. In this respect a child from the Zaskalnaya site resembles the Teshik-Tashian palaeoanthrope (Table 2). In this feature both finds from the Soviet Union resemble some European palaeoanthropes, but differ from those of North Africa and Southwestern Asia (for example Hauna Fteah I and II, Ksar Akil, Tabun I, and Skhūl VI) which are characterized by broad, shallow notches (Tobias 1967). However the range of variability of this feature is great so a much more detailed analysis must be made before stating a conclusion on the degree of resemblance between these fossils.

The dentition is the best basis for estimating an exact age[1] of the

---

[1]   The age was determined by V. M. Kharitonov and V. P. Yakimov.

child from **Zaskalnaya VI**. The number of teeth present, their development and stage of eruption, and the state of the masticatory surface were considered. Data on stages of eruption in modern children given by Rokhlin (1949), Gremyatsky (1949), and Zubov (1970), were used in our analysis.

In the fossil jaw the deciduous dentition is represented by second molars on both sides. The left dm_2 was found *in situ*, in its alveolus. Its resolving roots embraced the crown of the permanent tooth which was still embedded in the alveolar margin of the jaw. Thus, the permanent tooth was "saddled" by the milk tooth. The chewing surface of the milk tooth crown was quite worn. The right dm_2 was found isolated. The state of its roots and chewing surface are like the left dm_2.

The state of the permanent teeth is summarized in Table 1. The child from the Zaskalnaya site and the Neanderthal boy from the Teshik-Tash cave are compared on the basis of times of eruption of the permanent teeth in modern children.

Table 1. The dentition of children from Zaskalnaya VI and Teshik-Tash cave

Teeth	Times of eruption in modern children	The child from Zaskalnaya VI	The boy from Teshik-Tash cave
First incisor	8 years	Fully erupted	Fully erupted
Second incisor	9 years	Fully erupted	Fully erupted
Canine	11–12 years	Fully erupted but has not reached the level of occlusion surface	Developed but is embedded in the mandibular body, milk tooth has not been shed
First premolar	10 years	Appeared above the gum, milk tooth is absent	Has not erupted, milk tooth has not been shed
Second premolar	11–12 years	Exposed below milk tooth	Exposed below milk tooth
First molar	7 years	Fully erupted	Fully erupted
Second molar	12–13 years	Has not erupted	Has not erupted
Third molar	after 18 years	Only crown is developed	Only crown is developed

While closely resembling each other, the Zaskalnaya and Teshik-Tash finds show some essential differences. In the child from the Crimean site the canine crown is fully erupted although it has not completely reached the level of occlusion of nearby teeth. Further, the right and left permanent canines of the Teshik-Tash boy, although almost fully developed, are still embedded in bone. The milk canines of the Teshik-

Tash boy are preserved, their roots being considerably resolved and their crowns strongly worn.

The first premolar is also slightly more developed in the Crimean child. Its crown is either emerging through the gum or is in the state immediately prior to eruption. The corresponding milk tooth is missing, although we cannot be sure that this was so in the child's lifetime.

The Teshik-Tashian boy has milk molars with resolving roots on both sides of the lower jaw. The corresponding permanent teeth are exposed directly below the roots and are still embedded in the alveolar margin of the bone.

Some differences in the sequence of eruption between the two finds can be highlighted. Based on the degree of obliteration of crown surfaces Gremyatsky (1949: 180) ascertained that in the Teshik-Tash boy the first permanent molars had erupted before the incisors. Taking this into consideration we conclude that in the child from Zaskalnaya VI the incisors had erupted somewhat earlier than the first molars because the masticatory surfaces of these molars are intact while the crowns of both incisors are slightly worn. When compared with the Teshik-Tash boy the child from the Crimean site exhibits a much longer period between the eruptions of the canines and the third molars. While the third molars are equally developed, being in the stage of crown germs, the canines have already erupted in the child from Zaskalnaya. Per contra, in the Teshik-Tash boy they are fully developed but far from eruption.

The state of dentition in the Crimean child suggests that its biological age should be somewhat greater than that of the boy from Teshik-Tash. The latter's age was estimated at nine to ten years, according to its dentition. The Crimean child must have been approximately ten to twelve years old. Of course there is also a possibility that these differences in eruption time merely represent individual variations or depend upon sex, especially if the Crimean mandible was from a girl. The possibility that the mandible from Zaskalnaya VI might belong to a girl occurred to us when we first examined it. Although according to the state of the dentition the Crimean child is somewhat older than the boy from Teshik-Tash, it has a much smaller mandible (Table 2). The relatively small size of the teeth is another piece of evidence for "feminization" in the mandible from Zaskalnaya VI.

Measurements of mandibular breadth indicate that the Crimean child is significantly smaller than the Teshik-Tash boy and it approximates modern children. But in proportions of bicondylar and bigonial breadth both of these Neanderthal children are different from modern

Table 2. Some measurements (millimeters), angles (degrees), and indices (in percentages) of two children's mandibles from Zaskalnaya VI site and Teshik-Tash cave

Features	The child from Zaskalnaya VI	The child from Teshik-Tash cave
Breadth of the mandible:		
bicondylar breadth	109 [1]	122
bigonial breadth	66 [2]	83
Breadth index	60.5 [3]	67.2
Height of the body in the region of:		
symphysis	23??	26
foramen mentale	22??	—
second molar	20	21
Thickness of the body in the region of:		
symphysis	13	15
foramen mentale	13	—
second molar	14	16
Indices of robustness in the region of:		
symphysis	56.5??	57.7
foramen mentale	59.0?	—
second molar	70.0	76.2
Breadth of the ramus	29	31
Angle of the ramus	123°	125°
Breadth of the notch	28?	28
Depth of the notch	13?	12
Notch index	46.4?	42.8

[1] Modern children of the same age have on the average 92.6 millimeters.
[2] Modern children of the same age have on the average 68.0 millimeters.
[3] Modern children of the same age have on the average 73.3 millimeters.

children. In modern children the absolute difference between mean values of the two measurements is 24.6 (maximum 26) millimeters, while in the Crimean child the difference between bicondylar and bigonial breadths is 43 millimeters. In the Teshik-Tashian boy the value is 39 millimeters. The corresponding indices (bigonial breadth expressed as a percentage of bicondylar breadth) are 60.5 in the Zaskalnaya child (a girl?); 67.2 in the Teshik-Tashian boy; and 73.3 (average) in modern children. These values suggest that in the jaws of both the Mousterian children, the condyloid processes of the ramus have essentially deviated outward. This trait allows us to distinguish them from modern children and to confirm their assignment to Neanderthal forms of man.

The mandibular body in the child of Zaskalnaya VI is smaller and less robust than that of the Teshik-Tash boy (Table 2). This is further evidence that the Crimean child was female. A single foramen mentale is situated below the second premolar on the preserved portion of the left half of the lower jaw. In the Teshik-Tash boy a single foramen is located on the right side at the level of the interval between the first and second premolars. On the left side of the mandibular body the foramen is double. Modern man is characterized by a single foramen mentale.

That the Zaskalnaya child belongs to the palaeoanthropes is confirmed by many traits of its dentition,[2] including the highly differentiated second premolars, the presence of a distal trigonid ridge (especially marked on M_2), the talonid of the molars not narrower than the trigonid, M_1 and M_2 showing only rudimentary enamel cingula, the elongated form of molars, M_2 not smaller than M_1 in some features, and the presence of an anterior fossa on the molars that is especially marked on M_2. The number of cusps on the second and third molars is not reduced, thus marking another difference between Neanderthal and modern man.

As in the Palestinian palaeoanthropes the molar roots are not inosculated. The canines are small: $MD_{cor} = 7.3$ (left 7.2) millimeters, $BL_{cor} = 7.9$ (left 7.7) millimeters. The hypoconulid is situated symmetrically as in the Krapina palaeoanthropes. The protoconid is slightly larger than the metaconid and it does not project as it does in European Neanderthals. The milk molars were probably five-cusped, this trait being characteristic of palaeoanthropes and neoanthropes.

Measurements of the molars are given in Table 3. The mesio-distal diameters are "large" for M_1 and M_2, and "medium" for M_3, in comparison with values for modern man. The buccal-lingual diameters may be characterized as "small" for M_1 and M_2, and "medium" for M_3. These values vary from "medium" to "very large" in the palaeoanthropes we have studied.

Table 3.   Absolute sizes of molars in the child of Zaskalnaya VI site

| Molars | Measurements (millimeters) | |
	MD_{cor}	BL_{cor}
M_1	11.5	10.2
M_2	11.7	9.8
M_3	11.0	9.7

Table 3 shows the moderate reduction of the mesio-distal diameters, which characterizes palaeoanthropes by comparison with modern man. This is confirmed by the crown index, the values of which in all molars are smaller in the Crimean child than in modern man: $I_{cor} = 100x/VL_{cor}/MD_{cor}$. For M_1, M_2, M_3 the corresponding values are 88.6, 83.7, and 88.1, respectively.

[2]   Odontoscopic and odontometric analyses were performed by V. M. Kharitonov

The average crown module of molars $\left(\dfrac{m_{cor}\,M_1 + m_{cor}\,M_2 + m_{cor}\,M_3}{3}\right)$ in the child of Zaskalnaya VI is 10.65, which is greater than the average values of the crown module in modern man.

According to the relative size of the molars the Crimean child differs from modern man and is closely related to other fossil hominids. Table 4 and the third step-index by MD_{cor} show that M_2 is a key tooth.

Table 4.   Relative sizes of molars in the child of Zaskalnaya VI site

Measurements	Zaskalnaya VI	Modern man
MD_{cor}	$M_2 > M_1 > M_3$	$M_1 > M_2 > M_3$
BL_{cor}	$M_1 > M_2 > M_3$	$M_1 > M_2 > M_3$
m_{cor}	$M_2 > M_1 > M_3$	$M_1 > M_2 > M_3$
H_{cor}	$M_2 > M_1$	$M_1 > M_2$

The third step-index by MD_{cor} in the line of molars of the Zaskalnaya child is 101.7, surpassing modern man and resembling the palaeo-anthropes.

According to the second step-index by BL_{cor} (88.2) the child from Zaskalnaya VI also surpasses modern man. The same is true for the Krapina palaeoanthropes.

The value of the fourth step-index by MD_{cor} and BL_{cor} is within the range of variability known for modern man, but differs from Palestinian and Rabbatian palaeoanthropes (values more than 100 when $M_3 > M_1$).

The robustness of the crown ($Rb = BL_{cor} \times MD_{cor}$) changes in the line of molars in the following way: 117.3, 114.6, 106.7. This is characteristic also of the Temarian palaeoanthrope.

On the basis of our preliminary study of hominid skeletal remains from the Mousterian site of Zaskalnaya VI we draw the following conclusions:

1.   The mandibular fragments belong to a child of Neanderthal type. This is confirmed by the peculiar, non-*sapiens*, structure of the symphyseal region of the mandible, by the structure of the condyloid and coronoid processes, and by proportions of the bicondylar and bigonial breadths.

2.   The whole complex of odontoscopic and odontometric features also confirms that the Zaskalnaya child is a member of the Neanderthal type of man.

3.   On dental grounds the biological age of the Crimean child is estimated to be ten to twelve years.

4.   The size and robustness of the lower jaw and dimensions of the

teeth suggest that the hominid skeletal remains from Zaskalnaya are those of a girl.

Further morphological and metric analyses of osteological and odontological peculiarities in the child of the Zaskalnaya site may not only confirm the preliminary conclusions presented in this communication, but also clarify the position of the new find among other palaeoanthropes.

REFERENCES

GREMYATSKY, M. A.
  1949   Cherep rebenka-neandertalca iz grota Teshik-Tash, Yuzhnii Uzbekistan [Child's skull from Teshik-Tash grotto, South Uzbekistan]. *Paleoliticheskii chelovek*, 137–182.
KOLOSSOV, YU. G.
  1971a   Bagatosharova must'erska stoyanka Zaskal'na V [The multilevel Mousterian site of Zaskalnaya V]. *Arkheologiya* 3:50–58.
  1971b   Poperednii rezul'tati doslidzheniya must'erskikh stoyanok Krimu [Preliminary results of the investigation of Mousterian sites in the Crimea]. *Vi sn. AN URSR* 6:72–75.
  1973   Paleoantropologicheskie nakhodki u skaly Ak-Kaja [Palaeoanthropological finds at Ak-Kaya fell]. *Voprosy antropologii* 44:162–166.
ROGUINSKY, JA. JA.
  1954   Morfologicheskie osobennosti cherepa rebenka iz pozdnemustierskogo sloja peshery Starosele (predvaritelnoe soobshchenie) [Morphological features of the child's skull from the late Mousterian stratum of Staroselye cave (a preliminary note)]. *Sovietskaja etnografija* 1:27–39.
ROKHLIN, D. G.
  1949   Nekotorii dannye rentgenologicheskogo issledovanija detskogo skeleta iz grota Teshik-Tash, Yuzhnii Uzbekistan [Some roentgenogram dates of child's skeleton from Teshik-Tash grotto, South Uzbekistan]. *Paleoliticheskii chelovek*, 109–123.
TOBIAS P. V.
  1967   "The hominid skeletal remains of Haua Fteah," in *The Haua Fteah (Cyrenaica) and the stone age of the South-East Mediterranean*. Edited by C. McBurney, 338–352. Cambridge: Cambridge University Press.
ZUBOV A. A.
  1970   *Odontologija. Metodika antropologicheskikh issledovanij* [Odontology: methods of anthropological research].

Discussion

[Dr. M. A. de Lumley presented slides, showed casts, and summarized her paper.]

HOWELLS: Along with the La Chaise skulls the remarkable finds of the de Lumleys fill out the material of man in the Rissian. Madame de Lumley also believes that there were two lines of development during the pre-Neanderthal period. The question is "How did the Neanderthal form, of the classic variety, become set in the Würm and in the immediately preceding Interglacial? How might it derive from these?" The ground work has now been laid for judging all this.

[Professor Yakimov described remains of a Mousterian child from Zaskalnaya VI in the Crimea and showed a cast of its mandibles.]

Professor Marie-Antoinette de Lumley exhibiting and discussing casts of Tautavel Man

Professor V. P. Yakimov (left) discussing the mandible from Zaskalnaya VI with Dr. Phillip V. Tobias (holding cast) and other participants. (Photograph by George Sacher)

Biographical Notes

EMILIANO AGUIRRE (1925–) received his doctorate in Biology in 1966 ·
He initiated lectures on Quaternary Studies at the University of Madrid
(1964). He established a Department of Anthropology at the P. Universidad Católica del Perú (1967) and a Sección de Paleontologia de Vertebrados y Humana in the C.S.I.C., Madrid (1969). He is Associate
Professor of Vertebrate, Primate, and Human Paleontology at the
Universidad Complutense de Madrid (1971–). Professor Aguirre has
collaborated with F. C. Howell and P. Biberson in prehistoric studies at
Torralba and Ambrona, Spain (1961–1964), and with L.S.B. Leakey and
W. W. Bishop in Kenya (1968–1969). He is a member of the Workgroup
on the World Shorelines Map (INQUA, 1972–1973), the Subcommittee
on the Plio-Pleistocene Boundary and the Committee on Paleoecology of
Man (INQUA, 1973–). His research interests include Late Neogene to
Early Pleistocene mammals, taxonomy, and human activity on bone
fragments.

CHARLES K. BRAIN (1931–) was born in Rhodesia and obtained a Ph.D.
degree from the University of Capetown in 1958. His early work at the
Transvaal Museum in Pretoria was concerned with the australopithecine
cave sites. He then worked extensively on zoological topics (largely rep-
tilian and primate behavior) before re-starting work at the Swartkrans
australopithecine site in 1965. He was appointed Director of the Transvaal
Museum in 1968, a position he still holds.

SUSAN MARIE CACHEL (1949–) received a B.A. (1970) and an M.A.
(1971) from the University of Chicago. She is currently a Ph.D. candidate

in Physical Anthropology at the University of Chicago and is doing research on the origins of the anthropoid grade.

GLENN C. CONROY (1947–   ) was born in Boston. He received his B.A. (1970, Anthropology) from the University of California at Berkeley and his M.Phil. (1972) and Ph.D. (1974) from Yale. He has participated in several paleoanthropological expeditions to East Africa and Pakistan and is preparing a monograph on the primate postcranial remains from the Fayum, Egypt. He currently holds a joint appointment in the Departments of Cell Biology (Anatomy), New York University Medical Center, and Anthropology, New York University.

MARIE-ANTOINETTE DE LUMLEY-WOODYEAR (1934–   ) was born in Marseille, France. She studied at the Faculté de Médecine de Marseille and was awarded a doctorate in 1964 for her work on the paleopathology of prehistoric man. She subsequently studied at the Faculté de Sciences de Paris (Natural Science) and successfully defended a thesis on the pre-Neanderthals (1970). Presently she is Chargée de Recherche at the Centre National de la Recherche Scientifique, Paris, where she has been studying fossil man, especially Neanderthals and pre-Neanderthals, including the fossils from Tautavel, Lazaret, and Hortus which were uncovered during excavations organized and carried out in collaboration with her husband, Henry de Lumley.

ROBERT B. ECKHARDT (1942–   ) received his B.S. from Rutgers University in 1964. He then attended the University of Michigan, where he received an M.S. in Human Genetics (1966), an M.A. in Anthropology (1967), and a Ph.D. jointly in Anthropology and Human Genetics (1971). He was a Lecturer in Anthropology at the University of Michigan from 1968–1971, and at present is an Assistant Professor of Anthropology at the Pennsylvania State University. His subject area is primate and human population biology, with a major research interest in rates of evolution, particularly of polygenic characteristics.

WILLIAM WHITE HOWELLS (1908–   ) was born in New York and took his S.B. in 1930 and his Ph.D. in 1934, both in Anthropology at Harvard. After work at the American Museum of Natural History in New York, he taught anthropology at the University of Wisconsin from 1939 to 1954, and at Harvard from 1954 to 1974. He has since retired from teaching. Currently he is Curator of Somatology at the Peabody Museum, Harvard University. His most recent fieldwork was conducted in the Solomon Islands with the Harvard Solomons Project. His general books include

Mankind so far (1944), *The heathens* (1948), *Mankind in the making* (1959, revised 1967), *Evolution of the genus* Homo (1973), and *The Pacific Islanders* (1973). Multivariate analysis applied to recent and fossil man is a particular field of interest, his principal publication being *Cranial variation in man* (1973).

KATHERINE W. HULBERT (1909–) received a three-year special fellowship from NIGMS in 1966. She completed her Ph.D. at the University of Colorado in 1969 doing fieldwork in Kerala for her dissertation, "A study in human ecology: the sea-fishing people of the southwest coast of India." At present, retired from teaching, she continues independent research on the evolutionary implications of various ecological adaptations of primates, including man, convinced that the key to the unique hominid divergence from the ancestral hominid line is some AS YET UNDEFINED environmental adaptation which selected for alignment of the great toe and bipedal locomotion.

TEUKU JACOB (1929–) is Professor of Anthropology at Gadjah Mada University College of Medicine, Jogyakarta. Educated in medicine and physical anthropology in Indonesia, the U.S.A., and the Netherlands, he is a member of several anthropological and related societies. His research interest is primarily paleoanthropology, and in this pursuit he has studied almost all of the original pithecanthropine specimens from Java. Since 1962 he has been occupied with fossil man research in Central and East Java. His publications include works on craniology and dentition, the living Javanese, the Pleistocene hominine fossils, and Mesolithic and Paleometallic skeletal remains from Southeast Asia.

CHRISTOPHER G. JANUS (1911–) received his B.S. degree from Harvard in 1936 and did his graduate work in philosophy at Oxford and with George Santayana in Rome. Mr. Janus is the publisher of six volumes on Greek culture and is a founder of the *Greek Heritage Quarterly*. He is a member of the Visiting Committee for the Classics at Harvard. As a result of a visit to China shortly after that of President Nixon, he is active in a program to try to recover the long-lost Peking Man fossils.

VITALII M. KHARITONOV (1946–) is a Junior Fellow at the Research Institute of Anthropology of Moscow State University. His main publications are: "On the comparative systematic study of fossil hominids" (1971) and "A comparison of distinction scales between skulls of fossil hominids and modern mammals" (1973). Currently his special interests are paleoanthropology, human evolution, and the classification of fossil hominids.

A. P. Khatri (1932–) is Research Professor of Quaternary Studies in the Council of Scientific and Industrial Research at New Delhi. He is currently directing several research programs in connection with the exploration of physical and cultural remains of early man in the Siwalik foothills of the Himalayas, the Kashmir Valley and Himachal Pradesh in North India, the Highland of Bundelkhand in Middle India, and in the Narmada, Godavari, and Chambal Valleys in Peninsular India. He received his B.Sc. with Honors in Botany (1953) and a M.Sc. in Physical Anthropology (1955) from the University of Delhi. In 1958 he secured his Ph.D. from the University of Poona. In the past he has taken part in expeditions and excavations in southwest France (Abri Pataud at Les Eyzis and Regordou near Lascaux Caves), Ethiopia (1971), and Egypt (1972). His present interests include ecology, the behavior of living primates, and radiometric methods, as well as fossil primatology and Stone Age research in the Old and New Worlds.

Yurii G. Kolossov (1924–) is a Senior Fellow at the Institute of Archeology, Academy of Science, Ukrainian S.S.R. His special interest is the paleolithic archeology of the Crimea peninsula. He is the author of more than 50 publications, among them the monograph, "*Shaitan Koba, a Mousterian site in the Crimea* (1972).

Grover S. Krantz (1931–) was born in Salt Lake City, Utah. He studied at the University of Utah, the University of California, Berkeley (B.A., 1955; M.A., 1958) and the University of Minnesota (Ph.D., 1971) He has taught at the University of Minnesota and is presently Associate Professor at Washington State University. His work centers mainly on human evolution.

David Pilbeam (1940–) was born in England. He received his B.A. in Natural Sciences and Archaeology and Anthropology from Cambridge in 1962 (M.A., 1966), and his Ph.D. from Yale in 1967. After teaching at Cambridge for three years, he moved to Yale in 1968 where he is now Professor of Anthropology. His research interests include human evolution, primatology, and quantitative techniques. His major field areas are Pakistan and Kenya.

K. N. Prasad (1924–) was born in Bangalore, India. He received his

D.Sc. from the University of Mysore and joined the Geological Survey of India. As a geologist and paleontologist, he carried out extensive field surveys in the Siwaliks of the Himalayas. He was curator of Siwalik mammals at the Indian Museum, Calcutta, for a number of years. In 1965 he was appointed Paleontologist-in-Charge, of the Geological Survey at Hyderabad. Currently, he is Director of the Geological Survey of India at Hyderabad. His numerous publications include works on primates, Siwalik mammals, and Quaternary geology.

CANTEMIR RIŞCUŢIA (1923–) is a scientific researcher and professor at Victor Babeş Institute in Bucharest, Romania. He is a member of the Anthropology and Ethnology Commission of the Romanian Academy and was a Visiting Professor at the Braunschweig University (1972). He initiated and developed the photostereotomic method for morphological analysis of skulls, faces, and postcranial skeletons of man and other vertebrates (C. Rişcuţia and C. Petrescu: *Une nouvelle méthode d'investigation morphologique: la photostéréotomie*, 1960). He also initiated a novel method for the restoration of skulls and the morphophysiognomical reconstruction of faces and applied it to the following: Sangiran II (1967), Modjokerto (1970), Steinheim (1972), ancient historical Romanian skeletons, and modern forensic medical problems. He also conducts research on the population biology of modern inhabitants of Romania (Western and Eastern Carpathian, Danubian Region).

S. SARTONO (1928–) was born in Madiun, Java. In 1956 he received a Doctorandus degree in Geology from the Department of Geology, Faculty of Mathematics and Natural Sciences, Bandung, Java. He received his Doctor's degree in Mathematical and Physical Sciences in 1958 from the University of Indonesia. Since 1961 he has been Professor of Paleontology at the Institut Teknologi Bandung. He is also Head of the Paleontological Laboratory at the same institution. His fields of interest are paleontology and stratigraphy with a special interest in human evolution.

RUSSELL HOWARD TUTTLE (1939–) is Associate Professor in Anthropology and Evolutionary Biology at the University of Chicago and Visiting Research Scientist at Yerkes Regional Primate Research Center of Emory University. He received a B.Sc. degree (Anatomy, 1961) and an M.A. (Anthropology, 1962) from the Ohio State University and a Ph.D. (Anthropology, 1965) from the University of California at Berkeley. He has conducted field studies on nonhuman primates and associated fauna in Rhodesia, Ceylon, Kenya, and Tanzania. His principal research on the functional morphology and evolutionary biology of primates has been conducted at primate research centers, museums, and anthropological institutes in the United States, Japan, Switzerland, and Italy. He is the editor of *The functional and evolutionary biology of primates* (1972) and author of more than thirty scientific papers.

J. RIMAS VAIŠNYS (1937–   ) was born in Lithuania. He studied chemistry at Yale University (B.S., 1956) and at the University of California at Berkeley (Ph.D., 1960). Now at Yale University, his interests range from anthropology to zoology.

EMANUEL VLČEK (1925–   ) was born in Czechoslovakia. He is head of the Department of Anthropology at the National Museum in Prague, Czechoslovakia. His research includes studies on the skeletal biology of prehistoric and recent human populations, the ontogenesis of Neanderthal man, paleopathology, and the microevolution and classification of human groups.

CHRISTIAN VOGEL (1933–   ) is Professor of Anthropology at the University of Göttingen. He studied zoology, botany, geology, and physical anthropology at the Universities of Basel and Kiel. In 1964 he qualified as an ectuver in Anthropology with a morphological monograph on the skulls of catarrhine primates. From 1964–1972 he taught physical anthropology at the University of Kiel. In 1972 he was appointed Chairman of the newly established Department of Anthropology at the University of Göttingen. His present research is concerned with human evolution, especially with phylogenetic and functional aspects of the skull in nonhuman primates and hominids, as well as with studies on the social behavior and ecology of nonhuman primates. He has done anthropological and primatological fieldwork in India.

GUSTAV HEINRICH RALPH VON KOENIGSWALD (1902–   ) was born in Berlin. He studied geology and paleontology in Berlin, Tübingen, Cologne, and Munich. Between 1930 and 1948 he was paleontologist for the Geological Survey of the Netherlands East Indies in Bandung, Java. From 1948 to 1968 he was Professor of Palaeontology at the State University of Utrecht, the Netherlands. Since his retirement in 1968, he has been connected with the Senckenberg Museum, Section of Palaeontology, Frankfurt/Main. His fieldwork over the years has covered a large portion of the globe. In Java he worked primarily on Pleistocene stratigraphy and early man. He visited China in 1935, 1936, 1937, 1939 and, 1973 to study and collect fossil mammalian remains from Chinese drugstores. From 1946–1948 he worked in collaboration with Prof. Franz Weidenreich at the American Museum in New York. His other fieldwork locations have included East and South Africa, the Philippines, and Pakistan. His special interest is early man.

JOHN A. WALLACE (1940–) is Assistant Professor of Anatomy at Queen's University, Kingston, Ontario, Canada. He received his B.Sc. and M.Sc. from the University of Manitoba, and a Ph.D. in Anatomy from the University of the Witwatersrand. His present research interests are dental form and function in Miocene hominoids and the ultrastructure of early hominid enamel.

MILFORD H. WOLPOFF (1942–) studied physical anthropology and general problems of the relation between physical and biological sciences at the University of Illinois in Urbana, receiving a Ph.D. in Anthropology in 1969. Most of his research has dealt with problems of early hominid evolution in Africa, including studies conducted at the Transvaal Museum, the University of the Witwatersrand, and the National Museum of Kenya. His primary concern has been the relation of form to function, and the use of experiment and simulation in interpreting functional morphology. Other works of his have related to the interpretation of later Pleistocene hominid evolution, functional analysis of modern human variation, and problems in general evolutionary theory. He is currently an Associate Professor of Anthropology at the University of Michigan.

VSEVOLOD P. YAKIMOV (1912–) holds D.Ph. and D.B.Sc. degrees. He is a Professor and Director of the Research Institute of Anthropology (Physical Anthropology) of Moscow State University. His special interests include paleoanthropology, human evolution, and the origin of races. He has more than 100 papers in Russian on these subjects including: "Early stages of anthropogenesis" (1951), "Anthropological materials from neolithic necropolis by the Onege Sea" (1960), "Australopithecines" (1966), "Hominoids, hominids and the problem of the lower boundary of anthropogenesis" (1973). He is Editor-in-Chief of *Voprosy Anthropologii* [Problems of Anthropology], a member of the Permanent Council of USAES, an honorary member of anthropological societies in Czechoslovakia and Poland, and a member of the Society of Human Biology (England).

Index of Names

Index of Subjects

Aardwolf. *See Proteles* sp. *indet.*
Abbevillean culture, 169
Ascheulean industry, 381
Aegyptopithecus, 95, 136
Aegyptopithecus zeuxis, 136
Africa, 4, 5, 13, 21, 25, 34, 46, 50, 53, 65, 72, 80, 87, 90, 148, 154, 156, 167, 178, 183, 189, 190, 306, 347, 353, 386, 387, 393, 422. *See also* Names of individual countries
Agapornis (lovebird), 235
Ak-Kaya III, 419
Albumins, 78, 79, 132
Alcelaphini, 190
Aleut, 247, 248, 264
Alipur (Pakistan), 40
Allometry, 187–188, 285
Alouatta caraya, 247, 248
Amphicyoninae, 189
Amphipithecus, 21, 178
Amphipithecus mogaungensis, 26
Anagenesis, 109
Anancus, 25
Anolis. 187, 195
Antelope, 229–232, 238, 239
Ante-Neanderthals, 381–397
Anthus (pipit), 235
Antilope, 321
Antilopini, 190
Apataelurus, 188
Arago II, 381, 385, 386
Arago XIII, 381, 385, 386, 401
Arago XXI, 381
Archanthropes, 382, 383, 386, 422

Arctitis, 321
Asia, 21–30, 52, 72, 154, 156, 291, 306, 348, 353, 355, 358, 371, 386, 387, 393, 422. *See also* Names of individual countries
Asych, 385, 386
Ateles, 134
Atlanthropus, 386
Attock (Pakistan), 64
Aurochs, 420
Australia, 354, 355–356
Australian aborigines, 158, 218, 247, 248, 264
Australopithecidae, 168–169
Australopithecines, 29, 65, 105–107, 116–117, 123, 154, 226; body size of, 120, 278; canine breadth of, 287; determining sex of, 246–266; postcranial skeleton of, 276–278, 281; reduction in cusp height of, 214–215; sagittal cresting in, 274–276; sexing individual specimens of, 276–280; sexual dimorphism in, 245–281; speed of prey of, 285; temporal relationship of, to Giganto-pithecine, 121–125; tooth form and function of, 208–216
Australopithecus, 28, 48, 49, 50, 51, 52, 53, 72, 73, 76, 77, 78, 80, 113,117–118, 164, 166, 179, 361–362, 364; dietary adaptations of, 203–219; dietary hypo-thesis about, 184–185, 186; habitat distribution of, 28; sexual dimorphism of, 184; speciation in, 183–198
Australopithecus africanus, 50, 185, 197,